FREE TO BE
RESPONSIBLE

How to Assume Response-Ability

FREE TO BE RESPONSIBLE

How to Assume Response-Ability

Ben Thomson Cowles, Ph.D.

Foreword by Roger Shinn, Ph.D.

HOPE
Publishing House

Pasadena, California

For information address:
Hope Publishing House
P.O. Box 60008
Pasadena, CA 91116
(818) 792-6123
FAX (818) 792-2121

First edition

Manuscript Editor: David H. McElrath

Cover Design: Cristina E. Ortega

Book Editor: Faith Annette Sand

Printed by the Princeton University Press

Library of Congress Cataloging-in-Publication Data

Cowles, Ben Thomson, 1915-
    Free to be responsible : how to assume response-ability / by Ben
Thomson Cowles ; with a foreword by Roger Shinn.
       p. cm.
    Includes bibliographical references and index.
    ISBN 0-932727-28-X : $19.95. -- ISBN 0-932727-27-1 : $12.95
    1. Responsibility. 2. Free will and determinism. 3. Ethics.
4. Social Ethics.   I. Title.
BJ1451.C68 1990
128--dc20   90-36177
                                              CIP

Table of Contents

Foreword

The title of this book, *Free to be Responsible*, with the subtitle "Free To Respond," well expresses its two distinctive accents.

First, Dr. Cowles believes in human freedom. Against the psychological determinisms of B.F. Skinner and Sigmund Freud, to mention his two radically different examples, he argues that human beings are genuinely free to make significant choices.

He knows that freedom can be exaggerated, that there are bonds of necessity in human life such as time and space. He takes account of limits within the self, showing how the body puts constraints on freedom and he points to the limits that society places on individual freedom. It is refreshing to find a psychological discussion of freedom that emphasizes how severely some people's freedom is inhibited by poverty—an insight that seems obvious enough until we notice how often it is neglected in the literature of personal psychology. Human freedom is, in Cowles' echo of Paul Tillich's term, "finite freedom." But it is tremendously important. "Across the years we design a self," he says.

But second, responsibility (sometimes interpreted as response-ability) is equally important. The self is a responder—to other selves, to events, to nature, to values.

The traditional behavioristic pattern of stimulus-response (S-R) is not adequate for understanding persons. It is the self, not merely neurons, that responds, and the response involves the purposes and ideals, as well as the immediate needs, pleasures and pains of the person. Life is largely a matter of "responding responsibly."

So, far from opposing freedom to responsibility, Cowles says: "Responsibility presupposes freedom, and freedom can consist only in responsibility." This is not the familiar pop psychology of adjustment. Directedness is essential to selfhood. Purposes, values and ethical issues cannot be side-stepped.

In this age of "the new narcissism" it is good to hear a psychologist say: "When the self-centered pursuit of happiness becomes the chief purpose of a person, serious disillusionment sets in." For Cowles, the self and society are integrally related. "Our wholeness depends greatly on the well-being of the society in which we live." In his illustrations he moves easily from examples of individuals in counseling situations to events of political and international history.

Ben Cowles, who lived his early life in China and has been there again recently, never lets his vision so center on his own immediate friends and counselees as to exclude the wider world. We live, he says, "in one world with no place to hide."

This understanding of selves, society and nature involves a persistent religious sensitivity. The self, as responsible responder, lives by trust and commitment. It seeks to relate its temporality and its coming death to eternity. At times, Cowles writes of specifically Christian beliefs, as when he rejects both Utopia and Armageddon as adequate futures and relies on "a realistic Christian hope." But, avoiding all dogmatic assertions, he looks for religious insights in the histories and experiences of many peoples.

This book shows the footprints of a host of pioneering psychologists—for example, Freud, C.G. Jung, Otto Rank, Gordon Alport, Abraham Maslow, Erich Fromm, Erik Erikson, among others. It also shows the influence of such theologians as Tillich, Reinhold and H. Richard Niebuhr, Dietrich Bonhoeffer, Martin Buber, Soren Kierkegaard, and many more. It draws on insights of great literature from the ancient Greeks to modern times. But it is, above all, the work of a practicing counselor who draws insights from his own practice and experiences.

I commend it especially to those who in their concentration on personal fulfillment forget the wider world of history and politics, and to those who in their political partisanship neglect the personal dimensions of themselves and their opponents.

—Roger Shinn, Th.D., Professor Emeritus
Union Theological Seminary, NY

Preface

When I was a twelve-year-old my sense of responsibility was greatly tested. I lived in a city 600 miles down the coast of China from Shanghai. My ten-year-old brother and I had gotten what schooling we could in the area and the time had come to leave our parents and go to a boarding school in Shanghai. Despite some real dangers in prospect for the four-day ocean journey, the move had to be taken. If we wanted to continue our education, there was no alternative. Not only did we have to make the journey, but we also had to be away from our parents for six months. Conceivably we could have chosen not to go. Both my brother and I, however, were eager to take this giant step toward managing and enjoying our own lives.

Mother was much unsettled by the whole venture. Dad, on the other hand, knew that just as there is a time when baby birds have to leave the next, young sons come to a time when they have to strike out on their own. He counted out 110 silver dollars and poured them into a long, slender, matted, tube-like sack and sent me bicycling to the steamship office to pay for the two fares. Mother remained deeply apprehensive about her little boys. For one thing, it was the season of the great typhoons Joseph Conrad wrote about. For another, coastal pirates had attacked ships at sea on a number of recent occasions. The thought of those things only heightened the excitement for us. My brother and I were sure that we could respond adequately, if not courageously, to any such happenings. Unwilling to deprive ourselves of the experience and growth to be gained by this adventure, we were ready to take responsibility for ourselves.

Our parents came down to the ship to hug and reassure us as we began our journey. "Take care of yourselves and each other," Dad yelled to us from the dock. "Remember to be considerate of our hosts, the Chinese." Both of us were a bit embarrassed by this superfluous reminder, for he was only reiterating what had been said many times before and what we had innately sensed.

The voyage was to be an exciting one. Our British ship, only three months out of Glasgow, was the latest addition to the Butterfield and Swire Company's China coast fleet. From bow to stern it offered wonderful surprises: seamen working with freshly tarred hawsers and red-lead paint, fierce looking but kindly Sikh guards, smelly live sheep in pens covering the battened down forward hatch and crowds of steerage passengers milling about the aft hatches. The chief engineer took us into the depths of the engine room and the solicitous captain from Bristol allowed us up on the bridge.

Jeremy Bowlwer, correspondent for the *London Times* and a proud Lancastrian, was the only passenger who spoke our language. The other passengers in our class were a French couple, a Portuguese businessman out of Macao and a White Russian customs officer. The weather-beaten English journalist seemed grouchy in the beginning, but soon he warmed up and told us about his 14-year-old son back in England going to Eton. In the evening Bowlwer would interrupt writing his report on the current anti-British demonstrations in Canton, look over his spectacles and admonish us to be sure to take Latin and history in the school we were going to. In a tutorial way, he tended to become stuffily serious. "We've got to know the classics that fed our rich culture," he would say. "We've got to understand the forces that made the explosive and fast changing times in which we live." He mellowed as he saw how his wisdom went over our young heads. After meals he would try to engage us in a game of cribbage or backgammon.

We suffered no typhoons, although we did encounter some gigantic monsoon rollers. Despite the real danger of pirates, none attacked us. Instead our eyes searched the great China Sea looking, possibly hoping, to see pirates, but more intrigued with the unending string of islands and inlets dotted with picturesque fishing and ocean-going junks.

When we got to Shanghai, we did indeed encounter situations nearly as traumatic as our anxious mother had tortured herself imaginaing. Our ship arrived earlier than scheduled and unexpectedly docked on the opposite shore from the Bund—the broad and always busy street running along the north shore of the waterway. As our hosts had not be advised of the changed docking, there were no friendly adults there to greet us. To make matters worse, the hundreds of steerage-class Chinese who had been herded into cramped quarters on the cubicles of the aft deck grew ominously restless as the ship drew alongside of the dock. Even before the mooring was completed, they had begun their mad rush to disembark. It was a nightmarish scene. Holding their scant belongings and numerous children, they rammed themselves into the narrow gangway. To our horror we saw two toddlers wrenched from their mother in the stampede and trampled to death in the terrible melee. There was nothing we could do to help them.

The job of taking care of ourselves was by no means easy. We had to find transportation across the turbulent River Whangpoo to the International Concession and then on to the French Concession some 45 minutes away. The two of us were fluent in the southern Swatow dialect, but the porters, launch men and taxi drivers spoke only the Shanghai dialect and had difficulty understanding us.

The pressures of the usual throngs on the Bund were aggravated by a roisterous anti-imperialism parade with students shouting "Down with imperialism" and "Britons go home." Being respectful and manly with our hosts the Chinese, as our father had suggested, was difficult for they were the ones huckstering, jeering and nearly mobbing us in all the pandemonium.

We did make it safely to our destination and in record time, arriving at our host family's home hours before they had expected us. We explained the early arrival of the ship and began describing to them the scene—docking at an unintended berth, the deaths of the toddlers we had witnessed in the mad press to get off the boat, the precarious passage across the river, the long adventurous taxi journey through Shanghai traffic. Our hosts were aghast at our tale, for at any point in our various adventures, there could easily have been a misadventure. "Stop worrying," we told them, "We are here with you now."

Truthfully, we were so innocent and busy trying to be responsible we didn't realize how vulnerable we were. We both felt we had done a lot of growing up in the four days after we left our parents, but we hardly realized how blessed we were that early in life we experienced solid attachment, secure bonding and were encouraged to develop a sense of autonomy. What carried us through was our sense of what I've come to call "response-ability," a key concept in this book. There were no misadventures, largely because we were reasonably aware of the conditions and confrontations to which we might have to respond. We knew that in the rush and frenzy of such experiences, fear, self-pity and hesitancy are the reactions most likely to do one in.

I tell this story to illustrate what this book is about. In life we are pitted against situations to which we must respond. Our complex world summons the most accurate awareness we can muster and the most appropriate response we can make. As we move along through life, the demands for responsible responding increase and become more complicated. The choices we make can either be responsible or irresponsible. In the process we must see ourselves as whole persons with traits and capabilities necessary to make adequate responses. Our selves may be, as some psychiatrists claim, a cauldron of impulses determining behavior. But our selves are also autonomous and responsible. Through the understanding we get from identifying and fulfilling our *response-ability* we are able to live more meaningfully and with more satisfaction.

The account of my own successful adolescent voyage from Swatow to Shanghai was not told to suggest that life will always bring us to the safety of a friendly home after a perilous journey. Nor did that trip set me upon a life course that was nothing but a smooth ascent to many uplands. It did teach me, however, that we respond to our environment by dealing with all the actualities of life and that trial and error is probably the main way we learn, especially in the beginning.

Even when we are older, this continues to be the case. One popular notion holds that a college regimen is the royal road to developing responsible and well-ordered responses. Yet the truth is that as valuable as a university education is for the mind, responsibility is more caught than taught. The matters of the heart and soul are of a different order from those of the mind.

When we are dealing with the emotional part of becoming responsible, maturing seems to happen almost by osmosis. The mind does not exist by reason alone. Emotions help focus and enliven our thinking. We are affected more by the ideas and opinions of those who are charismatic, than by those who are not. My counseling and pastoral duties have taught me that success requires a melding of both clear thinking and genuine feeling.

In my education, I was strongly influenced by professors who evidenced living responsibly and sought to apply their beliefs. In college there were four who stood tall in my sight: Rufus Jones, Douglas Steere, Thomas Kelly and D. Elton Trueblood. In seminary I had the privilege of studying under such greats as Reinhold Niebuhr, Paul Tillich, Henry Sloane Coffin and George Buttrick. Russel Dicks and Roland Fairbanks provided incomparable guidance at Boston's Massachusetts General Hospital. And attending seminars at Harvard under the leadership of Gordon Allport and Alfred North Whitehead made a lasting impression.

These people were my mentors, challenging me with their brilliance, exuberance and creativeness. At the same time they sustained me with the power that flowed from their own faith, reasoning and searching. They were dedicated to truth, scholarship and humanitarian service and wanted to show people the essential relationship between what we think and feel, believe and do. Each one conveyed an impressive sense of personal accountability in this world. They seemed to use everything they had to the utmost.

These mentors inspired me to think that I, or anyone else, could follow in similar ways. If I would commit myself as they had and work as faithfully as they did, I would achieve whatever it was I was supposed to achieve with my life. They were my window on a way of life and *responsibility* that totally captivated my imagination. In subsequent experiences I found power from their examples, their ideas and their sense of responsibility. Their way was rarely realized, but I have never stopped celebrating it.

This book evolved out of my own journey to become a more effective responder and thereby a more responsible person. Whole communities as well as individuals are engaged in a similar struggle. It is the journey and work of life. Persons who take life purposefully and seriously struggle to find larger freedoms, more choices and opportunities. Likewise they want to feel effective as they try to become responsible responders to all the dimensions of life—within themselves, in the environment, with others and with their God. I found it so working at the Y.M.C.A. in the slums of Philadelphia and at Boys Clubs of Throggs Neck in the Bronx; it was as true in the mission field in China as it was in working among laid-back, self-seeking and frequently troubled Southern Californians.

This book is about the serious personal and social problems and opportunities, hurts and healings to which we respond. The effort is to address openly the predicaments confronting people as they work to enhance discipline in themselves and justice in society. Critical issues and perplexities we meet in the complicated aspects of our responding are identified.

The method used here is to outline mental, emotional and spiritual conditions that will guide us to find responsible responses as we search for patterns of thought, behavior and spirit that are fulfilling and significant. In the journey toward responsibility, responses and counsel came from almost every segment of society. I am deeply grateful for all the generous and unbounded help I received; it has given me an increasing awareness of the connectedness of all life, my own and that of other humans and creatures. Responsible people have helped me see more completely the importance of living in such a way as to celebrate the struggle for mutuality (the actual dynamic of justice-making) not only as an ethical ideal but as the very essence of who we are in the world and the basis of our survival.

This book is an exploration of new responses in relating genuinely and intimately to our authentic inner selves and to others. The suggestions you will come upon are meant to give you effective reinforcement so that the response of your mind, body, heart and soul will be productive and purposeful in these times of rapid and radical change. Some parts may sound overly philosophical, but the practical application of one's philosophy governs the responsible ethical response we make. Other sections may seem overly concerned with political and social issues, but our sense of responsibility is tested as we try to make appropriate response to surrounding political and social realities. Philosophic and cultural concerns are crucial in any consideration of responsibility.

Sections articulating religious convictions may trouble those with a secular bent. Yet again and again responsible people break through the tangles of daily problems and activities to search for deeper answers to the ultimate questions: Why are we here? What is the ground—and rationale—of existence? What is our destiny?

This book represents the quest for viable answers to such fundamental questions and the sharings of what key mentors, colleagues and clients discovered in listening to the promptings and chastening of a transcendent power.

The aim of this search-and-sort process is to stimulate you and me to become more responsible persons—and more responsive to the potentials of our inner selves, more concerned for the needs of others, more clearly expressive of our deepest convictions and thus better equipped to make rational and purposeful choices appropriate to our personal and social selves.

Whatever its roots, its purpose is to serve as an encouragement and guide to travel life's roads and face its roadblocks as well as its successes and failures. T.S. Eliot in *Four Quartets* wrote, "We shall not cease from exploring / And the end of our exploring / Will be to arrive at where we started / And know the place for the first time."

Hopefully, when you have come to the end of this book, you should have heard—and heeded—the most important of all: the response of your soul to its Creator.

Finding Reliable Guidelines
for Responses

"I'm back for one of your boomerang responses," said
Larry, a gifted and successful engineer.

"Boomerang response?" I asked.

"Yes, the last time I worked through one of my tough
decisions with you," Larry explained, "you directed responsibility back to me and encouraged me to become accountable
for my choices. I'm phoning because now I have a bigger
decision about an attractive job offer that has some negative
aspects on the options. I'm needing a second opinion to keep
me from going into a dead end."

I suggested he could come in the next day to talk at
length.

"Problem is, in a few hours I'm meeting the two
executives who want me to head up this innovative missile
guidance project. I have the necessary technical and adminis-
trative experience to handle the job, but the moral
implications don't square with my beliefs."

Obviously, Larry didn't need 30-second sound bites but
someone to explore with him the hidden depths of how the
defense industry affects not only his job opportunity, but our

society. Surely I ought to take a few minutes and listen empathetically to his concerns and offer him assurance.

"I'm taking better hold of new options," he explained. "I'm planning more carefully and following up on my decisions. Improvements of my ways of responding has put me in better shape financially and professionally. But I continue to question where today's sophisticated technology is taking us. Back in 1961 President Eisenhower cautioned us against letting scientific whiz kids make the nation captive of a 'scientific technological elite,' whose ingenious developments can carry the country toward disaster.

"The directorship of this guidance project," he added thoughtfully, "involves more than higher salary and prestige. What concerns me is its impact on society, what it doesn't do in relation to the homelessness, pollution, education, drug and alcohol abuse and other big problems we face. With the breakthroughs to greater freedom in Central European countries, the application of technology must square with what's right and wrong and how people can better relate to nature, the community and our religious convictions."

Both of us knew these questions deserved more than a few quick comments over the phone, and a momentary closure was called for. So I hastily encouraged him to compare the possibilities of the proposed position with his vocational expectations and goals. "You see that the opportunities of the new job," I observed, "entail greater responsibilities and more responsible management and ethical commitment. Yet, in regard to some of the questionable implications, you're able to separate the promise of technology from its potential threat. You're not blaming science and technology for making the world complex and impersonal, but still you struggle with your desire to stay in that field. You are meeting head on the ethical meanings of the job."

Regarding his seeking a second opinion, I recalled the account of the painter Paul Gauguin, who in 1897 did not look for guidance when he was struck with a series of seemingly hopeless decisions. He responded by deciding to try to

2

kill himself. Before doing so, he feverishly completed his last great testamentary painting and wrote on it—he said it was his signature—*D'où venons nous? Que sommes nous? Où allons nous?* (Where have we come from? What are we? Where are we going?) He then took an overdose of arsenic, but the dose was too large; he vomited and lived. Gauguin's survival was classic irony. In his attempt to duck responsibility, he found that he still faced his old difficulties and many new ones.

Knowing Larry's reverence for nature and responsiveness to the needs of others, I offered him further reinforcement: "Your ecological concern comes through in your dedication to wanting to live in harmony with nature. Also, your Peace Corps experience, combined with your social concern, moderate your motives and helps you look beyond your own success and welfare. It's great that you're looking for your own *internal* guidance system that will keep your decisions consistent with your ethical and religious convictions."

"Yes," Larry interrupted, "that gives me one of your 'boomerang responses' and enough instant feedback to last until I see you tomorrow."

Like Larry and Gauguin, we too confront questions about how we are going to respond—how we will use our freedom to choose and decide. Aware that we have this freedom to respond, most of us do not want to lose or neglect the responsibilities accompanying it. We look for more responsible direction to guide us as we exercise our freedom to respond.

External Pressures Require Response-Guidelines

In considering our vocations, we all meet serious questions about the possible responses outside demands make and the larger effects that follow. Physical, social and world happenings determine so much of how we respond.

Physical occurrences, for instance, often demand instant responses. Paramedics, called to the scene of an airplane crash, encountered a string of frustrating events that required a series of unanticipated responses. On the way to the accident, the team ran into a traffic gridlock. Managing to work their way clear and resume speed, they heard a rear tire blow out. With the spare frantically installed, they reached the area of the crash only to be turned back by the guards who explained that enough other units were already on the spot and that their dispatcher wanted them to return to the station. Each frustrating delay tested their "response ability."

Bodily injuries suffered in less violent circumstances stir up different responses. A sergeant in the Los Angeles police department wrenched her back moving cartons of stationery while on routine office duty. Suddenly immobilized and in severe pain, she cried out for help, though embarrassed, because her supervisor had told her to wait for an assistant to move the cartons, and also because the injury occurred under such unheroic conditions. The consequences of the accident involved her in a series of reactions that tested her guidelines for responding.

Family crises call forth other combinations of responses. Jerry Hails, a staff editor at the *Los Angeles Times*, writes poignantly of the painful choices he faced in his 96-year-old mother's last weeks. The family doctor calmly spoke of life's inevitable end, with its welcome release from suffering: "Your mother has lived a long time. She is tired and old and if she survives this illness she will be bedridden, a cruel punishment for a woman who has always been active and eagerly serving others." The doctor then spelled out the possible responses to this situation: The use of antibiotics could be resumed, or she could be readmitted to the hospital with its sophisticated life-support systems. "Or," he said, "you can make her as comfortable as possible with medication and let her go peacefully." The choice, the responsibility, was Jerry's. No one else could make the decision—a decision other families face as aging parents reach their moment of final crisis.

Inequities in our communities precipitate another set of responses. Census statistics and other demographic findings show gross disparities in our society: some people are under-taxed and others over-taxed; some are racially disadvantaged, others advantaged; some live in ghettoes, others live in mansions; some have too little to eat, others worry perpetually about their weight. Recurrent news articles tell about the trend toward affluence of the small "upper class," accompanied by a growing "under class," defined by increased poverty and corrosive effects which spread misery and madness in our cities. Minorities who did not make it into middle and professional classes in the sixties are left to fester in benign neglect.

Our political processes, particularly in our presidential campaigns, seem frustratingly ineffective. Attempted panaceas barely scratch the surface of our pervasive social ills and injustices. Instead of finding just responses, those who fall through the cracks of our pretentious economic and social systems experience social abandonment. Thus, we reap the dread harvest of terrors of hostage-taking, Apartheid's repression, escalated destruction of rain forests and the incurable twin scourges of AIDS and "crack" that burn through the social fabric like white phosphorus.

Our ecological profligacy, which might have been one of Larry's concerns, also challenges us to find new responses. We read recent World-Watch Institute Reports that point out, "We are borrowing from the future in a runaway binge of chopping, burning, draining, poisoning, leaving a wake of leaking landfalls, oozing lagoons, sludge, slag and waste plastics." Some manufactured products break prematurely, fail, or cause accidents and turn poisonous. Our air conditioners burn holes in the ozone layer. Our garbage travels the world looking for a place to rest.

The tragic events and conditions striking us from the world scene arouse other orders of responses: drought, famine and wars; 100,000 Mozambican civilian refugees killed by anti-government rebels reminiscent of the Khmer Rouge slaughter in Cambodia; Pan Am Flight 103 blown up in another outburst of terrorism bringing death or injury to a few, fear to many; a starving African or Asian mother sitting on a dirt floor holding a skin-and-bones infant trying to suckle her dry breast; and, multiplication of such conditions which renders one-fourth of the world's population hungry, illiterate, diseased and despairing.

Momentary twinges of conscience to such immense needs and suffering hardly do justice to the social concern we must address. We need to ask: How can we help alleviate the immediate tragedies, let alone the long-range programs needed to reduce the national and international seedbeds of such suffering? We come to the questions for which Larry sought guidelines: What are our responsibilities regarding the conversion of our Cold War economy and the goals to which technological expertise will be applied?

Consider America's opportunity for a wholesale conversion, not just cutbacks, of its economy which depends so heavily on defense industries: To forestall the United States from sinking deeper into international economic mediocrity and debt, military conversion offers a lifeline, not just a bonus. Experts agree that diverting research and development, capital and millions of workers to the military has retarded the U.S. economy. Redirecting military resources offers the only large, foreseeable new source of national competitive strength. More than a "peace dividend" is at stake here.

A large shift is possible and involves especially valuable resources for science, new products, managerial excellence, new capital and plain productive power. This prodigious opportunity is immediate, like an 80-yard pass when the home team is behind late in the game. "America is twiddling its thumbs," suggests the economist William G. Shepherd of the University of Massachusetts at Amherst, "if all it does is to debate the freeing of possible modest resources from future military budgets." Needed is a shift in economic priorities away from destruction toward the sustaining of and care for life—a shift the nature and degree of which we haven't even begun to contemplate.

Large issues emerge when we examine the purposes to which we put our technology. The most important technological innovation of the 1980s wasn't recombinant DNA or software or silicon chips or superconductivity. It was not manufactured by Silicon Valley start-ups, refined by the Japanese or found lurking in university laboratories. The greatest breakthrough of the past decade—and the one that will inevitably shape the 1990s—has been that we now think of technology as an independent force in its own right.

Developments ranging from computers to pharmaceuticals to materials science, are driven by the belief that everything can be engineered and scientists can shape technology into any form they want it to be. Nothing has to be taken for granted. Certain laws of physics remain immutable, but with genetic engineering, society is already re-engineering the laws of nature. Expectations of what technology can do are escalating. People assume their computers must become faster, cheaper and more powerful—and if American companies can't deliver, the Japanese will. Molecular biologists are expected to turn the genetic keys that unlock the cures for cancer. Detroit and Toyota are expected to manufacture cars that deliver more miles per gallon, while spewing fewer noxious gasses into the atmosphere.

Technologies have brought basic changes we hardly realize. Where the symbol of American engineering prowess in the 1960s was the Apollo space program, the symbols of the new engineering ethic can be found on an increasingly small scale, such as the silicon chip and the strand of DNA. Instead of engineering industrial mass, the focus is on engineering molecules and information. "The new technologies are dissolving disciplinary boundaries," observes Michael Schrage, science editor for the *Los Angeles Times*. Computer scientists now work with organic chemists to gain new insights into molecular structures. Electrical engineers now collaborate with neurophysiologists to design neural network silicon chips. Physicists work side by side with radiologists to map new ways to use magnetic resonance imaging scanners.

Science and technology are changing our outlook. "Scientists and technologists," says John Seely Brown, the director of Xerox's Palo Alto Research Center, "are now much more connected to the real world and not just the world of ideas," Scientists now use complex technologies to recapture simplicity. "The ten or more computers inside your car," Brown points out, "perform computations to keep things simple and reliable. Also they serve to keep you connected, helping you feel more attached." Computer technology provides a medium to integrate disparate information, manipulate it and even evoke and manage meaning. "These media amplify our ability to be reflective," says Brown. "We're going to be able to bootstrap understandings in a way we weren't before. We're moving from a world that worships analysis to one that worships synthesis."

Guidelines for Applying Technology

The challenge and serious questions that these technologies impose are mind boggling. Specialists now are concerned with how best to "package" and "integrate" the new technologies into forms that people can meaningfully use. The emphasis is less on discovery than design. Instead of just creating components and systems, technologists increasingly create environments and ecologies. "Instead of being conceived in mechanical terms," Harvard's Bell tells us, "We see a whole new sensibility: the new technologies are designed to offer more than just functionality. We now hear scientists and engineers using organic metaphors more and more frequently." Technologists want to become more like architects; designing environments that people live in and use. "Networks," says Robert Lucky, the executive director of research at AT&T Bell Labs explains, "now have to have some intelligence associated with them. The answering machine, for instance, becomes a new genre, a way people can give customized messages."

The technologies of the 1990s will differ from those of the 1980s. Technology is breeding a whole new concept of what can or cannot be done. Georgetown University humanities professor O. B. Hardison, Jr., author of *Disappearing Through the Skylight*, says, "The dynamic is that we're not going to be limited by history; we have the responsibility to make up new traditions as we go along." Technologists feel unencumbered by limits. The questions have shifted from "How?" and "Why?" to "Why not? and "How much?" Technologies of the '80s created a new consciousness of technology by offering a tsunami of choice.

In the next decade the emphasis will shift from choosing options to designing alternatives. Instead of selecting a personal computer because you like its interface, you will buy it because you can design the interface to your own liking. Manufacturers will build products in ways that enable you to customize them *yourself*—if that's what you want. In the 1980s, technologists programmed computers to perform tasks; in the 1990s, the computers will begin to program themselves and communicate with each other about what they've learned.

The revolution isn't just in the technologies themselves but also in how people see technology and how they will apply it. Technology is viewed as a powerful medium for personal wealth, political change and global competitiveness. "Technologies," asserts sociologist Christopher Lasch, "are political, demanding culture-wide decisions and no longer matters that are decided in a laboratory." Hence technology—as much as politics and culture—will become the medium through which society searches for meaning and expresses its values and priorities.

As these technologies continue to diffuse throughout society and become increasingly democratized, the range of personal responsibilities will be vastly expanded. In the 1990s, society will take more "votes" on what it wants its technologies to be and to do.

New Responsibilities Accompany Technological Advances

The ability to engineer new medicines, materials and systems—and do so with enhanced style and intelligence—confers new responsibilities. Choosing responsibly between the explosion of new alternatives promises to become increasingly difficult. "A lot of this technology is virtual—formal and a matter of essences," says AT&T's Lucky. "You have less time to delve into the reality of things; you have to take so much on faith. People will be forced to place greater trust in their own abilities." Our new expectations of technology will lead to new expectations of ourselves. The enhanced freedom provided by technology increases personal responsibility.

Fulfilling the new array of significant and complex responsibilities remains elusive and often evades our most dedicated determination. Some specialists contend this difficulty may well be a part of the high anxiety that Americans in all generations and every class have endured as the price of being an American. Not only Americans, but all people often are kept from achieving the promises of a new technology by the traumas of their lives. Something else impedes our search for appropriate response-guidelines for troublesome external pressures.

Internal Pressures Call for Response-Guidelines

At the same time that outside forces pressure us, we find within ourselves a host of unresolved struggles that call out for more appropriate and creative responses. Internal conflicts give us trouble in finding and living out the responsible life. Along with radically new responses for the social and economic problems in our own country or those abroad, we confront a host of emotional and spiritual confusion in individuals that also cry out for new responses. To feel at home in this planet, and even to survive, the chief two-legged species needs to put into practice what a majority of its adults probably understand in their more thoughtful moments. That's population control, CO_2 control, soil-loss control, drug-use control, living-on-credit control—in short, is self-control.

The unfinished business of facing and managing our angers, anxieties and other internal problems seriously distort our thoughts, feelings and behavior. Suppressed inner conflicts bully and skew healthy responses. Our sense of inadequacy and insecurity trigger feelings of doubt, keep us from making responses we know to be better, and hinder the realization of our potentials. Our well-intentioned responses easily go awry because of low self confidence and uncertainty about our priorities. Our deposits of time, energy and skill have not matched our withdrawals. When inner resources and adequate planning are insufficient, we become frustrated that our enterprises do not work out. Setting aside the consciousness in which we are rooted, we act impulsively. Self-centered, we assume that we are exempt from accountability. We do not risk developing new responses, and the moral and practical concerns mount.

As Americans, our prodigality with resources in our short history, is a case in point. We are beginning to have an uneasy conscience about our capriciousness and extravagant exploitation of our ecological inheritance. Europeans who settled the New World were presented with an entire continent abundant in material riches. They had the tools, the know-how, and the energy to exploit it. No such situation had existed before, nor will it exist again on our planet. But this unique situation was squandered. Particularly in the four generations since the Civil War we acquired some bad habits which permitted people to do as they pleased.

We have second thoughts about the way we live. We misuse the powers and resources that science and technology have provided. We continue in an obsessive urge to make more money to support our compulsive consumerism. Material objects and profits have become our gods. We are wasteful; we fragment the judgment of responsible economics and live beyond our means. Rationalizing our actions as socially, aesthetically, or politically necessary, we allow patterns of responding in our work place and homes to become skewed. The culture of alienation and despair, of greed and violence, being constructed for profit on the bodies of the poor, the elderly, the young and minorities is being masked as "kindliness" and "gentleness" by those who have learned to believe their own lies.

We allow our ethical responsiveness to become dulled, stuck in a rut of negative feelings. This leads us to make excuses for our failures and neglect of our innate "response-ability." The fruit of our unresponsiveness is that we are unable to face new challenges that call for faith and vision. Without sound guidelines and viable convictions our responses end up without direction or purpose. We can trim our own resource gluttony and the extravagant standard of living that makes our protestations to the Third World ring hollow, and we can invest in conservative technologies that will reduce our own consumption and share with peoples of other world communities.

At a deeper level, when we cast about for prescriptions and guidelines for "better living," we come face to face with human beings' darker side. "Everybody's got a mean streak in them," Terry Allen, multimedia artist, points out; "we all have to figure out where it is in us and how to get it into a box." Much of the work of psychotherapists and family counselors requires treating the wounds inflicted by men and women who abused them as children or as adults. Sexual, physical, emotional and spiritual violence against the vulnerable constitute an often unrecognized major crisis. In reaction to the sex-as-sin obsession, with its repressive, guilt-inducing sexual ethic, we now see generated a pornographic culture of eruptive sexual violence.

Cloe Madanes, co-director of the Family Therapy Institute of Washington, D.C., says, "The main issue for human beings is whether to love, protect and help each other, or to intrude, dominate and control, doing harm and violence to others." But the boundaries are seldom clear, for love involves intrusion, while violence can be done in the name of love.

Specialists Search for Response-Guidelines

The search for alternative and more responsible responses to both our outer and inner unresolved conflicts and confusions, denials and destructiveness are of central concern for biologists, psychologists, sociologists, historians, artists, futurologists, philosophers and theologians.

Biologists tell us that to live is to respond. They have developed a vast science on this premise. Exploring the responses of living creatures, they study structures, functioning, growth, origins, evolution and the distribution of organisms. The biologist Erwin Laszlo, an evolutionary theorist, affirms that "humans have the ability to act consciously and collectively in exercising foresight to choose their own evolutionary path." We are challenged, not by a strange and external fate, but by an inner awareness stemming from nature, history and an in-born capacity to make choices that can shape our futures. Laszlo adds, "In our crucial epoch we cannot leave the selection of the next step in the evolution of human society and culture to chance. We must plan for it, consciously and purposefully." In the same vein, the biologist Jonas Salk affirms that our most urgent and pressing need is to provide that wonderful instrument, the human mind, with the wherewithal to image, and thereby create, a better world.

Psychologists, likewise, demonstrate how we respond to physical and psychic stimulation. They study responses of individuals' mental and emotional processes and behavior. The full range of human capacities and expressions involve responses—perception, cognition, volition, behavior, aspiration and faith. Each field of human activity is investigated to find ways to manage responses and defuse our tendency toward denials, procrastination and other self-defeating mechanisms.

In addition to studying human pathologies, psychologists are concerned about ways of developing creativity and ever more effective levels of performance. The psychologist Erich Fromm reminds us that "conflict makes for problems that demand solution—the response of unfolding our creative powers. Some responses remain simple actions based on specific issues and others involve dealing pragmatically with political, social and ethical problems arising in the community." Another psychologist, Abraham Maslow, has studied the "peak experiences" of gifted persons to discover how exceptional performances in thinking, feeling and doing can be cultivated and extended.

Sociologists focus attention on the crucial importance of human response. They show that the interaction between responding persons provides the basis for society. They point out that in whatever way we look at personal and social intercourse, we see that to be human is to respond. All human interaction—good or bad—is actuated and driven by response. Response is at the heart of all personal expression and human intercourse. To live, as the poet Jorge Luis Borges says, "is to respond within the webbed scheme of social and natural existence." Even in radically dissimilar human exchanges, response remains central. Social scientists agree that certainty about where we as individuals and as societies are headed require more effective response. By making responsible responses, within the extent of our freedom to respond, we lend zest to individual life and social settings.

Historians tell us that "responsibility," now so familiar a word in moral discourse, came into general use in the languages of Western culture only in the 17th century. In the late 19th century, two works gave the term a central place in the lexicon of morality: F. H. Bradley's essay "The Vulgar Notion of Responsibility and Its Connection with the Theories of Freewill and Determinism" (1876) and Lucien Levy-Bruhl's study of the problem of freedom, *L'ideé de Responsabilité* (1883). As its etymology suggests (from Latin *respondere*, "to answer"), the most obvious meaning of the term is accountability, being answerable for one's behavior. Thus, it is within discussions of the conditions requisite for moral liability to praise and blame, punishment and reward, that the term is most frequently encountered.

Historians speak of the essential function of our collective memory. In history, Page Smith explains in *Redeeming the Time*, "we find the concrete reality of day-to-day living, wherein we may be healed and reconciled." What we have said and done in our history, in our "autobiography," as Eugene Rosenstock-Huessy puts it, is in large part what (and who) we are. The study of history helps us respond to a larger realm than any that we can dwell in simply as contemporaries.

Abraham Lincoln once noted, "We need to know where we are and whither we are tending." He claimed that from the past we learn how we came to "where we are and find help in choosing and deciding what we wish to make of the future before its arrival." We gain strength, he said, "as we respond by naming our problems and giving order to the chaos ahead which waits to become our cosmos." Today we are faced not only with giving order to that imminent chaos but also with dealing realistically with the singular threat of nuclear annihilation.

Art works are essentially responses to human experience. Interpreting how artists rely on responses, Mircea Eliade, explains that responding invites "the act of participating in the artwork of creating." That is, artists choose and decide to respond creatively. Eliade tells how artists, during moments of creation, fulfill the fundamental human instinct toward transcendence. Artists, as all persons with ethical concern, seek responses that are consistent with their values and faith. The craving to be freed from the limitations of one's humanness is satisfied by what many creative persons call "passing over into the Other." When, momentarily tasting transcendence, they break the bonds of individuality, their creative experience becomes universal. In that experience they are freed from human frailty and even from the ultimate frailty: death.

Playwright-turned-president, Vaclav Havel, a noble artist thrust into prominence in the thrilling months since tyranny's icy grip on Eastern Europe began to loosen, searches for guidelines for responsible responding. Addressing a joint session of Congress, he dealt with democracy and the responsibilities of the human spirit: "Without a global revolution in our sphere of human consciousness, nothing will change for the better in the sphere of being. . . . We still don't know how to put morality ahead of politics, science and economy. We are still incapable of understanding that the only genuine backbone of all our actions, if they are to be moral, is responsibility—responsibility to something higher than my family, my country, my company, my success." Havel noted, "When Thomas Jefferson wrote that governments are instituted among men, deriving their just powers from the consent of the governed, it was a simple and important act of the human spirit. What gave meaning to that act, however, was the fact that the author backed it up with his life. It was not just his words; it was his deed as well." Democracy, the new Czech leader added, "in the full sense of the word will always be no more than an ideal. One may approach it as one would a horizon, in ways that may be better or worse, but it can never be fully attained. . . . You, too, are merely approaching democracy."

Futurologists who study the options ahead are much concerned with possibilities and portents, the directions and purposes of human response. More than prognosticators, these investigators see responses as coming in the content of unfulfilled tasks and highlight how people in their choosing and deciding, create their future—destructive or creative.

Alvin Toffler, author of best seller *Future Shock*, writes of the bold projects many nations are engaged in for progress and international cooperation as the pivotal year 1992 draws near. Western Europe projects the "European Community,"

Central European countries begin to build democratic forms of governments, the Soviet Union is astir with "Project Perestroika," Nicaragua elects a new regime, and Japan is heavily engaged in projecting a new vision for itself in the coming decade. Toffler notes that "the major powers of the world are vigorously pursuing master plans for survival in the next century. The very existence of all these projects will alter the global balance of power and raise the stakes involved in all political, strategic, and economic competition." There is one notable exception, however, the United States. "The United States," Toffler observes, "not only lacks any clear strategic project for the years ahead but seems unaware that it might need one."

And what do philosophers—those who aim to see life steadily and see it whole—tell us about responses? They probe the "actual" and "potential," as well as the authentic and genuine within human responses. The search is for the perennial responses people make to questions about the "reality" underlying all temporal phenomena. Their search for "essence" in response provides a variety of findings. Plato held that the search for essence, or basis, of response came from thought and particularly from "ideas" which are forms or archetypes of all concrete things. He argued for the independent reality of ideas as the only guarantee of objective scientific knowledge, feeling and behavior.

"German thinkers in the 18th century probed what they called the "thing-in-itself" as the source and motivator of responses. Responsiveness, as seen by Immanuel Kant, linked this search with the effort to understand the human mind's active awareness. The mind's response, which issues in behavior, is continually active, not simply passive. Responses flow from the dynamic processes of the mind, which constantly interprets the content and significance of the data that flows into it. This theme in philosophy has been confirmed by recent work in the psychology of perception, the philosophy of time, and the sociology of knowledge.

Philosophers tell us that the act of responding involves accountability. Responsible action, they say, is the voice of ethics telling us to do and not to do certain things. Our responses are not dictated by Fate—the inevitable lot to which we are assigned by a power beyond our control. Rather, they are guided and empowered by ethical considerations which include responsibility and responsiveness to an internal awareness formed, as Laszlo said, by nature, history, and our own freedom to respond and participate in shaping our futures.

Philosophers also point to a second and deeper etymology of "responsibility." Within the word for response is hidden the Greek word for "promise," recalling the practice of reliably performing one's part in a common undertaking. In this sense, responsibility refers, not merely to the conditions for imputability, but also to the trust-worthiness and dependability of the agent in some enterprise. The guidelines for accountable behavior come from a base that must at once be practical, philosophically reasonable and religiously sound and committed.

Reason and Knowledge Claim to Balance our Responses

Reason and knowledge, their champions hold, supplement and give meaning to what we see and hear. In struggling to act responsibly, experience cautions us to question the information our senses both give and do not give. Some messages of the senses seduce us, creating an illusory reality. Candy, cigarettes and liquor may satisfy our tastes, yet they violate what is best for our health. Madison Avenue woos our sensuous responses to buy beyond our means. Reason warns us against being sucked in, but the Sirens of Glamor and Desire are hard to resist.

More than caution us about the limitations of our senses, reason receives and sorts out impressions we receive from experience. By reason we are helped in our responding to assess and manage the personal, natural and social conditions that enter every act and decision. Reason works to enable us to grasp and transform reality. Like computers, which translate figures and information into "computer language," reason takes the data our responsiveness receives and organizes and translates it into meaningful patterns and symbols that express and communicate thoughts and feelings. Reason, its champions maintain, provides the substance and vehicle for mental, aesthetic and practical responses.

Knowledge also serves as another possible guide for our responding. As the record of what is perceived, knowledge includes both empirical data and that derived by inference or interpretation. We often must wait to respond until we better understand our stored data. Without such pauses to cultivate sharper awareness our responses are like those of shoppers in a bargain basement, jostled and compulsively grabbing at a garment that fits or is momentarily in style.

Of course individuals at best know only the tiniest bit about the inner and outer world. No one person can hope to grasp all the essential facts about, say, violence, anxiety or pity, that are needed to make a single wise decision. On the one hand, knowledge becomes fragmented so that our world seems to be disintegrating before our eyes into ions and electrons, photons and quarks, and other such invisible elements. On the other hand, knowledge becomes collective in the weakest sense, and scientists become like men and women in a crowd, looking for one another, each holding a single piece of an expensive, indispensable computer or software program.

Our awareness tends to be only what our eyes and ears tell us and what our minds conjure up. Our perceptions cover only a subjective, material point of view. A deeper consciousness, a deeper knowledge, is needed to tell us about ultimate, unshakable truth, about the spiritual reality that is the very basis of our most responsible actions and awareness.

A new synthesis must be achieved. This task is not confined to the relation between two sciences or between philosophy and psychology as a secular enterprise and theology as a sacred wisdom; it concerns the relation between human beings' own efforts to civilize themselves and God's intention and guidance—the relation between culture and faith. Responsibility lies in searching for a quality of self and development of a world order tolerant of diversity, truth, justice, and the welfare of persons.

Religious Support for Responses

In spite of the revolt of the intellectuals against religion and some reduction in the influence of revealed religions, strong voices among the inheritors of Hebrew-Christian, Buddhist and Islamic traditions reaffirm that we need renewed religious conviction.

These partisan advocates claim responses based on solid faith can discipline us for the lengthened foresight demanded for today's crises and for the years ahead. Plato, great thinker and teacher that he was, persistently sought responses based on truth, beauty and goodness. Toward the end of his life he published his final convictions that not only does a divinity exist, but also the divine element in the world is to be conceived as a persuasive and not as a coercive agency. Plato further held that the soul before it entered the realm of Becoming existed in the universe of Being. In due course, released from the region of time and space, it returns to its former abode. After a season of quiet, of assimilation of its earthly experiences and memories, refreshed and invigorated, it is seized again by the desire to keep in step and on the march with the current world. Human beings, according to this view, are urged to respond in ways that are in tune with cosmic forces and purposes.

Wisdom from the Middle East reminds us that in a similarly transitional and revolutionary time—the sixth and fifth centuries B.C.—the Hebrew prophets drove home the message that renewed religious conviction offered the only unconditional base for relevant responding. One of the prophets, Micah, who believed "Yahweh" to be the central and ultimate deity, delivered the classic statement about response: "He has showed you, O man, what is good; and what does the Lord require of you but to do justice, and to love kindness, and to walk humbly with your God? (6:6-8)"

In the same century, from an entirely different culture in North India, Gautama offered another religious base for responding. Disillusioned and unfulfilled by the sensual excesses, pretensions and unexamined narcissism in his father's luxurious palace, he left his wife and young son to search for more adequate responses. Seated beneath a pipal or bo tree, he meditated on how to achieve reliable truths that would guide him to fitting and sound responding.

In time enlightenment came: "Birth, sickness, age and death are sorrows—all in the world is sorrow and suffering." In a final Noble Truth he found the basis for responding: the way to end craving lies in the Eightfold Path of Right Views, Right Resolve, Right Speech, Right Conduct, Right Livelihood, Right Effort, Right Mindfulness, and Right Concentration. By such steps Gautama, who became known as the Buddha, decreed a path of spiritual improvement based on acceptance of the Four Sacred Truths and on such things as avoidance of ill will, malicious talk, lust, and hurt to living things.

In the West, 2,000 years later, the 17th century authors of the Westminster Confession, raising the question: "What is the chief end of man?" answered in the Hebrew-Christian tradition, "The chief end of human beings is to glorify God and enjoy Him forever." This affirmation has been for centuries the baseline of human responsiveness in the Western world. At the knife edge of the present, responsiveness is not dead to the power that religious conviction can lend to them. This is true, despite the way we have allowed our responses to become underpinned with the accepted secular metaphysics and the prevalent insistent narcissism.

In retrospect, as responsive persons heard it, we can see that the primal scream of the 1960s was a great inarticulate cry of hunger for the spiritual nourishment that sophisticated knowledge, technology and modern megapower failed to provide the soul. "Signs are in evidence," writes Theodore Roszak in *Where the Wasteland Ends*, "that the social conscience is back and that the young will now be marching on Washington again instead of vrooming their BMWs on the fast track out of business school." Contemporary theologian, Robert McAfee Brown, writes in his book, *Spirituality and Liberation* (1988), "It is significant that within our own upward mobile and success-oriented culture, the appeal of a new and powerful spirituality is on the rise." *Forbes* magazine (1988) surveyed leaders of the nation's 100 largest corporations and found "most of these executives called religion an important influence in their lives, and claimed that their faith helped to guide them in their day-to-day responses."

The etymological meaning of *religion* is "to bind us back" to our sources. Religious believers and all citizens of our planet need to respond to the awesome mystery of the scientific story of our origins. Matthew Fox reminds us that "the archetype of the Cosmic Christ encourages us to reverence our origins and to reverence our divinity and our responsibility as co-creators." As Meister Eckhart put it, "Though we are God's sons and daughters, we do not realize it yet."

A well-grounded faith provides the deeper and wiser view of the 'nature and destiny of man,' to use the title of one of Reinhold Niebuhr's books, without for a moment relaxing the fight for peace and social justice. A sturdy faith, Niebuhr suggests, helps us avoid the dismal pitfalls of self-adulation and self-hate. Americans are helped to see that our remarkable accomplishments have been, first, "on behalf of humanity" and, second, the consequence of "grace." They have been bestowed on us, as trustees for mankind, by a beneficent Providence. Firm convictions of this sort bring insights and power and give us courage to choose and decide, to find and go through new doors.

Accumulated Wisdom about Guidelines for Responding

But where does the compass settle? In the direction of the physical sciences, or the social sciences? Even though we are schooled to find grounds for responding in both these directions, neither emphasis fully satisfies our search. Many feel insecure in the presence of science. They say they have never had an aptitude for mathematics or chemistry or engineering, and are fearful they will not understand what they read and hear everyday about quantum physics, or gene splicing, or quasars and quarks. Others, like Larry, whose bent is toward science and technology, are not comfortable in fields of the liberal arts. They have little sensitivity or appreciation of art and music, literature and drama, of history and philosophy and the classics. Neither of these great combinations of human achievements in themselves provide the ultimate synthesis to give direction and purpose for our responses.

Similar questions raised in other generations involved simpler circumstances and perhaps less threatening consequences. Human irresponsibility did not include the possible snuffing out of the human race. Our age of space technology, microbiology and particle physics, when we explore both the infinitely large and the infinitely small, demands increasingly responsible responses. We are over-whelmed with the gamut of new social and scientific developments. The momentous events ushering in the 1990s so fills the mind—let alone the front page and television screen— that history seems to be sprinting across Europe at a speed never before known. The profound changes we are experiencing comprise an intricate dance between the death of old systems and the rise of a new culture. The required basic restructuring calls for new understanding and new responses.

We are not helped by reverting to worn out, irrelevant ideologies. During the last three decades the West, by permitting the Cold War to be debated in ideological terms (the merits of capitalism over communism, etc.), obscured the more profound point, the moral one. In an age of an electronic revolution, communism was attempting the impossible—trying to create an advanced technological society while mandating ideological uniformity. In domestic affairs, we allowed the right to create this same ideological trap for the left: Engage in a listless and unproductive debate over the inadequacies of an ideology, namely "liberalism," while avoiding the moral question of what is right and what is wrong.

Likewise, a nation's purpose is discovered not by consulting ideologies, but by reviewing its history and searching the hearts of its people and enlisting their responsible participation. At the same time a trap lies in the democratist temptation, the worship of democracy as a form of government and the concomitant ambition to see all humankind embrace it. Like all idolatries, democratism substitutes a false god for the real God, a love of process for a love of country. We live in a fallen world, a world in which it is always tempting to rely on an ideology for our salvation. When a shift away from one ideology takes place, we are tempted to assume that the victorious counter-ideology will now save the world. However, what we are seeing is not a victory of ideology, but a groaning toward new structures.

War stands out as our greatest idolatry. In the 1980s we enacted Gauguin's frightening irony on a global scale. We brought to a crescendo a world that has been preparing so long and so carefully for its own nuclear self-destruction that a successful ending is virtually assured. If the order comes to go, we go. All together. "Where have we come from?"—We have come from an antique civilization, led by warriors and shaped by more than 14,000 wars against often illusory enemies. "What are we?"—We are human beings, who at the most critical time in our long history, at last can grow up, recognizing that instead of giving way to mutual destruction we can call forth the amazing array of creative and constructive responses we have successfully developed in other areas of our social life. "Where are we going?"—On, and on, as part of the great chain of human existence. With Gauguin's questions echoing, we must respond to assure our survival beyond the nuclear age.

We must respond by examining and deciding to end war, to develop and extend the creative forces at hand, and to turn around our destructive pattern of interacting. But if, in changing (as we must to survive), we do not hold stubbornly to the roots of the idealism of our faith, we will be sucked into a funnel through which our theological vision will narrow and, in time, become rigid and false. Sustaining life requires us to respond not with counterfeit stereotypes or high sounding rhetoric, but with tested theory and realistic action, i.e., "firmly based" and appropriately applied responses. Our responses today must be substantial enough to confront the threat of a nuclear holocaust and take hold of opportunities opened when historic events fling themselves headlong into the future.

These key disciplines provide a speculative attempt to outline people's responsible responses toward themselves and their distant posterity. Most scholars agree that responses involve the entire range of our personal and social natures. In responding we express our thoughts and feelings, needs and hopes, as well as our reactions to the world around us. Responding and responsiveness bridge the gulf between our finiteness and our aspirations. In spanning the gulf, the nature and scope of our responses manifest the essential quality of our life. Each great field of human examination ventures to work out a concept of nature that links the scientifically ascertainable "is" and the morally binding "ought." We need these objective imperatives to save us from the excesses of our malevolent tendencies and at the same time draw out our Promethean positive potentials.

The axiom of responsibility in the personal and social crises we face requires that we harness our broadened powers and direct them for the common good. The lengthened reach of our responses moves responsibility, with no less than the fate of the race for its object, into the center of the ethical stage. We must open our eyes to what is at stake. We must take the step of involving ourselves not only in appreciating this confluence of events but also in meeting its challenge. The solution itself is not a pleasant one. It demands the ability to overcome our own prejudices and confined responses.

Compare the issues confronting someone in Gauguin's time with those of Larry's at the close of the 20th century. Previous guidelines for ethical responses, as Hans Jonas, a 20th century philosopher, observes, developed from premises "that the human condition, determined by the nature of man and the nature of things, was given once for all; that the human good on that basis was readily determinable; and that the range of human action and responsibility was narrowly circumscribed."

People a hundred years ago were geared to direct dealing with others within narrow limits of their space and time. Their image of human nature and their patterns of responding generally were found enshrined in the teachings of revealed religions. Not so today. The pattern of our responding rests increasingly on the trust we have in secular reason, the technological tools we have created and our changed doctrine of general being.

Larry and many others raise serious questions about the adequacies of such foundations for our responding. Confused and pressured in a time of rapid change, we search for personal and corporate responses that express "purpose and direction." Finding no lasting fulfillment in the rat race of modern capitalist society, many outwardly successful people seek ways to overcome the competitive pressure and attain a measure of serenity that will fill the emptiness and counterbalance the chaos around us. Other observers hold to an insistent yearning for higher ground and sense that there is a mystical power, external to us yet still closer than breathing, which can illumine our way with responses that will take us out of our tunnel into the light of a new day.

Our ability to respond involves the responsibility to continually explore how this endowment will be applied and guided. This "freedom to respond" requires actions we choose, awareness we cultivate, and a moral sense that we are accountable for the way we respond. The chosen action, or *response*, refers to the answers we give to the stimuli we receive from outside ourselves; cultivated awareness, or *responsiveness*, has to do with the quick and accurate recognition of stimuli; and the sense of moral accountability, *responsibility*, includes the obligations to apply our values and assume accountability for the consequences. The three aspects of responsible responding—responses, responsiveness and responsibility—are intimately interwoven.

The quality and power of our responses depend on our responsiveness and sense of responsibility. Responses, expressed in behavior, thought and feeling, emerge from responsiveness. Responsiveness, as empathetic receptivity, provides fuller and more accurate readings of the world, history, other people and our own inner promptings. Responsibility monitors and evaluates the realistic information we receive, then motivates thoughts and behavior. Responsibility also weighs the consequences of responses and renews a sense of purpose and meaning for them.

Responding that is undergirded and enlivened by religious conviction, enriches and empowers by giving responses vision and direction. The challenge and risk before us calls for sharpened responsiveness, clear reasoning, broadened knowledge and deepened religious faith. Christian living, for example, consists of putting faith into practice. Christian theology shows that faith is real only when it is lived. Faith is genuine only when the person's responses are responsible. Christian faith is a way that must be traveled in readiness for battle against attacks and temptations. It is real only as something ever newly claimed, ever newly received in listening to the word of grace. We understand the cry, "Lord, I believe; help thou mine unbelief!"

The ethic of responsibility is not one of withdrawal and defensiveness in the face of the realities of personal and social life. It holds, rather, that God calls individuals, not by calling them away from the urgent needs of social and civic life, but by summoning them to work within the world, redeeming and reforming its structures so that all persons might live freely and responsibly. The moral life is not merely a life of accountability to God's preordained law, it is a response to God's invitation to live in the world and to enter into the solemn undertaking of redeeming the world in concert with its creator.

Summary

The fact that freedom and responsibility are tied together confronts people with an inescapable anomaly. The more choices we have, the greater is our freedom, and the greater our responsibility. The struggle to be more free is universal, as individuals and societies. But the more free we become the greater the threat of the follies of libertinism and the excesses of license.

The consequences of undisciplined ways of life, sooner or later, leave us bound instead of free, out of control and responding irresponsibly. Addicts began as free agents, free to choose alcohol, drugs, over-eating, violence, crime or some other over-indulgence. On the other hand, higher and deeper intimations press us to keep searching for guides to more responsible responses. We sense that we are not contingent entities, but the representatives of a necessary metaphysical aspect of the universe. Responding human beings are a necessity if the universe is to exist. The ability to respond clearly and positively characterize human beings. Our senses tell us so, our reason confirms the experience and our faith underpins it. It is part of our nature to ask: What is the bedrock for our responding to existence?

At the end of the 20th century many voices and concerns call for more relevant and creative patterns of responding.

Contemporary social scientists, Physicians and Psychologists for Social Responsibility, some church bodies—to name a few—recognize that circumstances far more complicated and lethal than those confronted by people at the end of the 19th century now demand new guidelines for responding. "The drift of irresolution," writes Gary Hart about the new ethical demands, "is not in our interests. Clearly we must think and act anew and turn the confluence of events that have developed." The altered, always enlarged nature of human action, with the magnitude and novelty of its works and impact on our global future, raises moral issues about our responding for which past ethics has left us unprepared. The changed nature of human action calls for a change in the basis for our responding.

The responsible—persons continuing the search for new systems of responding appropriately in the interdependent planet Earth—must commit themselves to a program with specific assignments. They need, says Albert R. Jonsen in *Responsibility in Modern Religious Ethics* (1968), "to enter into the task aware of its potential and its risks, willing to be blamed if it is performed faultily and rightfully claiming credit for its probity. In addition, the moral quality of a person grows out of the commitments made and stood by: persons form their lives in certain ways and come to be identified by others as responsible for themselves and their actions."

America enters the 1990s awesomely alive with the opportunities of being *free to be responsible*. The spread of its pluralistic and democratic society—a victory for American ideals and policy—promises a world bound more tightly together, largely at peace, and freer to concentrate on improving the well-being of its inhabitants. The country is shrugging off the malaise and shrunken visions of the 1970s, partly because the 1980s turned out so much better than the voices of doom predicted. A world of increasingly interdependent nations requires shared power, a new international order and commitment of all peoples to give loyal and responsible cooperative responses.

If it follows an irresponsible course, America will lose ground to cutthroat competitors, megabyte by megabyte. It cannot afford to allow its national purpose to become a vessel, emptied of original content, into which ideologues of all shades and hues are invited to pour their own causes, their own visions. The nature of power is continuing to change as the world becomes more interdependent. If the United States remains the leading power, it will have to cope with unprecedented problems that no great power can solve by itself. Many new issues in international politics—ecology, drugs, AIDS, terrorism—involve diffusion of power away from large states to weaker states and private actors. These issues will require cooperative responses. How to manage this transition to interdependence is the real challenge of being free to be responsible.

For the United States, as Joseph E. Nye, Jr, Director of the Center for Science and International Affairs at Harvard says at the beginning of 1990, "the universalism of a country's culture and its ability to reestablish a set of favorable rules and institutions that govern areas of international activity are a critical source of power. This and other 'soft sources of power' are becoming more important in world politics at the end of the century."

Key questions become: Will enough of each new generation learn sufficient self-discipline to avoid the excesses of either unproductive hedonism or uncreative author-itarianism: (That means enough self-discipline to demand that their children be basically well educated, to save more than they borrow, to require that both politicians and consumer products live up to their promises or be dropped.) And, will people of all cultures gain the kind of spiritual underpinning that provides both individual stability and concern for the larger human family?

Judeo-Christianity has consistently stressed responsibility in the sense of accountability: God as creator dictates a law and will judge accordingly, human beings are summoned to find God's law and freely obey it. They are responsible, that is, accountable before God's judgment. The relationship between response and responsibility serves for theologians as a fundamental metaphor for the relationship between God and humanity: humanity must *respond* to God's call and intention for the world. In God there is life, sustenance, power, reconciliation and resurrection. Away from God is loneliness, fear, shame, guilt and uncertainty. Human beings are free to choose either way.

This book identifies some of the critical issues and perplexities we meet in the many and often complicated aspects of our responding. In exploring how we exercise the freedom to respond we hope to find ways that lead to a fulfilling instead of wasteful life. The search is for patterns of thought and behavior that open our present and future to more satisfying and significant living. The aim is to define mental, emotional and spiritual conditions that will help us give responsible responses as we work, create and love.

The phenomenon of response will be examined in following chapters dealing with how our freedom to respond is both unbounded and bound, the importance of awareness or responsiveness, how we are to respond to conditions and forces we cannot change, what the great world faiths affirm about responses, involvement as the "intimate response," and how responding presumes responsibility.

C H A P T E R

Responses Unbounded, Freedom Qualified

Responses come in unlimited variety, but our *freedom* to respond is limited by many moderating factors. Our individuality and the society of which we are a part come forth as we respond to confrontations—as minor as our reactions to the checkout line cheat who tries to leapfrog the queue and as major as a nation facing war. Though our responses are unlimited, the circumstances of responding narrow our choices.

Our Unbounded Responses

Countless responses—simple or complex, casual or deliberate, public or private—occur by the second. The response may be a simple "yes" or "no" reply to a question or an elaborate exposition for an inquiry about a complicated subject. A response can be a quick gesture of approval or disapproval, or it can be the flowing movements of a conductor directing an intricate choral antiphonal.

Inner responses often help to keep our behavior in line. In his prayers one night, a 13-year-old named Tommy asks

God to help keep secret his encounter with marijuana that day. He is responding to some hard nudges of conscience.

In response to an overflowing toilet a housewife frantically calls a plumber. Responding, a journeyman with 20 grimy years of crawling under houses and fine-tuning water closets comes and works with deliberate efficiency, coupled hopefully with the right tools the first trip.

A husband and wife often respond differently in the same situation. When John and Mary go to their mountain cabin in the Catskills, John cannot wait to get into his hiking boots and walk out into a storm looking for wildlife in trouble or, in better weather, checking up on a screech owl refuge on a remote trail. On the other hand, Mary cannot wait to curl up in the window seat with a cup of hot chocolate and the latest Tim Conroy thriller. When John comes in breathless with excitement about a new family of screech owls or a black-hooded night heron he spotted in a birch tree, Mary barely listens to him. Nose-in-book, she wants to find out whether another missile threat has been foiled by NATO forces.

Responses break through in many ways as people express their individual interests and priorities. In the neighborhood Mrs. K. and Mrs L. may respond quite differently when they get a call from Mrs. J. to come to a reception to meet Bob, the school-board candidate. Mrs. K. turns down the invitation, not because she does not like Bob, but because she feels frumpy in the only dress she would consider wearing to the fashionable gathering. Mrs. L. on the other hand accepts Mrs. J.'s invitation because she'd like to lobby for funds to build a backstop at the Little League field.

The timing and nature of responses remain crucial for businesses and services. In the marketplace the motto, "respond and thrive," provides a sound strategy that works miracles for the companies that rigorously practice it. Retailers not responsive to customers don't thrive. Unresponsive clerks or receptionists cause customers to become disaffected and go elsewhere. A seemingly infinitesimal Nielsen sampling of responses helps the media determine what television programs the networks will show the rest of the season. The response of a few hundred govern the viewing fare of millions!

Community and national happenings stir up particular and differing responses. We see John Kenneth Galbraith responding to a major shift in the economy or political situation. Bishop Desmond Tutu marches with his colleagues to protest the latest human rights violation. Martin Luther King, Jr. leads the 1955 bus boycott in Montgomery, Alabama to make a stand for civil rights. Polish workers stage demonstrations against legitimate grievances. Each of these represent responsible responses.

Countless other responses go unrecognized: The ambulance attendant comforts a stroke victim. The postal carrier brings the mail to the door of a shut-in instead of leaving it in the mailbox. An unheralded woman refuses to stand aside in the crowd demonstrating for Solidarity. An unknown Good Samaritan protects an elderly lady bullied by street toughs. Each of these demonstrate the conscious choice to respond.

Response's Unbounded Components

To live is to respond with thoughts, feelings and aspirations to the inner and external demands we meet. Through our responses we express the entire range of our personality, our social nature and our hopes and spiritual yearnings. When we track the workings of either the simplest or the most complex human reaction, we run into a nest of questions about the power and persuasiveness, quality and elegance of our responses.

Since the first glimmer of human thought, questions have been with us such as: Why are we what we are? Why do we do what we do? Why do we feel what we feel? These whys and wherefores of our innumerable responses have continued to perplex humankind. Some answers explain simple actions and specific issues. But beneath the superficial questions we find more complex ones about the pragmatic patterns of responding. Answers to such questions display the unbounded richness and power of responses and give us handles for understanding and managing them.

Physical circumstances contribute both to the wide variety of our responses and to the restraints surrounding our freedom to respond. We think of the way children, on seeing a play yard, want immediately to explore it. There is the batter responding to the pitcher's slider and the tight end reaching for the quarterback's bullet pass over the goal line. But the children may not be able to get in to play because the gate is locked, the batter may strike out and the quarterback may overthrow the receiver.

Biologists examine the nature of our physical organism and how this condition affects the ways we respond. Sigmund Freud, originally a physiologist specializing in the study of the nervous system, established his interpretations of human behavior on what he called "the organic substructure." Since his work a century ago, sophisticated studies have further demonstrated how our bodies follow the imprint of genes. Physiologists, with their studies of the intricate interactions of muscles, organs and glands, teach us much about how our bodies respond. A seemingly simple response like a leg-jerk, when the doctor taps one's knee, actually involves a complex process. The tap stimulates receptor nerves, the brain decodes the impulse, decides on a response and activates nerves to communicate movement of the leg. To appreciate and discipline our responses we must accept the fact that in responding we maintain a continuous give-and-take with our complex bodily functions.

Similarly, the social environment puts complicated "spin" to our responses. Close at hand are parents, brothers, sisters and friends, who place obligations and expectations on us. Our response is demanded when the couple next door asks us to join a plan for a Neighborhood Watch. Schools, hospitals, churches and other organizations evoke responses which can be varied and complicated. Effective communal response is enhanced and broadened by "responsive" and "responsible" public leaders. In turn, we hold these leaders accountable for their competence and ethics and for the way they respond to citizens and changing conditions.

Likewise, business managers and industrialists depend on responding to the needs and wants of customers and clients for their existence. Questions about effective ways of responding determine systems for sales, advertising, marketing, producing and delivering items and services to people. The application and control of responses is vital in research, planning and goal setting. Leadership style, training, incentives, establishing standard values—all provide ways of encouraging and guiding responses.

The makeup and expressions of our personalities—our psychology—contributes yet another crucial constituent of our responses. Hobart Mowrer, past president of the American Psychological Association, in his article "Freedom and Responsibility" wrote, "The desire for response is universal among human beings. It is seen especially in the closest relationships: marriage, which involves the demonstration of affection, the sharing of interests, aspirations and ideals of husband and wife." Melanie Klein, pioneer British psychiatrist, put it another way, "To be alive is to be free to respond. The hunger for response and the need to respond launches and powers the growth of individuals and the development of the race."

Thoughts, feelings and convictions also provide the origin and stimulation of responses. We become aware of these inner promptings when we take our responses off "automatic" (under control of the central nervous system) and put them on "manual" (examine them with our thoughts). We cannot predict how any one of us will respond to given stimuli because our mental and emotional reactions involve the complicated processes of desires, intentions, memory and self-reflection.

Desires, for instance, give impetus and power to responses. The need for food or drink, male or female companionship, or a manner of occupying leisure time demands satisfaction. In responding to our wishes, we become frustrated when our desires reach into more situations than we can respond to. At other times, an element of cowardice may creep in and render us unwilling to define and express our desires. We may try to escape into rationalization, justifying our preference for response "A" rather than response "B" by holding "A" to be more agreeable and affording greater insight and mastery in some field. Perhaps "A" involves less conflict than its rival. More complex responses occur when unconscious desires, directly opposite to what a person seems to want, press for open expression and try to get into the driver's seat.

Intentions, another combination of mental and emotional stirrings, also have a strong influence on our responses. They work powerfully to accomplish their partisan aims. If a decision is intended, something is decided; if the intention is love, some thing or person is loved; or, if it is hate, the response becomes hate. Intended responses are further complicated because they are more calculated and extended. They have to be pulled into line with our priorities and values. Since the process involves weighing our convictions, making intentional response must also affect one's convictions. Making intentional responses to people and events is neither simple nor easy, but we are helped to keep our intentions and values in balance as we respond by our memory.

Memory is at work in our responding to remind us of the values we hold and the lessons learned from past mistakes. "Memory," writes Norman Cousins in *Human Options*, "is the proof of life. Nothing really happens to a person unless it becomes memory." A stimulus invites an initial reaction, but subsequent considerations set in motion our memory. This was the case with 13 year-old Tommy.

Response is measured by the ability to transcend personal memory. We, too, in recalling past responses, see patterns which enable us to act according to our values and to define the essence of our personality. This essence may be impaired, as in the case of the rapist or child-molester whose blighted pattern of responding cannot distinguish the acceptable from the unacceptable. Responsive people, who reach into memory for a conscious reference are guided in determining what they *ought* or *ought not* do. Memorable words and phrases call up significant past events and etch the present into the future. Metaphors, slogans, catchy quotes, suggests Stanley I. Kutler at the University of Wisconsin, "contribute to the resonance and recall of events, offering images that groove into the hard disk of individual historical recollections."

Self-reflection utilizes memory to develop, guide and enrich responses. In this self-examining process we say to thoughtless impulses: "Wait a minute! Stop and look at important considerations memory reveals." This inner searching mirrors our genuine selves and shows us the memory of ourselves, our ongoing genetic substance. Self-reflection clarifies and strengthens our sense of *oughtness* by providing a baseline for appropriate responses.

This inner searching shows us when our self-benefiting motives may get in the way of our ideals: a deserving charity or church may get our approval but not our donation. With self-reflection we can turn behavior around to put money and effort behind praise of a worthy cause.

When we look at people's interactions, we see that their responses are unbounded, varying with the times, circumstances and individuals. However, these same diverse factors that arouse our responses more often than not include restrictions of our freedom. The learned boundaries established in our family background, the limits of our social and physical surroundings, and the close parameters of our faith, all prevent us from willy-nilly thinking, feeling and doing as we please.

A Family Illustrates Its Response Limitations

Bright-eyed, a pair of beribboned pigtails flying, five year-old Annie ran up the steps half a flight ahead of her mother, LeAnne, her grandmother, Iris, and her step-grandfather, Dave. With a smile, she ran toward the counselor and greeted him with a hug and a kiss.

"Down in the play yard," she said, catching her breath, "there's a big Noah's Ark! Can you unlock the gate and let me climb in?"

Having no key to the yard, I did the next best I could do and took her to a window where she could see the old boat and told her how it was built. On the way back to the waiting room, she agreed reluctantly to stay there and color while her mother and her grandparents talked with me in the next room.

"Last week went better," Grandmother Iris started. "But all hell broke loose last night. Returning from a church meeting I found LeAnne, 25, carrying on a word battle with her 23-year-old younger brother, Bob, with whom she has fought since she first began to talk. I intervened when the outbursts escalated and the two sounded close to coming to physical blows."

"Mother!" LeAnne broke in, "Again you're blaming me and putting me down before you've heard what happened. The fact is Bob, self-righteous and critical as always, said my bad temper and inconsistency lead to my not landing a teaching position during these three years since graduating. He kept on calling me 'a 25 year-old leech,' still living off of parents and branded me 'a shameless wench' for shacking up with no-account Scott and getting pregnant with Annie out of wedlock, and repeating it all now by sneaking off weekends to sleep with Steve, another fifth-class citizen.' He pushed all my hurt buttons. And I'm not going to take such abuse lying down!"

"Okay, okay." Iris broke in, "So, last night I was wrong in blaming you. I'm sorry."

"See, Dr. C.! This fourth of my six children may be the brightest and the best educated, but she's the fastest at lashing out against the rest of the family."

"Incidentally," Iris continued, pointing to the chart on the table outlining the birth order of the siblings and listing each of Iris' and Dave's previous spouses, "You had better write in 'Scott,' Annie's natural father."

s LeAnne burst in, "Mother! Why must you always bring up Scott? You know I don't want his name mentioned around Annie. She's already confused enough about all this father business. Right now she's calling my current friend, Steve, 'Daddy.' Annie's blood father has never been anything but trouble. The less Annie knows about him the better."

"A fact is a fact, LeAnne," snapped Iris. "You did have Annie by Scott. Furthermore, you've never told me you wanted word about her father kept a secret."

"You never leveled with me about who my natural father was" LeAnne cut in. "The word leaked out accidentally from mouthy Auntie Sue just in time to add more confusion to my fouled up adolescence."

Defending herself, Iris explained, "Your stepfather Winn and you had a positive relation from the time you were a toddler. I didn't want to do anything to damage the support he gave you and the love you showed him. I had my hands full raising the five other children as well. I did the best I could for you."

"Your 'knowing the best for me' always means trying to get me to go your way," LeAnne blurted out. "You did it last night, pushing me down and backing up your little 23-year-old favorite son."

"LeAnne," Iris countered, "from even before you were born, you've been a kicker. As you grew, I tried to help you become less antagonistic, but your track record hasn't been all that good."

" 'Track record'? Who are you to talk? Four husbands, and having two of your six babies out of wedlock!" snapped LeAnne. "See, Dr. C., how hysterical and immature Mother is. She's just like her meddling and scatter-brained mother in Albuquerque!"

"I can't take any more of this," Iris sobbed, and burst into tears. "I give and give, only to have the helpful things I do thrown back in my face. LeAnne cannot communicate without stirring up hostility. She always goes for the jugular. She's stirred up so much trouble lately, I've twice told her to move out. Each time her stepfather, Dave, reminds me of the hard fact that until she lands a teaching job she and little Annie would be out on the street. So I renege, brace myself and let her stay longer."

Suddenly little Annie came in bringing a handful of drawings. "Are you fighting again?" she intervened and innocently tossed in a bomb with the question, "Grandmom, why won't you let 'Daddy' Steve come over to our house?"

Iris managed to smile, gave Annie a big hug and assured her, "We'll be going home soon, but now please go on back to the other room and do some more pictures."

"Yes," LeAnne broke in, "exactly why is my Steve so unacceptable? How long am I going to have all your flak about him?"

"As long as he continues in his old ways," Iris shot back. "His track record in the 30 months you've dated him has worsened. He's still on drugs and alcohol. He's unstable and irresponsible, uncouth and unappreciative, unemployed and unemployable and refuses to get job training."

"You don't even know the man," LeAnne fired back. "You judge and reject him without giving him a chance. All his life he's been deprived and hounded. He deserves encouragement instead of your steady stream of rejections. It doesn't matter to you that he's about the only person on earth that believes in me and helps me feel wanted and needed. You don't care that the chemistry between us is super. He's basically smart and sensitive.

"And where does this family go from here?" Dave interrupted, pulling his chair closer into the circle. "I've had it up to my eyebrows with this constant sniping and feuding. While you two go at each other's throats, I'm churning inside, sometimes mad as hell, other times ready to cry out of pity for all of us."

"Okay, where can we go as a family?" asked Iris, now more exhausted than exasperated.

"Each of us better start tending to his or her own unfinished inside business," continued Dave. "I see myself mirrored in you two. My way of responding is out of whack. I shoot off my mouth before I've heard the other side. I let my anger spew out. I've not made peace with my own mixed-up 30-year-old daughter. I dump my frustrations from work on the family and I spend too much supporting the addiction to my model railroad hobby."

Dave continued, "You two are much alike. You charge into each other's weak side making inner uncertainties worse. We're all too defensive and waste a lot of our energy protecting ourselves. We twist facts instead of facing the way things really are. Refusing to be open and empathetic, we distance ourselves from the ones dearest to us. We're spinning our wheels and wasting time and energy we could use to cooperate and enjoy one another."

Turning to LeAnne, he said, "What bugs us about you and your Steve is how you are wasting your education and limited funds in a relationship that cannot go anywhere but down."

"LeAnne, you said you wanted to forget the mix-up over 'the father business,' " Dave continued, "All of us have a biological father, but not all have an emotionally supportive father. I remember that I missed having a father who would help me develop a firm will and a sense of what is real and the capacity for *facing reality.*"

Concluding his lecture, Dave added, "When we sweep our unresolved hostilities toward our parents under the rug, the rest of our responses go haywire and we respond as if we never had a father to provide us with a solid presence and a sense of direction."

Little Annie was back at the door, tired of waiting. "I don't want to color any more," she said sleepily. "Let's go home. . . . Please."

Annie was right. It was time to go and the family gathered itself together and left.

Responses of five year-old Annie were wonderfully simple and direct. Things, places and people brought out transparent words and movements. The Noah's Ark was for exploring, the paper for coloring, the office was a new place to investigate and the different mood and reactions of her mother and grandparents gave her a circle she wanted to share in. When she walked in on the mother-daughter battle, she called it as it was—*fighting*. We can say her responses— until she got tired—were unbounded.

LeAnne's responses at age 25 were complicated. With little enthusiasm for being "dragged" into the counseling session, she resisted reacting with the family. She threw her responses into defending herself, countering condemnation and warding off the threat of being thrown out of her mother's home.

LeAnne's ambivalence added to the pressures of her uncomfortable circumstances: being dependent, but wanting to be independent, living under the same roof yet feeling estranged. Locked into the family, she still felt excluded. Educated in cognitive skills, she lacked empathy. Feeling vulnerable with no money, job or spouse, she responded in a defensive and self-assertive way. Unemployed, she needed parents to supplement her welfare check and baby-sit her daughter. All this made LeAnne especially vulnerable to her parent's criticism. Uncertain of her identity, vulnerable and insecure, she responded impulsively, and often damagingly to herself and others.

The two grandparents, both in their 50s, responded in their habitual ways developed from decades of coping with their jobs, families of origin, child rearing, work, hobbies and their religious convictions—their survival. Iris, lacking self-confidence and self-reliance, subordinates her own needs to those of the persons who depend on her. At other times, needing reassurance and being inclined toward self-indulgence, she responds by manipulating and making demands. Dave, on the other hand, has some awareness of his "unfinished inner business." The resulting responses get him into trouble in his family. With his perfectionism and insistence on rules, he tends to insist that others submit to his way of doing things, and lacks awareness of the effect this has on others.

Boundaries of our Freedom to Respond

Questions about whether we are free to respond deepen as we probe the nature and limits of human interaction. The question of exactly how free we are simply will not go away.

Are we free to respond? Responsiveness clearly and positively characterizes human beings. We are aware, capable of sensing, thinking and acting reasonably in the light of knowledge. However, do not natural and social environmental conditions enter into every event, act and decision in ways that leave little room for the human will to guide or even influence our responses? How determined are we?

Many circumstances force us to recognize the limits of our freedom to respond: often our clearest thoughts and best intentions make no difference in the course of events. The responses we can manage often seem sealed by an implacable fate, as if we were fenced in and the exit gate were locked. Involuntary and spontaneous responses are blocked by predetermined conditions as the determinists tell us, and the eternities created by the imagination appear pitifully ironic against the shadow of inevitable death.

The ages have known past civilizations that were much concerned with whether humankind is free to respond. Throughout history most people have had precious little freedom, but as societies developed and their cultures became more sophisticated, the nature and extent of freedom became an issue of ever greater significance.

The Greeks, for example, initially thought of freedom in terms of a person's capacity for self-determination. Freedom to respond was seen as the liberation found in returning to one's self and recovering self-control. Freedom meant freedom from slavery, freedom to express self-will within privileged citizenship in the Greek *polis*. In due course they found that questions about freedom are not problems only *of* the self but problems *for* the self. Asking questions about freedom leads one to examine the relation of the self to itself and to the world. Responses, the Greeks concluded, stemmed not only from desires and other emotions, but from reason and sharpened consciousness as well. Inquiries about free action and will took them particularly to questions about how to use reason to overcome the world's ambiguities and, finally, with finding a place beyond the world to which people can retreat. As the *polis* declined, freedom came to be viewed more as liberation through reason from the tyranny of the affections and fate. As confusion and pessimism increased, responses were curtailed and freedom could be had only as individuals escaped to their heavenly origin through a super-knowledge called *gnosis*.

In other cultures, at different times, freedom became increasingly a central political concern. In China, for example, the establishment of each of its long line of ruling dynasties was marked by dissatisfied groups who sought to free their country from regimes that had become moribund, corrupt and oppressive. In Western societies, particularly from the 18th century, the achievement of political and social freedom became people's *cause célèbre*. In time freedom was extended and built into habits of common life and became buttressed by institutions and law.

The 20th century has brought an explosion of political and social freedom for Westerners: women's suffrage and later women's liberation, minority and other human rights and the relinquishment of colonial domination. But the triumphs of science and technology, paradoxically, have hemmed in some of that freedom.

The challenge of deterministic theory to the concept of free will cannot be taken lightly. Much about human origins, genetics and anatomy remains cloaked in mystery, so that a deterministic explanation of certain aspects of human nature must be taken seriously. Many contemporary scientists meet the conflict between determinism and free will by limiting it to resolvable empirical problems in physics and biology. Consciousness becomes an immense number of coordinated symbolic representations by the participating neurons of the neocortex. Neurobiologists describe how information from the senses passes to a region of the cerebral cortex and activates responses electrically.

Mechanistic arguments against our being free to respond do not consider all the evidence. To reduce consciousness to an action of organic machinery does not rule out free will. The emotional centers of the lower brain are programmed to pull the puppeteer's strings more carefully whenever the self steps onto the stage of the neural drama. Even if the mind is basically a pre-programmed computer, it is unlikely that the program is powerful enough to predict precisely how any individual person is going to act. Deterministic approaches concern themselves with what *is,* especially what is seen and measured. This approach of the physical sciences has made phenomenal contributions in many areas of knowledge and technology, but has proven inadequate in providing insight into the spiritual side of human beings. Humans are more than the chemistry and physics of their bodies. They are not rule-dependent flesh or robots, bounced here and there by fixed physical circumstances.

Fortunately, the mind is more than a comprehensible biological computer. We are capable of enormous varieties of self-generating feelings, beliefs and thoughts which require responses. How, for instance, can we talk about love among identical, though differently programmed computers? If we are biological computers, our experience of love must be some kind of illusion. More importantly, what about the ultimate questions on the meaning and purpose of life? How can we have personal purpose when "we" do not exist with freedom to respond? Edward O. Wilson, professor of entomology at Harvard University reminds us, "The mind is too complicated a structure and human social relations affect its decisions in too intricate and variable a manner, for the detailed histories of individual human beings to be predicted in advance by the individuals affected or by other human beings. You and I are consequently free and responsible persons in this fundamental sense."[1]

Wait a minute, insist the determinists who argue that freedom affirmers also wear blinders. Determinists say the contradictions and resistances our fast-changing age, and many other evidences reinforce the argument against our being unconditionally free to respond. One paradoxical way our freedom to respond is restricted arises from the burgeoning of options available in modern Western consumer-oriented societies. The glut of choices often diminishes our freedom with action-slowing inertia or with a paralyzing indecision. Furthermore, the information explosion reduces us to focusing on stereotype television programs while particular periodicals give us little time for reflection. Our material abundance often imprison us. We accumulate

---

[1] *On Human Nature,* p. 77

more things than we can ever use and we are easily enslaved by the need for more ready cash that we do not have.

What freedom we enjoy often is diminished by what Martin Marty, professor at the University of Chicago, calls "the tribal preoccupation with self." That is, in our communities we tend to narrow our freedom by letting our local connections and ethnicity reduce us to becoming exclusive. The Afrikaners, themselves once victims of British imperialism and persecution, have developed an ideology through which they see themselves as the "Chosen People." They have been persuaded by the bizarre comforts provided by the brutal system of racial privilege that the African is a subhuman being created to serve white interests. Marty observes that in the United States we have brought ourselves to the point where the Blacks say if you aren't Black and oppressed, you don't have the vision. The Moral Majority says if you aren't one of them, "you don't have *the* vision."

In our cities tolerance and cosmopolitanism often get lost among the "warring tribes." People who seek to escape the banality and limitations of life in a small town find urban permissiveness and anonymity posing new difficulties. They arrive in the "Big City" to find themselves lost amid the crush of humanity. Suffering isolation and estrangement, they cannot be sure that the person next to them is safe getting to know or is a homicidal maniac.

In many situations the freedom to respond reasonably, purposefully, or fulfillingly is almost impossible. Troublesome happenings we face or hear about daily put a heavy weight on the NO side of having any real freedom to respond. As terrorists carry out death-games with hostages and currencies rise and fall amid rumors of a third World War, we look in horror and feel we are not free. The crucial question of whether we are free to respond, then, draws both a YES and a NO answer.

NO, say the determinists, claiming that prior influences control people's decisions. Amid such bewildering contradictions and failures today, saying NO to the freedom to respond becomes almost automatic. So many of our responses trap us in dead ends. Persons in this camp argue against the possibility of free will and continue stubbornly to hold that complex natural, personal and social phenomena result from specific pre-determined causes.

YES, say others, just as vehemently. To deny the YES-side of freedom throws us into the pit of pessimism. The YES-side stirs us with hope that we can find a way to live within the ambiguity of human freedom and exercise wisely and responsibly the freedom within our reach.

To say YES about our freedom to respond is reinforced by our common sense. Of course we are free to respond. The little girl playing with her doll is free to respond with fantasies, the boy on his skateboard is free to feel excited, athletes are free to exercise their skill, parents can entertain high aspirations for their children and grandparents are free to respond with pride as they share pictures of their progeny. When thirsty we respond by going to the nearest water fountain to drink; when cold, we turn up the heat or put on a sweater; and when we are in church we bow our heads and offer supplication. YES, we are free to respond.

When the sun is shining and we are assured of living within a loving blanket of human relationships and supported by the promises of the divine, then we say YES, we are free to respond. With family and friends, clients and customers, co-workers and neighbors, we perform *as if* we are of course free to respond. Beyond the individual circumstances, entire societies, even history itself, revolve around peoples' freedom to respond. Conceivably, if George Washington had responded differently and chosen to become king of the 13 colonies, our nation might be an oligarchy today, instead of a democracy.

Nevertheless, the arguments for the NO-side of our having free will persist. The free will we do enjoy remains bound by definite conditions. Existence is just like staying alive on the freeway. The perilous fast lane in which we move requires split-second responses. We are "free" as long as we stay in our lane, keep with the flow and give correct signals. Speaking metaphorically, traveling on the threatening freeways of life, we are "free to respond" in any way we wish: YES, but to live and not jeopardize others; NO, we are not free to respond in any way we please.

To the determinists who argue NO to freedom to respond it can be pointed out that there is a difference between fortune and choice. A tested answer for meaningful living remains: fortune or fate happens to you, but choice comes in what you do about it or how you exercise your freedom to respond.

In the final analysis, neither determinism nor free will can be proved. As long as freedom cannot be disproved, we will continue to debate about it. Responsible living, however, can never rest on the consideration that we are able, 100 percent of the time, to respond exactly as we desire and intend. The point is: We are responsible for our responses within the range of where and how we are free to respond. The continued mystery—yet reality—of freedom provides our last hope for a life of meaning and purpose.

Freedom and the Courage to Decide

The sequence of choice-decision-action is crucial in the exercise of freedom. To be free to respond builds upon the assumption of the individual's being able to choose between options, make a decision about it, then act on it.

Along with the question of whether we are free to respond, we must ask: Can we *choose* with confidence and purpose to move from our desire and will to responsible thoughts, feelings and behavior? Put another way, the question asks whether we can move from self-reflection to reason and knowledge, from wisdom to appropriate responding and finally from these steps of freedom to reach a consciousness of who we are and where we are headed; i.e., a consciousness of our identity and destiny.

"Freedom is experienced as deliberation, decision and responsibility," asserts Paul Tillich.[2] He defines deliberation as a process of self-reflection in which we weigh our arguments and motives. Decisions occur when persons, after struggling with their motives, *choose* a response. Decision calls for courage, because to decide cuts off possibilities. To decide one particular "true" or "good" course means excluding countless other possibilities. It is a risk, rooted in the courage of being a free person.

In deciding, then, we must not only evaluate the precision of our responsiveness, but whether we possess the *will* to alter nature and history. In our daily life, whether we are free spirits will be less important than whether we believe we are, because the *belief* in free choice is itself a potent determining force in human affairs. To believe in our freedom to decide lifts us out of the chaos of mere conjecture and gives us a unique dignity among the species. In deciding, as on the freeway, we must exercise our freedom to respond within the webbed scheme of natural and social conditions.

When challenged about our decisions, we cannot ask anyone else to give an answer. Each of us is responsible for the response decided upon; we are expected to justify and take responsibility for the decisions we make. Our accountability for how we choose weighs heavily upon us. The obligation that flows from our freedom both defines our responsibility and lends a fatal light on all our actions and beliefs. Albert Camus held that deciding whether to commit suicide or to live is unavoidable. "When we decide to live," he claimed, "through our responses we accumulate the quantity and variety of experiences that guide and give meaning to life." He urges that by deciding and responding

---

[2] *Systematic Theology,* Vol. I, p. 184

we answer the fundamental question whether life is worth living.

To find courage to affirm life, the individual must struggle to overcome the paralysis of indecision. The response of personal decision is particularly urgent when trauma strikes and threatens existence. I cannot hope to hitchhike on a community or state decision. I must decide both to affirm life and to survive. I must choose and decide to survive.

The experience of Eddy dramatizes the pain and urgency of decision. Now an adult, he remembers the shattering days of his adolescence 20 years ago. Parental abuses drove him out of the home into Juvenile Hall and then into a mental hospital. The hurt and fear of his youth remained open wounds. "Being trained 'never to fight,' " he explained, "I was defenseless. In the Hall I had to figure out ways to survive. Those years in that jungle ground me up and almost wiped me out."

"One day," Eddy related, "I came into my cell and found one of the bigger toughs beating up on my small roommate. The fellow was broad-shouldered and a head taller than me. Suddenly thoughts of safety went out the window and I kicked the bully in the rear as hard as I could. He wheeled and belted me. I got off the floor and stood my ground. Completely surprised, he backed off and never bothered me or my roommate again."

"I surprised myself," continued Eddy. "It had taken me a year to pull together enough inner strength to decide to resist. From that day I began to respect and assert myself."

Though small of stature and weakened with feelings of inadequacy, he drew himself together in the crisis saying, "I'm the only one like me and I'm the only one here-and-now to defend my roommate!" If Eddy had not decided and discovered these inner staying powers, he would never have survived in the jungle community in which he found himself.

Summary

Thus human expression, in all its variety, moves on responses. This phenomenon of response begs for understanding, management and guidance. To render responses intelligible, controlled and directed, we must confront the paradox that responses may be unbounded, but our range of responding has boundaries.

The whys and wherefores of our innumerable responses will continue to perplex us. Biologists, it was pointed out, tell us about the organic basis for our responses; sociologists outline how our complex social environment affects our responses; and psychologists trace the way our thoughts, feelings and convictions influence how we act and react. Dave and Iris' family system reveals each member's hunger for intimacy and acceptance and the differing responses they make within their generational context.

Responses, then, express personal motivations, social exchanges and reactions to the conditions of our physical environment. In describing another person or characterizing a country, most often we capsulize their typical responses saying, "She's so helpful and caring," or, "They're all isolationists/imperialists." We find persons "special" who respond specifically and sensitively to our concerns and aspirations, while persons are "not so special" when they respond with superficial clichés to our agonized recounting of a purse that has just been stolen or the accident that disfigured our child.

Since responses express our reactions to the physical, social and psychological environments in which we live, our responding defines our behavior and our behavior is our responding. By responding fittingly and as completely possible, wholeness and health are enhanced; in turn, our wholeness and health empowers and guides our responses. This "health" renders our responses more appropriate and extended, progressive instead of regressive. This wholeness comes as a gift from the effective functioning of our total persons—body, mind and spirit. In this way we realize our full potentials.

In estimating the extent of our freedom to respond, many circumstances force us to acknowledge that our freedom to respond remains limited. The question of exactly how free to respond we are simply will not go away. The arguments of determinists and our own experience of resistances and failures curtailing our freedom reinforce the fact that human beings are not unconditionally free to respond. In the final analysis, however, neither determinism nor free will can be proved. What we can affirm is this: human beings are responsible for their responses within the gamut of where and how they are free to respond. Though something of a mystery to us, the reality remains that freedom, to the extent we have it, provides our last hope for a life of meaning and purpose. We find that the crucial question of whether we are free to respond draws both a YES and a NO answer.

The endowments of the eyes, ears and other senses give us the capacity for responsiveness. The endowment of our mind gives us the capacity to manage our responses. The deepening and enriching of our responses can be a fruit of our emotional and spiritual health.

Being able to give responses to our inner stirrings as well as to the society and physical world which cradles us, brings us face-to-face with ethics. Having the endowments of the senses and the mind, we have the responsibility to justify our decisions. Eddy, responding appropriately in the crisis he confronted, acted responsibly. He evaluated the nature of the crisis and determined to use his *will* to alter the situation. With his freedom to respond he could either regress or progress. In recognizing that he was not tied forever to fixed ways of responding, Eddy risked developing and applying new responses. In exercising his freedom to respond he lifted himself out of the chaos of insecurity and indecision and into a new self-confidence.

Life offers the adventurous possibility of fulfilling our unique human endowments: to serve as faithful stewards of ourselves, our society and our world. Our appropriately grounded responses remain unbounded. Our expressions of them, however, continue to be moderated by a wide variety of conditions. As desiring, reflecting and intentional persons, we are accountable—we must respond responsibly. Granted, our degree of freedom to be responsive and the decision to take responsibility for our responses must be our preëminent concern. One of life's central questions becomes, How is this concern carried out in a consistent and fulfilling way? For this answer we must consider *awareness* and *responsiveness*.

C H A P T E R

Awareness and Responsiveness: Basis for Responding

The total experience of *awareness* prepares us to make fitting responses. Whether we are putting together breakfast or preparing a banquet, how well we manage to respond depends on how well we initially receive and take stock of the immediate situation.

Accepting and evaluating our experience involves a step-by-step process. First, we find at work an *alert sensibleness,* aroused by the knowledge gained in sensing and perceiving the "what" and "who" we confront. A second force at work is *consciousness,* which emphasizes recognition of something or somebody and an assessment of the nature and qualities of the object, situation or person before us. The quality of being *cognizant,* a third element of awareness, stresses sure knowledge and the recognition of it. This facet of awareness includes a discrimination or recognition of the objective characteristics that affect the interaction taking place. *Watchfulness,* or *vigilance,* a fourth aspect, implies acute perception of what is potentially promising or dangerous.

Two other qualities, deeper and more global, affect awareness. Having a *vision* of the big picture prepares us to respond aptly. Seeing the totality of life, we are more able to picture events and people in perspective. Still another condition, *openness to the transcendent dimension of religious experience*, enhances responsible behavior and social values.

Responsiveness, combines awareness and freedom. Responsiveness begins with sensing carefully and correctly incoming messages, as well as our own inner promptings. We receive these messages through our senses. Responsiveness requires precise and exact attention, taking accurate account of situations. In their fullest awareness, people respond precisely and openly. This more effective responsiveness readies us for timely, suitable responses.

Awareness as Alert Sensitivity

Being truly sensitive to our surroundings is a remarkable process we too often take for granted. Sensitivity consists of immense numbers of simultaneous and coordinated symbolic representations by the participating neurons of the brain's neocortex. To classify this marvelous capacity of approaching things and people as the action of organic machinery does not underestimate the power of the process. In Sir Charles Sherrington's splendid metaphor, the brain is an "enchanted loom where millions of flashing shuttles weave a dissolving pattern." Confronted with our surroundings, we draw on our knowledge having each solution grounded in a separate body of facts and approached with a quiver full of different theories, with all the responses connected in a great complex web.

Seeing and hearing do the yeoman work of cultivating responsiveness. By refining our seeing and hearing we sharpen and make more appropriate our responses.

The scriptures warn us about people who "have eyes but see not and ears but hear not." Many of us "having eyes, see not." For varied reasons we may limit what we see. We may be myopic; we may not see distant objects distinctly.

When a man sees an attractive woman walk by, his attention may be on her stylish dress or regal manner. His responses stem from habits and systems of how he sees women. His manner of "seeing" arises from his physical and emotional feelings as well as his memory and imagination. Social restraint, conditioned by education and moral instruction, tempers his response. If he is a gentleman, he considers the possible feelings of the woman. Responses aroused by present desires may be reined in.

Seeing responsibly, therefore, requires focused attention. It calls for seeing more than what is visible on the surface. The particular and ephemeral must be sorted out from what is general and constant.

Phyllis often complained of not being heard. She said, "People don't listen to me. My husband doesn't pay attention to me. Often I tell him, 'Harry, if you'd only grunt to let me know you're listening to me!' " Suddenly, she asked the therapist, "Dr. C., are you *listening* to me?" Phyllis not only doubts that *anyone* listens to her, she herself listens poorly.

"We all suffer to some degree from deafness," observes Frederick Buechner in *The Hungering Dark.* He notes that we find it hard to hear what other people are saying to us—either hard in the sense of difficult or hard because it is painful. Often we are deaf to the subtleties. We hear only the words, or only what is comfortable to hear.

Somebody remarks about the weather and all we hear, or allow ourselves to hear, is someone talking about the weather. But what the person feels reaches deep: "I'm lonely. Be my friend, for heaven's sake. Speak!" or, maybe, "I know you're lonely."

If we listen responsibly to other people, whether on the surface the talk is about the weather or predicting the outcome of the Super Bowl, we begin to realize they are talking about themselves. One way or another they are saying, "Love me," or maybe "Hate me," or, "Pity me."

Whatever is said, the implication is, "Listen to me. Know me. Accept me."

We are helped to respond appropriately and responsibly when we interpret accurately and clearly the meaning of what we see in and hear from people.

Awareness as Consciousness

Consciousness of one's self is an essential part of awareness and responsiveness. The central responsibility of personal consciousness is to identify, develop and express one's uniqueness. In becoming aware of one's inner reality, individuals become at home in the scheme of things and react toward others more genuinely. We learn about our inner or "essential" selves through appreciating and using the many powers of consciousness. Our "self" achieves consciousness by rearranging our thoughts, feelings and actions. In this process we pull together and reconstruct our experience so that personality is continuous with consciousness. We do more than "just be ourselves;" we take responsibility for tying our behavior to our consciousness. In cultivating and appreciating our personal consciousness, we take responsibility to be aware of the origins and fuller dimensions of our self.

Deeper consciousness provides the guidelines and source of strength we need in becoming more responsible responders. The consciousness which enables us to make a positive reintegration of our life experiences, Paul Ricoeur suggests, includes at least three levels: the organic (*bios*), the person-to-person (*thumus*) and the cosmic (*logos*). The first level of consciousness devotes mental energy to *things* in the natural world that satisfy our needs and pleasures. The second level focuses attention on our responsibility to *ourselves and our relation to others*. The third level concentrates our mental involvement on our intuition of the meaning of what is most important in life.

Artists, poets and saints give expression to these levels of consciousness. Van Gogh's painting, for example, illustrates the effort to pull together these three levels. At the same time he sketches a chair, he portrays a man sitting in that chair and thus projects the figure of one who "has" and is "in" this represented world. He gives the man identity and places him in relation to other people. Through these things and relationships human dignity and self-regard are formed. Then there is a third, or cosmic dimension which seems to reach out to find the key to human wholeness as a conscious individual.

Responsiveness as consciousness, a century after Van Gogh, is harder to cultivate and nourish. Technology has developed along with an intensifying problem of fractured consciousness. Writing of the "dissociation of sensibility" that characterizes our age, T.S. Eliot noted that we are like our poets who have become "masters of diction" but who are no longer "explorers of the soul." In Greek mythology the gods sometimes punished human beings by fulfilling their wishes too completely. We are paying the price for a seemingly effortless achievement and our excessive confidence in things (the *bios* level). We are being pushed back to the cosmic/psychic frontier and to the discovery that our responsibility for deepened consciousness reaches beyond concentration on the physical/organic. Responsibility for our self-representation, as we confront daily life, must focus on our social and cosmic roots. In his *Phenomenon of Man* Pierre Teilhard de Chardin, the Jesuit paleontologist, envisioned our consciousness as calling forth a greater integration of the person's total powers—a condition in which we have responsibility for an expanded consciousness.

An illustration of the demand for an "expanded consciousness" is given by specialists in their fields of academic studies. Foreign policy specialists distribute the responsibility of greater awareness and more responsible actions to improved international relations on citizens and whole departments of government as well as on leaders. Specifically, according to Professor Hans J. Morgenthau of the University of Chicago, "without drastic domestic reforms in thought and action—deepened consciousness and more determine commitment—American foreign policy will continue to stumble." He cites what happens when this more realistic awareness and determine action is missing: a strange and ominous apathy appears that precludes a lively concern in public affairs without which democracy itself loses vitality and tends to ritualize our civic life.

Psychologists, in studying the mind and the emotions, find a variety of approaches to exploring and sharpening consciousness. Ways to enhance disciplined behavior are found by studying people's quirks and phobias, as well as the inclinations and creativeness. Monitoring each stage of our development shows that consciousness is commensurate with the extent of our capabilities. In maturing and increasing our freedom to respond, our consciousness expands. Deepened consciousness and committed action enables us to respond to options that are generative instead of addictive, positive instead of negative. Deepened consciousness adds to our sense of responsibility and helps us own our past and acknowledge that we are products of our parents and teachers. We are helped to change from being antique to being real and contemporary. Dedicated and committed action based on deepened consciousness presses us to push back the boundaries that limit our development.

Social scientists tell us that with the rise of individualism and the decline of traditional values, people are increasingly in need of a broadened and deepened consciousness of themselves and of the meaning of life. It has become increasingly evident that a new and more adequate consciousness is needed to limit and restrain the destructive side of individualism and provide alternative models for how we might live.

Many Americans, according to the observation of Robert Bellah and his associates in the book, *Habits of the Heart*, are devoting themselves to disciplines, practices and "trainings," often of great rigor. The deeper consciousness reaches for something that transcends even the best of "steps." Consciousness, in its fuller dimensions, seeks relationship to the total field of energy which is the ultimate condition for all phenomena, persons and nations.

The deepest consciousness commands us to align all our tasks and interests to the fulfillment of a transcendent promise.

Cognizant Element in Awareness and Responsiveness

The unique human capacity for cognition—the ability to obtain knowledge—accompanies the sensing and perceiving that leads to awareness and responsiveness. To be "cognizant" is to have conscious knowledge in the form of recognition and apprehension. It includes the range of what one can know or understand.

When we try to learn how to respond appropriately, the outcome must not only reflect the desires of persons but must present an accurate picture of reality. We may *know* that "honesty is the best policy," but until we practice honesty in daily life, our knowledge and then our responsiveness is neither complete nor responsible. Platitudes and words about values may float beautifully around us, but they are not responsible actions until applied through experience.

Our problem with knowledge reaches beyond the overwhelming volume and variety of the information glut. Reliable knowledge, the kind essential for helping us make appropriate responses, does not automatically order itself. Mere bits of knowledge laid end to end do not necessarily lead to wisdom. "Multiplicity," cautions W. Macneile Dixon in *The Human Situation* (1941), "does not contain a reason for unity." Even science, with its remarkable achievements, aims not so much to open the door to everlasting wisdom, but to set a limit to everlasting error.

When circumstances become overwhelming, the sharpened awareness and responsiveness we seek eludes us. In such moments our awareness becomes "jammed," locked in an unworkable position, our responsiveness is frozen. To recover, we may need to pull away from the pressures by seeking rest and perspective. To become cognizant we are helped when we return to the "well of wisdom" to consider how the past heroes responded at significant turning points in history. An Abraham, a Hercules, or even that mythical Paul Bunyan can highlight the importance of people experiencing a fresh awareness that clears the way to express their freedom to respond. This happened in the evolution of the race with the acquisition of fire and in the eating of the fruit of the tree of knowledge. The traditional stories of great ancestors form the "mythologies" that can help open up our clogged responsiveness. This works because the union of the cognitive and aesthetic functions is fully expressed in mythology. By recognizing our mythologies we see the human face in events and become more responsive.

Our knowledge is intimately tied to the crisis of our limited responsiveness and our uncertainty about ourselves. Our responsiveness must expand to enable us to respond in ways appropriate to the holistic nature of thought and behavior. No such thing as a purely physical, emotional or mental reaction exists. We cannot isolate a "pure response" of either senses or reason. Elements of the body and personality are interrelated as we respond. Thus knowledge of our potential for "wholeness" can strengthen our motivation to strive for health. Also, with the deepened knowledge we gain from greater self-awareness, we are more able to fit new findings of science into a more realistic view of the world.

The philosopher George Santayana, with his hard experience and exquisite sensitivity, was an uniquely aware and responsive person. His biographer John McCormick reports,

"All came clear when Santayana got a handle on the 'essences.' Examples of essences include the quantity *pi*, the color blue and the human face: though not graspable, all three exist. Each helps us to order our world and respond to it appropriately." The knowledge Santayana sought was an awareness that pressed beyond the message of the senses and even the order of the mind, to lucidity and truth.

Watchfulness and Vigilance as Part of Responsiveness

To be observant and alert is essential to awareness. The birth of modern science with Copernicus, Kepler and Newton, came in the 16th and 17th century as these and other researchers became increasingly and more accurately observant.

Ecologists are calling for new responses after a period of mindless squandering of our natural resources. In their vigilance, they call for increased consciousness of what needs doing: establishing a consistent advocate of responsible grassroots activism to reduce acid rain, nuclear waste disposals, air and river pollution, attacks on endangered species and the likelihood of nuclear war—the ultimate environmental threat.

Social scientists sound warnings about the dangers of destructive forces in contemporary society. There was a time in the development of our nation when under the battle cry of "freedom" separation and individuation were embraced as the key to a grand future of unlimited progress. In our deeper consciousness we are concerned that the individualism that has marched inexorably through our history may have grown cancerous.

The quality of watchfulness and vigilance needs to be applied not only to seeing and warning against ominous possibilities, but also alertness to positive opportunities.

Consciousness is deepened as we push back the "fence" that limits our development. The challenge of responsiveness includes living as effectively and positively as possible within the bounds of our particular level of growth and at the same time pushing back restrictive boundaries and opening gates to new and creative responses.

Clinical experience has shown me that individuals grow in awareness and responsiveness as they decide to become watchful of themselves. In their vigilance, or discipline, of themselves, they expand their awareness in four areas: 1) awareness of need and opportunity, 2) awareness of life, 3) awareness of identity, and 4) awareness of integration or wholeness.

The initial "personal vigilance" has to do with the recognition of the legitimacy of our individual needs. Our elemental needs are for food, clothing and shelter, as well as emotional essentials such as security, affection and a sense of belonging. Parents have to be "vigilant" to appreciate that babies grow, not because of cribs that keep them hemmed in, but by their receiving the nutrients critical to physical and emotional health. Vigilance about the self is important for the maturing adult. We establish ourselves as an "I" involved with other "I's" by our common needs and our cooperative effort to meet those needs. We are watchful of self as we engage in an open-ended quest to substantiate ourselves and our connection and worth with others. Recognition of the legitimacy of my essential needs is one way I justify *myself.* Vigilant about my needs and potentials, I make an authentic and appreciative judgment about myself. I am aware that I am enriched by the fulfillment of basic needs and gain a sense of personal self-direction.

A second condition for growth in awareness and responsiveness comes with the recognition of the paradox that the world will not automatically give me what I most need: love and acceptance. It is a fact of life that people are in competition for the fulfillment of their needs. Vigilance requires that we leave behind those relationships which do not nurture and to which we therefore cannot respond. Persons need to turn decisively to those aspects of life which have vitality and to which response may be given. The individual learns how to receive from that which is truly a nurturing source of life and learns how to respond and to be open to life's possibilities. Likewise, fuller awareness of life comes as we grasp that the span between birth and death is not solely subject to our direct control. We must accept the fact that every encounter in our lives places us at the borderline between responsibility and irresponsibility. Vigilance regarding our condition requires that even though we share some responsibility for our lives through the mere fact of our existence, we are responsible to the Creator for our lives. In a Nazi prison, condemned to be hanged, Dietrich Bonhoffer was aware of this truth when he wrote, "The bold stroke which is done on one's own free responsibility for his life is the only kind of a deed which can strike at the heart of evil and overcome it. The man of duty will end by having to fulfill his obligation even to the devil."

A third way in which awareness and responsiveness grows comes from consciousness and appreciation of one's identity. "With the awareness of one's identity," claims Rollo May in his book, *Man's Search for Himself,* "we become more free to respond. Responsibility takes on new meaning." He says further, "In this awareness we recognize what it means to be able consciously to choose to live. In the process of choosing ourselves we are able to become more self-disciplined and to take charge of our life."

I need to be watchful of my identity because it is the sum of my intentional acts, my responsible responses. I must give answers that pay serious attention to the full spectrum of personality. My origin, for instance, is not simply a question of conception, gestation and birth, but where and how I will live my life or apply the lessons of my history. People who struggle to locate identity and work out who they are no longer try to "escape from freedom," but respond responsibly and thereby relate to the outside world in cooperative ways.

The individual's identity involves maintaining an equilibrium between the extremes of action. The world, for example, is divided into doers and stoppers; of these the doers are often the most amoral, and the stoppers tend to be the most preachy. While the doers are in danger of exercising too much freedom, the stoppers tend to restrict freedom that has been won.

A fourth discipline for enhancing awareness and responsiveness has to do with moving toward a sense of wholeness. Achieving the integration of our experiences and total powers enables us to cope with what Chardin called "the perplexification of man's functioning in the modern age." Watchfulness and decisiveness are the price we pay for this greater integration. It requires an efficient channelling of energy and the loving acceptance of ourselves.

These four phases of growth in awareness and responsiveness parallel the development of people's "responsible freedom." In the first two stages need is perceived, knowledge is gained and skills are cultivated. The crucial middle stage is accountability—a dynamic requirement when the individual after attaining competence and independence becomes responsible to a deepened self. The final or reintegrative stage finds individuals focusing intellectual and emotional abilities on those aspects of life that are increasingly meaningful. Responsible participation in this growth process, as Piaget writes, "gives life challenge."

The challenge is to remain vigilant. Vigilance is necessary since the whole is composed of opposites that push and pull against union. We see the dynamic tension coming together when male and female create new life, and in the mysterious play between sound and silence that creates the rhythm we recognize as intelligible speech or music. We see this wholeness in persons who give up symptomatic living for explorative and creative living. Depression gives way to curiosity and interest in the unknown. Self-esteem and feelings of worth are raised and the ability to make responsible choices is increased. Ezra, from the Old Testament, was challenged to remain vigilant when with one hand he worked with a trowel rebuilding the city and with the other he wielded a sword to ward off enemies. Our forbearers had to be vigilant while forging a new nation. Now corporations have to be vigilant to maintain their competitive edge while avoiding takeovers. Husbands and wives must be vigilant to generate and keep growing a supportive and loving relationship as well as maintain a yard and a house. As father and mother they need to keep vigilant to nurture and provide for the family.

Each person is challenged to work against the inner threats of neglect, self-indulgence and irresponsibility. When we sabotage our power to be free to respond, we self-destruct and become aliens in a strange and empty world. Unabashedly we often exhibit demonic traits. We act, not out of faith in a Higher Power, but from our self-centeredness. The challenge to remain vigilant continues in all aspects of our responsiveness. Only then do we approach fulfilling Julian Huxley's claim that people of faith are "the axis and leading shoot of evolution."

Awareness as the Vision of the Big Picture

To be responsible in relation to the world beyond ourselves is a big order. Relating to extended communities and other peoples requires commitment and the application of thorough knowledge and disciplined skill. Responsiveness calls for our making a persistent effort to be aware of and understand our place in the community.

Help in coming to appreciate our place in the world is given by an increasing number of researchers in the hard sciences and in the social sciences. Two biological anthropologists at Harvard University, Melvin Kronner and Edward O. Wilson, illustrate such efforts. Kronner, in *The Tangled Wing* (1983), and Wilson in *On Human Nature* (1979), have developed guides to what we know about the biological roots of human behavior. To better understand why people react toward things as they do, integrative scientists invoke methods and findings of almost every field of study.

Responsiveness to the world beyond ourselves calls for "reality testing," which is the process of distinguishing a present perception from a present act of imagination or act of remembering. Clinicians in diagnosing ask: Is this person seeing something as it truly is or just imagining it? Reality testing has particular significance because confusion between the real and the imagined can be disastrous in the real world.

Responsiveness requires making objective evaluations and judgments of the world outside ourselves. Children, for example, actively experiment to determine how far they can modify a thing or process and how far it resists modification. Through such trials the child gradually learns to distinguish between the self and external reality. As reality testing develops, falsification is reduced. Objects, people and events are seen accurately and meaningfully; thoughts and behavior conform to the hard facts of life.

The fully aware individual must honor and participate in what is universally human. I have a responsibility to my neighbor who conversely has a responsibility to me. The deepest social truth is our mutual responsibility. The scope of this mandate extends to the contribution we owe to the culture of which we are a part. We cannot hide behind the claim that we are unrelated either to the first or the last human being. We inherit the guilt of our forebears and our children die for our wrongs. Perhaps they die vicariously even for those who were mere bystanders in the great struggle of life.

Responsiveness in the complexities and tensions of modern societies requires careful balance of individual and collective action. The mending of strained relationships may require substantial reshaping of a person's or group's patterns of responding, as South Africa may suggest.

Our responsibility to be responsive to the Big Picture is vastly extended in an age such as ours. With the information explosion and the increased array of alternatives, we find more opportunities to become more free to respond. Awareness in no way can be limited in time to the knife-edge of the immediate present or in space to one particular local situation. The deepest consciousness challenges us to align our tasks and interests to the fulfillment of a transcendent promise.

Responsiveness and Religious Experience

Responsiveness, with its sharpened awareness, needs the balance of reason and knowledge, but it also needs the anchoring provided by religious experience. When, beginning with the 17th century, religion was replaced by scientific rationalism, Theodore Roszak observes that, "something vital went out of experience." Whenever and wherever the human spirit feels stifled by its "secularization of consciousness," or by the device-filled world it creates, responsiveness becomes dulled.

People of faith witness to the transformation that comes to those who commit themselves to an awareness that goes beyond mere sensory perception and external satisfactions. The hunger is for an undivided consciousness that consists less in telling stories, adhering to myths, making pronouncements and observing rituals, and more in being related effectively and practically to a fellowship that leads to personal and social healing.

Persons who pride themselves on being strictly practical and rational frequently are uncomfortable with the supernatural world. Such persons may be surprised to find that responsible behavior and social values can be advanced when undergirded with religious experience.

Observation of religious ceremonies may heighten responsiveness for some. A bar mitzvah service, or the call to weekly prayers, beg for a sense of responsiveness. Persons of faith who engage in social action, witnessing from their sense of justice, illustrate an enhanced order of relationship through religious experience. Likewise, a pastoral counselor blends theological and psychological insight. Dedicated to the conceptualizing behavior, the counselor works empathetically for the client's present and future out of concern welfare.

Responsiveness, in part, is being able to see oneself in the new light which comes with religious experience. Responsiveness results when the self reacts positively in life to its interpretation of the "Higher Power." When people seek guidance for their activity as they respond to the demands of their human freedom within their religious experience, they react responsibly.

In the history of Western culture, the relationship between responsiveness and religious experience has the potential of clarifying, supporting and empowering people. The religious experience to which responsiveness answers is not limited to church membership, acceptance of particular creeds or even living by the Golden Rule. It is living out of a vital faith that arises out of a mysterious Source of order and meaning, transcending all the disorders and ills of nature and history—faith in the holy God who is related to the world as creator and renewer.

Our responsiveness leads us to recognize religious experience as not only legitimate, but as a central fact of history and culture. This comes to us when we appreciate why and how religious faith has persisted for the last three centuries following the first triumphs of modern science. A child-like trust in a "loving heavenly Father" is a precious experience which will soon be dissipated if maturity cannot convert this basic trust to a faith that transcends all the paradoxes of life.

People are the most incongruous of creatures because they are children of nature and yet create history. History, however, cannot satisfy our search for meaning because we have a freedom which transcends history itself. At the same time, this freedom never completely frees us from either nature or history.

Responsiveness lays upon us the crucial business of affirming, even if not solving the mystery. An error of modern empirical disciplines is the belief that mystery is merely the realm of the unknown, which will gradually disappear as science enlarges the realm of the known.

Responsiveness grows out of the wholesome interaction between religious and secular life. Without the religious view of the incongruous individual, there is a temptation for secular disciplines to interpret people in the dimension of pure nature. But without the constant influence of rational and empirical disciplines, religious life would degenerate into obscurantism. Without an emphasis on the universality of natural causation, religion is tempted to create childish securities under a "special" providence. An example of the latter is the Rev. Pat Robertson's grandiose expectations of winning the presidential nomination in 1988.

Responsiveness faces us toward yet another facet in the interaction between religious faith and the empirical disciplines. Kant regarded the intelligible part of human beings as the lawgiver and the "sensible" part of humans as law observer. But human beings, in the integration of body, mind and spirit, are both lawgivers and law observers. Thus, religion is related to the sense of moral obligation because this sense is derived, not from pure intelligence, but from an imaginative construction of the ultimate meaning of human existence.

Summary

Responsiveness, as we have pointed out, includes a combination of acute awareness and the human capacity for being free to respond. Responsiveness prepares the way for making relevant and fitting responses. This total awareness by which we accept and evaluate our experience and ready our responses is a many faceted process. We sense the object and person as accurately and completely as possible and allow the experience to lay hold and "grab" us. Then we engage the combined faculties of mind, feelings and determine will to process what we have sensed and perceived. Next, we apply that "determine will" watchfully and vigilantly. This takes us out of ourselves and our tight locales into ever-widening circles of experience and influence. Fulfillment of responsiveness is not realized once and for all. It is a dynamic response, always happening. A continuing struggle for the individuals, it is a process of doing-undoing-redoing and for society, an ongoing revolution.

A final step in the full-orbed challenge of responsiveness as we have explored it gains its uniqueness and its imperative force because God willed and created freedom in human beings. In fact, it is not humanity, but God, who cannot get on without responsiveness. The freedom to respond and its corresponding responsiveness and responsibility come as a privileged gift. From mysterious powers beyond ourselves, we find the responsiveness to move toward greater individual and social wholeness given by Christ who says, "Take up your cross and follow me." This ultimate challenge is unique in our life in that it includes the stark facts of suffering and death—not as the negation happiness, but as the voluntary shedding of the mortality necessary to put on immortality.

Coming to Terms with the Givens of our Environment

Our freedom to respond is conditioned by the nature of our social and physical environment. Forces and powers of society and nature bestride us like conquerors. Costs and demands of daily living and a host of other expenses burden us. Constraints of our social relationships and the influences of history enclose us. We are surrounded by the unchanging facts of chemical elements, biological structures and the laws of physics. We know it is disastrous to light a match near inflammable chemicals, to violate the biological limits of our bodies or to try to defy the law of gravity by jumping off the Empire State building expecting to land intact. We know very well that our daily allotment of time is 24 hours, no more and no less. Early we discover that the social and physical environments upon which we depend confront us with countless facts and entities many of which are unalterable.

Certain given forms interlace our experience and enable the mind and our senses to lay hold of reality. These givens or categories tie together social and physical happenings and our awareness of them. They make it possible for us to hold in balance the opposing forces we confront, such as the affirmative and negative elements, as well as freedom and destiny. Not always apparent, but nonetheless real, these "realities" or "given" aspects of being, appear implicitly or explicitly in every thought, feeling and action.

People find an ordered and meaningful world in which to live in spite of inner contradictions within the social and physical environments. The operative fields that encompass us, at the same time that they may overwhelm us and bring death, also can be harnessed and can give us life. For all its tensions and contradictions, the real world provides us with what we need to survive, starting with simple necessities— food, clothes, shelter.

We hesitate to think of people and things that fit into our lives as "contingencies." As for our social environment, we confront many unchanging elements. We relate to people as persons-to-persons and to things as users and managers of their functions. For example, we think of our families and our community as giving us assignments or roles, which are more like reasonable requests than inescapable mandates. As for the physical environment, from the alarm clock that wakens us to the bed we lay on at the day's end, things surround us. We agree with the Chinese in calling "things" *dung hsi*, or all that is between East and West. Until we get introspective, we simply take the people and things in our lives for granted.

To be responsive, sensing and perceiving fully to the givens of our social and physical environments is a bigger order than we may at first realize. Social and physical forces give us a world to live in whose order and meaning are not always easily evident and it is difficult to make a determined and persistent effort to be responsive to them.

Nevertheless, more than recognition, more than sensing and even more than understanding, the unalterable aspects of the social and physical environments must be *accepted.* Reason can degenerate to rationalization, emotion to hysteria and behavior to misbehavior. Reason divides up parts for meticulous analysis, while acceptance takes in the whole, grasps the unity. Emotion easily flies to extremes, but acceptance works to achieve a balance. Behavior easily jumps in and pulls out, while acceptance stays in and becomes involved.

Acceptance of the unalterable facts and conditions of the real world accomplishes several tasks. Acceptance, in confronting the givens, serves as the starter and the finisher of our responses: a starter, in that once an object or person is accepted, reason, sensing and action can begin; a finisher in that once the findings of reason, emotion and action are all in, the positives and negatives of the objects or persons, are *accepted.* Acceptance, in receiving and assigning validity to the givens, imparts meaning and impetus to our thinking, sensing and doing.

Responding to Limitations

Our experience tells us that in accepting the unalterable conditions and facts of the real world, our freedom to respond meets specific boundaries. The particular nature and boundaries that mark the situations we are summoned to accept and respond to are difficult to determine. The ceiling on the potential of human expression is not known. The wisdom of the ages has it that the limits of our individual lives and our environment are derived from creation and destiny.

Can we identify the human limits set by creation? The Declaration of Independence suggests that human beings were created "equal" and with "inalienable rights." The assumption that people are equal, or even that they have inalienable rights, does not provide us with a clear picture of either the nature or the extent of their equality and rights. Even less is said about how greater equality and human rights can be achieved and guaranteed. The most definitive declaration we can make is that human beings are created *finite.* The Declaration and other proclamations like it express the aspiration to raise the ceiling of our human potential. The Declaration expresses the hope that existence is the fulfillment of creation and gives creation its positive character. Christian realism emphasizes the split between the created goodness of things and their distorted existence. But "realism" in practice is paradoxical, because the Good is not considered an arbitrary commandment coming from the outside but the inner essential of reality. Only the inner essential structure of reality, God, is good.

We tend to be guarded about accepting destiny as an influence and determinant of our boundaries. We balk at a conception of destiny that ties us to a meaningless fate or puts us in a spaceship hurtling to who knows where. More acceptable is the premise that sees destiny as necessity combined with meaning.

The boundary, then, is the recognition that people are threatened with the loss of freedom by the necessities implied in their destiny, and they are equally threatened with the loss of their destiny by the contingencies implied in their freedom. They are in danger of trying to preserve their freedom by arbitrarily defying their destiny and of trying to save their destiny by surrendering their freedom. To lose one's destiny is to lose the meaning of one's being.

How can we know, accept and respond appropriately to the limits imposed by our creation and destiny? No quick and easy answer can be given. We gain suggestions, however, from people who are responsive to the crucial importance of this question and have worked out realistic responses in their lives.

Janet Baker, the world-renowned mezzo-soprano, tells about her struggle learning to live with all the limitations of her career as an opera singer. She may want to be free of wardrobes, rehearsals and schedules, but these are conditions she cannot change. Instead of lamenting them, she accepts them and, if anything, takes them as challenges. She works to keep her frustration from becoming an invitation to despair.

Her virtuosity comes forth as she responds creatively to the inescapable parameters of her musicianship.

Each life, regardless of status or location, is similarly bounded. Each of us must cope with external conditions according to our own abilities. When we estimate them carefully and respond to them creatively, instead of imprisoning us, they can serve as vehicles for expressing our endowments and destiny. When we deal effectively with these inescapable qualifying conditions, we gain a feeling of satisfaction and often find new alternatives opening to us.

Once we understand the unchangeable factors imposed by the real world, we must choose how "human," in the fullest sense, we will decide to remain. This is never easy. If we decide to commit ourselves to principled action, there is no escaping the way the concept of right and wrong is found in our social and physical environments. To accept, understand and respond to these environments is to accept the full predicament of the human condition.

Adversity proves a harsh teacher of the limitations imposed by our environment. The realities of daily life become especially obvious when we have difficulty confronting them. The pinch of a tight shoe or the devastation of an earthquake focuses attention on small or great troubles. A long-active, middle-aged professional stricken with Parkinson disease explained to his colleagues how his advancing disability forces him to face a whole range of adaptations to the real world that he had always taken for granted. "Before, I could think of and perform several tasks simultaneously," he said, "but now I have to concentrate hard on what muscles and balancing movements I must exercise to sit down or get up. I have to calculate carefully my space and time. I no longer have my old energy, and what strength I still have is hard to control and apply correctly." He talked also about disciplining himself to exercise regularly lest his muscles atrophy further. "It's as if everyday I have to battle my limitations and fight against the reality of death."

Jim, 55, caught in the staff changes of a large company following a merger, faced the sudden end of his 28 years of creditable service to the corporation. He told how he felt when he looked around his emptied warehouse on his last day. "The little kingdom I built up with such hard work and which had become so important to me was no more. For years I had worked to create that service department, picking and training the staff, developing policies and procedures, gathering equipment and supplies. The empty space mocked me. Now not only are the inventory and office cubicles gone, my economic livelihood is gone as well. I had only two more years to be eligible for retirement pay and benefits." Throughout his 28 years with the company, Jim knew about these conditions, but when these "contingencies" reached a particular point, he was expendable and was terminated.

Months later, having gained perspective on his termination, Jim reflected, "I now see some of the conditions of my job I'd neglected to deal with. Who you know, for example, is important, but I failed to keep up and establish new "connections." My assumption that I had tenure because of my seniority was unrealistic; the best of positions ephemeral. Management teams, instead of going on forever, are subject to quick changes. I took it for granted that my innovative work in the service department would assure my permanence with the company. I thought I was immune to the effects of buy-outs and increasing pressures created by foreign competitors. When push came to shove and all these forces combined, I was 'shoved out.' "

Jim was able, however, to transcend his initial responses to the desolation of his vocational plans. He reached back into his history to tap buried experiences and aspirations. In his twenties,he had been a medic and had survived imprisonment by the Japanese during World War II. He now enrolled in community college courses to become a male nurse. "In this new test of my survival," he reported, "I had to face the changed conditions and I had to look for changes *I* could make."

Responding to Problems in Our Social Environment

Numerous problems in the American society demand a realistic response. The urgent need to coordinate the efforts of government and the will of citizens to develop a solution to the current predicament of rural America is but one example. The government is obliged to purchase and store millions of pounds of dairy products and billions of bushels of grain, but cannot get food to the needy in cities everywhere. Farm-lending programs force farmers out of business and depress land values for those who remain. Hard facts have to be faced when American farmers produce food in extraordinary abundance—enough to feed starving millions around the world—but face hunger in their own homes. We should thank farmers for their efforts to apply the realism they derive from being close to and dependent on the soil, but we citizens and our government stand judged together for not dealing more realistically with this segment of our economy so crucial to our society.

Another problem is in the gross and widening economic inequalities. Excuses for not dealing with these widespread inequities are many. One holds that the long silent war between those who have and those who can't get has persisted for a millennium. To admire and even protect those who have gotten, and at the same time be sympathetic to those who could not, does not deal with the problem head-on. Adjustment to the resources of the earth cannot be right when some wear thousand-dollar suits while others are in rags.

Exorbitant expenditures for continuing the arms race presents another immense social problem. The enormity of this worldwide problem was outlined in a recent issue of the *Manchester Guardian Weekly*: "In a world where one in three adults still cannot read or write and one person in four is hungry, military spending of the USA has reached $800 billion a year, despite the existence of enough nuclear weapons to kill every one twelve times over." The article continues, "Forty years of the arms race has cost between $4-5 trillion to produce 16,000 megatons of explosive energy, compared with the eleven megatons which killed 39 million in World War II, Korea and Vietnam. Since their use would mean global suicide, they represent the 'ultimate absurdity' as well as an ominous threat to security." The arms race, then, looms as the ultimate social problem.

The gap between basic needs of people and provision for supplying them is even more evident in developing countries. Although some Third World nations have faltered on their debt payments, many of the creditor nations have been unrealistic about the interest rates charged.

Nigeria is a case in point. A magnet for all the poorer West African nations on its borders, Nigerian cities are bursting with job-seekers and clogged traffic. Nigeria seemed to believe that its oil money guaranteed a prosperous future. For several years toward the close of the 70s Nigeria was the world's leading importer of champagne.

Nigerian realities in no way matched its bloated fantasies. Its politics was rough and often sleazy. Political figures, some of them people who—in the appalled assessments of ordinary middle-class Nigerians—would not have been able to hold down jobs in the "real world," were making and flaunting huge fortunes. Despite profits from rich deposits of oil, national affairs drifted into a fool's paradise and the country continued to be racked by political instability and corruption.

Recently Nigeria's finest writer, Chinua Achebe, in *The Trouble With Nigeria,* gave a realistic picture of his country. Crying from the heart, Achebe wrote, "Nigeria is *not* a great country. It is one of the most disorderly nations in the world," and then concludes, "The Nigerian problem is the unwillingness or inability of its leaders to rise to the responsibility, the challenge, of personal example which are the hallmarks of true leadership."

A similar note is struck by Helmut Schmidt in his book, *Grand Strategy for the West* (1985). With the same realism that was one of his strengths as chancellor of West Germany (1974-82), he describes proposals to overcome what he sees as a dangerous absence of cohesive policies. He observes that soon after the initial period of unity in a common cause, governments begin to fracture. These crucial institutions of society are subject to "routinization," the exhaustion of ideological energy and other kinds of threatening developments. Citizens and their leaders, he holds, are not disciplined to see distinctly and face squarely "the way things are." Nations as well as individuals need to confront the specific demands of the real world. This weakens intellectual standards, personal and social cohesion and individual's spirit of sacrifice.

As with individuals, societies can "lose their compasses" and their responsiveness to the facts of the real world. Although regression is never far away, with determined and coordinated effort, remission of the ills can be achieved. On the national scale, ingrained attitudes and organizational patterns make any major shift in priorities difficult. Any shift needs to address serious problems in coordinating the many facets in government.

Facing Realities in the World of Nature

The totality and parts of the material world we call "nature" evoke the full range of human responses. To live involves unending curiosity about natural conditions. We respond with questions about the near and the far and the small and the great. Our responses have to be magnified to encompass the infinitesimal and telescoped to address the infinite. Each response to the material environment rests in some way on our estimate of what our existence is all about and how we are to approach our finite and historical life. Thus, some responses arise from elementary survival and utility concerns while others emerge from feelings of curiosity and awe. Realistic responding is shown in honesty with which we face nature's facts and forces.

Survival and utility responses to the physical environment started with the beginning of human consciousness. For Western cultures the articulation and analysis of these kinds of responses came with the Greeks 2,500 years ago. For example, in responding with understanding to what a human artifact such as a knife or a bowl is and does, they were not concerned with its size, weight or mass. Only the qualitative arrangement of its material parts into something that "cuts" or "holds food" was important, and once they knew that qualitative form, they could respond appropriately to the material elements of which it consisted.

The approach to the physical environment of Western people is a rich amalgam of its scientific method and its philosophic, psychological and religious heritages.

Modern Western society chose the empirical response and became deeply invested in sensory experience united with a mathematical and scientific discipline. Our primary responses rest on the confidence that whatever variability and sheer materiality the contingent world of physical experience might reveal, it nevertheless contains an order which can be measured and manipulated. Hence scientists do not guess at the purpose or even utility of an object; rather they study the object as they experience trees, rocks and stars in their mass, acceleration, physical composition and relations. They see nature as presenting conditions and events liable to occur, but not with certainty. Response to nature's "contingent reality" is made by examining it from the outside as it is perceived by our senses and responds to our manipulations. Because of the orderliness in nature, valid responses to it must be orderly and consistent with our experience.

Philosophers look to another range of responses people give to nature. They raise metaphysical questions such as: "In or behind the changing things that make up existence, is there any substance or principle which is always there? Has such a basic thing always been there? Can it be said that from this elementary substance all things have come? Put another way, this view asks: Is there one fundamental and permanent substance which underlies the world we experience? Is there some principle that gives natural things and forces the reality they seem to possess? If so, what is it?

Psychologists study from a different perspective the myriad ways people respond to their organic and inorganic environments. They examine how the material world requires continuous adaptation and change in human responses. Health, housing, mobility, the realities of space and time, powers of life and death responses. They study how these realities of the material world set boundaries on our freedom to respond. They are concerned with the honesty, courage and persistence of our responses to the immediate physical environment.

Personal responses to nature tend to be less scientific or metaphysical and more aesthetic. Throughout the evolution of the species, the order and variety of nature has called forth responses of appreciation and creativity. Appreciation includes abiding strictly by natural laws as well as by the unbounded awe that nature stirs. The phenomenon of beauty in the tiniest and most immense aspect of the universe thrills us.

Another response to nature comes with the questions it raises about the meaning and significance of human beings. People are alternately troubled and inspired as they respond to nature and realize their weaknesses as creatures. Caught in the mighty facts and forces of nature, responses move in the direction of questioning the significance of people themselves. In confronting natural conditions, individuals are taught the lessons of dependency and contingency as well as lessons of temporality and mortality. Sometimes curious, sometimes serene and at other times frantic, we raise ultimate questions about how we as individuals are related to the universe. We ask about the meaning and the destiny of our own existence. These are existential questions in which we ourselves are deeply involved.

For persons of faith, nature teaches about the Creator God and it evokes awe. These people see that nature and the supernatural as aspects of the same reality. Nature expresses the law in process and the supernatural expresses the end to which it tends. Creation provides the believer with an answer to the deepest questions about the meaning and purpose of our finite life. In this response the meaning and dependence flow from the glory and power of God who created and governs the heavens and the earth.

Facing our Closest Given: our Bodies

Our bodies are the closest given of our environment and command our special response. Such an integral part of ourselves and with so much of its functions occurring automatically, it is easy for us to take our "self" for granted. Out of necessity, we tend to the body's requirements for food, shelter and physical care, but full responsiveness to the realities of the body includes awareness and appreciation of its individual uniqueness and its limitations.

Amazingly, in the array of highly specialized and intricately related internal organs, each body has its own biochemical structure and function. The laws of the organism are extraordinary: They relate first to chemical compounds within the body, then the chemical reactions between them. The genes are made of DNA (deoxyribonucleic acid) with analyzable molecular configurations. When the simplest of these living cells form, the new complexity depends not merely on the number and diversity of cells, but on their interrelatedness.

The body has both a history and is history. Beyond understanding and caring for the health of our bodies, we have responsibility to be aware and appreciative of the history the body represents. History, as the struggle between space and time, continually affects the body. The body occupies and functions in space and has its own cycles of living and dying. Taking full consideration of the complexities of the body enables us to have an accurate perception of ourselves as both separate and related to our environment and others.

All the while the body maintains an amazing homeostatic balance. This delicate system is one of the body's safety factors, protecting it from being swallowed up by its surroundings and enabling the body to swing back to a poised normality after an upset. The homeostatic balance serves to coordinate the body's organs and systems and at the same time keep them functioning within their limits. It is a magnificent but precarious balance.

Responsible responding is accomplished as we respect the body's systematic and automatic series of actions directed to survival and health. Health itself is the bonus the body gives when its intricately structured organs and its complex systems are functioning optimally. We respond to the health of our bodies "on the move," because the body is constantly changing. It is continuously in process, continually growing, maturing and dying. Biological research shows that each separate human body, like every snowflake, is unique. We respond to the body in wonder, remembering St. Augustine's observation that people "go abroad to wonder at the height of mountains, at the huge waves of the sea, at the long course of the rivers, at the vast compass of the ocean, at the circular motion of the stars, and they pass by themselves without wondering."

Facing the Reality of Space and Time

Space and time are all-pervasive and immediate that we are surprised if asked how we respond to them. Common sense tells us that to exist means to occupy a particular space and time and that our responses to them come automatically. This led the 18th century German philosopher Kant to call space and time "forms of intuition." With that we would agree, for they are classifications of experiences grasped without benefit of reason.

Whether or not we grasp these essential givens by intuition or find them as we order our experiences, space and time are both ubiquitous and commanding. Space and time are givens that require special responses. Thus, when pressed, we realize that even though they are universal, in responding we continually work hard to hold our share of space and time. To assure our identity and position in life, we want confirmation that we have space within the universe. Similarly with time, in our anxiety over the brevity of life, we frantically try to hold on to it, grasping at a self-affirming present and feverishly working to assure a better future.

We try to control space and time by measuring space's dimensions and blocking out time's intervals. Confronting these givens in this way enables us to face ourselves and relate to the world. In our responsiveness to space and time we see and react to our "inside" selves. Upon self-examination we may say, "We must move from this place, since it is time to find a new and more rewarding new job." At a deeper level, our responsiveness to space and time helps us to unite anxiety with courage. Our inner response to space and time enables us to relate to the outside world and to unite "being" with "non-being:" unite what *is* with what can become, unite the actual with the potential.

Responding to the Reality of Space

Space presents an all-pervading reality that calls for particular and disciplined responses. The phrase "all-pervading" is apt, because space is the stuff our planet whirls through and also the locale where subatomic particles exist. We are conditioned to follow Euclid in seeing space as three dimensional: length, width and height. But we live in additional dimensions: "social space," or the region we occupy in the community, and "inner space," or the region of our personalities. Space possesses the inescapable condition that

87

both sustains us and also fences us in. It helps us organize and structure our lives as a basic class by which we store our knowledge of the world and then provides an arena for our involvement in the world. As the arena of our lives, space affords us an area for work, play and achievement.

We cannot avoid responding to the space-aspect of life. But the phenomenon of space requires responses that function within the limitations of the particular, marked-off area in which we are located. Being circumscribed in this realistic way, people feel pressed to provide and protect space for themselves and their loved ones. In meeting the contingencies of space, the responses of people are infinite in number and variety. We may chafe at limitations our particular space imposes, but we learn to accept the boundaries that cannot be changed. With unbounded ingenuity, humans try to push beyond the limits of their existing space. Nuclear physicists to probe submicroscopic space of atomic structures and astronomers to explore interstellar space. Sociologist and psychologist focus on responses to characteristics of space beyond its strictly physical characteristics.

"Social space" is the area of life where we make connect with others. It identifies individuals' need for a place in community and gives them a presence with others. Social space encompasses the various locations in which we live, places and situations where we work, play and live. The Old Testament gives special meaning to the "covenant" relationship as an essential privilege and responsibility. Likewise, Chinese culture, which sees persons in terms of their relationship to a community than as discrete individuals, stresses people's obligation to contribute to "social space." This assures both the present collective identity and an essential enduring link with ancestors.

The restrictions imposed by repressive societies upon persons' social space, though frequently painful, may not be insurmountable. Social scientists point out that people who live in poverty or under despotism suffer from reduced social space. Conditioned by inadequate knowledge and skills, motives are stunted with self-fulfilling fatalism that buffers against hopeless circumstances but itself helps to perpetuate their reduced "space." Similarly, even in more democratic societies, when boundaries of the status quo are fixed and limiting, individuals may become unwilling actors bound to dull roles. When our individual environment shrinks, the boundaries of the self may be restricted to a small circumference of choices.

Though limited by society's boundaries, within their social space human beings enjoy some degree of freedom to respond. Even within such social restrictions, given human creativity and courage, persons may not remain bound by the confines of their immediate treadmill. Others, by training and modeling of positive attitudes and values, learn liberating responses to social situations. With their self-produced cultural envelope they restate causes and effects into effective means and ends.

Personal space marks the territory of one's self. It is a space fully as real as a living room space. It is the field of one's individuality, with positions, directions and magnitude. A baby, for instance, in turning a toy so that the handle is toward it, sees space as an arena for movement. Space is found between the baby and the toy. The baby's own body has a particular or personal space in that it is a permanent focal point to which other objects are oriented. An adult's psychological space becomes increasingly complex, widening from only elementary motor movements to fields of personal thoughts, feelings and activities. Within the boundaries of our personal space, goals, energies and values are combined and kept at work.

The more complicated responses that well up from our "inner space" are frequently described in spatial terms. Explosions of anger are spoken of as persons "blowing their top." Persons who are hypersensitive and easily hurt may be referred to as being "brittle" and "out in left field." When Jay, a 32 year-old lithographer, talked about his inner confusion and loneliness, he spoke graphically in spatial terms. Explaining how his ribald behavior and fantasies ran counter to his puritanical upbringing, he described "trying to put back together his 'lower' and 'upper mind.' " He said, "They were once together, but now the 'lower mind' with its memories, wild urges and far-out ideas, seems to be trying to trip up my 'upper mind,' " He added, "I'm having a battle in 'my space.' My 'lower mind' moves in to push out my reason and direction. I need to be pulled up, and it's very hard, because the further down I go, the further up I have to pull myself."

"Personal space," or "inner space," a figurative expression handed down from the ancient Greeks, pictures the person as a container of experiences. In using this expression they tried to show how no mental or spiritual area was separate from their concept of the corporeal. *Phobus*, for example, became *fear*, an experience seen as an effect "inside" us. As these concepts became more sophisticated, it was evident fear could not be inside a body, so they posited a container called "inner space." This provided a convenient mode of self-reference. Changes in behavior were explained by private dynamics in that special realm of inner space. "Depth" came to be used to describe the more sought-after human qualities. Heraclitus used the figure of inner space in referring to "deep thinking," "deep knowledge" and "deep pain."

In contemporary psychoanalysis "depth" provides the comprehensive term required to describe the unconscious. As a physical analogy the term "depth" proves helpful in that it avoids value judgments. When a person's inner space and depth perception becomes skewed and garbled, we have a strong indication of emotional disturbance. One way clinicians check mental stability and the grasp of reality is to test the client's space perception. When the spatial orientation is confused and out of sync with the way things are, the person has difficulty answering correctly the question, "Where am I?" This confusion may point to a disordered mental state. Describing the unconscious' faulty intake, we can refer to the bodily experience of having one's eyes "out of sync," a condition called "binocular retinal disparity." Psychologically, the quality of our life space is better when we think and feel binocularly, i.e., when we experience in depth and pick up more subtle perceptual clues.

Findings of dynamic psychology reinforce our intuition that under the surface, in the "depths" of life, we touch a fuller dimension of mental, emotional and spiritual processes. In going "deeper," we move from the temporary and external to the more permanent and basic. Going "deeper" fosters growth rather than regression and works for wholeness in persons and communities.

The religious response certainly wells up from a person's "inner space," but one must be consistently aware of the tentativeness of finite space. Religious experience teaches that no finite being can rely only on "space." Not only must we face losing this or that space because we are "pilgrims on earth," but eventually we must face losing every place we may have had. In the Old Testament, Job expressed this awareness when he said, "Its place knoweth it no more." Thus, in death we experience a loss of space. To be this finite is to be insecure. But faith in the eternal God gives courage to respond positively to the negatives of eventually losing our "space." God is neither endlessly extended in space or limited to a definite space. God is Omnipresent—in and beyond all space.

Responding to the Reality of Time

Time, a complex continuum in which individuals and societies are inextricably immersed, surrounds us with another reality commanding our response. As with space, *time* raises hard questions of how to understand and cope with the mystery of our finitude. Time is a reality requiring responses of acceptance and compliance as well as understanding.

We do not wonder for long what time has to do with our

life. When we cannot check the hour on a clock or the day of the month on a calendar we feel lost. We readily admit having a problem getting on the freeway at six a.m. before all the lanes clog up. For most of us, time plays a large and central role—sometimes menacing and sometimes creative.

We know that time also uses us. Time pushes us before we are ready into youth and adulthood and then sends us careening, unwillingly, into old age and death. In the drama of life, temporality plays with us like puppets, bringing us on to the stage, moving us ever more speedily across it and yanking us off when it so chooses. Time is no abstruse problem for the physicist and astronomer—it is one of the fears that haunts every human being, demanding response.

When we respond to time by trying to understand it, we are both fascinated and bedeviled by its mysterious character. Subjectively estimated, time includes both the direct awareness of duration and judgment of the intervals based on the number and kind of experiences that have intervened. Since time never stands still, even the present moment cannot be pinpointed. Another aspect is the way time is direct, irreversible and predictable; we can forecast precisely what time the sun will rise tomorrow.

Through the years people's understanding of and response to time has changed markedly. Ideas and applications of time have moved far beyond mere chronicity—matters of clocks and calendars. One constant, carried over from the Greeks, has been that time is not just a chain of arbitrary intervals, but a progression of dynamic changes from past to future. Contemporary approaches have taken into account new empirical data presenting conditions such as duration, synchronism and instantaneousness. A new concept of time, as inseparable with space, was essential to Albert Einstein's breakthrough theory of relativity. As a result of his pioneering theory, scientists work in a four-dimensional continuum called "space-time." This insight affects each of us; we can no longer respond by seeing time simply as periodicity, but must look at the time-flow of the minutes and hours as enduring advance and related intimately to space.

"Social time," comparable to social space, requires particular attention. Few influences are more powerful and pervasive on individuals and cultures than their perspectives on time. Children learn a time perspective appropriate to the values and needs of their society. They simply "pick up" their society's time concepts as they mature. "If people do not keep pace with their companions," Thoreau observed a century ago, "perhaps it is because they hear a different drummer." We use the phrase "the beat of a different drummer" to describe any pace of life unlike our own. The drummer's beat in the industrialized Western society has become dominated by a preoccupation with the future. Savings banks and insurance agencies became viable only after people had developed a sense of an extended future.

The clash of time perspectives accounts for some of the misunderstandings between North American and Latin American countries. How this occurs was described by Robert Levine and Ellen Wolff in their article "Social Time."[1] Latin Americans see us as obsessed with working, efficiency, rationality, delaying gratification and planning for what will be. To us, they are inefficient, lazy, imprudent, backward and immature in their obsession with making the most of the moment.

Psychological processes are strongly influenced by our temporal perspectives. Motivation, emotion and creativity all have critical-time dimensions. Individual behavior is regulated by subjugating the urgencies of the present to the learned demands of past and future. Without an articulate sense of the future, expectations and goal-setting reduced. Without the response to time, in which the past blends into the present, how could we establish a sense of self that is stable through time or extract causality and consistency from possibly coinci-

---

[1]   *Psychology Today,* March 1985.

dental, random events in our lives?

Psychologically, the present moment offers unique opportunities for responding. The experience of time, as either past or future, gives persons a sharpened self-awareness. But the present, requiring the person's perceptions and attention to be focused on the immediate, finds the self especially open. The present moment requires the response of concentration and persistent application of all one's faculties. When the *I* and the *Now* are fused the I and Thou relation is reinforced. The responding self centered in the *now* is one that knows itself as *having been* and also as *going into* the encounters of life. As the present moment is responded to positively and openly, the self is relieved of anxiety over its transitoriness and is encouraged that we live in a sustaining time.

Ethical decisions are influenced by the factor of time. With the world being one of action, persons moving in time, as in space, move within the context of moral considerations. The response of courage is required to deal with the anxiety about the transitoriness of life. This is difficult because of vanishing reality. The feeling that our existence is slipping ever more rapidly away from us into nothingness, menaces our sense of meaning in life. We know we are mortal, but we struggle continually against this awareness. We can respond more positively to the onrush of maturity and old age if we feel that our life and work have accomplished something—be it a good book, a successful business enterprise or having contributed to a "cause" beyond ourselves which lends meaning to life.

Responding ethically in the *now-time* provides a moment of awakening. It is a moment for gaining more skills, more wisdom and for moving on intentionally to have a share in determining the future. The Chinese proverb, "People and places have their period of time and destiny," suggests that responding responsibly to the immediate moment requires that we see time as integral with personal, community and spiritual experience. Responding fully to *now-time* gives us a moment's dialogue with colleagues, friends and the stranger we may meet. The "fuller" response involves establishing an appropriate and meaningful relationship. A major problem of ethical and creative relationships, as Langdon Gilkey notes, "Is so to understand and appropriate our own essential temporality that it ceases to be a source of anxiety to our life and becomes the condition for courage, creativity and zest in the face of the new—even the new that may displace us."[2]

The Hebrew-Christian tradition affirms that created time, directs its movements and unites with eternity-and-time to redeem and fulfill time. In this faith, concrete finite existence is given an eternal meaning which does not absorb but enhances the uniqueness of individual persons. This faith generated the powerful interpretation of time and its character that completely transformed our Western world. On its basis the whole latter-day edifice of the belief in historical progress was fashioned. The eternal source and nature of time requires of people just, righteous and obedient responses to God. The now-time takes on special significance and opportunity as an immediate crisis. As a "boundary event," between past and present, the occasion summons the response of accepting the will of the Creator and Redeemer of time.

Summary

As days pass and history deepens, promises of a future with new events and relationships open. We see and respond to a variety of people and countless of physical things and events as a matter of course. Common sense tells us responding to our community and to the "things" of the physical environment is as natural and spontaneous as

[2]   Gilkey, p. 241.

breathing. Yes, we grant, we depend on social relations and on the things of the physical environment, but we would insist that our responses are not so much an acquiescing to the givens of our environment as they are a matter of controlling them. We point out that the race and its many cultures has been achieved by the manipulation and conquest of the forces and powers of our social and physical environments.

Effectiveness in life depends greatly on perceiving accurately the unalterable characteristics of the forces that surround us. We must respect the restraints that the social and physical environments place upon our freedom to respond. Within the parameters of personal capacities, the unalterable facts and realities of our social environment must be dealt with. On the other hand, exercising discipline and determination, we must deal with the unalterable conditions and causations of our physical environment. The more fully we are responsive to the nature and workings of these environments, the more appropriate will be our responses.

Acceptance of the realities of our social and physical worlds can be surprisingly liberating. In accepting the hard givens, the contingencies of these realities can strengthen us and become stepping stones to new experiences. Contingencies taken as restraints hold back thoughts, feelings and action; accepted as realities, they can open opportunities for new responses. As we assess and cope with the limiting conditions and respond positively to them, we will find that these surrounding givens can sustain and empower us. Acceptance opens the way to truth. "Seek truth from facts" was Deng Xiao-ping's dictum of acceptance in 1978 when he launched a wholesale revision of the catastrophic Cultural Revolution. (Would that he had kept to this dictum instead of permitting the tragedy of the June 1989 Tienanmen Square massacre.) Acceptance of truth brings wisdom; acceptance of reality provides an honest and solid foundation for experience and responding.

C H A P T E R

Responding to Unseen Givens

Philosophers and theologians consider space, time, causality and substance as four elemental categories. These "ultimate notions" call for a balance between the fulfillment and power of history, between the future and eternity, between "being" and "non-being." In dealing with each of these categories we can exercise two complementary responses: impulses that are both positive and negative and orientations that are both outward to the world and inward to the self. They are as essential and meaningful as the *yin and yang* concept.

These principles are illustrated in other paired elements: individuality and universality, dynamics and form, freedom and destiny. Tillich aptly illustrates how each of these three polarities and their parent categories express the union of being and nonbeing which arouses in people the double response of anxiety and courage.

Reality of Superhuman Energies and Powers

We must respond to many insistent forces and powers. Physicists tell us movement occurs when a "vector quantity" meets an object. Force exerted is *power* and we measure it in terms of the strength and the rate at which work is done. When something accelerates because it is pushed or pulled, the pressure is power and the application is force.

By analogy we speak of the force and power of the charismatic or prophetic person. Force and power impinge in myriad ways in our personal lives. In responding to natural forces and historical movements, people experience the realities of psychological and social powers. These pressures not only affect behavior, but cause motion and produce also change.

The energies and powers we usually meet include physical and life forces. These physical, social and spiritual energies both sustain and destroy. They can help make the world go around and empower us individually. Likewise these energies, as in earthquakes, can wipe out entire populations. Social scientists point out that the interaction of force and power affects our social, mental, emotional and spiritual lives. Their efforts to define and gain specific control over these realities is comparable to the management of energies and powers achieved by physicists, engineers and biologists. Nevertheless each of us must respond to the inner and outer pressure we experience as a result of these factors.

Responding to the Reality of Life-forces

Life-forces determine conditions and exert energies that fix the terms of many of our key responses. As living creatures we owe our beginnings to life-forces. The pumping heart is both an organ and a power that sends life-sustaining blood through the body enabling other organs to turn food into cells, growth, strength and energy.

In its simplest form this life-force is found in a paramecium. Under a microscope we can see movement, a system for receiving nourishment and processes for reproduction. In more complicated organisms the biological force animates more differentiated behavior—feeding, establishing territory (space), mating and caring for the young. In higher reaches of development, in human beings, these life-forces are organized into complex systems.

Our responsiveness arises from the life-force that brings about personality and gives it qualities that sustain and animate individuality. It is the only integrative drive or power that remains unchanged and undivided through all layers and stages of growth. This central force, which Carl Jung calls the "primal libido," is the dynamic basis for our personality system. We say of strong personalities, "there's a forceful person," or "there is a dynamic and influential person." The evidence of an inner awareness of self arouses our response.

Forces and powers of a similar kind operate in social structures. Energies and authoritative influences are at work in every aspect of life. Force and power empower society to justify control and have the authority to do so. As for the source of these energies and powers, the infant sooner or later asks, "How did I begin?" Early Greek thinkers in raising the same question answered by saying power is *being*, the fact and ground of existence. They held there is no being without power. For Plato the idea of existence as being, or "being-itself," points to the power of being in everything and above everything, the infinite power of being.

Psychologists meet the question by building on the concept of a biological life-force and adding systematic explanations such as Adler's "will-to-power." Philosophers of life, such as Nietzsche with his *superperson* and Bergson with his *élan vital,* emphasized the element of energy and force in all living things. Tillich gave recognition to the enormous power of the biological life when he called it "the power of being."

Responding to the Inevitability of Change

To be alive is to be inextricably caught up in change—the sequence or condition in which there is a break from uniformity and constancy in quality, quantity or degree. The world continues to change even as we walk, breathe and think—as we read these words. We all are engaged in radical change that confronts us both with amazing opportunities and increasing risks. "Everything flows," remarked Heraclitus, the Greek philosophers, in 500 B.C. In the same period the Chinese philosopher Chuang Tze taught, "Nothing is permanent. We are immersed in constant change." In this century major change has escalated in all walks of life. Charles de Gaulle said in 1960, "The world is undergoing a transformation to which no change that has yet occurred can be compared, either in scope or rapidity."

Change in the last five decades, particularly in Western societies, has passed the threshold of social tolerance. Change is occurring at such a pace that it disrupts ordinary habits of living, destabilizes institutions and creates intense personal conflict and distress. We can learn new skills to meet changes providing they are purely mechanical or intellectual, but it is difficult to learn new emotional attitudes and new beliefs.

Some changes are superficial. We read about them in the morning paper. While interesting as an account of happenings, the citing of externals provides little understanding of the self, the community or history. These news reports say little about movements at the deeper levels that initiate and shape those events—and where our social institutions are changing and our beliefs are being modified. Beliefs and values that hold individuals and societies together change much more slowly; as they do, they shape everything else. Changes at these foundational levels of purposes and goals are hard to perceive and harder still to accept.

We are helped in living with change when we recognize that change is the way we grow and maintain health. Biologists tell us every cell in the body changes within approximately seven years. Between childhood and adulthood a gradual but marked alteration occurs in the body, mind and spirit. Changes mark each succeeding stage of life.

The responses to the need for change vary. A successful executive may finally say, "After careful consideration I see more clearly the mess of my personal life, but the price of change is too high," and then proceed to reject change as did the rich young ruler whom Jesus told, "Go, sell all of your goods." Since change is threatening, people tend to be reluctant to change for they fear what change might bring— dampening the spirit of adventure. For many the certainties of secure city life are preferable to the uncertainties of distant and unknown places.

Venturing as a pilgrim like Abraham, is an act of faith, yet such venturing is a high risk—high yield. Avoidance of stagnation and the spirit of adventure move together. Responsible persons are not naïvely seeking Utopia or awaiting Armageddon, but living in the world where God carves the rotten wood and rides the lame horse—even at times creating upheavals and new opportunities driven by hope. The response to change must be acceptance and the realization that it involves the essence of life and in the process they grow and develop new formulas for living.

Responding to the Realities of Oppositional Forces

Oppositional and negative force must be responded to. Our social and physical environments include stubborn resistances, stolid obstinacy, "sin" and death. Karl Menninger observed, "Not everything outside the human organism favors our purpose; not everything is edible; not everything is healthful; not everything is usable; not everything is friendly. To live is to be beset with ceaseless threats, obstacles and challenges as well as opportunities." Centuries before, St. Paul said, "We contend against principalities and powers."

Since actions tend to produce equal reaction, we have to exert pressure to be positive and to exercise our freedom to respond. We must wrestle with things, people and forces that negate and cancel out our best efforts. To live is to risk being dragged back; to try to change is to face resistance. Often our effort is blocked by those working at cross-purposes.

Sometimes we are caught unwittingly by complicity with forces responsible for the extension of gross inequality in the distribution of goods, which perpetuates misery and poverty. On our streets we see the spread of muggings, murders and rapes. In our physical environment we are caught in droughts, famines and earthquakes. Such negative forces can disrupt productivity, stability and creativity.

Resistances, subtle or not, account for another form of oppositional forces and powers. In carrying out an accustomed task or relationship, colleagues can turn balky and uncooperative. With "passive-aggressive" types, resistance is expressed indirectly rather than directly. Among individuals or groups, the demands for adequate performance in both occupational and social behavior are met with procrastination, stubbornness and intentional inefficiency. The consequence is pervasive occupational and social dysfunction.

At other times, instead of passive-aggressive resistance, the flow of life is suddenly disrupted by threats or outright opposition. The braking or drag on progress is occasioned by political, social or economic counterforces. Progress is subverted by individuals or groups that cling to outworn patterns of actions. Resistance may come as a reaction to the unexpected—such as a catastrophe or a crucial decision for which we are ill-prepared. Responses to such traumatic disruptions are thrown off course by doubts and questions. How is this peril or obstacle to be overcome? What is the alternative? Why do I have to confront such horrible adversities at this time in my life?

Other resistances arise from the "sins of omission." Priority emphases are pushed aside by preoccupation with lesser concerns. Well-intentioned persons can default in their role of exemplary living. In institutions, persons can carry on as if trouble were invisible, losing themselves in paperwork or unproductive committee meetings. Hesitancy alone may block new risk-taking.

Not all oppositional forces are exterior. Inwardly, we often work against ourselves. The personal dimensions of resistance include the complicated negative forces of fear, guilt and anger. If an unresolved resentment or feeling of hostility is left untended, sparks can ignite an entire well of violent rage. Such responses of uncontrolled outbreaks are both contagious and synergetic: persons and groups are easily infected and the difficulty escalates.

Persons dominated by negativity, when faced with a serious emotional trauma such as rejection or serious conflict, are rendered insecure, inept and otherwise emotionally disabled. Their past choices, having been confused and ineffective, render them reluctant to make new starts. Their state of inertia worsens their emotional and mental problems. They narrow their options to escape into unreality—which can be manifested in suicide or violence against others. Resisting suggestions to seek psychotherapy or pastoral guidance, they cut themselves off from available help and allow their problems to become more aggravated. Neurotic negativism feeds on itself.

Malicious communities led by distraught and misguided persons tend to breed antisocial individuals and groups like Nazi Germany under Hitler. This malignant concentration of oppositional forces frequently is labeled "evil," the work of a personal devil who personifies all negative forces. The psychological drag or dark side within us is what psychiatrist Carl Jung calls the *shadow*—the converse in the unconscious of whatever people or society have emphasized in their ego.

Psychiatrist Franz Alexander called this inner tendency to resist change *psychic inertia.* St. Paul identified an *inner voice,* something within that destabilizes the self so that "The good I would do, I do not do; and the evil I would not do, that I do." By denial, rationalization and projection, we excuse ourselves and resist what we know to be right and refuse to change our ways.

Persons of ethical and religious sensitivity take these social oppositional powers seriously. Moralists, for example, find responding responsibly becomes the effort to achieve the purpose of the "right" in the face of resistance from adversarial forces. Morality in any mode is the effort to find ways to deal with evil, the source of negative forces.

Impulsive violations of religious or moral conviction represent the ascendancy of negative forces. The Greeks called it "missing the mark." Such an act could be choosing mundane and purely self-serving pursuits instead of greater and more universal concerns. In the case of individuals living out personal and social pathologies, we see how such defaults in responsible behavior eat away at integrity and effectiveness. Being in the grip of negative powers when aberrant behavior becomes a pattern is much more serious than having committed an error in etiquette. Superficial apologies or cosmetic changes in personality may prevent retaliation and even assuage guilt, but this is not enough. As Jesus and the Hebrew prophets stressed: Those under the influence of negative forces and powers need a radical change at the center of their lives. Emotionally divided and deeply confused persons need to experience a fundamental change at the core of their being.

Responding to the Inevitability of Death

The inescapable fact of death casts a shadow on our becoming what we would like to be. It is not easy to see anything good in death. To be dead is to be snatched from the world of space and time, buried in Stygian darkness, becoming dust and then nothing. The common response, augmented by cultural bias, is that death is deplorable, evil and always premature. Of all things that move us, observes Ernest Becker in *The Denial of Death,* "one of the principal ones is the terror of death." To talk about death is to invite alienation, denial and fear.

All responses of life are affected by the fact of death. It engulfs children, the middle-aged and the elderly. In developing countries people respond fatalistically to the high toll often exacted by flood, famine or revolution. Responses differ with different conditions: a widow grieving the loss of her husband responds differently from grieving parents who lose a teenager to overdose.

The responsible person must take existence as a life *and* death matter. St. Ignatius taught that daily meditation on death for a few minutes has a corrective and healing effect. Some day the bell will toll for me. It often tolls for someone who was to others the very essence of life's meaning. When a beautiful person close to us dies, it is an intimate, often overwhelming experience. In viewing death, we sometimes visualize the long and arduous course by which the personality developed and journeyed to its ultimate end on earth.

Death, the threshold of eternity, is a personal and a communal experience. Each of us must face it alone, yet all must face it. There are no natural boundaries to the experience of love and beauty. There are no comprehensible limits to the truth about death. Goethe on his deathbed cried out, "More light, more light!"

Responses to death, however, are not all negative. In a paradoxical way death gives significance to life. Some declare, "I don't get an infinite number of chances, so I'll make the most of what years I have." Swift said, "It is impossible that anything so natural, so necessary and so universal as death should ever have been designed by Providence as an evil."

The profound meaning of death demands responsible responses. Taking death seriously invokes the deepest sense of life's meaning. The fact of death presses the living to become more responsible and intentional in their behavior.

A new set of responses is called for as biomedical technology extends life. We may now grieve over deaths that could have been prevented had adequate health care services been available. We are also plagued by decisions whether life should be prolonged in cases of the seriously disabled. In either case, as death approaches the individual is challenged to respond responsibly when human potential diminishes.

Responding to life's most stubborn reality, though difficult, is imperative. Death is not merely something that takes over after our earthly life, it is that power which dominates our present life and one of the fundamental aspects of existence. Martin Luther's hymn says, "In the midst of life we are surrounded by death," or as the Swedish say, "We on earth live here prisoners under death."

Theologians suggest various responses to death. Martin Heidegger locks in on death as the terminus and hence the guarantee of our temporality. Death, he holds, is life's Big Event. Contemporary writer Norman O. Brown maintains our fearfulness of death-in-life precludes our enjoying life's fullness. Christians affirm that in the experience of a "resurrection" this fear is broken. The responsible response to inexorable death leads us to look to a super-individual factor in the personal élan, as Bergson called the life-force. The ultimate response to death is to be responsive to the transcendency beyond.

Responding to the Reality of History

History commands our serious response. Because most of us are preoccupied with the present, history may be one of our most neglected realities. Born into the history of parents, grandparents and culture, we remain enveloped in the blanket of our origins. In childhood the preoccupations of family, friends and school forge our history. Our responses during these times take our history for granted, assuming we are central to it. As adolescents, our responses begin to modify the history imposed on us, sometimes resenting it, often trying to remake it as we form our own identity and struggle to find recognition from our peers who for a time comprise our history.

In maturing we enter more seriously into the structure of history, striving to link ourselves with others and assure our place in some community. Through our vocations, marriages and the causes we support, we become involved in the wider dimensions of history. Our responding progresses from entering *into* history to becoming absorbed by it and eventually to going *beyond* history. We partake of history, then, in trying to mold it discover we have to accept it and finally in our death we are cast from it into we know not what. Before we are ready, we scramble to "tie into" history so that through history we may somehow move into eternity itself.

The suggestion of "tying into history" raises the hackles of those who compulsively concentrate on the immediacies of the present and who feel looking into the past is like driving via the rearview mirror. Due to a less-than-exciting experience in school, some have an aversion to history claiming, "It's just a matter of remembering a list of dates." Others agree with Henry Ford who once said, "History is the bunk," implying that concern for the past diverts time and energy from the fierce demands of today.

History, as the flow of life and human events, never stands still. More than the chronological record of selected past events, history must be seen as living within the flow of one's own life span as part of he whole flow of the human race. As we "tie into" history, we proceed (time) and reside (space) in the ongoing events. To respond with choices and actions is to affect the course of both our personal life and our society.

Consider the perspective we get from 19th century history. It generated the unfolding of a vast expanse of human horizons and a great increase and distribution of knowledge. It brought the emergence of newly awakened intellectual energies in scientific investigations, exploration and mercantile development. In studying this period, we are introduced to nationalistic political systems festering with deep antagonisms between states. Common people were awakened to a new and more profound social justice. Such a review throws light upon terrible wars, remarkable technological achievements and widespread social upheavals. It enables us to respond more effectively through a comprehensive historical understanding of the modern world and the forces that have molded it.

When our response is to "tie into history," we become involved in the process of change, in of the moment-by-moment occurrences of daily life. The changes we encounter contribute to the essence of history; history is rooted in change. As we grow we participate in history's unfolding. Only people, says Soren Kirkegaard, make history. Paradoxically, even though Henry Ford at one time considered history "bunk," in developing the way to mass produce autos, he *made* history. Each of us in responding to change makes history.

Likewise each of us has a history to which we had better respond positively. Those who deny or ignore their history are doomed to see the world as commonplace because, except at extreme times, they are going to live among commonplace people who have come to that conclusion. The only way to realize the substance of human experience is to reach out beyond the years we have into the years of the past, into the significant experiences of the human race. Nations, peoples and cultures also "have a history," as they respond to new concentrations and unifying forces that gather power in human affairs. These larger circles of society, as with individuals, cannot afford either to deny or ignore their history.

As the focus of human activity, history synthesizes and strengthens our personal and social stories. The anthropologist Kluckhohn explains, "History is a sieve that filters and a lens that focuses human experiences." Tillich sees history as "the totality of remembered events, which are determined by free human activity and are important for the life of human groups." It is humankind's living memoir—our deep archetypal rootage in the dynamic process of the ages. History serves as the arena of a person's responsibility. We are accountable for the history we are making in our lives. By our "open" responses we contribute creativeness, and by our responsible responses we strengthen direction in history.

Countless sages have counseled us on responding appropriately and wisely to history. Past history sheds light on present predicaments. "The person who is in doubt about the present," wrote the great Chinese thinker Tung Chung-shu centuries ago, "should examine ancient times." He added, "The one who does not understand the present or the future, must look at the past." The antithesis of Henry Ford's "history is bunk" assertion emerges in Santayana's oft-quoted phrase, "Those who refuse to learn from history are doomed to repeat it."

History surrounds us as a continuous necessity, giving significance to Carl Jung's observation (1937), "To denounce history and to be unhistorical is the Promethean sin." "Each culture," notes Kluckhohn, "embraces those aspects of the past which, usually in altered form and with altered meanings, live on in the present."

Philosophers see history as the intersection of space and time, the carrier of meaning and purpose, while psychologists see it as the arena of accident, freedom and change. Prophets view history as the flow of human events that point beyond itself and invites the workings of God.

History often begins as a unique event, with "the color of blood, the flash of glory or the stench of abasement." To those who have specifically bled, prevailed or lost, to be remembered only in a perfunctory way is as intolerable as to be forgotten. Witness the pain of the Vietnam veterans whose nightmares are ignored in the dovish or hawkish analysis of national miscalculation.

To breath new life into the present and future is the best use of the past. The best example is the persistence of dedicated Christians in preserving the galvanizing message of the historical Christ from becoming bland orthodoxy or naïve biblicalism. The language of the Bible and of dogmatic tradition is tied to an ancient, outdated world utterly incomprehensible to today's person whose habits of thinking and speaking have been drafted by science. In particular, those who know something about history are aware that church dogma is a historical phenomenon, resulting from a complex historical process.

History prepares us for the future. Abraham's basic dignity, self-esteem and confidence that God was leading him into a promising future were rooted in history. History leads us into the future, writes Teilhard de Chardin, "for the simple reason that every increase of internal vision is essentially the germ of a further vision which includes all the others and carries still further on."

The findings of neurobiologists suggest that the culture of each society arises from genetic rules of human nature. The prospect is that the human species can change its own nature, and history will greatly affect that change.

Responding to the Prospects of the Future

To talk of the "reality" of the future appears inappropriate. How can the future be "real?" If looking to the past is anachronistic, looking to the future is premature. Let the future alone as the time that will be; it is only in the present moment of history that we can express our freedom in our natural and social environment. Even in metaphysics and mysticism we cannot step outside our here-and-now.

How people respond and work out their salvation within the present *now-time* is powerfully influenced by the fact that there is a future. It is more than crystal-balling— predicting the nature of possible happenings. Forecasting the future is an educated guess of what the present conditions will bring about. Present behavior, in large measure, is action in the light of the future which individuals envision or project. The raw material for their action comes from remembered ideas, events and models. Their response is grounded in their view of particular pasts.

Human beings are the only creatures capable of "futurizing." Only they are able to distinguish between what is and what ought to be and plan responses that will achieve the values and hopes cherished. This accounts for the rise and preoccupation with the notion of progress in the 19th century. People became increasingly impatient with injustice, ignorance and poverty. In the expansive atmosphere of the century, progress became the catch-all term for any change or movement in society. In its fullest sense, progress meant growth toward something in the future which is different and hopefully better than life in the present. It also became a watchword of institutions, industry and science. One large corporation advertises: "Progress is our most important product."

Speculation over the future has always been a popular pastime. Few have nothing to say about possibilities that might develop next week, next month or next year. At its worst, prophecy lies in the arts of magic and, at its best, in the vision of the prophets. On the basis of pure hunch, or on reflection by the more serious, individuals devise outlooks that are projections of their personal and community history. Those with prophetic insight feel in their bones what is going to happen, but even the wisest and most intuitive are only able to estimate the general drift of coming affairs.

Science has made possible accurate prediction in areas of specific expertise or knowledge: astronomers can foretell the movements of the stars and comets; meteorologists can, within wide margins of error, forecast the weather. But the science of human behavior is not yet complete enough in its analyses or exact enough in its quantitative assessments so that anyone can speak with intelligent assurance about humankind's future. Wanting changes for the better has not abated in the 20th century. In the first 50 years, in spite of two terrible world wars, optimism regarding the future prevailed. People viewed the technological and humane orders in society as hopefully converging to create a world where, in spite of conflict, it would be more effectively managed and directed to serve individuals and communities.

Marxists deal with the future as if it had already occurred. They speak of "knowing" the outcome—"the classless society." Others, like theologian Berdyayev in his book, *The Meaning of History,* expand the Hegelian picture of a "dialectic of history," seeing in our present era the loss of integral and organic experiences in our historical order. They see a second period in the challenge given to the established order. After a fateful and menacing disruption, hopefully, a third period will come and a new history emerge.

Today people tend to feel a particular restlessness and uncertainty. These feelings push us toward a growing awareness and sense of responsibility in the full dimensions of *time.* People have dreamed, seen visions and prophesied with compulsive eagerness. Visions of what lies ahead are frequently mirages, not telephotographs; nevertheless, all responsible people have long had an eye on the future.

This response of optimistic expectancy is an important strand in the web of Western societies. It makes for a concern over individuals' responsibility for the future. As an attitude and way of perceiving life, optimism regarding the future has been central to human progress. It determines to a degree not yet charted the way human beings think, play and respond to life and death.

In the last three decades in Western Europe and the United States specialists have spent an increasing amount of time and money drawing up predictions and programs for the future. Bertrand de Jouvenel and his *Futuribles* group in France pioneered in charting a variety of future possibilities. In America the Academy of Arts and Sciences developed a Committee on the Year 2000 under Daniel Bell which was expected to lay out various potential futures. Such entities tend to assemble and format facts about the immediate past into a chart of possibilities for future production—or warfare.

These efforts in *futurology* coincide with the advent and burgeoning of computer science with its capability of processing ever larger variables. Among the other accompanying factors contributing to these studies was the acceptance of the idea that history has no iron-clad laws, that the future belongs to human beings and that greater freedom lies in the future. As a new breed of thinkers, those engaged in these projects try to do more than make judgments based on guess-like stabs into the future.

Their work differs from that of pre-scientific days when no distinction was made between "the future" and "the ultimate stage." Unlike ancient seers, they are rigorous analysts who examine the laws governing social, political and economic trends and their effects upon one another. They also seek to present a sober and reasonable vision of tomorrow and point out that attempts to envision a fanciful and static future without change would be a frivolous and regressive exercise. Human beings have a particular responsibility to consider and prepare systematically for the future.

These futurologists believe that both Utopia and Armageddon give us futile scripts which lead to misguided action, frustration and immobilization. Three scenarios are chief among others now envisioned: 1) secularization stemming from increased industrialization, 2) the proposal to decentralize society, and 3) predictions of a no-win eventuality.

Two of these are optimistic, one pessimistic. The two optimistic views are in conflict: that we have been witnessing growing industrialization and technology; and increasing centralization. The movement was away from traditional religious grounding toward a materialistic and utilitarian base. A second scenario, which arose in the mid-70s, is presented in the Report for the Club of Rome's Project, *The Limits of Growth*, which cited the need for a society that will be more decentralized and will give greater care to the environment.

A third scenario is the combination of the two. Advocates of this projection point out that the future is not all applicable to human purposes. The tragic sense in life will not fade away simply because there are some who are incapable of comprehending it. Progress is not automatic; it can be thwarted. The human story likely will eventually end.

Several lessons emerge. Each scenario suggests there are wrongs that need righting. Each relates to our ethical and belief systems. Furthermore, these studies remind us that our future is not exactly unbounded. Space and time pose inescapable limitations. In responding to the future, even when our vision of it is the clearest and we have at hand the findings of the most skillful and experienced analysts, still we only "see through a glass darkly." The future may well be in God's hands, moving in the direction of the fulfillment of the divine will as the Hebrew-Christian believes, but this does not mean that the future automatically turns into God, or even *toward* God. Serendipity and chance will continue to play their part in considerations of the future.

The response of looking to the future is the recognition of today in tomorrow, as history is the recognition of yesterday in today. When people prepare their next steps in space and time, they are searching for and getting ready for a usable future.

The Hebrew-Christian response is much concerned with people's future. The teachings of the prophets looked to the future to vindicate the present and in so doing made humanity impatient with injustice, ignorance and poverty. When Utopian scripts were provided in a Christian context, the basis for optimistic views of the future were reinforced. More than a simple optimistic outlook, this view of the future became *hope.* The Swiss historian Jakob Burckhardt, writing about the future, observed, "From the one point *accessible to us,* the one eternal center of all things, we look to our tomorrows. Through our suffering, striving, doing—as we were, as we are and as we shall be—through our acts we contribute to our future."

The faith that God, as the eternal agent and center of history, gives the future meaning and a plan for its fulfillment provides a solid theological basis to prepare for the future. For those of this confidence, the future is directed to personal renewal, community service and extended mission. High risk is involved in the application of this scenario of Christian hope. "Go for broke," says this imaginative projection which focuses on the God whose essential character is futurity. It is God in Christ who moves toward the world with demand and promise, and Christ's resurrected life which is a sign of affirmation and a call to radical appraisal. Persons are called, nevertheless, to act responsibly in the sight of God and to fulfill divine purposes for the future they do see.

The confident and committed response to these foundational convictions gives to the future the substance and quality of destiny. Since freedom is a part of these convictions, destiny is more than an inevitable or necessary fate imposed by a strange external design or power that determines what shall happen to persons. In responding to the future one must take into consideration that a person's destiny is the span and condition of existence into which one is born. Sidney put it, "seeing the way things are." Destiny points to the complex combination of internal and external circumstances in which people both find themselves and have a vision of the persons they could become.

Destiny is much more than the dark fear of a formless future. Rooted in our responsiveness and centered selfhood, destiny gives a concreteness to our future in the same way that it gives concreteness to the here-and-now. Our response to the future rests securely on the fact that we have a destiny and that by virtue of our freedom to respond we participate in shaping our destiny.

Along with destiny, *eternity* must enter into our consideration. Eternity embraces the conception of a personal fellowship in an undiscovered sphere of being where our hopes and ideals can find ultimate fruition and fulfillment.

Such a surmise is beyond the reaches of futurology. We can only accept the concept on faith and hypothesize about it. Goethe wisely said, "An able person, who has something regular to do here and now and must toil and struggle and produce day by day, leaves the future world to itself and is active and useful in this." Right! People in their normal senses do not think habitually about death and its aftermath. The present is where life is with its specific and measurable substance.

Recall how Thornton Wilder's character, the Stage Manager, puts it in the play *Our Town,* "I don't care what they say with their mouths—everybody knows that something is eternal. And it ain't houses and it ain't names and it ain't earth and it ain't even stars. . . . Everybody knows in their bones that *something is eternal* and that something has to do with human beings. All the greatest people have been telling us that for 5,000 years and yet you'd be surprised how people are always losing hold of it. There's something way down deep that's eternal about every human being."

We are not positing for or against immortality, but we are searching for the guidelines of how each of us can live a fuller and more engaged life. Most of us have a high resolve to become responsible persons. But we procrastinate and hold back. Kierkegaard urged immediate and full commitment: "Take hold to will this one thing." Death and eternity are considerations which both threaten and challenge us. Far too many of us deal with this challenge like children picking at the piano with their jerky one-finger rendition of Chopsticks, hesitantly, without cadence or command.

Imperatives Presented by Life's Unseen Givens

Space and time, forces and powers, history and the future—all provide intangible forms or categories that call for responses. As givens they are what the philosophers see as bearers of the distinction between essential and existential being. Although essence and existence are philosophical terms, the experience and the vision behind them precede philosophy.

Moralists and theologians give strong emphasis to the distinction between essence and existence, which religiously speaking is the distinction between the created and the actual world. The tension and balance between the two is the backbone of the whole body of religious response in thought and action.

On the one hand, these categories can be responded to as "essentials." It can mean the universals which characterize a thing and the ideas in which existing things participate. It can mean the original goodness of everything created, as well as the patterns of all things in the divine mind. But the ambiguity lies in the variation of the meaning between an empirical and a valuating sense. In addition to the fundamental nature of a thing, "essence" offers the basis for value judgments.

On the other hand, these unseen categories can mean the possibility of finding a thing within the whole of being. It can mean the actuality of what is potential in the realm of essences. Existence is the fulfillment of creation; existence gives creation its positive character. Christianity has emphasized the split between the created goodness of things and their distorted existence. But the good is not considered an arbitrary commandment imposed by an all-powerful Existent. Novelists are great when they respond to the distinction between essence and existence. In their responsiveness to the full range of human expression, they observe how differing people relate in different ways to the same stress or conflict, dramatizing that to be human means responding uniquely to the essentials of life.

Regardless of the variability of how people form their patterns of behavior, they demonstrate how all must make some response to the conditions surrounding them. As people express their freedom in the complex tapestry of their diversity, they are formed in the ways they respond to the conditions of their particular environment. While free to give differing responses, individuals are responsible not only for their responses but also for the personality they develop in the process of responding. People exist in factions, interest groups and sects that differ with one another over the most profound aspects of what they consider to be "right" or "wrong." So what do we do in a republic when my values do not match your values, when my ethics, theology and views don't agree with yours? When that occurs, we do not have to respond by ignoring present realities. In what is being called postmodern, post-Enlightenment times, we are challenged to respond with other strategies.

In a world steadily more complicated and fraught with resistances, responding responsibly becomes ever more exacting. We may wish for new geographical frontiers or an overpowering imperial authority that would eliminate the confusing complexities of life, but even if such events would occur, given our "response-ability," we still stand under the obligation to face squarely the cosmic and societal realities that shape us. The fact that our freedom must operate within the limits of a particular space and time makes more urgent our learning to respond appropriately and purposefully. Risk, as well as adventure, accompanies us in this effort. But we must give some response to it.

To meet responsibly the essentials of space and time, forces and powers, history and the future requires strong, enlightened and confident persons. The responsible person responds from a stance of *autonomy*—the quality, or state, of being self-governing. The autonomous individual risks being a responsible self. Responsibility carries the liability that we will be called upon to answer as the primary cause for a particular act. Responsibility requires a consistent and purposeful meeting of the realities of existence an. It calls for a trustworthy approach to the forces and powers that the environment presents.

The autonomous person, applying strong attributes to living, reinforces the larger community. Andrus Angyal talks of an "autonomy drive": the response of an individual to try to master the environment and to imprint an acceptable purpose on it. The will and capacity of human beings to do this is powerful. The danger lies in the ease with which autonomous responses can become dominating. Asserted responses must be balanced by increasing responsibility.

Summary

Close corollaries of the main givens influence every aspect of our social and physical lives. These have to do with superhuman energies and forces, history and change, as well as the future and eternity. Unseen, but nonetheless real, these given aspects of being, or "realities," also appear implicitly or explicitly in our thoughts, feelings and action. These categories also help us find meaning in the innumerable events and circumstances that we meet moment after moment.

Our destiny is the condition into which our decisions emerge. Included in that global response is body structure, psychic striving and spiritual character. Such total response draws on individuals, communities, and the environment which has shaped us and the world itself. The effect of our former decisions and our plans for future decisions become involved. One of the first conditions we meet is the necessity to limit our choices. We do this by eliminating the possibilities that do not agree with our priorities.

The response to unseen givens, according to the New Testament, can be described as a realistic hope or faith, i.e., confidence in things unseen. Responding in this way, paradoxically, enables people to go beyond their usual boundaries. In social outreach, artistic expression and spiritual searching, individuals consistently go beyond the limits of previous accomplishments.

The response of confidence in unseen realities that we call faith was one of the cornerstones of Teilhard de Chardin's prescriptions. Considering this self-transcending response of human beings, he spoke eloquently of how "among all the energies of the universe, consciousness is a dimension to which it is inconceivable and even contradictory to ascribe a ceiling or to suppose that it can double back upon itself. There are innumerable critical points on the way, but a halt or reversion is impossible." By sharpening self-consciousness and preserving their humanity, individuals exceed themselves. Something new comes into being through our grasping and shaping activity. Out of creative thoughts, feelings and spirit, new realms emerge.

Involvement: Deeper Engagement in Self and World

A Spanish proverb says, "It is not the same to talk of bulls as to be in the bull ring." Outside the ring the matador appears photogenic in his colorful regalia. He looks handsome, strong and confident. Inside the ring all these appearances give way to facing the reality of the red eyes and lowered horns of the charging bull. To survive, every moment demands consummate skill with absolute attention and split-second agility.

The difference lies in being a self-contained observer or a whole and committed person actively engaged in the process. Involvement means entering and responding to the conditions and demands of self and environment. People who involve themselves and cooperate to create a new world, more than self-centered onlookers, find more personal fulfillment and are favorably remembered in history.

The response of becoming involved is much more than a rhetorical exercise or dramatic pose. Involvement is the whole self responding to the circumstances immediately at hand. With freedom to respond in gear, thoughts, feelings and spirits combine to decide and act. In relating to people, involvement begins when people listen not just to words but to intentions and hungers and then share themselves. Involvement entails converting hopes for the relationship into operational terms.

Involvement serves operationally as a bridge from the self to the world of objects and persons. In the process of involvement, our self-understanding and self-image is strengthened and our linkage and contribution to the world is confirmed. Involved persons are not limited to being passive and quiescent, but are outwardly-directed, active and reactive. The heart of involvement in the arena of life is the dynamic interaction of people responding simultaneously to self and their world. The bridge of involvement cannot be built with fantasies or wishful distortions, but requires carefully engineered plans, solid foundations and the disciplined use of resources.

Peter Drucker, a contemporary social philosopher, sees responsible involvement as more than a fancy new method of rearranging old conditions and orders. He proposes a "responsible absorption" in a new role as persons accountable to themselves, their communities and the universe. He presses for a fresh view of the universe as one of risk rather than of chance or of certainty. Involvement is connecting the individual's consciousness with the outside world. It is a creative uniting of our inner lives with life's givens. Involvement is a closeness of persons' thought-feeling-behavior to the actualities of the world and the universal principles which sustain them.

Involvement also serves as a bridge between the self-world and the universal principles which undergird our lives and our environment. In becoming involved we get an internal signal that warns us against mask and disguise. Perplexed and haunted by fateful pairs of opposites—such as life and death, truth and falsehood—we are possessed with an enigmatic impulse to span the chasm between them. Uncomfortable with an isolated self-containment, we follow a built-in quest for involvement in reality. Involvement, in its naïve and solemn meaning, draws us with magnetic fascination. We reach from what we know about the physical world, history and the life forces to the less known principles and orders that underlie them.

When we ask, "What is reality?" we ask Pontius Pilate's question, "What is truth?" The more deeply engaged in life we become, the more we gain the insight that perhaps our most precious acquisition as humans is not only the capacity to understand and manage life's givens, but respectful and grateful involvement in durable truths. We realize that we must protect ourselves from the tendency to give up our freedom to respond and fall into the chasm of alienation and enmity. Involvement bridges the chasm of this and their frightening possibilities that lead to internal disintegration.

Involvement in the fluid interactions of life challenges us to make multi-dimensional responses. Our personality structures, our strivings and motivations and our ethical and religious convictions are all called into play. Involvement challenges us to transform the passive world of impressions into the active world of planning and developing. To survive we develop forms and styles to balance opposing forces and create order in place of chaos. We learn to respond with moral poise that readies us to reckon with the past and keeps an openness to the future. The sense of being involved gives strength and assurance that leads us beyond confusion to some order and meaning, beyond despair to confidence and hope.

Venturing from Fantasy into Reality

How do we grow into involvement? From birth, we become involved with mother and mother with us; thus begins reciprocity and involvement. At first, it is the fundamental relationship that provides the infant with an enveloping security in which the infant is the center of life. Before a perception of "I" and "non-I" develops, there is a transitional phase during which a soft cushion toy, the edge of a blanket or a lullaby provides a sense of cohesion and comfort when mother is suddenly not close. But when mother is even for a moment not at hand, the absolute is suspended. In the first "separating," when mother's warmth and protection are no longer immediately all around, the baby is thrust into an arena. The inevitability of the disappointment and pain of separation throws the infant into reality and provides the beginnings of a sense of identity—an awareness of one's boundaries and the outside world. The imperative of attending to the business of life begins.

Child psychiatrist Donald Winnicott, working in the Paddington Green Hospital in London, observed some of the later stages of how babies become involved. He put spatulas within reach of infants and noted how they reacted. First the infant, becoming aware of the wooden object, touches it, then hesitates. After a moment's waiting, the baby puts it in the mouth and chews it. In the second stage, the babies grip the spatula and show satisfaction in having it in their power. Next, the infants drop the spatula as if by mistake. If it is picked up and returned, they are pleased, play with it again and drop it once more.

The baby's brand of selfhood, of emotional economy, of trust or distrust, of passive or aggressive intentions are shown in this sequence. As the infant goes from the spatula to other objects, these first "possessions" become elementary aspects of reality that are crucial in the process of self-organization. In growing, the child's ego builds up a more or less constant and enduring self-image. This "sense of self" that emerges in the process of increasing involvement in the world is created out of the forms provided within a given culture.

Involvement with reality makes us aware of our existence and leads us into becoming individuals. We, like the infant, test the new realities we meet. The Chinese phrase *ch'u jieh* which means "to be born" and "to be in the world" provides an instructive insight. It is associated with the phrase *ch'u shir* which implies an imperative "to manage, control or attend to the business of life." Once born, we are in the world. And in the world our maturity is marked by the need to manage, control and attend to the business of life. After giving new conditions full awareness our responsible response is to open ourselves to become involved in the world.

The process of maturing takes us through difficult struggles as our involvements become ever more complicated. In each stage of growth and individuation, the elemental process of becoming involved is repeated. We see the object or persons and are attracted, then we come to grips with them. In trying to stand on our own feet we repeatedly test our capacities, as if to reassure ourselves. The happenings we experience in our becoming involved are destined to be a part of the internal logic of the psychic organization that forms our "self."

Despite the endless current of change in the self, where the ebb and flow of differentiation continues, there is normally an overall experience of inner consistency. Disparate units become integrated into workable forms in the light of early identifications. The self, in reaching out, expands its ability to test reality. In the process of meeting new situations our sense of identity, strengthened by our feeling involved, is like the unchanging form of a musical theme throughout the transformation and variations which unfold in time. As our involvement with circumstances and people increases our "ego core" becomes stronger and more confident. This identity lends stability to the flux inherent in our freedom to respond.

By the choices we make we define and redefine our unique essence, our identity. This definition and redefinition occurs through what the philosopher Whitehead calls the "actual occasions" of our involvement. He suggests that like organisms, these occasions grow, mature and perish. We saw this development with Jim, described in the last chapter, who was laid off and at 53 had to find new work. When all seemed lost and life became "parched and empty," he had to struggle to define and redefine himself. The American author Tom Keen declares, "People are born into a question, the answer is not thought or felt; it is lived. One's living is one's answer." In living the answer Jim found himself.

The Struggle of Involvement as We Mature

In the last nine years of her young life, Sydney ran into enormous difficulties trying to find meaningful involvement. From childhood, unsupported by her family, she had her hands full just surviving. She ran away from home at age 15, seeking a caring relationship. Instead, she stumbled into a series of abusive affairs, resulting in pregnancy out of wedlock. She struggled with being a mother, then a wife and her persistent effort to "find who I really am." At 22 she felt swamped tending her toddlers, keeping house and helping her husband start a new business. The many chores gave her burdens but little meaningful participation and needed support. "Involvement," she said, "means more than being busy. It means finding ways to be a more adequate mother, wife and neighbor."

"But how do I get into life?" Explaining why she felt uninvolved, Sydney continued, "I'm on a merry-go-round instead of 'in life.' Round and round I go with my children, up and down like a calliope repeating the same tune. It's not the real thing. Round and round my life goes, day in and day out, without improvement and without me finding out where I stand or what life's *really* about."

Sharon, another over-burdened and unsupported woman, faced heavy odds in her life. At 35, she was frustrated and depressed. "I'm letting a meaningful life rush by. I'm drifting in the storm of activities; blown about, with no bearings," complains Sharon.

A full-time teacher and mother, she receives only sporadic help from her live-in alcoholic mate, who continues to stall marriage even after fathering their two children. Her seven year-old daughter is diabetic and her five year-old hyper-active son is a problem at kindergarten. Her blue-collar mate is frequently laid off from his oil field job, so Sharon is the primary breadwinner of the family. Though affable when he is sober, he is irresponsible, procrastinating and indulging in self-pity, guilt feelings and absenting himself for weeks.

Sharon cannot count on support from her immigrant and divorced parents. Her mother, who lives nearby, is a persistent meddler and her father is dying of lung cancer. Neither parent is strong and objective enough to give either sound counsel or emotional backing: they tend to add to Sharon's load of low self-esteem and damaged confidence. Her house, for which she pays an exorbitant rent, is tiny, poorly arranged and is surrounded by belligerent neighbors. Teaching in a district where the socio-economic structures are deteriorating and racial antagonisms are explosive provides daily crises in her classroom. She says, "I'm not geared into life. In time and place, I'm weighed down instead of held up. My activities seem like draining distractions with little renewing connections."

Now, at mid-term in her eighth year of teaching, Sharon is pregnant for the third time. She enjoys teaching, is good at it, and her salary provides the chief support for the family, so she needs to continue teaching as long as possible before taking maternity leave. She will not consider abortion. She sizes up her situation, "I don't have freedom to choose about having this unplanned third child. The decision is already made. As far as working out a decision with the father of my children, it's next to impossible. No approach I make seems to reinforce our relationship and bring about a healthy two-parent family. I've weathered eight tumultuous years with him and he is the father of this new baby. I'm in it up to my eyebrows. It's high time I face the obvious fact: *I am involved,* so I'd better make the most of it."

In a steadier and more focused light she was able to see herself more clearly. She found in a co-dependent group others who shared her emotional needs for recognition and acceptance, for appreciation and respect. Another teacher in one of the groups gave her a helpful quote by William Blake: "He who would do good to another must do it in minute particulars." Seeing the significance of her particular and immediate involvements brought her a sense of meaning and purpose. She was helped to look inward with more confident self-reflection, and outward by testing her past and present to better prepare for the future. This new look at herself and her involvements paid off with boosts to her ego. As she became more objective about her involvements one-by-one they seemed to become less of a load. Sharon, in time, began to find some answers to her questions about her place in life.

A therapy group of seniors, ranging in age from 64 to 80, began with a common complaint of feeling "out of it" and no longer attached. They demonstrated that becoming meaningfully involved in life cannot stop at 35 or 45 or 55. In their pilgrimage, each admitted dragging their feet as their determination to "jump into the flow" of life lost momentum. On this day, with six of the regulars of their number absent, four zeroed in on ways to become more involved in their generally mundane existence. The four were Janet, a 65 year-old widow; Harvey, 60, a lay worker with the Salvation Army; Jerry, 61, a retired pathology technician; and, Sybil, a 64 year-old grandmother.

It was a week before Christmas holidays, which frequently brought them loneliness and frustration. On this day the four put aside their usual complaints and self-pity and focused on the business of getting more active in "the business of life."

Jerry mustered courage to challenge Janet, asking, "What did you do with your usual 'hang dog' look?"

Janet smiled, sat up straighter and met the taunt head on. From the time of her childhood in Iowa, living on an isolated farm, she had responded to many rough and raw experiences by withdrawing. She was so unhappy and confused that a year earlier she had attempted suicide three times. In recent months, however, she had begun to feel more positively about herself. So now, surprising the others, she expressed an unexpectedly strong affirmation: "I've stepped out and forward. And getting into life is not as scary as I've always thought. There are a lot of good forces in my life that will keep me going if I only let them."

Sitting a little forward, she added, "I'm beginning to enjoy eating, meeting people, volunteering to work in a day-care nursery and reading detective stories at night. Life is something I hang on to now. I'm not as torn up by the civil war that was going on inside me."

Next to her was Harvey, a chronic complainer whose old themes had become an inhibiting habit. Unaffected by Janet's unusual positive responses, he said, "I feel worthless, so muddle-headed I'm afraid of losing my mind. I'm so indecisive even God must be getting tired of me."

Fireworks broke out when Sybil, across the circle tried to agree with him and suggested that he shut up and bow out of life. Harvey jumped to his feet asserting, "No! No! People have to go on! Even animals have an urge to survive. There's something inside a person that pushes and pulls to keep living."

Jerry, the retired technician, spoke out, "There's something in our bones that drives us to keep alive. Even our simplest acts are powered by urges to stay alive."

Sybil introduced another angle. Having recently taken up oil-painting, she ventured to say, "Ask an artist or musician why he or she creates and you'll be told there's something down inside—call it a life-force, if you like—that bubbles up for expression on a block of stone, a sonnet or on a piece of canvas."

"Wait too long for life to start and it'll be over," Janet put in. "When I was little, I remember, I ached with the simple fact that I was not a grown-up and that my life on an Iowa farm was uneventful. I would never want to repeat my childhood years because of that awful sense of waiting for something special to happen. Life was so close I could touch it by the time adolescence arrived. By then I knew that the only way to get any relief was to hitch my wagon not to stars, but to some ordinary country landmarks I knew I could reach. When I'd get to the landmark I'd ask, 'That's all?' Then I'd realize that *is* all, and that's O.K. Since then, I've aimed and reached new landmarks. And now I see that somehow, without knowing it, I've traveled through five decades of my existence."

All of these four had in their own way and in their own time come to recognize that they were free to respond in new ways of involvement. At their age, they could not procrastinate much longer to work on the realization of their hopes. They needed to start *now* to change their patterns of passivity and uninvolvement and enter life's arena. Not only in group, but in their lives they had to decide to rise out of their slumps and begin to taste a confidence that there was a future in which they can have an influence. They sensed that when they become involved in life they can take part in change and direct their future and shape their destiny. If they neglected their freedom, they wrote off the chance to change and assured a declining future.

Regardless of age, where is our chance to change and assure an ascending future? Hall and Lindzey, in *Theories of Personality* (1981) suggest, "Just as persons are born with the capacity for seeing the world in three dimensions and develop this capacity through experience and training, so people are born with many predispositions for thinking, feeling and acting according to definite patterns and contents." Thinking, feeling and acting are the essential ways in which we become involved.

Involvement as Thinking: What and How We Know

Organizing our thoughts about self and our environment, then using that process to confront and cope with reality provides one of the important ways of becoming involved in life. Thinking through and trying to gain knowledge helped Sharon find answers to questions that perplexed her. When she started testing reality she said, "I've had to look squarely at basic things." She was responding to her need to see the conditions and forces bearing down on her more clearly in fuller perspective. The "world-consciousness" she reinforced her responsibility. She found that involvement is thinking her way *into* and then *out of* life's problems. The questions Sharon raised are key questions.

Humanity's most probing thinkers from Pythagoras to Wittgenstein have developed entire systems of thought as avenues into involvement. They have outlined ways to reconcile the solid ground beneath our feet with the airy possibilities above our heads—the real versus the ideal. For millennia philosophers and religious leaders have worked to think through how to connect the individual's own consciousness with the outside world and with the world's organizing principles. They search for ways to enhance people's involvement in the essentials of life.

Plotinus long ago gave one prescription for what he called "reasoning into involvement." He said, "Knowledge, if it does not determine action, is dead to us." Centuries later, the 17th century French philosopher and mathematician Descartes, indicating the involvement of "knowing," put it another way when he said, "I think, therefore, I am." The British empiricists stressed that we are truly involved when we *sense* accurately and fully the facts, movements, events and persons around us.

Other philosophers see the characteristics of existence, which they call "structure of being," essential for understanding involvement. To ask about "being" is to raise questions about the one-and-the-many or the individual and the universal and other such essential opposites. Involvement, these thinkers hold, must look at the process contrasts to structure. Sharon, keeping her nose to the grindstone, was tied to the structure of her existence. All the static forms became "draining distractions." As she was helped to see the "process" of life, she was better able to feel "involved" and handle her many responsibilities. Becoming aware of her involvement in existence she exercised her freedom to respond in the sequence of her personal and communal history.

Involvement, then, includes our bodies and our psychological selves. Our bodies serve as agents to involve us in our "being" and our "existence." Our life-forces give energy and substance to our thinking. The brain provides the control center for the body and for our thinking. Where the body will go, sit, walk, eat, exercise, feel or make love is largely motivated and guided by our willful thoughts. Our thinking influences our emotional and spiritual health. So we emphasize an inner mental machinery when dealing with personal difficulties.

From the time of the ancient Greek philosophers, Western people have relied on logical thought as the basis of their approaches to involvement in the world. Two ways of mental involvement come from modern brain research. The indications are that the two hemispheres are specialized for different modes of consciousness—one rational, one intuitive, which work in complement. The left hemisphere is predominantly involved with analytic, logical thinking. Its mode of operation is primarily linear and sequential. The right hemisphere seems specialized for holistic thinking. This hemisphere is primarily responsible for our orientation in space, artistic endeavor and recognition of faces. The left hemisphere processes information about nature analytically and sequentially; the right processes it more diffusely and demands a ready integration of many inputs at once.

Scientists, who once contended that sense perceptions are the only admissible basis of human knowledge and precise thought, now concede that actions and reactions of objects or persons may not always be predicted on the basis of natural law. Heisenberg's Uncertainty Principle states that one cannot determine the position and velocity of an electron exactly. This suggests that electrons in an atom do not consistently follow the same pattern. Electron Two may follow Electron One, but Three may break rank and Four might take still another path. These observations have a bearing on the question of human freedom and our capacity to become involved: in a cosmos where everything can be predicted, there would be no freedom; we would have to accept the rigidity of inviolable laws of nature and society.

The psychological quality of life for those who read and think is markedly superior to that of those who don't, but cultural illiterates do not *know* what they are missing. Some Americans don't know where the Pacific Ocean is. A greater deprivation than geographical ignorance is ignorance of the customs and involvement of people of other cultures. Involved understanding is the only way of seeing through the facts that inundate us. Understanding is what the ancient Greeks regarded as a moral trait, a sign of character. The same remains true today. If involved understanding is replaced by memory banks, then our future is in peril. We will have forgotten how to think.

Involvement as Feeling: Affect and Becoming Involved

Through *feeling* or *affect* we become involved in sensation and consciousness. Distinct from "knowing" that is based on left brain activity, "feeling" is attributed to right brain activity. Carl Jung distinguishes an *active* and a *passive* feeling and says passive feeling happens when content excites or attracts the feeling, compelling a feeling-participation. Active feeling, on the contrary, confers value from the person—it is a deliberate evaluation of contents in accordance with feeling and not with intellectual intention. Being loved, for example, would be undirected and a passive kind of feeling. Loving, however, is an active feeling and is directed.

Feelings arise in many ways. We receive impressions from our five senses. Affective states—the more active feeling experiences—include desires, cravings and interests which are reinforced often by thoughts. Traditional psychology distinguishes pleasure and non-pleasure, liking and disliking. We speak of feeling as the coloring of experience, the evaluating aspect of our adjustment to our environment.

The physical world, which inspires a rich array of feeling responses, provides unlimited opportunities for rich involvement. On the practical side, environmentalists urge the response of careful stewardship, while industrialists press for the development of resources. The wider universe, viewed through the lenses of spacecraft, turns out to be not only scientifically interesting but compellingly beautiful.

The feeling responses of poets and saints, naturalists and environmentalists is the arousal of the human sense of beauty—attributed by the religious as the handiwork of God, by philosophers as identified with the true. These same appreciators of nature see both its beauty and destructiveness which leads to a deeper consciousness and more realistic involvement. Tolstoy expressed this bifocal view when he said, "Nature is a friend you will never lose until death and even when you die, you disappear into nature."

Feeling responses serve as important doors for estimating and approaching people coming to mental health clinics. Ruth's pain, anger and sadness all showed from the moment she opened the counseling office door. She looked her feelings! Stoop-shouldered and dowdily dressed, she dragged in, eyes barely visible under her lowered head. Making it to the chair seemed tedious. Her monosyllabic responses to my greeting betrayed her suspicion of male authority figures. Although only 29, her pervasive negativism gave the impression of someone double her age. The unraveling of her convulsed and sad history was labored. The referral from jail, where she was awaiting trial on the charge of murdering her 22 month-old son, gave a glimpse of the many set-backs and batterings she had suffered.

The youngest of nine children, she had been sexually abused repeatedly by her father, her uncle and three of her brothers. Ruth's love-hate feelings, so precariously repressed, had accumulated. As an adolescent these contradictory feelings became terribly confusing. How she wished to love and be loved! Thoughts and behavior became devastatingly tangled. As the years passed she sought love with one man after another, only to have each relationship sour and fail. Hate settled in as an act of will and in time it became lethal and almost devoured her until her hating began to tear up the wish to love and be loved. Her damaged feelings skewed her thinking and values and made it hard for her to see facts and people straight on. Having encountered abandonment and abuse throughout her life, she tragically has been pushed into the habit of inviting abuse.

In spite of her serious deprivations, Ruth decided to seek a new life. Correcting her poisoned feelings, deep hurts and strong hates, will be difficult. The healing of such feelings will take her into a long journey of psycho-therapy and religious confession. The way of reconciling, along with gaining clarity of thought and values, will take much discipline.

Involvement in the Way We Act and Function

The response of involvement is expressed in the way we act and order our lives. This refers to responses of the whole person, not just a stray physiological activity. Each component of the body has its own special way of reacting. When our stomach feels the pangs of hunger, we look for food. The seeking constitutes involvement through behavior. Human behavior is multi-natured and multi-determined. In becoming involved, people's behavior can be healthy or disordered and manifest a variety of levels: genetic, physiological and environmental. Behavior stemming from past experience and present environmental situations interact to deter involvement. Powered by the "life-force," described earlier, people through their behavior "enter into" involvement with others and the environment.

Psychologists are the specialists who probe how psychic forces and patterns affect behavior and involvement. Freud frequently wrote of the "impetus" and "pressure" exerted by psychic energies seeking involvement in persons and societies. The special feature of human life is to be *engaged* in activities and relationships. The source of this "life-drive" is bodily and mental process stirring action. The internal manifestation of the drive is the discharge of an emotion and the external expression is behavior.

Jung describes a psychic force, or a "libidinal energy," that influences behavior in the interactions of life. When this energy is removed from one activity or interest, it reappears in another. Behavior, he said, depends on the movement between opposite forces within the psyche. We become involved in life as we cope with tensions such as those between thought and feeling.

Karen Horney claims in *The Neurotic Personality of Our Time,* that in Western culture there are four principal ways the life-forces influence behavior and bring about deeper involvement. 1) People's behavior aims to gain affection and avoid hurt. 2) Others seek power in the form of success, possessions and status in the hope these qualities will provide security and pleasure. 3) Others use submission to protect themselves. 4) Still others withdraw emotionally out of fear of inadequacy. Driven often by more than one of these motivations, the responses are especially noticeable in the behavior of people under stress.

Otto Rank advanced another interpretation, claiming the separation experience at birth, the "birth trauma," had two opposing affects on people's becoming involved in life: 1) a strengthening of the emotional binding to the mother and 2) a striving for *will* toward freedom and independence from any one person. The fear of individualization is the fear of being alone, of loneliness or the loss of kinship with others. The life-force expresses itself in the individual exercising an act of *will*, which for Rank is "a positive guiding organization and integration of the self that utilizes creativity and controls the instinctual drives.

In the last three decades, questions about how the life force works in the development and functioning of self have been reframed. Old issues have been given new approaches by advocates of ego psychology. Two from this group, Kohut and Kernberg, suggest that the life force within us is predominantly self-concerned. This instinctual energy shapes and differentiates the self in the process of social and cultural changes. Issues arise and involvement occurs, they say, in every critical exchange among persons who are face-to-face participants in a close-knit or primary group—in the workplace, school and home.

Kohut contends that the life force influences behavior in two ways: One is the advancement of the "grandiose self," the other, its glorification of the "idealized parent." Kernberg sees the neurotic person as painfully and obsessively absorbed in self-concern, self-reference, seeking reassurance and admiration. Persons can burst into rage when disappointed and turn freezing cold toward others in a defensive effort to fuse the ideal self and the actual miserable self-image. In maturing, the self seeks to differentiate between these exaggerated images and looks for its own uniqueness.

Involvement and Struggle with Freedom and Change

1) Freedom and Involvement: We are able to become involved in the world by virtue of human freedom. Our involvement in societies depends on the degree of freedom we enjoy. Our parents' and our own special achievements in freedom have chiefly been in the areas of political, economic and technological freedom. Freedom in that context is commonly taken to mean exemption from unpleasant and onerous conditions and unrestricted access.

The limits of our freedom place limits on our involvement. We are never completely free or independent. No behavior is altogether free of influence from previous conditions. Prior decisions or unforseen circumstances can block our becoming involved in a new project. Freedom and involvement with it, may be limited by conditions of space-time, contingencies of nature and mores held by society. Jean-Jacques Rousseau's historic formulation that humans are born free, yet everywhere are in chains, expresses a paradox for involvement as well as for freedom.

The responsible involvement of autonomous person's includes more than being able to choose and decide between options. It must include applying, protecting and extending their freedom. Being self-governing, we have both the ability and responsibility to become involved in life. In the gift of human freedom responsibility and involvement are linked.

Freedom to respond and the responsibility to become involved may be our birthright, but like any capability, it atrophies if not used. Freedom requires work; it must be applied and revised continually. In democracies, for instance, we are free citizens. But unless we exercise our involvement in the political process, demigods rush into the vacuum caused by our irresponsible citizenship. Getting involved in the democratic process necessitates voting and writing our elected officers. Likewise, our freedom to get involved, being vulnerable to attack, must be protected. Freedom muzzled and locked up is no longer free.

Involvement in society requires struggling against the yoke of restrictive laws. Where there are abuses of freedom, governments are required to take measures to correct the condition. Where freedom is hampered by political oppression, communities need to struggle to free themselves of tyranny. Where persons are limited by neurosis or psychosis, mental health workers seek to free the impaired person from their emotional bondage. The freedom which involvement needs is not only to be "free *from,*" as Erich Fromm has pointed out, but also "free *to*" work toward worthy goals. Such involvement exercises our capacity for *creative acts*—not merely for reactions. Involvement is eloquently expressed in our capacity to formulate ideas and goals and seek to realize them while paying attention to the spiritual sources of freedom.

2) Involvement as the response to change: To be involved in life is to be immersed in change. We are caught in an acceleration of radical change that presents both amazing opportunities and increasing risks. Our involvement in the runaway changes of the last half century has had a jarring and disruptive effect on individuals and societies. Alvin Toffler (1970) described "the dizzying disorientation brought on under the shattering stress of the premature arrival of the future."

In such times the changes in life's arena test our capacity to respond with new patterns of involvement. We can learn the required changes providing they are mechanical or intellectual, but it is difficult to learn new emotional attitudes and beliefs. Often we can cope with superficial changes but not those at deeper levels, such as the values and beliefs we share.

Becoming involved in the changes at the foundational levels of society's purposes and goals meets with stubborn resistance. Even harder tasks for us arise when insights about ourselves or our involvement with others demand a personal change. Where successful people might resist being involved in a necessary change, others, considered less advantaged, might find the necessary discipline and persistence to forge new patterns of living. Such persons venture as pilgrims like Abraham of old leaving the certainties of secure city life in

Ur of Chaldees daring to risk the uncertainties of far away and unknown Canaan. In each break that change brings, old freedoms are challenged and new freedoms are created that lead to new stages of involvement.

3) Involvement in the possibilities of the future, destiny and eternity: The manner and mood of perceiving the future strongly influences people's attitude toward their present involvement and their outlook guides people in responding to life and death with more effective thought. The view of things to come, pessimistic or optimistic, affects decisively the future of individuals and societies.

Futurologists are the specialists who detail how we can involve ourselves in preparing for the future. The future, they urge, is not merely to be seen or even outlined, but to be *planned* for. Human beings, as the only animals capable of distinguishing between what is and what ought to be, have a particular responsibility to prepare seriously and systematically for the future. They recognize that their task is neither to predict nor detail our tomorrows, but rather show how people who hold to a realistic hope move beyond the shortcomings of deterministic and anxiety ridden scenarios. This hope is not the same thing as "knowledge about the future." Involvement, through action and change, is implicit in the term "hope."

Some futurologists suggest that having a sense of responsibility to look and work positively toward the future and prepare for it has a profound theological basis. These would agree that God, seen as an agent and the eternal center of history, gives meaning and a plan for the future.

For the Christian, hope rests on the conviction that a particular person serves as a model for the future. Jesus Christ *is* the hope of the world. This is the victory that *has* overcome the world. The gates of death *will not* prevail. For Christians the promise is manifested in their involvement in the world. Something *does* happen. The promise is that nothing shall separate us from the love of God in Christ—and nothing does. The community is sustained by witness to the fulfillment of that promise.

Involvement with planning for "things to come" gives the future the substance and quality of destiny. Given our freedom to respond, destiny is more than an inevitable or necessary fate imposed by a strange power outside ourselves. As we involve ourselves in planning for the future, our destiny becomes the whole condition out of which our decisions emerge.

Along with questions of destiny, *eternity* must enter in to the consideration of involvement. This is not something that belongs to the future alone, for it is not to be understood in terms of simply an endless continuation of time. It is already present, a dimension of reality different from those knowable by the five senses, a promise present in the degree we can see time as a never-ending stream, without beginning and without end.

In the process of involvement, eternity embraces the conception of a personal fellowship in an undiscovered sphere of being where our hopes and ideals can find ultimate fruition and fulfillment. Involved in considering it, we see eternity as a condition that is a duration without a start or a finish. Granted, having no hard facts to conjecture about eternity, we can only accept the concept on faith and hypothesize about it. But to consider our destiny and eternity is part of the risk-taking required of our extended involvement.

Involvement as Risk Taking

All aspects of involvement—thinking, feeling and acting—include the factor of risk. Consider the penchant for the young to participate in sports that pose various hazards. A taste for danger is common to all people. Involvement includes the risk of danger since many situations present difficulties we may not be able to overcome. Failure and the prospect of being pulled out of involvement is one of the serious risks we take.

Involvement leads to vulnerability which in turn brings the risk of trouble and pain. Paradoxically, even though danger lurks in involvement, we seem to welcome a certain amount of risk. Dr. T. Glynn Williams, associate director of the Maryland Psychiatric Research Center, observes that human beings do not appear to be created to be safe and if there is no risk and danger in their lives, someone will create it. This is the them of the book and movie, *I Never Promised You a Rose Garden*, which describes the difficulties and costs of achieving emotional health and loving relationships. Nor did Jesus promise his followers a rose garden, promising to save them from the risks of involvement. Paradoxically he said, "I come not to bring peace, but a sword; I have come to set a man against his father and a daughter against her mother" (Mt 10:34). What could be more risky than responding positively to the challenge, "Take up my cross and follow me?"

Risk enters the paradox of imperfection-and-incompleteness vs. perfection-and-completion. In our involvement, risk is derived from the tension between permanence and change. Persons who cannot face imperfection and lack of fulfillment suffer guilt and anxiety. They struggle for the assurance that eventually perfection and fulfillment will be achieved, but the risk is that involvement in life's arena cannot provide this guarantee. Likewise, venturing from fantasy to reality is risky. When idealism is not balanced with realism, the risk is great that grief and misunderstanding may ensue. There is risk in carrying youthful enthusiasm and eagerness into adult life. "Youth has been called a perishable talent," wrote E.A. Gutkind, "but the creative individual is an imperishable juvenile." The young's eagerness and optimism upon a disillusioned establishment could provide the magic to turn around a despairing civilization.

Involvement is impossible without risk. Life goes on only when people risk "doing what has to be done." Not to change is also risky—we may become stultified and ossified. Envisioning and working for a more livable society is likewise risky. Risk is involved in changing "thoughts and purposes" we have become accustomed to. New meanings need to be recognized.

Responsible individuals must develop stronger disciplines for risk-taking in a world crying out for drastic measures to rescue a desperate civilization faced with the numbing prospect of spreading poverty and famine, war and other human disasters. Political and organizational controls are in themselves often not enough.

Modern pagans hearing the message of God's risk in accepting the unacceptable often do not want to risk becoming involved in a religious prescription, because the term "God" and the problem of being accepted or rejected by God has little meaning for them. Taking the risk to surrender one's own goodness to God, however, is the central element in the courage of the religious. We tend to feel more fulfilled if we try ourselves to conquer the ambiguity of good and evil. But try and try again, we fail until we feel "accepted," even with our faults and failures, by the Creator. We find when we feel accepted personally, it is easier to accept others. But, our big risk is to relinquish our insistence on "doing it ourselves," and gaining acceptance through our own efforts.

Risks increase as the perils are met in moving towards becoming a more responsibly religious persons. In religious experience this is moving through "justification" (being accepted) and on to "sanctification" (being renewed). Luther pictured the problems of a line moving upward toward perfection as arising from persons being thrown back into estrangement and ambiguity. This up-and-down experience was one that Luther himself struggled with. In his risks of faith he swung between moments of courage and joy and of doubt and despair. In a larger context he found it risky to be involved in a restrictive institution unwilling to risk change.

Summary

We have traced a wide range of ways people respond within themselves and toward others in the process of involvement. These strategies for responsible involvement, looking at ourselves and relating to others, rest on our ethical guidelines. With the guidelines of our values or ethical convictions, we are enabled to become involved by choosing and taking action while minimizing the possibilities that do not agree with our priorities.

This entails identifying and engaging in the forces and causes working for justice, rightness and equality. Involvement with these causes lends them power. Likewise, power for ourselves and others comes from applying human values. The nourishing and supportive use of moral power abets our neighbor's power and makes for an integrative use of our strengths.

The linkage of value with involvement reinforces internal unity and external security, and helps to make our behavior effective and responsible. Responsible involvement requires us to decide between the surplus of available options and act with positive responses. Then we must face and take responsibility for the consequences of our involvement. Positive and intimate involvement of this sort places unique responsibilities on us.

In the '70s the celebrated anthropologist Margaret Mead cited two major tasks of involvement determining human survival: The question of *responsibility* for power and the *need to develop* reliable moral and spiritual curbs to prevent humankind from triggering their self-destructive powers. On the first point, she indicated that any definition of science as a means of giving us *dominion* or power over nature, tends to compound human responsibility and the task of curbing exploitation. On the second imperative of involvement, Mead points to the "cosmos-sized risk" we face because we not only have knowledge of good and evil, but we also have the absolute power to destroy the earth and ourselves. Here is perhaps the greatest challenge to change that humankind has ever confronted—the risk to trust, one nation to another, that none will commit nuclear forces to destroy the earth.

Ernest Troelsch, innovative German theologian of the first decades of the 20th century, wrote perceptively of the fuller aspects of involvement, positing that connecting the depths of human nature with the realities of our environment was our ethical responsibility of "choosing, deciding and making our history." He stressed that involvement was living, day by day, in a way that was concerned with the direction, quality and meaning derived from being immersed in what he called "a purposeful new movement." Involvement in life's processes, he said, was being accountable for our being created free to respond. We are personally accountable for responding responsibly in the involvement open to us.

First, we need to respond responsibly to our selves. Often this requires revising our view of ourselves. We need to be aware of our misery and our grandeur; on the one hand acknowledging our limitations, faults and foibles, on the other hand steadily going beyond the boundaries of previous accomplishments. Out of self-awareness and self-conservation can come self-transcendence that leads to an individual's fullest involvement.

Second, the positive and intimate experience of love remains one of the most powerful ways of involvement. The boundaries of power and love overlap each other. Love motivates the person to want to do what the loved one wishes. Living in a world dominated by giant technology, persons must be able to assert the power of love plus the power to express it—if they are to survive. Authentic religious experience reinforces this: faith requires courageous and loving responses.

Third, when we deal directly with life as we share our-selves with others responsibly, when we truly become involved with another person, we listen not just to words but to the language of the heart. We look for thoughts, feelings and behavior of the other. We become involved when we can convert off-hand statements and generalizations into opera-tive terms. We ask: Have we respected free will—ours, as well as others? Did we risk innovation in cultivating new relation-ships? Are we committed to accepting responsibility for life?

Accepting Responsibility for Life

If this is a moral universe, then the free are the responsible. When we take responsibility for the appropriateness and quality of our responses, we find an answer to the recurrent question: How can we achieve acceptance and integrate our powers to go on from where life seems to leave us? We begin to see how we can contribute constructively to a confused world and find great ends that have socially useful outcomes for God and God's children everywhere.

We may revolt against the hereditary chains forged around us and complain bitterly about the prison walls of unfavorable environment which limit our powers, but always there is a third element on which the whole of life turns—our personal and responsible response. Unthinking heredity and an uncaring environment will definitely have an effect on us; however, what we make of our given situation is the determinative matter. Ultimately, we are responsible for our life.

It is the courage and strength of the believing individual to take on the responsibility for action. Even though no realistic worldview holds that the enigmas of life can be solved here and now, the great world faiths affirm that no person can be freed of responsible decision no matter how difficult and lonely it may be. The Christian faith goes further and says in all the darkness and contradictions of life, still we are to speak the 'even so.' In responding responsibly we are to involve the entire range of our personality, our social nature and our insistent yearning for higher ground. Responsibility is accountability within ourselves, toward others and toward the higher ground to which we are committed.

Living responsibly is a process of fulfillment based on a satisfying sense of personal adequacy and self-esteem and a growing circle of meaningful relationships. There are five essential expressions of self-action. 1) A positive response from awareness, 2) action that reacts to the subjective perception of "what's going on" in the world, 3) individuals' accountability for their action, 4) a concern for and commitment to the community of which we are an inescapable part and 5) the challenge to link ourselves to the all-commanding purpose Jesus demonstrated to be the requisite of discipleship. Thus responsibility entails a sense of obligation to self, life's "givens," intimates, community and a commitment to a central and integrating purpose.

Responsibility is not the performance of duty, but includes the quality and thrust of a life rooted in its origins. It is growing with "the grain" and "the flow" of our lives from the cosmic to the personal. Laws about what's "right" and "good," or even what's "reasonable" and "magnanimous" mark minimal responsibilities. Fuller responsibility is an adventure and a celebration of our unique individuality and our freedom to respond. Rules, developed to guide our personal and civic relationships, are helpful as we search out our responsibility to our destiny.

As we move to fulfill our destiny, we become more responsible. True, we are formed by nature and history, but that gives us our freedom to participate in shaping our destiny. We can comprehend both the minuteness of our environment as well as the millions of galaxies. By dedicating our self-will to this overarching and undergirding purpose we find a freedom which enables us to live in freedom from fear and in freedom for responsibility.

To further identify responsible responding we need to consider 1) immediate areas where responsibility applies, 2) counter actions which resist the expression of responsibility, 3) examples of individuals seeking to be more responsible and 4) formulations that philosophers have proposed for responsible responding.

Where and How Responsibility Applies

The application of responsibility begins with taking on accountability for one's responses. The exercise of this endowment is rooted in one's "response-ability." The state of West Virginia has set up "responsibility criteria" as part of its laws governing custody matters and which parent will be given primary care of the child. The state awards custody to that parent, if otherwise "fit," who 1) prepares the food, 2) changes the diapers, dresses and bathes the child, 3) takes the child to school, church and other activities, 4) makes appointments with the doctor and generally watches over the child's health, and 5) interacts with the child's friends, school authorities and other adults engaged in activities involving the child.

To be responsible is to serve as an agent to improve the health and welfare of oneself and another. Taking this responsibility is reinforcing but can be risky. Risk comes from the outside when associates may criticize or attempt to block your responsible responses, and it may also come from within because fulfilling responsibility can become a burden and at times stir feelings of inadequacy. It is also reinforcing for it can cement relationships and bring a sense of satisfaction for the opportunity to exercise skills and provide the opportunity to help another.

Responsibility goes hand in hand with obligation—which carries a personal accountability. Even if we do not answer to someone else, we have to satisfy our own question: "Why do we do what we do?" Responsible responding involves duty, commitment and reliability.

At a deeper level, responsible responding occurs in the context and direction of divine activity within people's lives and provides the resources of human renewal. What God is doing in the world to make and keep human life human releases behavior from the frustrating impasse between irrelevance and relativity and forges the authentic behavioral link between freedom and responsibility.

Responsible responses are crucial for society. The need is to apply the resources of personal freedom responsibly to the craft of social conduct. We need both responsible leaders and responsible participants. Communities are kept alive and stimulated by the responsible "bridging" of the individual's freedom to respond with the requirements of the social systems.

In considering where and how responsibility is applied, we recognize those who demonstrate the quality even before we are able to describe it. We see responsible behavior when siblings are supportive of one another and when neighbors join in worthy community activities. We call them *responsible* for they respond in ways that help people and communities accomplish their purposes. They serve as agents to bring about greater health of body, mind and soul.

Escapes from Responsibility

In *The Life We Prize* Elton Trueblood discusses the differing reactions to coping with the stress and strain of modern life. "It appears that the most common reaction is that of some form of escape and especially the effort to escape responsibility." Ogden Nash, in a more mischievous vein, penned the verse: "Why did the Lord give us agility, if not to escape responsibility."

This satire focuses on a grave tendency of our time to run away from life's demands instead of meeting them with willing shoulders. We may magnify our infirmities so that we refuse to develop life's remaining gifts. An alibi persistently held is the last stronghold of those who blame fate for their lot and in the process avoid responsibility. Each of us, one way or another, is sorely tempted to soften down or sneak around the titanic fact of responsible living.

One way to evade responsibility is to blame natural forces. Fire, lightning, flood or any other circumstance of the elements may be used as an excuse for not responding responsibly. A popular song decades ago lauded "Doing What Comes Naturally." Current novels refine this theme repeatedly: nature made me this way; I have these urges and drives; it's really not my fault; I wasn't responsible; the urge was there and I simply satisfied it.

Another common device to avoid responsibility is to blame persons and conditions outside ourselves. "One of our worst defects and our best fictions," said the Peruvian writer Mario Vargas Llosa, "is to believe that our miseries have been imposed on us from abroad, that others have always had the responsibility for our problems." In the mazey world of his brilliant novels are compact descriptions of characters pinning responsibility on someone else. Just like King David asked Nathan the prophet, we demand, "Who is the scoundrel who did that awful deed?" To our own dismay, we like him hear the prophet Nathan's judgment, "You, O King David, are the person!"

David's life is a classic account of the full range of human responsibility and irresponsibility. When still a lad, David carried the responsibility to stand against Goliath. As a youth, with his life in jeopardy, he had to elude the murderous pursuit of the demented King Saul. When still a young man his people placed on him the mantle of leadership. In his advancing years he increasingly bore the heavy responsibilities of administering a precariously united small kingdom, mediating over a contentious court and fractious generals, raising and leading armed forces to hold back besieging Ammonites and Philistines. Continually the compounding "evil in his own household" confronted him with the need to model the moral insights of his people and balance his sensuous impulses with his religious sensitivity. The account of the tremendous struggles of this remarkable hero of responsibility describes bluntly his shadow side and spells out his slump into gross irresponsibility.

After satisfying his lust for another man's wife, David arranges for her husband Uriah, a brave and faithful officer, to be killed in a contrived battle maneuver. When Nathan boldly targeted the irresponsibility and perfidy of the king's taking of Bathsheba by telling a parable of a poor man and his one little ewe lamb who fell victim to the greed and lust of a powerful neighbor, David saw the moral responsibility as applying to another and asks for the identity of this deceitful person and added, "As the Lord lives, the man who has done this deserves to die." Nathan's fearless answer rolls in, "Thou art the man . . . You have had your loyal officer, Uriah the Hittite killed with the sword of the Ammonites and taken his wife to be your wife."

The consequences of David's irresponsibility escalate. The son conceived of his sin dies seven days after birth and shortly the treasonable plot of his cherished son Absolom is revealed and foiled at the price of the death of this beloved son. The infection of irresponsibility seriously weakened David's insights and judgments, leading him into disastrous miscalculations—removing his indispensable and loyal general, Joab, replacing him with the rebellious and treacherous Amasa. David's neglect of responsibility resulted in needless acts of violence and impractical political strategies. Never again was he capable of the same combination of diplomacy and courage in dealing with the affairs of state.

At the heart is a record of the breakdown of family morale and the irresponsibility of a devoted but vacillating husband and father, unable to deal with his household as a responsible spouse and parent. He failed as a mediator of the justice and mercy of God which, as a sinner, he himself had received.

Sabotaging Responsibility—Irresponsibility Infected

Pervasive as is the human quality of taking responsibility, it has a powerful companion counterforce: *irresponsibility.* We like to see ourselves as the responsible person we want to be, yet frequently are embarrassed and nonplused by our irresponsibility. Like the contradictions of being alternately genuine then phoney, we are responsible and irresponsible. We subvert responding responsibly in many ways. Confronted with decisions, we excuse and rationalize our negligence and back away instead of face a problem head-on.

Readily we develop all sorts of resistances that hinder responsible action. St. Paul's experience is our own: "The good that I would, I do not; and the evil that I would not, that I do." A high school senior, within eight weeks of finishing, jeopardizes graduation by not getting out of bed early enough to attend a first period class. Asked by a counselor to explain this self-destructive habit, the adolescent admits: "I really don't know myself. It's important for me to get to class but still I don't show." A struggling young attorney admits that her great need for approval often leads her to give soft instead of firm responses which hinders her practice and keeps her from collecting her accounts receivable. Carried over into her marriage this fear of "rocking the boat," keeps her silent, but their marital problems, instead of going away, build up and explode.

Within conflict-ridden families, irresponsibility takes many forms. When family members are unwilling to see and correct their share of the chaos and pain, resistances accumulate and barriers increase. The result stifles the capacity to work out alternative behavior and cultivate intimacy. Each feels that if it weren't for the other, they would have a pretty good marriage. They tell the therapist, "Doc, I wish you'd straighten out" the spouse. Grown children, out of college, continue to live at home. Quarreling and not helping with family chores or expenses, they say, "We've got our own activities and expenses to tend to." At 16, the youngest is dissolute and self-centered, doing poorly at school, not helping around the house and adding to the tension says, "Who cares?" Each member is irresponsible in not clarifying their own identity and role in the family. Although dependent on each other, each is assertive at the expense of the others. Their communication is more towards attacking than toward supporting. Each feels either controlled and/or defeated by the other members, while continually trying to control or counter-control the other.

Less conflicted families are also afflicted with irresponsibility. Several films in the mid-80s, such as "Lost in America," "Desperately Seeking Susan" and "Almost You," have featured young marrieds disillusioned with upward mobility and infected with a radical desire to be (gasp) *irresponsible.* These films show our society's conflicting patterns of interacting similar to those of many dysfunctional families: mixing both centripetal—a tendency to leech off the family—with centrifugal force—a tendency to fling themselves away from the center on which they are dependent.

A supportive and guiding response is necessary to cultivate mutual concern. Japanese writer Michihiro observes one difference between Japanese and Americans: "In the U.S., you say, 'I'm O.K, you're O.K.' In Japan, we say 'We're O.K., therefore I'm O.K.' " The Japanese tend to identify their own welfare with that of their family and country and it is significant that "We" precedes "I".

The sum of our personal, family and community irresponsibility adds up to "the infection of irresponsibility." When the emotional immunization system breaks down it renders us vulnerable to emotional and societal disorders. Symptoms may be conflicting fears, resentments and feelings of inadequacy. Negative emotions develop from failure to fulfill a trust or be faithful stewards of resources. These destructive feelings can push us toward irresponsible behavior. When disease or the disablement of advancing age overtake us, we may not have at hand responsible medical care. By attending to preventive measures we learn that health is not just the absence of disease but a state of well-being that extends beyond normal readings of medical tests.

Our careless stewardship of the potentials of young people, minorities and the expanding number of senior citizens also reflects the irresponsibility syndrome. Young people without confidence, direction or faith wonder what is the point of working and ask, "What does it all mean?" An increasing number decide life is worthless and commit suicide. Others turn to drinking, drugs, promiscuous sex and cults. In the shadows of our great universities, there is a growing attraction to other-worldly mysticism, religious fundamentalism or cynicism. Johns Hopkins President Steven Muller notes, "The failure to rally around a set of values and nurture self-accepting and fulfilled persons means universities are turning out potentially highly-skilled barbarians."

Similarly the potentials of minorities—Blacks, Hispanics, Asians and native Americans—are as great as they are varied. Responsible development of their uniqueness coupled with bridges for more realistic blending into communities is urgently needed. Likewise the wisdom of the increase of the elderly in our population, offers additional human resources that are underdeveloped.

Irresponsibility also finds its way into our politics. Our democratic society is weakened by persons whose preoccupation with self-centered interests and pleasures prevents their participation in voting. Many citizens fail to acquaint themselves with the crucial needs and issues of neighborhood, state or nation. The result is that elected officials can sidestep their responsibilities, fill their own pockets and expand their personal influence rather than exert time, energy and skill tackling issues of prime concern for their constituencies. History shows us that communities and nations begin to weaken and stagnate when citizens succumb to political irresponsibility.

Irresponsibility takes a toll in our careless stewardship of the economic system. To be responsible in the fabric that supports our livelihood requires more than guaranteeing profit for a few. Complex economic issues—such as people's jobs, work morale and benefits—must be worked out responsibly in the larger context of environmental conditions. The irresponsibility of individuals—from senior executives down to minimum-wage employee—undermines the health of the economy. A group of influential executives, when asked by California's Senator, Alan Cranston, what single factor most limited their company's capacity to expand, answered *irresponsibility*. Most reported that their biggest problem was the dearth of responsible employees. This situation is potentially catastrophic for a democracy, because a self-governing nation urgently needs people prepared to make choices, assume responsibility and act positively on the values to which they are committed.

Our careless stewardship of the earth's resources also contributes to corporate irresponsibility. In the name of "development," and "utilization," we exploit oil, ground water and other irreplaceable elements of our natural environment, regardless of the needs of future generations. Our wanton use of land despoils forests and endangers species. Our machines and chemicals pollute our streams and oceans. Such irresponsibility is a sin against both the delicate ecology of the earth and the needs of others with whom we share this planet.

Evidences of More Responsible Responses

Conscientious people have deep concerns over the crisis arising from our individual, communal and global irresponsibility. Such people realize we have neglected the lessons of history and want to rescue the future for themselves, their communities and posterity.

"Wow! Did I ever have responsibility come down on me seven years ago when, at age 20, I found I was pregnant," said Lena in a therapy group. "I had gone out with a handsome fellow from church in his new van. He was from the right side of the tracks, had a good future. He was tender and showed me a super time. Weeks later when I told him I was pregnant, he took off fast. I was devastated at first. The prospects of raising a new life by myself made me feel as if the world had come to an end, but after many sleepless nights, I decided to face the music head-on and told myself, 'Okay, responsibility, I'll meet you on your terms.'" And she did.

Young people in "delayed adolescence," like Lena, frequently have a hard struggle managing their dramatic expansion of freedom and responsibility. The horizons of novel experiences and exciting liberty unfold as new opportunities open—some are safe, some are perilous. It is a time of intense self-consciousness as they realize how "free to respond" they are. With this recognition they come up against the consequences of their ability to respond. Questions like "Who am I?" "What do I want out of life?" and "What do I value and believe in?" become unavoidable and urgent.

In the Orthodox Jewish Bar Mitzvah ceremony boys give significant responses to such questions when they declare, "Today I am a man." The adolescent is saying in effect, "From this point on, don't blame my father if I conduct myself badly. Blame me, for I am responsible."

As we mature, demands for more complicated responses increase and tax our freedom to respond in more responsible ways. "I consider my primary responsibilities to be twofold," observed a Los Angeles judge. "First, I am accountable to the populace, which includes the defendant before the bench, the defendant's family and associates. Second, I must be faithful to the laws which make this court an institution of society." Pausing a moment, she added, "Completing my tenth year on the bench, new questions emerge, such as 'Am I applying my broadened experience to the community at large as well as remaining genuinely myself?' I am seeing responsibility as strategic in both community cooperation and personal fulfillment. Responsibility to the community comes through as the need to help resolve conflicts; responsibility to individuals as the need to train them to better handle ordinary matters such as managing time and handling stress."

Similarly, in reviewing his 20 years in the field, a social worker noted, "My sense of responsibility has deepened. In graduate school I felt responsible to complete the expectations of parents and assignments of supervisors. Now, with clients, I no longer see my 'responsibility' as requirements from outside, but more as an inner necessity to respond appropriately to people's needs. To respond realistically I have to check myself repeatedly to make sure I'm responding with sensitively and consistent to my values. With my supervisors, I find I pay a price for being responsible; the more responsible you are, the more responsibilities will be given you."

Responsible behavior can be seen in many places. At the entrance of a picketed supermarket I overheard a picketer voice his feeling, "We didn't have to volunteer for this monotonous walking back and forth, but I figure this pacing is more than just union duty—it's duty for ourselves and our families." One of the others chimed in, "Yea, our picketing is part of making democracy work. It's standing up for our rights when management plans to fire us veterans and hire younger workers at lower wages." Sensing my interest, she handed me a brochure, saying, "Here, this spells out what our union stands for." Listed were five responsibilities they pledged to assume: 1) to provide the skilled workers needed to maintain the operation of the store, 2) to maintain high standards of competent service, 3) to assure members a voice in union decisions, 4) to not interfere with the flow of goods in ways harmful to the community, and, 5) to get jobs done, even if it takes extra time and effort.

Similar statements of responsibilities are held by professional people. Their publicized pronouncements recognize responsibility to provide competent performance, honest dealing, loyal support, continued growth and community betterment. Taken seriously, vocational responsibility includes efficiency, reliability, integrity, concern and job security and survival.

The response of survival lays upon the living a special responsibility. We do not know whether human responsibility extends beyond the grave, but we do know that this side of the grave we have a responsibility for survival and that throughout the whole of living nature death performs its work, silently but relentlessly, in every living cell, intent on ultimate destruction of the living being and the end of freedom. To exist is to be constantly in search of a responsible response to the immanence of death.

Survival looms as a particular responsibility for political prisoners. Reynaldo Arenas, the refugee Cuban author of *Hallucinations,* considers responsibility to be much like Eddy found in juvenile hall—the obligation to "keep from being wiped out." Arenas, telling of his suffering under torture recalls, "I had to fight the inner enemies of survival as well as the outer torturers. Just as I was about to give up, I remembered the story of a friar during the French Revolution who after the imminent terror of the guillotine was asked, 'But what did you do?' He answered, 'I survived.' I clung desperately to the thread of being responsible to remain alive. Somehow my torturers were not able to stamp out that feeling. When it came down to the wire of expiring I had to conserve my deepest self, or die."

An awesome sense of responsibility persists in the face of death. A fellow chaplain was comforting a dying sergeant in a Vietnam jungle. Little was left of what had been a powerful and handsome man, yet the capacity to give a responsible response remained. Short clipped phrases came through: "What the hell was going on with us, Chappie? It was my responsibility to take my platoon through the mine field. My men are wiped out. What did it accomplish? What can I do now that the goddam Nams have blown my leg off?" With his response fading, he asked, "Will I make it? What about my wife and sons?" And with his last gasp he whispered,

"Come on, we've got to move out." All the way to the door of death he was a responsible person.

Searchings of the Learned for Responsible Living

Answers to practical questions about the process of responsible living require defining principles. Estimates of responsibility, in the last analysis, flow from our philosophy and from what we consider to be the nature, ground and destiny of human existence.

For thousands of years philosophers and theologians have searched for the conditions and boundaries of people's responsibility. Thinkers have examined a wide spectrum of the hows and whys of our freedom seeking a person's responsibility not in transient opinions or superficial answers but rather in the rhythm of what they considered to be eternally true. As responsible persons they were concerned to respond to life within the movement of history, with its ultimate destruction and eternal recurrence and its polarity of principles and energies, discovering that responsibility based upon insight, wisdom and conviction dictated a way of life that could pattern itself after the cosmos and the purposes of the Creator.

Plato and his student, Aristotle, mark the epitome of great Greek thinkers and responsible persons. Speaking of responsibility, Plato told his followers, "Let us take hold of life and remodel it." His soberer successor, Aristotle, said, "Let us first know more of life and meanwhile serve the king." For Plato, responsible responding to life involves a two-fold process of thinking: establishing general ideas and classifying them by logical divisions. He explained the physical world as possessing only relative reality. The supreme idea is the Idea of the God, with the cardinal virtues being justice, self-control, courage and wisdom. As a responsible citizen in Athens, he sought to realize his political ideals. As a responsible author, he completed 35 dialogues, 13 epistles and other works. His writings constitute one of the most influential bodies of work in the history of the Greeks. So subtle, searching and wide-ranging is his thought that almost all the problems of subsequent philosophy are traceable in his dialogues. His writing shows him to be a responsible character of singular dignity, urbanity, humor and aristocratic distinction.

Aristotle located human responsibility in the natural order, in the movement toward an orderly structure or form. He believed that people are able to choose to pursue that quest and so fashion and fulfill their destiny. Responsible people must recognize and deal with the distinction between matter and form. We confront this distinction in the continual process of change where what a thing (the "actual") is projected into what it may become (the "potential"). Movement is toward a purpose which is God—an existent, good substance, the "first cause" and "final cause" of the world.

Aristotle's responsible responding breathes through all his elaborate thought system, his dialectical thinking and his approach to the whole range of human experience. His intense sense of responsibility is seen in his remarkably accurate and comprehensive biological researches. He enlisted over a thousand investigators to make close observations of natural life and assist in the classification of findings in reports that were encyclopedic. As a teacher he was renowned for his thoroughness and universality and for his effective training of selected students, the most illustrious of whom was none other than Alexander the Great.

Centuries later the Stoics held that responsibility rested in working to realize the Socratic ideals of virtue, endurance and self-sufficiency. Responsible responding to events must be with reason, not passion, and must cope with enduring pain or adversity.

Aquinas, theologian of the 13th century, did not question whether people were free to respond. He felt actions could only be called properly human which proceeded from a deliberate will. As a person he was responsible, humble and charitable in his conduct and profoundly spiritual in character. A clear, sharp and comprehensive thinker, he viewed responsibility as recognizing that reason and faith differed in their procedure, but they could not deny each other's findings. The responsible person distinguishes between *act* and *potency*. Act may be described as that which exists and potency as the capacity for being. In this respect, ice may be said to be water in potency, but water is water in act, similarly water is steam in potency and steam is steam in act. He saw human responsibility as a hierarchy of potency and act, each act being a potency of a higher act, ascending to God, who is pure act.

Responsible responding for the German philosopher Leibnitz (1646-1716) occurs when people live within "the laws of harmony," with body and soul acting together in "complete correspondence." He held that the universe is the inevitable choice of the best from among all possible and conceivable combinations of "monads" (independent psychical beings, creative units of force that make up the world). In responsible movement toward perfection there is an evolution from the potential to the actual. Human responsibility, then, was a corollary of liberty which he said "consists in the power to do what one wants to do." Accordingly, our sensations are "thought in the process of becoming."

In the same century English philosopher John Locke, like other great systematizers of thought, was the personification of persons' freedom to respond. He not only formulated an all-embracing philosophy, he lived it out. Trained as a physician, he also served in civil posts, became a political philosopher and was exiled to the Netherlands on suspicion of being a revolutionary. Locke helped to draw up a constitution for the colonists in the American Carolinas. In his theory that people enter the world not equipped with ideas but minds that are blank and ready to receive ideas, he became the founder of British empiricism. His germinal thoughts about democracy strongly influenced Rousseau and other French activists as well as Thomas Jefferson who shaped the justification of the American Revolution. Responsibility lay in exercising individuals' liberty.

Responsibility was seen by Rousseau as the obligation of human beings as *citizens*. He and other kindred spirits in the 18th century believed in the goodness and worth of people and emphasized the deep need of human nature for emotional space (freedom) and insight (to shed light on responsibility). As members of society people were to be obedient to government and law. Some political theorists of this persuasion argued that individuals should freely surrender their absolute power over themselves to the people as a whole, creating an indivisible, infallible, "popular sovereignty" functioning as the general will or general responsibility.

In the next century the English Utilitarians, John Stuart Mill and Jeremy Bentham, held that human freedom to respond entailed responsibility for what individuals deliberately will. Responsibility meant doing what one desires. Mill understood this as maximizing pleasure and minimizing pain. They also saw the social dimension of responsibility consisting of people doing what will produce the greatest good and benefit for the greatest number.

Responsible responses involved blending idea and form for Hegel, who was one of the most influential philosophers of the 19th century. For him mind and matter are not dual; they are modes of the same fundamental thing, which he calls the Absolute. Responsibility lies in relating to and helping the realization of the Absolute. The Absolute does not transcend the stuff of life but exists in it. Responsible responses, serving as the subjective, act upon the objective and are in turn affected. All is result and potentiality at the same time. The universe develops by a self-creating plan that is powered by an active "world-soul." As responsible responses become rational and logical, Being unfolds. Hegel contended that people are not made free by abstract will-power, but by the efforts of their whole being, by becoming "energized in the depths of their total personality." This responsible self-determination works from the inside out.

Responsibility proceeds "from the inmost depth of personality and is empowered by the spiritual life."

Karl Marx, Sigmund Freud and Carl Jung exercised powerful influence on the 20th century. Though not professional philosophers, each was dedicated to understanding the nature and limits of human responding and defining responsibility in the full range of human experience.

For Marx, individuals have only limited freedom to respond, because economic conditions determine history. Like Hegel he believed that history would eventually culminate in an age of reason. Unlike Hegel, Marx believed the utopian aim would not come about through idealism but by the force of the production, development and management of material wealth. It is as productive agents that people are free to respond. Responsibility is with the "proletariat," the association of productive agents. During the period of proletarian dictatorship, the individual's freedom to respond is restricted in order to exert force to correct their property-less condition and prepare the way for a society without special privileges to any class. A freer humanity will be ushered in which no longer needs power politics and use of force.

The concept of responsibility rooted in people's free choice was repudiated by Freud because of his loyalty to rigorous reason, strict scientific method and a thoroughgoing materialism. He saw people's regressive patterns of thought as determining the drama of life. Feeling and behavior block new and more fulfilling expressions of life. Their fixations and lack of plasticity inhibit change, while their egos are caught in murderous crossfire between id and superego. Then they develop crippling guilt not from an inborn sense of sin but from a fear of losing love.

In his life, Freud was singularly free to respond. Living in an era saturated with scientific materialism and Victorian hypocrisy, his theories were expressions of this ethos. At the same time he was free enough to stand back and look at himself and take responsibility for his own disturbing fantasies and obsessions. He also took responsibility for employing his materialistic premises to destroy the idols of his day. In his long years of clinical practice he labored responsibly, innovatively and unceasingly to relieve the confusions and suffering of people bound in neurosis or psychosis. Working by analysis, he relied strongly on the process of *insight,* an inner ameliorating process that could "free up" unfree people. He worked intensively on the assumption that people were free to respond with more fulfilling and more responsible responses.

In contrast to Marx and Freud, Carl Jung gave more credence to people's freedom to respond. Recognizing our age's obsessive rush to become free from collective restraints, Jung observed, "Possessed by a heroic idea of absolute freedom, many people strive for the god-like condition where every attitude is intentionally chosen by themselves."[1] He saw the need to seek a deeper and less self-centered freedom, one that would be more directed and responsible. The greater freedom he envisaged accompanies the process of drawing the fragmented and chaotic pieces of the person's unconscious into an integrated whole, enabling the conscious part of personality to become aware of itself and the way it works. The conscious mind is responsible for the person's experience of identity. It enables us to adapt to the environment. The self, in maturing, seeks to balance extroversion/introversion and the functions of thinking and intuiting. This process, or the "journey into self," as Jung called it, is a continuous and lifelong responsibility. This journey into *individuation* involves persons becoming a homogeneous and autonomous being with the realization and integration of all the possibilities immanent in the individual. Human experience may be a maze in which to wander to destruction or a laboratory for the creation of consciousness, depending upon the way the freedom to respond is exercised.

---

[1] *The Structure and Dynamics of the Psyche,* p. 332.

Jung viewed freedom as he viewed aspects of nature. On the cosmic level, freedom operated to balance the tension between opposites, e.g., the "conservation of energy" and the "space-time continuum." He proposed the principle of *synchronicity* in an effort to integrate a "causal connection" by which we observe a "constant connection through the effect of causality," and an "inconstant connection through meaningful happenings." On the level of psychologic processes he saw freedom not as a fixed entity or force, but as an essential part of the psychic energy operating in all activities of life so a crucial function of freedom is to achieve an equilibrium and integration between contending inner forces.

"Responsibility," Jung wrote, "as the *sine qua non* of the subjective reality of the world serves as a bridge to all that is best in humanity." When the unity of consciousness is disrupted and complexes take over and impede the intentions of the will, we experience "diminished responsibility." However, when grounded in the structural elements of the psyche, responsibility powers and monitors symbols and acts as a *transformer* converting psychic energy from "lower" into a "higher" form. Responsibility carries conviction and at the same time expresses the content of that conviction. Experience of the archetype seizes and possesses the whole personality and is naturally productive of faith.

Combining Jung's "integration," with Tillich's "correlation," can serve well to pull together the concepts about responsible responses of thinkers from Aristotle to Freud. Jung sought for integration to give a positive evaluation of the human predicament. Thus in his approach to freedom, he worked to pull together the clinical process of psychology and the happenings and movements of history and culture.

Tillich's method of correlation affirms that "the question of human existence" is developed by analysis and a parallel theological search. Aimed to avoid what he sees as the pitfall of separating the Christian message from the cultural situation of our day and the inadequacies of idealistic liberalism, Tillich begins each topic with a philosophic analysis of some aspect of the human's actual existence, ending with a question to which the Christian revelation gives a symbolic and paradoxical but finally adequate answer: Reason and Revelation.

Combining Jung's *integration* and Tillich's *correlation* using knowledge and logic and faith and revelation, offer approaches that help us find the synthesis of experience sought by the philosophers and the "coordination" contemporary systems theory aims to achieve.

Thinkers and theologians in finding meaning in misfortune, criticism and ultimately death, inevitably confronted issues regarding responsibility. The ways they struggled to live out their insights give us courage in our own journey. In seeking to affirm the unique human endowment of being free to respond and be responsible, they help us gain clarity when we are confused with life's relativities. The conceptualizing of freedom and responsibility provides us light when our way grows dark with despair and gives direction when we are driven alternately into no-win situations.

Guiding Principles for Responsible Living

Responsibility springs from our freedom and the fact that we have the capacity to respond—*response-ability*. Human beings are not born into the world simply to breathe and eat. The scientist Lecomte de Nouy, in his book *Human Destiny*, puts it well:

It must be demonstrated that every person has a part to play and that he is free to play it or not, that he is a link in a chain and not a wisp of straw swept along by a torrent; that, in brief, human dignity is not a vain word and that when man is not convinced of this and does not try to attain this dignity, he lowers himself to the level of the beast.[2]

---

[2] NY: Longmans, Green & Co., 1947, p. xix.

Gifted with the freedom to respond, a major obligation of life is to use our response capacity in ways each of us can be freed to realize more of our potentials. To be responsible is to create, relate and participate in shaping our destiny. To be responsible is to respond in ways that help ourselves and others clarify and accomplish these purposes.

Responsibility then is moral living; living to see and get a handle on trustworthy responses. It is defining the good in our obligations to ourselves and to each other in our relationships. There are at least three kinds of situations in which we attribute moral responsibility to individuals: 1) In recommending a person we say that person is responsible. 2) We also say that person is responsible for a particular worthy deed. 3) Or we say that person is responsible for accomplishing a project. It is assumed that the person is free to respond, be responsible, and choose to do the worthy act and accept the responsibility to accomplish the project—and also free to choose not to do these things.

Religiously based moral living goes further: it challenges us to reach for more than we think can be done with our own strength. Responsibility in moral living points the way to the symbolic dimension of life, i.e., what we "ought" to do and be. But power and purpose for *doing* what we see we ought to do requires considerably more. Ethical responsibility grounded in religious experience takes us beyond simplistic definitions of the "good" and the "bad." Jesus did more than he ought to have done. His supreme responses and quality of life reflect the taking of responsibility to respond on the basis of trust and faith in his relationship to a Higher Power. When people seek direction and power from their religious experience as they commit themselves and bear the burden of their human freedom, they are responding responsibly.

We do not commonly relate moral responsibility and religious experience. The two may seem incongruous and even contradictory, at least in opposite spheres. Moral responsibility has to do with the attitude and behavior of human beings; religious experience has to do with our responsibility to our belief in a transcendent Creator and governor of the universe—to the finite and the here-and-now or to the infinite and the eternal. The one is approached by calculation, self-will and scientific reason, the other by symbols, grace, trust and faith.

In Western cultures it does not necessarily follow that persons who have had a "religious experience" are responsible, or that persons who are responsible are religious. A vital "religious experience" is not limited to church membership, acceptance of particular creeds or even living by the Golden Rule. It is rather living out of an empowering faith rooted in a mysterious Source of order and meaning. Such an experience comes in surprising ways.

Mary, an executive in her mid-40s, had struggled unsuccessfully for ten years to overcome her worsening alcoholism until she became involved in an Alcoholic Anonymous program. There she discovered that religious experience and the practical response of sobriety were closely related. "In our groups," she reported, "we are challenged over and over again to face 'the Higher Power' and with that help to take responsibility to keep our sobriety and perform responsibly at work and in our homes. Responsibility, Mary reported, was monitored and reinforced by two indispensable aspects of religious experience: trust and faith. She found how hard it was for her to "take inventory" of herself as one of the Twelve Steps followed in her A.A. group. "We are responsible to face up to the incongruity of our own existence," she said. "People are the most incongruous creatures because they are children of nature, yet we transcend nature. This transcendent power is something we must lean on, or trust." She went further, "Regardless of how responsible I may be in my various roles in my family and community, I am not a whole, responsible self until I accept the ultimate response of trust. I've had to take another step of trust and say with confidence that 'God is *good,* especially concerned with human beings and the One in whom we find our greatest fulfillment in responsible responsiveness."

Others who have come close to suicide and pulled back tell of "clinging to a thread of faith." As they realized life was a gift of the Creator, their faith was strengthened. As faith grows they gain a vision of transcendent meaning in life beyond suffering and failure. As they recover faith in themselves, their world and their God, they respond with greater responsibility. At a time when his faith had waned, Martin Luther told of his struggle, "I am free to respond either positively or negatively to the assertions of religious faith." But as he trusted what faith remained, it grew until he was able to affirm that faith is the essential element of religious experience.

This responsible way of trust and faith in God is often praised and even worshipped, but less often practiced. It is repeatedly threatened by neglect, self-indulgence and irresponsibility. Hopefully Julian Huxley was right in affirming that people of faith are "the axis and leading shoot of evolution," but most of us do not take the faith journey. Instead, we exhibit demonic traits. We act, not out of faith in a Higher Power, but from our self-centeredness.

Persistent self-concern violates the religious vision of an ultimate moral fulfillment as we have it in both Jewish and Christian Messianic hopes. It is true that this vision is so pure that it seems irrelevant to the problems of individuals and collectives, but it is significant that both biblical religion and modern social learning agree that we are dependent upon and have responsibility toward our neighbors. Modern political theory takes the insistent ego striving for granted, while Christian theory has been realistic ever since Paul confessed: "There is a law in my members which wars against the law that is in my mind."

The problem of making responsibility more specific is related to the moral and social questions of how to reach a tolerable harmony among self-regarding individuals and collectives. It is increasingly urgent in a technical and nuclear age that standards of discriminate judgment be the indirect instruments of the love commandment. "Let love be the motive, but justice be the instrument," said the late Pope John. Coming from a God of love, the freedom to respond issues ultimately in unfettered love. The response of love welling up from unfathomable depths is the kind of love God wants from people. One expression is humility—not servile submission—but the interaction of persons with inner freedom that overcomes the evils of life. The response of this sort delivers spiritual peace and serves as a means of union with powers higher than our own.

Christians hold the belief that in the life and death of Jesus they are given the ultimate model of responsible living. Being human Jesus experienced joy and suffering; being divine his responses were attuned and empowered with the energies and purposes of the Creator. His is a responsible life, obedient and trusting to the Father and at the same time outgoing and loving to the people. Following his death and resurrection, through the Holy Spirit, he continues to respond to people as the Comforter, Counselor and Friend. His responsible life, deepened with sensitivity and extended with healing and guidance, enables people to find wholeness, joy and creativity. Responsibility lies in discipleship with Jesus and rests in a condition where the element of grace and freedom is maintained, so the cross is not primarily a symbol of an ethical obligation but of an ultimate permission.

Christian theologians who search for the sources and traditions of their faith have discerned as many ways of associating Christ with the responsible life as ways of associating him with the ideal or obedient life. Some theologians stress responsibility derived from the model of unswerving commitment to God seen in Christ, others see responsibility issuing from Christ's humanity, or his existence and responsiveness, while others affirm responsibility as the required response to the essential nature of God as freedom and process.

Biblical scholars consider responsibility to be a function of the spirit of limitless freedom which pervades the Gospels and the Epistles. "Then are the children free" (Mt 17:26);

"You will know the truth and the truth will make you free" (Jn 8:32); "Christ has set us free for freedom" (Gal 5:1) and "the Spirit of life made me free" (Rm 8:2).

Barth asserts that freedom and its consequent responsibility rests upon individuals to accept the gift of the Spirit which enables them to become "creatures of the grace of Christ." Responsible persons stay "as close as possible to the *Word* and listen to it and follow its guidance."

Niebuhr in his landmark book, *The Responsible Self,* concludes that the Bible gives commanding authority to the Christian on the matter of responsibility. He sought, however, a larger place for critical reflection about Christians' actions. Responsibility, as Niebuhr sees it, "affirms God is acting in all actions upon you. So in human responses, respond as if they are God's actions."

For many thoughtful and committed Christians, human responsibility occupies a central place in their system of thought. Responsibility emerges from the mystery that finally gives persons their unique identity. The fundamental word, therefore, is the personal name. Language respects the fact that the union between persons takes place in freedom and mystery. Responsibility is found not in people's freedom *from* self or the world, but in freedom *for* the whole self involved in the world. "Responsible (religiously) based freedom," Dietrich Bonhoffer wrote from prison shortly before he was hanged, "displays itself in the self-examined life and of action and in the venture of a concrete decision." Human beings can choose between living their lives as God has shown them or going their own way. Responsibility lies in responding to choices by "taking charge of our life," and "getting our act together," and responding to a "higher order and power."

Responsibility Rushes Out At Us

Trying to understand responsibility, as we have observed, is like trying to drink from a fire hose. Responsibility rushes out at us as a quality, a force, but also as an obligation. It permeates every significant expression of life. For persons of faith, responsibility is God at work.

Few of us have the gamut of responsibilities that rested on King David's shoulders, but each of us can identify with his dual struggle: outwardly to meet obligations to country and family and inwardly to control explosive impulses. We may not have the range of mandates that surrounded him, but we are susceptible to the infection of irresponsibility. In our personal lives few of us have our sense of responsibility as sorely tested as the dying sergeant.

We cannot survive unless, at an early point in our lives, we are willing to stop blaming others, excusing ourselves, and take responsibility for ourselves. Integrity and direction are more available to most of us than we allow ourselves to think. Many of us are disposed to hold the external situation more responsible than we should for the moral ambiguity of our lives. It is easy to rationalize our failures and omissions and say, as television celebrity Flip Wilson used to say, "The devil made me do it."

We are most truly persons in moments of decision, particularly those in which we make decisions of genuine consequence for the future of ourselves and others. But making responsible decisions is no simple task. The philosophical, moral and legal questions of responsibility involve more than logical knowing. Carrying out one's responsibility is complicated by the fact that it is judged by values accepted in a society under given circumstances and these guidelines are not easily discernable. To cope with the counteractions that resist the expression of responsibility we are helped by associating with individuals who are seeking to be responsible, but responsible persons are not always available.

Fulfillment of responsibility is not realized once and for all. It is a dynamic response, always happening. A continuing struggle, it is a process of doing-undoing-redoing and, for society, an ongoing revolution. Given the recalcitrance of our fallen humanity, the Spirit of God can impart the new reality of Christ to us only in the form of a continuous engagement with our spirits (Rm 8:15) and which ones of us maintain a "continuous engagement?"

Clear thinking about responsibility provided by sages and saints helps us gain stability and maintain commitment amid contending and hostile forces. When we feel alternately abandoned and then overburdened with the demands of many choices, we can be reinforced as we draw on available guidelines for responding responsibly. We are reminded of how human beings can bring to bear capacities and forces more complex and inward in character than the causality of the natural world. The sages and saints show that we are not made free by abstract will power alone. We experience ourselves as free for the simple reason that the category of causality is not always applicable in immediate experience. But we find freedom to respond does not mean an absence of causation: freedom means that persons are organisms who can to a degree control their own future.

Summary

What, then, can we conclude about responsibility? It is both the management and giver of power. The powerful response can be manipulative and Machiavellian. It also can be exercised as reflective consciousness which harnesses our impulsivity. Responsibility as power is the ebb and flow of freedom's privileges for the expansion of human consciousness. It is a force that enriches freedom with discipline and knowledge as well as spontaneity and creativity. In its fulfillment, responsibility is power committed to love and to God's voice.

Responsibility is truth, which like a laser beam penetrates to the center of facts and to the heart of persons. People who give true responses do not sit around evading and criticizing. True responses expose error and mediocrity. Responsible responses are not those of the arrogant who are convinced that they have *the* last word, but come from people who consistently search for a higher truth.

Responsibility is memory, persons reflecting upon themselves and the vision of forbearers. It is recalling and having respect for lessons learned in the struggle to be realistic about life and self. It is seeing our entanglement in inner destructive forces along with our striving for higher consciousness. Responsible responding recognizes our roots in family and community of origin.

Responsibility is creatively risking the unknown. It finds the new in the old and the old in the new. To respond responsibly is to express our being by creating a needed sequel to being responsible. To respond responsibly to the multiple choices confronting us, we are called upon to do something new, to push into a forest where there are no well-worn paths. To live into the future means to leap into the unknown and this requires creativity and courage.

Responsibility also is hope. Such hope holds to the vision of a better future in families, businesses, institutions and governments. Responsible responses include hope because we were created to hope; to live is to hope.

Responsibility is love, turning survival into joyous celebration rather than boredom. Loving responses are those of people who have an active and truthful concern for neighbor and self. Loving responses are responsible by binding people together in tender attachments and in efforts that enrich individuals and communities. Responsibility is to accept life as the arena of God's work of love.

Ultimately, responsibility is God at work. It is trusting God not only as a belief system but as an immediate presence. Responsibility is not an other-worldly condition, rather it is having one foot in the world and the other in a steady search for ways to practice the presence of God. Responsibility is awareness that fulfilling that presence is to live in loving relation to God, neighbor and self.

Human responsibility, as we have explored it, derives its uniqueness and urgency because God willed and created freedom in human beings. In fact, it is not humans, but God who cannot get along without freedom. The freedom to respond and its corresponding responsibility comes as a gift from the Creator. From beyond ourselves mysterious powers work to move us toward greater individual and social wholeness given by persons like Christ who says, "Take up your cross and follow me." This challenge is complete in a way that no modern conception is because it includes the stark facts of suffering and death—not as the negation of happiness, but as the voluntary shedding of the mortal necessary to put on immortality.

The Self:
Our Closest Given

An immediate and personal given—the self—envelops us as an inescapable fact. Closer than breathing and nearer than our beating heart, it comprises our total personality. As such, we had better accept the self because it is the psychic structure set of mind emotions and spirit in which we live and spend eternity.

What we really *are* never quite fits any model or analogy. The self is more than a bundle of habits, more than a passive deposit of after-thoughts from the day's behavior. More than an internalized conscience or "ego-ideal," the self finds expression in a variety of self-governing structures. William James, the famous psychology professor at Harvard at the turn of the 19th century, described the *self* as "the sum total of all that a person can call his, not only his body and psychic powers, but his clothes, house, wife, children, ancestors and friends, his reputation and works, his lands, forces, yacht and bank account."

Fascination with the self begins early and the estimation of its expressions continues until life's end. In 1968 Mahler observed, "The infant's inner sensations form the core of the self." The crystallization of the "feeling of self" starts the establishment of one's sense of identity. The infant looks in the mirror and says, "That's me." For the young, those in their prime and the elderly, the self flows as the totality of personal being. The young look at the self in its dawning realization simply and factually. Those midway in life explore its nature and destiny. The elderly reminisce about how their selves have fulfilled three score and ten years.

Talk about the self provides an important means of communication. A friends may say, "As far as myself is concerned, I had a great weekend." The bruised and troubled may say, "I've gotten myself into a bad fix;" or, "I've got to get myself together." And, those in ultimate desperation confess, "I'm ready to kill myself."

More precise definitions usually picture the self as a living organism and effort is made to appreciate the global aspects of the self and do justice to the broad spectrum of human qualities and functions.   To explain the evidence of the separate expressions of ego-states, theorists have found it helpful to discuss shadings and differences between self and other, between superego, ego and id and between parent, adult and child. The outflow of research and publications on these subjects has brought the term *self* back into vogue. As currently used, the concept of *self* generally refers to the central, integrating structures and functions of personality.

When we hear *person,* we transform it in our mind's eye into a particular sort of human, but exactly what it means is not always clear. We may speak of a favorite actor or a political figure as *persons,* knowing full well that they may be different from what their image projects. The problem comes in trying to assess what a *person* is genuinely like. "Pay no attention to that person behind the curtain," said the Wizard of Oz to Dorothy. But today aspiring pols never stop to think that political wizards may actually be frauds hiding behind the curtain of their reputations. In trying to reach an accurate estimate of the nature of humankind, we are suggesting a more specialized entity which we choose to call the "self."

We are convinced that we must pay attention to the person behind the curtain.

Classifying and Naming the Selves

In describing the self we try to name and type its many characteristics. Naming the self's features and parts offers a way to estimate human nature. In talking and thinking about the "self" we use many different words: person, individual, psyche or just human beings. We search for words adequate to describe appreciatively the variety and complexity of people. "Words slip and slide", wrote T.S. Eliot, even when we do not want them to, making it hard to say precisely what we mean—making it hard even to know exactly what we mean.

Putting different selves into classifications helps us identify and remember people's uniqueness. Some are only mannequins in a store window standing with an artificial pose. Other selves fall into groups that we associate with certain ages, lines of work or income brackets. In doing so, we begin to make assumptions and value judgments about people. It is not enough to give a person's address, date or birth, telephone and social-security number. The self is not complete when seen as a bundle of statistics.

In every language the word "self" is full of subjective meanings. The Chinese phrase for self, *tze ji*, is rich in suggesting the private, intimate, natural and independent. In English over a thousand combinations of forms and literary usages are available to distinguish the subtle influences pervading the stated meaning of the "self." We talk of self-interest, self-adjustment, self-contradiction and self-confidence. In literature we read of "selfsame material," "better self," and "to thine own self be true." However we describe it, the self is an inescapable fact and a reality we had better accept because it is the totality of who we are.

Observing people in public places teaches us much about the façades of selves. Once during my college days I did this on a crowded Philadelphia subway. Before the crowds began rushing in, it was easy to spot Kretschmer's constitutional types—the frail, the athletic or the rounded physique. The more passengers we took on, the more I had to abandon such academic classifications. As the train rushed north under Broad Street, the externals of the surrounding humanity brought other perceptions: a carpenter with hammer slung from his overalls, a business person with attaché case trying to read the paper, a well-dressed executive and street person lugging two enormous sacks. The adventure of observing and wondering about the nature of people went on. What was revealed in their faces? their posture? their clothing? Why are there so many biological differences: tall/short; slender/overweight; cheerful/glum; healthy/sickly?

Typing selves helps us understand people. If we are careful to avoid arbitrary pigeonholing, we are helped to perceive them better. As we see people on an elevator, walking the sidewalk, at a podium, we inevitably evaluate and compare. In maturing we learn to distinguish between people's exterior and interior, their potentials and their limitations.

Researchers go beyond superficial typing of selves and make more sophisticated distinctions. Pavlov observed that some individuals manifest relatively strong excitatory tendencies and weak inhibitory tendencies, while others reverse this pattern.

Our Responsive Self: Our Closest Given

The self, our nearest and most intimate given, is not a thing but a living organism, unique for its higher functions of thinking, feeling and aspiring. As a unitary being, the self's qualities are focused in an authoritative center.

The self's striking contrasts and ambivalences make the exploration of its nature and meaning both complicated and fascinating. Transparent and roiled, grand and grubby, magnificent and miserable, the self is also capable of sublime aspiration and stunning accomplishment or failure, despair and violent destruction. Responses are conditioned by differences in mental and emotional endowments plus the reinforcers or inhibitors that are at work in the self.

The self is aware of itself, sensitive to the "me" and aware of the self presiding over any awareness of the world or of the spirit. But the self is also aware of being a responsive person, designed to confront and give meaning to space, time, ideas, hopes and other human lives. The self is also required to exercise stabilizing controls over itself, providing correction and direction. At this point the self can reach beyond itself, pushing beyond the limits of the past and present, rising above the restricting emotional responses such as fears, guilt and narcissism. The self seeks to rise above depleted motivation and straitjacketed habits. It reaches for sharpened awareness, disciplined knowledge and moral sensitivity.

As a direction and centering executive, the responsible self seeks better understanding of its actions, thoughts, feelings and convictions. The activity of the self in its moment of reflection is directed toward the acquisition of understanding assurance and faith. Instead of the solitary "I," the self must function on the basis of the "you-and-I." It feels an imperative that initiates and empowers persons to reach out for meaning beyond itself and especially to communicate concern and love. The experience and direction that come out of this responsible search leads to a deeper sense of community and one's relationship and obligation to it.

The self must be approached in its communal dimensions, always giving consideration to the essential relational nature of persons. Self-realization alone is impossible. The individual is also a self in the community, the world and in relationship to the Creator.

The self is aware that it has a role to play in the community. It is part of space, time and society. The self forms its own reality in reacting to the physical and interpersonal worlds. Without these particular realities, selves are empty forms. With these realities, selves assume uniqueness and significance. By keeping related to their space and time and community, selves are given sustenance to keep open to new possibilities for change. In their relating as selves, people gain a sense of identity and significance.

The self has a built-in yen to venture beyond itself in reflection, imagination and religious exploration. Although it is our "closest given," because of its personal awareness, the self is enigmatic. We experience our selves as both subject and object. We can probe its nature with our senses, our thoughts and with our imagination make pictures and analogies of it. These approaches are the ways of empiricism, rationalism and metamorphism.

The self also is *spirit-conscious.* In its full freedom and awareness, the self reaches beyond emotionality, rationality and imagination to find a more comprehensive meaning of life. A capacity for awe, described by Rudolph Otto as "the idea of the Holy," this religious consciousness is as common as speech and more encompassing than reflection. The inner life of the spirit is not merely technological, nor condemned to a servitude of practical and predetermined ends. Spirit-consciousness confirms both the self's awareness of its uniqueness and rallies it to make responsible responses and thus gives it a new system of meaning.

Perennial Questions About the Self

Through the centuries people have striven for a deeper understanding and control of the self. The child asks, "Why am I me?" The psalmist asked, "What is person?" Shakespeare's Hamlet queried, "To be or not to be?" Heidegger, Jaspers, Marcel and other philosophers have made sophisticated probings into the meaning of the self.

The perennial questions involved in self-awareness run the gamut from the obvious to the impenetrable. The easier ones—"What and who am I?"—and the more difficult—"What rights and obligations do I have or what is my destiny?"—are needed to enable persons to act, think and feel. Answers are also needed to help individuals define their uniqueness. In this way individuals can become increasingly self-aware and realistic about their strengths, qualities, worth and responsibilities.

These basic questions about the self occur frequently in clinical situations: "How come we foul ourselves up so often?" asks an intelligent young grandmother, seeing the mistakes of four generations. A 40-year-old human-services worker with four children who is a part-time graduate student struggling amidst the mounting pressures asks, "Why does life have to be so complicated and demanding?"

We often learn much about the *self* from our own and others' responses in times of confusion and stress. When limits crowd or threaten, people become increasingly aware of the fractures and weaknesses of their individuality. We see distinct degrees of ego-integration and a capacity to handle difficult situations as well as various levels of self-understanding and evidences of how the *self* operates. We see signs pointing to the self's drives and motivations. One self may be hypersensitive, hurt by any experience, while another is under-sensitive.

Many persistent questions about self remain unanswerable. Clinicians are trained to gather details of their clients' histories systematically and review with colleagues their estimates and progress reports. In this way the therapist stays with "the human document" and tries to piece together more truths about the self. But details of life's accidents, unless representatively symbolic, hardly begin to tell the full story of the self. They may form only its collective clutter, the peripheral trivia, but not the individual substance.

The need is to move qualitatively into the unknown. Rather than inquire into the bits and pieces, one must seek origins, patterns and dynamics. The longer and better one knows another, as in deep analysis extending through months, the less can be said with certainty about the roots of the person's troubles or potentials.

Across the sweep of life, friends, loved ones and therapists keep searching for accurate and holistic understandings of the self's structure and processes—learning how it moves from awareness to thinking and valuing and from considering to deciding and acting. We want to discover the self's integrity and its strengths and its confidences and esteem.

The consummate capacity of the self to be free to respond and become more responsible is one of the hallmarks of humanity. Fulfilling human uniqueness means taking up the challenge to explore how the self grows, relates purposively and becomes more responsible. The self is not a static center as long believed, but is uniquely endowed by its capacity for freedom and ability to choose and decide. In the 15th century Giovanni Pico della Mirandella wrote the *Dignity of Man* pointing out that humans were special among God's creatures in that they were not confined to one level. According to Pico, humans contained within them the capacity to rise to angelic heights or to descend to brutish levels—and the corresponding responsibility to choose on which level their lives will be lived.

As selves we have the responsibility to *be* and to *become* more responsible. This is an essential part of living. We can acknowledge our potentials and work to develop and maximize them. In becoming more responsible, we raise our self-esteem. Power wells up from deeper levels of personality, which brings forth promptings of the mysterious supernatural world which is often more real than any regressive fixation on childish fantasies.

The way in which I am aware of how I perceive and act on my responsibility defines my uniqueness. The responsibilities I confront in my life have many dimensions and forms and are peculiar to myself. As such, I act on them in special ways. In coping with the resistance I encounter, I reveal my individuality.

To become more fully human we have the responsibility to develop an "ego-picture," a self-image—an accurate, adapting and flexible estimate of the unitary *me-and-I,* the image we see in the mirror of our relationships and the reality stemming from our feeling, thinking and acting. Ours is the obligation and responsibility to keep growing an "ego-picture" of the self in the world and the self within-the-self. We need this in order to decide, act and derive satisfaction and meaning from our individual styles of being.

The Enigma of the Self

The self's perplexing ambiguities and its great variety of expressions make it enigmatic. Although it is the immediate physical and psychological organism in which we live and move, it encompasses extremes that are not easily reconciled. The riddle of how various contrasts are held in unity proves vexing. In spite of the puzzlement it presents, probing its secrets is singularly rewarding.

One initial aspect of the self's enigmatic nature is found in the difficulty of reaching its core. The question becomes, How are we to approach the self? Its immediacy and close-ness renders it particularly hard to examine. Each of us, jealous of the self we have evolved through the years, tends to protect our inner being and present a "façade" to all who inquire. The psychoanalyst, Franz Alexander, talked of the self as "the concealed connection of existence." In his work as a clinician he observed how the contradictory nature of the self's polarities tend to throw us off the trail of our reach to understand and direct it. Working with his clients he repeatedly saw how the self resists giving up its inner secrets, especially the well-guarded secrets about its anxieties and unresolved conflicts. The troubled self wards off relief if the new clarity threatens the protected secrets.

Cognitive approaches can analyze the enigma of the self, but never quite fathom and explain its inner secrets. The reasonable and logical view of the self does not always get a handle on the experiential actions and feelings. The begin-nings of idealizing the self go back into Greek history. The Platonic-idealistic personality sought an "essential" or "ideal" view of the self. It was thought that the multiple experiences of the world are centered in the self and that the self knows no other world but the one it can perceive and appropriate in thought.

In the 19th century philosophers expounding idealism again carried much influence. For Fichte and Goethe wholeness of personality became the central quest, as if the understanding of all things human and in the cosmos hinged upon it. The emphasis was not upon civilization as community, but upon civilization as developing the idealized self. The whole personality as an inward unity was seen as the ultimate unifying factor that could prevent the breakdown of civilization.

The idealization of the self did not, however, get at the enigmatic nature of the self. The catastrophes of the 20th century have piled up objective evidences of the failure of this thought—which was unsuccessful partly because idealism could no longer cope with the increasingly antipersonalistic tendencies of the present era. Thinking of the ideal self, bunching good hopes together and pressing for "harmonization" tends to squeeze out the spiritual reaches of the self and suppresses the essential nature of human beings. Under such a regime the spirit can turn demonic, as in the Nazi perpetration of the Holocaust.

When powers of despiritualization run amuck, the negative "spirit" can estrange soul from body. Harmony becomes simply a rhetorical phrase or a pure postulate devoid of substance. Chaos develops and threatens the integrating powers of the self. In Dionysian rapture, people reach greedily for their last chance to retain their wholeness—be it in power politics or eroticism—in order to remain at one with themselves and the cosmos. Idealism fails to act as a cohesive agent.

Another puzzlement arises from the fact that the more we learn about the self, the more we see how much more still remains to be learned. Gordon Allport observed that the more he studied human nature the more convinced he became of the uniqueness of the individual—and the more pessimistic he became finding how wide the gap was between their potential and their actual behavior. This discouragement is reinforced by the current focus in much psychotherapy upon pathology, rather than health and strength and the self's higher powers. There are numerous studies of criminals, but few of law-abiders; many cases of fear and few of courage. Hostility tends to be our focus.

A.H. Maslow held to a "holistic-dynamic" or "holistic-integrative" theory of personality as a fruitful approach to coping with the enigma of the self. Writing about the overemphasis of psychology on the negative aspects of self, he said, "It has revealed to us much about persons' shortcomings, their illnesses, their sins, but little about their potentialities, their virtues, their achievable aspirations or their full psychological height."

The self continues to be an enigma. Fundamentally, the self is neither a disease nor a superhuman. Much of the structure and functioning of the self is still unknown. We know much about the DNA programming of the genes, but many of the self's inherent characteristics elude us. These are mysteries which spur our continual search for the structure and meaning of the self.

Deeper and More Systematic Approaches to the Self

In spite of the limitations of rational and empirical methods, they do provide an ordered and scientific approach to the self. Specialists in the behavioral sciences, using refined cognitive methods and more precise instruments for measuring responses have succeeded remarkably in developing a science of the self. These systematic approaches to the self, as both subject and object, include: 1) observing the self as a living document, 2) analyzing its patterns and systems and 3) viewing the self in comparison and in direction.

Psychiatry, with the empirical emphasis of its clinical preoccupation, has relied heavily upon impulse and action.

The various histories of the unconscious before Freud repeatedly remind us that well-hidden physiological and psychological forces were always cooking up a new broth of trouble—more charitably, "creative inventiveness." When Freud observed patterns of behavior and thoughts which came from seemingly hidden springs of potential, he was extrapolating a series that had begun with the medical psychology of Hippocrates and other Greeks. He, like the experimenters among the Greeks, was proceeding on practical clinical experiences.

Stressing the rational studies of the self pursues the principle of immanent truth, which holds that propositions must be free of inconsistencies and, within a given system, must not contradict one another. In the search to comprehend the self, however, a strictly rational approach may not reach the self's invisible reasons, feelings and decisions.

Consideration of the stages of self-development has helped provide a canvas wide enough to capture much of its fuller dimensions. The mature person has moved effectively through each of the stages of growth of the self. The *self-system* begins as the infant becomes aware of being appraised by its parents and develops as the individual interacts with others. It is further formed in the process of attempting to relieve the tensions arising when felt needs are not satisfied. The individual whose intimacy needs satisfied will not have to use up resources for protection from anxiety and guilt. Instead of maintaining a defensive stance, the person will have a sensitivity to the needs and intentions of others and will cultivate the ability to collaborate with others.

Many experiences suggest the importance of the "ego-picture." This includes both the façade we present to the world and suggestions about our "inner core"—an awareness of how we function, decide and act. The pattern of our life comes from both our chromosomes and the way we are nurtured. The self we grow into becomes our life-world with which we pursue our destiny. As we see ourselves accurately and appreciate our individual styles of being-in-the-world, we derive increased satisfaction and meaning in our lives. People need a personal picture of the world that facilitates the business of living. Psychiatrist Otto Fenichel stressed that, "Our picture of the self stems from both external and internal perceptions." It is formed by what people tell us and what we derive as feedback from everyday experience.

The fruitful approach for psychology is *not* for it to become *less* empirical and rational, but *more* open to the knowledge-giving qualities of metaphor and mythology. A less encapsulated discipline, one which makes the most of *all* the cognitive processes at our command, will be able to embrace the reality of the self with greater awareness.

Psychologists' Descriptions of the Self

In the last century, innovative psychoanalysts, psycho-therapists and personality researchers have produced a wealth of factual data and complex conceptual systems regarding the nature and functioning of the self. The three giants of psychology—Pavlov, Piaget and Freud—as well as hundreds of other brilliant and creative minds have caused in this relatively short period, a far-reaching revolution in our self-knowledge. Few other fields of human endeavor are as encompassing and difficult to define as studies of human nature. Unlike those in other scientific fields, these specialists who investigate human nature systematically extend their investigations to both the subjective and objective world of the individual and examine peoples' patterns of responding to nature and society. All aspects of human nature—its drama, banality, consistencies and inconsistencies—are taken as grist for their mill. With infinitely varied human beings as their subjects, it becomes increasingly difficult to gain consensus as research digs deeper.

In the multiplicity of impressions which form the content of human life, persons have always sought some principle of order as a point of reference to which each fragmentary experience can be related and into whose lines of force it can be fitted in such a way that the chaos of events and circumstances takes on a pattern which gives coherence and meaning to life. Those who venture into strange and unexplored realms need a thread of Ariadne to guarantee an unbroken connection with the familiar world and the promise of a way back when the adventure is finished.

Psychoanalysis initiated by Freud began largely as an esoteric theory of the mind, exploring its abnormalities and patterns of change. Controversial from the start, it has undergone revisions and, in the hands of the human potential movement, fundamental transformations. Besides being a therapeutic and intellectual system, psychoanalysis is also a theory about the transactional immediacies of everyday life—a mode of understanding the relations between the "I" and "the social other" by interpreting such ordinary happenings as dreams and slips of the tongue. Psychoanalytic ideas have also made their way into entertainment, the media and political life and thus have become part of our social existence—a series of unrecognized and often unspecifiable assumptions about life.

It is common in this day for persons to be plagued with bewildering thoughts and feelings about the self. Ours is a confusion that psychiatrist E. Mansell Pattison calls "the cultural cloudedness of consciousness." If we are to survive, function and find meaning in life, we cannot exist in a relativistic ennui, but must be able to construct an appropriate picture of self and the world. There are many ways to do this, but I must choose *one way* to be which must be normative *for me,* although it may not be for others. To walk through the dimly lit forest of life, I must blaze my own trail. The same must be true for others.

Communities are bands of wanderers who aid each other to discover more about themselves. Mental health workers and pastors are particularly committed to this sort of mutual aid. The careful searchings into the nature, expressions and dynamics of the self are their special concern and discipline.

These professionals provide insights on particular behavior and entire systems of personality theory. Findings of representative psychiatrists and psychologists offer a wide variety of perspectives on ways persons are free to respond.

Freud and his key contemporaries: Sigmund Freud postulated that the self is controlled by two opposite and contending forces: the pleasure or life principle and the pain or death principle. He observed that the self is also powered by "hormic" driving forces—behavior is only partially explained in purely mechanistic or physicochemical terms. It is characterized by a striving of urge towards a purposeful goal. The self is not merely a surface entity, but a central fact of personality. "Each primal situation is one in which the self is an individual 'cell,' reflecting the essence of the social aggregate of which it is a part. It responds to and within each primal situation encountered by means of sensing, thinking, feeling and acting. Under this surface portion of the self lies a deeper layer of psychic experience, the unconscious. Evidences of this unconscious arena emerge in dreams and delusions, hallucinations and everyday slips of the tongue."

Freud viewed the self as an individual unit. "The total life of an individual," he asserted, "becomes a dynamic whole." As such, the self, called "personality" or "the ego," or "psyche" can be studied with scientific methodology. Behavior is powered and determined by the unconscious force of "libido" which especially expresses sexual energy. He identified the contending forces which keep personality in an unstable truce as the instinctive drives of the primitive unconscious *id,* the inhibitive power of the socially-introjected *superego* and the reality-testing *ego.*

Consistent with 19th century thought, Freud ascribed to reason the central role of arbitrator between these instinctual drives and the prohibitions of society. The *id* is the powerhouse of personality and the "psychic reality." The *superego* strives to direct unconscious forces into channels of appropriate expression, but the empirical *ego* is the nearest approximation to the current meaning of the self as an operational expression of a person's uniqueness.

Offshoots of Freudian theory apply his basic model of the "oral," "anal," and "genital" stages in emotional development and amplify his concept of the dynamic self. Differing interpretations are given for the motivational processes by which personality takes shape and responds. Paul Schilder, a disciple of Freud, visualized the core of the self as a three-dimensional image which comes: 1) through the senses; 2) as unique awareness, and 3) as an experience of the individual's particular identity.

Sando Rado regarded the responding self as "the integrative apparatus of humans." It is the faculty that adapts to the world and enables persons to control their motivations and behavior. The self-image is formed as the person focuses attention on the equipment that is used to control the environment. Changing as it develops, the responding individual, the "action self," starts in infancy by attributing limitless power to its willed action. Responses become tempered as the person moves into adulthood struggles for emotional self-approval, self-confidence and self-esteem.

Carl Jung shared Freud's view that the self is the dynamic totality of our personality. In identifying its structure and functions, however, he gave dissimilar descriptions and ventured into different areas, notably the primordial origins and cultural influences affecting the unconscious. For Jung, the Self, spelled with a capital, is equated with the *psyche* (total personality) and encompasses more than the *ego* which controls the consciousness.

Instead of seeing the self as the battlefield between the superego, id and ego, but rather seeing these parts as analogies, Jung saw the Self as a growing and adapting set of functions. "Self" was the "empirical ego-personality" and more than just a cauldron boiling all our repressed experiences and the unconscious was more than some universal consciousness. The Self holds the past, present and future of each individual *and* that of the race. Most importantly, the

Self includes original models—which he calls archetypes—that embrace both conscious and unconscious elements. His experience taught him that it was more appropriate to see the Self as being aware of both our unique natures and our intimate relationship with all life. The Self is uniquely made up of inorganic organic and cosmic matter; it is also that within us that connects with all life.

Picturing the Self as the entire person, Jung sometimes speaks of it as "the inner voice," "the personality that is being," or our "essential potential for creativity." In *The Integration of Personality* (1939) he notes: "The Self is not only the center, but also the circumference that encloses consciousness and unconsciousness." In a later work, *Answer to Job* (1954), he describes our ego-consciousness as "the ascendancy of the 'complete' or total human being, consisting of the totality of the psyche."

The Self brings a feeling of "oneness," of reconciliation with life, which can now be accepted as it is and not as it ought to be. In explaining this, Jung says, "Only that which acts upon me do I recognize as real and actual." The Self responds to the empirically real. Essential is that the Self is in turmoil and misery because of the discord and disunity among the forces warring in its depths. Written large, this inner struggle has global consequences, for the modern person "has lost the metaphysical certainties" of medieval cousins and "set up in their place the ideals of material security." But Jung also saw the Self as "the new center of personality" growing toward *individuation* as we achieve unity out of the contradictions of our nature. Operating in this double way, it ensures a new and more solid foundation for our personality. As the principle of unity toward which the individual strives, the Self manifests and animates our behavior and is our ultimate goal.

Jung differed from Freud in his view of the unconscious as the original mold of the personality and not merely the repressed part, holding that the psyche communicates through images rather than concepts and that these images take the form of analogies and parables that represent the meaning of a given situation. He considered the symbolic approach to dreams and other unconscious manifestations as the most rewarding means of comprehending the language of the psyche and of describing its dynamics.

An "objective psyche" is identified by Jung in his later writings as compared to the "collective unconscious" of his earlier reference which gave rise to serious misinterpretation. The objective psyche is the totality of *a priori* psychic prefigurations and predispositions, the whole substratum of autonomous psychic functioning. This reservoir of intrinsic and rational psychic existence gives birth to consciousness; it exists prior to the conscious mind and continues to function together with or despite consciousness. It is autonomous and has laws unto itself. The objective psyche may contain many elements that were once conscious and have become unconscious again—through repression, for instance. The unconscious as a whole cannot be thought of as a mere relic of consciousness.

Jung posits a personal unconscious, again differing from Freud who referred to experience that was once conscious but was subsequently rejected as repressed material. The personal unconscious holds attitudes, urges and feelings that have been repressed as incompatible with our ego ideal. These are experienced in personalized form in dreams and fantasies as the individual's unacceptable and repressed other personality.

Responses, according to Jung, are expressed either outwardly or inwardly by two contrasting attitudinal types of people: the extrovert and the introvert. In the extrovert, the conscious energy ("libido") habitually flows toward the object, but there is an unconscious secret counteraction back toward the subject. The opposite occurs with introverts: they feel as if an overwhelming object constantly wants to affect them—from which they continually have to retire; everything is falling upon them, they are constantly overwhelmed by impressions, but they are unaware they are secretly borrowing psychic energy from and lending it to the object through this unconscious extroversion. Others who are extroverts make their relationships with the world through intellect, feelings, sense perceptions or intuitions. The introvert draws back and hesitates in a definite way.

Responses are processed according to what Jung calls the person's "most developed function." There are four cardinal functions which we use to orient ourselves in the world (also to our own inner world); *sensation,* which is perception through our senses; *thinking,* which gives meaning and understanding; *feeling,* which weighs and values; and *intuition,* which tells us of future possibilities and gives us information of the atmosphere which surrounds all experience.[1]

Two chief elements of the objective psyche are the archetypes—the *à priori* energy-field configurations that express themselves in typical representational images and in typical human emotion and behavior patterns—and the complexes that surround them—defined as feeling-toned ideas, these may develop as a result of long-term conditioning of early traumatic experience. However, their structure derives from an archetypal model—they are based on transpersonal and universal forms of human experiencing. A "mother complex," for example, develops as the result of the conflict between archetypal expectation and actual experience with the real woman who functions in a motherly role.

Jung sees the "archetype"—of which the Self is the greatest and over-arching one—as an original model or type. It is an inherited idea or mode of thought derived from the experience of the race and is present in the objective psyche (or collective unconscious). Archetypes control our way of perceiving the world. The material contained in this area is derived from the person's ancestors, and therefore from the entire human race. The whole history of human psychic functioning, the collective experience of humanity, is the

---

[1]   *Psychology Types,* p. 568.

inheritance of each individual. In all cultures archetypes are expressed in similar themes such as The Old Wise One, the Earth Mother, the World Tree, Paradise Rebirth, the "persona," "shadow," anima and animus.

Jung wrote that the form of these archetypes "is comparable to the axial system of a crystal which predetermines the crystalline formation in the saturated solution, without itself possessing a material existence." He adds, "The archetype possesses . . . an invariable core of meaning that determines its manner of appearing always only in principle, never concretely."

Like the contents of all creative spiritual energies, archetypes are relatively autonomous and cannot be integrated simply by rational means, but require the art of arriving at the truth by disclosing the Self's polarities and contradictions and overcoming them. Expressions of the archetypes emerge in dream symbols, which in the form of mythological motifs have portrayed psychic processes of transformation since the earliest times.

Individuation, the process of forming and specializing the nature of the self, is accomplished as the archetypes are integrated so as to provide the systems of the Self equilibrium and stability. Individuation, therefore, is a process of collective psychology in which differentiation takes place. Its goal is the development of the individual, the Self. Individuation is the road to health, the self incorporating healing archetypes, representing greater wholes, which are crucial in the transformation of personalities. Striving for wholeness, opposites are drawn together: all that is felt to be good and bad; maleness and femaleness; the four functions of thinking, feeling, sensation and intuition; the conscious and the unconscious. The process of developing the personality toward wholeness moves toward being finalized in middle age, but no one ever achieves a complete unification.

The aim of Jungian treatment is to develop within each person the creative potentialities, even if only the creative potentiality for living. The therapist, trying to help people find new meanings within, does not so much tell them about themselves as put them in touch with themselves.

Alfred Adler saw the total personality or self in terms of our being "unitary persons" and "individuals." At a time when it was fashionable to view people in a deterministic light as driven by instinctual impulses beyond control, Adler claimed that the self constantly strives to improve its life and said we try to establish goals for our thought and activity.

As individuals, we develop life-styles or life-plans which provide a common, unifying thread that ties together all bodily systems and perceptual experiences. For Adler the self was a "prototype," or the carrier of our individual and unique life-style. Our responses in adapting to the encounters with the material and social order are worked out in the self. Blockage of the "wish to be a complete person" and the frustration of an individual's "guiding principle" may result in our developing an "inferiority complex," or some other of the self's deviations.

In short, the "Individual Psychology" of Adler is a psychology of use, not of possession. What mattered for him was not what endowments we have, but what we do with the gifts we have. He saw the self as essentially altruistic, cooperative, creative. His portrait of the self was satisfying, hopeful and complementary to more pessimistic views. He sought to restore a sense of dignity and worth to the self. In his eyes we are responsible beings and our actions and attitudes demonstrate our purposive answer to the work and play, pleasure and displeasures of life. We are not completely bound by hereditary, environmental or conflicting inter-psychic forces.

Adler urges us to realize the tremendous power and strength within our individual self. Human beings frequently are considered small in time and space, like grains of sand on the beach, "coming from dust and becoming dust." Adler countered with the insistence that now we are in a better position to appreciate our potentials and recognize how we use our capacities only minimally. He showed how to release these immense inner energies in outlining a means of freeing us from our deep inferiority feelings which we have allowed to become the basis for our normal functioning. He viewed individuals as free agents, each able to decide and choose. This confidence in people's capacity to change gave Adlerians their proverbial optimism. "Everyone can change," Alder said, "but we cannot be sure everyone will decide to change."

Post-Freudians: Sullivan, Reich, Alexander, Horney, Guntrip and Rank: In the second quarter of this century personality theorists confronting new clinical findings and changing cultural conditions were pressed to move beyond classical views of the individual as caught in a fateful struggle with instincts. Increasingly, consideration had to be given to seeing persons as organisms in interaction. Advances in physics were being made as events were viewed in terms of their relations. New vistas opened in sociology as crowds were looked at as more than groups of persons and society was appreciated as more than a compact entered into by discrete individuals for their mutual benefit. The new generation of psychoanalysts of necessity adapted classical notions and therapies to meet the flood of intensified physical and cultural problems such as alienation, lack of individuality, urbanization, automation, poverty and the search for values.

Harry Stack Sullivan has given us one of the most comprehensive statements describing people as biologically- rooted but socially-interacting organisms. In clinical situations he applied his belief that the "I" is not a fact but an act. Also, he put to the test his conviction that the person we commonly refer to as an individual is the result of the social process, the derivative of the myriad experiences with people from the moment of birth.

Sullivan, along with Adler, maintained that persons are motivated to respond by "aims as well as causes." In his estimate, the self is organized around interpersonal *events* rather than intrapsychic energy. "Personality," he stated, "can never be isolated from the complex of interpersonal relations in which the person lives and has being."

To be a self is to have the capacity and freedom to respond. He distinguishes three "modes" of the self's responses: One of these—amorphous and without form or character—he called *prototaxis*—is undifferentiated and unrelated as in the primary experiences of the infant or of a regressed psychotic. A second state—structured and with distinguishable characteristics—he called the *parataxis*. This way of responding included differentiated experience, such as the awareness of concomitance or coincidence, accompaniment or accidental sequence. A third and higher level of responding called the *syntaxis* occurs when previously unassimilated masses of life experiences are integrated into a whole.

The healthy self, according to Sullivan, responds in syntaxic ways. The self-system, by discharging tensions in acceptable ways and preventing more massive outbursts of anxiety, maintains the individual as an effective functioning entity. The increasing power and confidence felt with regard to one's security will give rise to a feeling that Sullivan called self-esteem. A minimal amount of self-esteem is required to deal with the realistic feelings of powerlessness and helplessness that are evoked in a person. In the therapeutic process responses are dealt with not only to uncover repressed or dissociated material but also to serve as a learning process that assists the restructuring of new patterns. The self is strengthened as a social system, in ways similar to how Martin Buber encouraged the "I-Thou" development rather than as a "mind" proposed by the older idealistic traditions or as a "substance" with attributes advocated in thinkers within the Aristotelian tradition.

Wilhelm Reich, another psychoanalyst, researched the self's psychic energy and ways mental disorders manifested physical symptoms. He developed a view of the self that identified the central role of energy in its functioning. He sought to associate the sexual drive or libido, which Freud saw as an abstract psychological force, with concrete energy flowing through the physical organism. This approach led Reich to the concept of what he called "bio-energy," a fundamental form of energy that permeates and governs the entire person and expresses itself in the emotions and in the flow of bodily fluids and other biophysical movements.

Reich's view of bioenergy comes close to the Chinese concept of *ch'i* in which life-giving forces flow in pulsating wave movements throughout the body. Like the Chinese, Reich emphasized the cyclical nature of the organism's flow processes and saw the energy flow in the body as the reflection of a process that goes on in the universe at large.

Franz Alexander, another brilliant disciple of Freudian psychoanalysis, was an intuitive clinician as well as a creative thinker remembered for his remarkable approach to the study of the influence of emotions on chronic diseases. Using motion pictures to create stressful and life-like situations, he demonstrated how organ neurosis is not an attempt to express an *emotion* but is a physiological *adaptive* response. This observation called into question the classical concept of pathology which considered disturbed function as resulting from disturbed structure. Alexander showed how disturbed function can cause disturbed structure. Elevation of blood pressure, for instance, under the influence of rage does not relieve the rage but is a physiological component of the total phenomenon of rage. Thus fear related to conflict over dependent attitudes causes frustration or a threat to security and provokes rage leading to intense, usually unconscious, fear of retaliation, which must be repressed. Such states of fear and rage produce persistent autonomic excitation. Or consider the process of our becoming tired: Fatigue, like pain, is largely a subjective response to excessive and prolonged physical or mental activity. It has, however, a physiological concomitant. Emotional participation, interest and zest are important factors in the feeling of fatigue. If people are bored or resent a certain activity, they may feel fatigued quickly, whereas a keen interest in a strenuous task may prevent fatigue for a long time.

Alexander viewed the self as "a special part of reality" and stressed ways in which the connections within the self are like those in the external world. He held that "every intuitive comprehension of a truth, if it is accompanied by the subjective feeling of its being a discovery. . . is a kind of recognition of one's own self mirrored in the outside world."

Psychotherapy's chief objective, for Alexander, is to provide what he called a "corrective emotional experience." An intellectual understanding of one's neurosis must be combined with emotional experiences which stabilize and enliven new patterns of life. Fresh understanding undergirded with a new emotional experience gives the person a feeling of mastery, and this in turn encourages the mobilization of repressed material which before could not be mastered by integration with the rest of the conscious personality. A primary function of psychoanalysis is to help persons straighten out the tangled relations between themselves and their world and help them accommodate their "drives" and "desires" to reality.

Karen Horney, much like Sullivan, emphasized environmental and cultural factors in the formation of the self and in the origins of its dysfunction and held that the self's health or sickness and its tendency to respond or withdraw depend largely on whether there is sufficient motive and power to propel us out of ourselves into the arena of the world. She found the seeds of neurosis in conflict between the pulls-and-pushes within us. Some, for example, tend to "move toward," others to "move away from," and others to "move against" someone or some situation. In personal relationships, people tend to "fight," "take flight," or encounter the other and "work it out."

Horney made extensive observations about the experience of suffering and noted that not all suffering was masochistic but frequently was an unintended byproduct of neurotic conflict. She showed how suffering may be the only way the self sees it can protect itself against imminent danger. By self-recrimination, for example, we can avoid being accused and accusing others, by appearing ill or ignorant we avoid reproach and by belittling oneself we avoid the danger of competition. The suffering we bring on ourselves is at the same time a defense, an adaptive maneuver. The healthy self moves more effectively toward others when inner desires, interests, motivations and values are nurtured and applied to life. Given a chance to express our unique life-force, we develop our potential—our "real self," instead of our fickle "idealized self."

Harry Guntrip, an English psychoanalyst and theologian, with his mentor W.R.D. Fairbairn, sought a psychodynamic theory of the self. He emphasized the search of the ego for security, which it can find only by dealing satisfactorily with its "bad objects" while maintaining reliable relations with its "good objects."

Guntrip starts at the center of the self, the ego, and depicts its strivings and difficulties in its endeavor to reach a supportive object. In his book *Object Relations and the Self* (1969), he cites clinical evidence supporting Horney's picture of the healthy and responding self that "persons whose self was integrated and strengthened by a firm sense of identity are more capable of accepting moral responsibility and social education." Emotional health and the ability to respond positively comes as persons experience themselves as "whole selves *and* as they become 'morally congruent.' " This condition is approached when, within themselves and with others, people have honestly dealt with guilt and defined clearly their values and goals.

Otto Rank stresses an element of "self-determination" that influences responding. Freedom and growth towards the essential and positive responding self comes as persons step from the fated to the self-determining attitude, from the withdrawn to the positively responding self. The exercise of one's power to make reasoned decision is not selfishness, but responsible controlling of one's own actions. Instead of pulling away from the environment and others, the positively responding self accepts willingly its own individuality and moves responsibly into the outer or "real experience," world. The positively responding self is able to do this by having tended to the inner clarification and restoration that is helped by psychotherapy and spiritual renewal.

Rank thought that people were powerfully motivated by their "imagined self" or "other self," which is the self persons want to be, but are not. Persons "self-create their own fate," he said. The pleasurable, for instance, will be struggled with consciously. The individual wants the pleasurable, yet there are inner and outer conditions that hinder the pleasurable experience. The amount of pleasure experienced is determined by whether the persons have an outer or inner ideal by which to create themselves and their destinies. As important as is the interplay of will with feelings and thinking, he holds that responding individuals try to break away from the persons they have become and did not want to be and begin to listen to the "other, more responsible self." Rank contends that "neurosis presents less a medical and more a moral problem." Neurosis stems from dissatisfaction and guilt over having become something other than the genuine and responsible being the person had wanted to be. The positive response required is psychotherapy and spiritual renewal which releases and builds the self by giving the needed philosophy of life and faith in the self.

Holistic estimates: Gestaltists and Kurt Goldstein stress the need to see responding as a function of the total personality, rather than on the basis of a fragmented or "part-process" view. The special weight given the whole self of Gestalt psychology emerged as a reaction against reducing the self to pieces or components of analytic orientations. Its special contribution was the clear formulation of the thesis that the whole is more than the sum of its parts—which can be understood only after the meaning of *whole* has been discovered.

Goldstein, following his work with brain-damaged patients, saw the self's impairment as a disruption of wholeness. In working with the injured he utilized his special skills as a neurologist in combination with a Gestaltist emphasis of encouraging persons to put their separated or projected parts back into a unity, pointing out the Dr. Jekyll and Mr. Hyde in each person. He sought ways to help individuals rid themselves of the bestial Mr. Hyde and at the same time respond to both aspects of the self and integrate these separate elements into a more united individual. Responsibility is for the person—either Dr. Jekyll or Mr. Hyde—to stop playing lawyer and blaming the other person, to stop projecting or imagining that someone else is experiencing an emotion that the self is feeling and hiding.

Gestalt psychology accents the dynamics of perception. In responding to its environment which it sees as "a differentiation field," the self finds its identity. This approach reinforces the stress Harry Stack Sullivan gave to the relation between the individual and the interpersonal whole or context within which the self is shaped.

Kurt Lewin, for example, developed his "field theory" and applied it to the way individuals and communities respond, emphasizing the pattern of present influences acting upon a person at a given time as perceived or interpreted by the individual. He drew diagrams of the "life space" of persons, with symbols to represent all the significant regions, forces and barriers present—i.e., the persons and events which might influence the behavior of the person. Gestaltists see the behavior of a person as functions of the quality and kind of relationships characteristic of the total personality. Conversely, what happens to one affects the whole field in which one participates. The responding self is an organic whole, a *Gestalt.*

Goldstein highlights the self's quality of intention and declares that the individual is motivated by "one sovereign motive," an inner pressure toward self-realization. He found that brain-injured soldiers were handicapped in their capacity to grasp abstractions and when asked to go beyond the familiar they suffered severe tension. Healthy personalities have the capacity for freedom and the ability to cope with anxiety and bear pain and grief. The "preferred-patterns" which make up their selves have "positive motive-systems." These motive-systems are powerful inner forces which press for self-preservation and push us to reach for self-actualization. In the healthy self the tendency toward self-actualization acts from within, overcoming the disturbances arising from the clash with the world—not out of anxiety but out of the joy of conquest.

Humanists: Maslow, Allport, Erich Fromm, Angyal. The humanistic approach to the responsive self is relatively new and less well formulated than many other theories of personality. In contrast to psychoanalytic and behavioristic approaches, humanistic psychology is primarily concerned with those human capacities and potentialities that have little or no systematic place in the other positivistic views. Qualities to be enhanced by the responding self include love, creativity, self-growth organism, higher values, basic need-gratification, self-actualization, being, becoming, transcendence, objectivity, autonomy, meaning, fair-play, psychological health and responsibility.

Existential psychotherapists have lent their support to humanistic interpreters of personality. Rollo May holds that part of the problem of Western persons comes from the resistance, avoidance and repression of concern with *being* human, to the extent that they may even lose the sense of being, a situation which is related to collectivist and conformist trends in our culture. He sees part of the solution in "intentionality," a factor in all psychotherapy and also at the heart of consciousness and key to the problem of wish and will. Humanistic approaches to the responsive self agree when May asserts, "It is in intentionality and will that the human being experiences identity."

Abraham Maslow developed the theme of the self as free to respond with striving for release and expression of its possibilities. With unyielding trust in the self's intrinsic nature, he maintained that responsibility consists of a person moving toward identifiable goals of maturation. Persons can experience increasing enlightenment so that the self is free to make choices compatible with life. Persons have the responsibility to become "congruent with reality," and grow and actualize themselves. Unique selves, the heroes of the race, were more completely "individual" than ordinary persons. Yet these special selves were thoroughly socialized and identified with humanity. Pathways to the self becoming more autonomous and responsible include a steady and accurate perception of reality and the development of comfortable relations with it. People need to accept their inescapable relatedness to others and to develop their capacity to problem-solve in the present and plan for a fulfilling future. These efforts require the continuing freshness and sharpened awareness that creativity gives.

Maslow and other humanistic psychologists are especially concerned with reconciling opposing forces of the self—the tension, for example, in the pull of conformity against innovation and change. Responsible responding is a fruitful way of coping with such tensions. Franklin J. Shaw said, "Human beings can become something other than creatures of either conformity or rebellion through reconciling the opposition between them by means of a concept of responsibility, one which allows for both possibilities."

The self as *Gordon Allport,* another esteemed psychologist and Harvard professor, put it, "is the dynamic organization within the individual of those psychophysical systems that determine unique adjustments to one's environment." The many facets of these dynamic and infinitely varied systems make the study of the self extremely complex. He held that the self's purposive responses proceed under their own steam. The self-sustaining, contemporary systems grow out of antecedent systems, but they function independently of them. These systems make up the self's central core.

According to Allport the striving for "realization" is a pivotal factor in the self. The self reaches for more than tension release, catharsis or even comfortable adaptation. The quest is for *meaning* and *direction* which he calls "appropriate striving." In unhealthful motivation, unbalancing mechanisms in the self have the upper hand. Dissociation is at work along with repression, compulsions and other pathological expressions. Normally the balancing mechanisms dominate, making for an essential harmony and integration in the personality system. Under such conditions, the ego seems to be in full control; this is the "active ego" at work in the self.

Erich Fromm, out of the breadth of his social emphasis elaborated in *Escape from Freedom* (1941), espoused a "sane society" which would be more suited to the human condition and not frustrating to basic social needs. He spoke also of the urge for transcendence—a person's need to rise above the animal nature. From this dual concern—human being's social needs and their reach for transcendence—Fromm focused attention on the differences among selfishness, self-love and self-interest. In each he found an incessant tension between altruism and self-centeredness. The attitudes toward others and toward the self, far from being contradictory, help give unity and substance to the self. Love of others and love of the self are not alternatives, according to Fromm. One's own self "must be as much an object of one's love as another person." The affirmation of life's happiness, growth and freedom is rooted in the capacity to love: to care, to respect, to act responsibly toward others. Individuals, Fromm posited, who are able to love productively, love themselves too. If they can love only others or only one other, as the love-smitten romantic, they cannot love at all."

Andras Angyal gives a poetic interpretation of the self which he calls an organized and patterned process. He holds that persons respond as unified, dynamic organizations which tend towards increased autonomy. The self is a *specific* psycho-social organism; it is autonomous, asserting itself actively, instead of responding passively as a physical body might, expressing itself in spontaneity, self-assertiveness, striving for freedom and mastery. It struggles for centrality within its surrounding world. The self also seeks a home, striving to become an organic part of a greater whole.

Transpersonal psychologists who represent an emerging "fourth force" within the larger group of humanistic mental health workers propose that the enigma of the self should be met head-on. They champion a range of *ultimate* human capacities and potentialities they think have been neglected and recommend facing and harnessing these "other side" aspects of the self. The concern is for the self's becoming more "fulfilled." Meta-needs must be addressed and satisfied, and they encourage experiences which enhance ultimate values, peak experiences, ecstasy, mystical experience, wonder, transcendence of self and cosmic awareness. They meet the enigma of the self less with causative factors in personality, involving the past, than with *being* (present) and *becoming* (future) and have a growing interest in transcendence and the transpersonal rather than being limited to the immediate, the given, the here-and-now.

The function and structure of responding—Pavlov and Piaget. The Russian Pavlov and the Swiss Piaget have pioneered in two different areas of psychology. Both are similar in the magnitude of their contribution to the understanding of the self and the ways it responds—Pavlov by his innovative studies of how psychic processes are related to physiological processes provided new light on the functioning of the self in terms of classical conditioning and Jean Piaget, in multi-volume and monumental works, describes the complex makeup of the self and how it develops. Though not a mathematician and not as strict a laboratory researcher as Pavlov, Piaget was no less a meticulous experimentalist and an especially careful observer of the responses of the self, of the intellectual development of children and of how the component parts of personality fit into configurations.

Pavlov took issue with the psychology developed by the renowned German pioneer Wilhelm Wundt as a "science of consciousness" and study of subjective states. From his extensive experiments in physiological conditioned reflex,

Pavlov developed a method which provided both for the induction of stress and the measurement of emotions as correlates of physical stress. In his experiments with stress related to excitation and inhibition, Pavlov distinguished three types of responses: The "hysterical," who are dominated by inhibitory feelings and are timid, shy and submissive; the "centralized," who cope effectively with inhibitory and stress conditions and try to respond in a balanced pattern; and the "normal," who alternate between the inhibitory and excitational stimuli, sometimes responding to the one or the other.

Pavlov followed Hippocrates' theory of four temperaments: the sanguine, phlegmatic, choleric and melancholic. The sanguine and phlegmatic types are normal and central; the sanguine is energetic and productive and the phlegmatic is quiet and persistent. Manic-depressives and neuresthenics belong to the choleric, excitable type; hysterics and schizophrenics belong to the melancholic type. Later on Pavlov added three more types—the intermediate, the artistic and the intellectual—which he found in societal responses. A combination for the four Hippocratic types with the three cultural types permitted a greater variability in describing patterns of response.

With the discovery of the conditioned reflex, Pavlov contributed both a new research tool and a conceptual model for exploring the relations between external and internal responses and events in the behavior of disturbed animals. Experimenting with a great variety of stimuli and applying progressive reductions in conditioning, he found the variety of stimuli which can elicit a given reflex is almost limitless. One series of findings monitored the point at which an animal ceases to make approach responses to a formerly rewarding situation as a result of the withdrawal of the reward. In defining this process and conditioned reflex, he succeeded in giving his answer in operational terms. In higher-order conditioning, a response is progressively associated from one conditioned stimulus to another. Complex interactions in the brain would be established and these could account for complex acts and for higher mental processes.

Jean Piaget gave an illuminating description of how the self developed and how it is structured. His extensive studies led him to conclude that the self was unique in its wholeness and its capacities to regulate and transform itself. *Wholeness* has to do with the interdependence of elements; a structure is more than an aggregate in which independent elements are mechanically associated but do not affect one another. *Self-regulation* refers to the way the self responds adaptively to influences from outside and at the same time manages to maintain its integrity. *Transformation* is the way the self persists even as it must constantly change and is capable of developing new patterns of behavior.

For Piaget, goal-seeking responses require "adaptation"—a process by which we can change both aspects of our external environment and the balance of our inner forces. He speaks of "adaptive responses" as balances between the active and passive parts in our adjustment to our surroundings. The most complete and complex of these responses in our efforts to master environmental conditions is found in problem-solving behavior. This interpretation of Piaget allows for more human freedom than Pavlov's theory that only if conditioning is of a complex nature would some of the higher centers and functions be involved.

Pavlov's work had greatest adherence in his native Russia and continues to be a dominant influence in Russian psychology and psychotherapy. His theories, with those of Piaget, have had a powerful influence on the Western social scientists' premises for their theories of behavior, learning, intelligence, memory, creativity and psychotherapy.

Emphasis on person-self-identity—Carl Rogers, Heinz Kohut and Erik Erikson. Carl Rogers epitomizes the "open self" kind of responding self. Whatever problems or clients he confronts, he consistently points persons to a responsive life that is receptive, accepting, genuine and congruent. He suggests that below the level of the problem situation—be it trouble with family, spouse or employer, with one's uncontrollable and bizarre behavior or frightened feelings—lies one central search: we seek to answer, "Who am I *really?*" "What's with *Me?*" "How can I get in touch with this real self underlying all my surface behavior?" "How can I become myself?"

In this search persons are helped with healing and self-realization by a client-centered therapist—one who senses, understands and accepts the thinking, feeling and direction of the other person. Having such an experience of genuine and non-possessive love, persons become more themselves. In an accepting and intimate relationship, one's personhood is experienced fully, new elements are discovered and limits extended. The self is experienced in a way that Rogers likens to "pure culture." For a moment, persons *are* their fear, their grief or anger, their kindness, tenderness or love.

Such experiences of the self are not easily achieved. Both the intense individualism of the West and the binding communalism of the East make us vulnerable to aberrant emotional patterns of behavior. Disturbed involvements with others lead to disturbed relations with ourselves; inner disturbances create social disturbances. When we are given or cultivate the opportunity to become less defensive, more open and self-assured, Rogers claims "insight and self-understanding come bubbling through spontaneously."[2]

This is the "freeing up" and strengthening of the self that is the objective of Rogerian psychotherapy. We become liberated to look at old facts in new ways—an experience of discovering new relationships among familiar attitudes—and of bit by bit coming around to a new orientation. One of Roger's clients who felt herself "imprisoned in feminine demands," once freed up to see a new orientation, told about the fresh insight, "I'm a woman. I'm going to accept it, not as fate, not in a spirit of submission, but as meant for the best. I can probably do a lot more good by being myself and

---

2   *Counseling and Psychotherapy,* p. 40.

developing my own talents rather than trying to do something else."[3] Where formerly she wanted complete self-control, now she wants more "to be myself."

Rogers explained that this woman gained "insights" in at least four areas: She came to accept a more realistic view of her abilities and her ultimate goals. She achieved acceptance of her own inhibited social desires. She admitted her hetero-sexual desires and she shifted from a repudiation of her feminine role to a rather complete acceptance of it. In light of her new orientation and clarification of possible courses of action, with strengthened self-assurance she decided and took positive steps to move her self in new directions.

Heinz Kohut, a Chicago psychoanalyst, similarly found deep disturbances of self-esteem in many of his patients and concerned himself with how these persons suffered an inner emptiness, loss of initiative and destructive tangles in social and sexual aspects of their lives. Repeatedly he found the self's inability to regulate the sense of worth and confidence kept persons at levels insufficient for normal functioning. When threatened with punishment, denied love or removed from those important to them, these individuals' lives had ceased to have meaning. Without the usual reward-providing and approval-giving relationships into which to channel their energies, these people were unable to keep their self-esteem and their self-cohesion. Persons with these kinds of distur-bances of the self were particularly difficult to help since often they were unable to pinpoint their complaints. The self-observing function of the ego appeared to be impaired, suggesting Ludwig Binswanger's description, "the eye, as it were, cannot observe itself."

Kohut applied Freud's, Melanie Kline's, Fairbairn's and other classical psychoanalysts' approaches in new ways and concluded that the complicated disturbances he was confront-ing stemmed from "impaired primary selves." He posited

---

[3]   Ibid, p. 192.

that during infancy these persons were improperly or insufficiently bonded or insecurely related to parents, especially to their mothers. This lack caused emotional disturbances of greater importance even than gross traumatic events. Therapeutic revival of these unfulfilled childhood needs allowed his clients to gain insight into the nature of their psychological imbalances. In respecting and attempting to picture themselves as part of the therapist, people began to feel strong and worthwhile and, in time, learned to gain mastery over the former imbalance.

Kohut pictured the self as unitary, but not singular, since it is composed of many "sub-selves" and is more like a federation of parts, each of which struggles to express the affective needs of individuals. People are driven compulsively by powerful emotional needs and pulled by equally powerful and creative urges. When these needs are unrequited and the urges are blocked, serious trouble develops. The affiliative intimacy a mother can provide needs to be regained. The support, energy, protection and sense of values a responsible father can provide needs to be reconstituted.

Much of the preliminary work leading to the research on "narcissistic disturbances" done by Kohut and his colleagues came from advances in meta-psychology pioneered by M. Hartmann in the 1950s. Hartmann differentiated some of the ego. Among the more important, he cites (1958) particularly the individual's relation to reality. People's mental health depends strongly on the effectiveness of their reality-testing, the organization and control of motility and perception and the development of a protective barrier between external and internal stimulation. The "ego" refers to the functions of the self which enable it to respond to itself and act toward the environment in acceptable and self-fulfilling ways. Kohut's careful work in describing the adaptive responses of personality, much like that of his mentor Hartman, contributes a view of the self as a totality. He sees the self not only in the id, ego and superego—as Freud set forth—or even as one of the agencies of the mind or the emotions, but as the total person, including the form and contents. This formulation helps therapists become more specific in diagnosing and more effective in correcting emotional troubles of "borderline" patients.

Erik Erikson's approach to the self provides a unique combination of imaginative clinical description, rigorous thinking, gentle humor and deep humanity. His genius for applying personal and cultural empathy with communal and individual intuition led him to a concern with the self's unifying goal, i.e., its pressing drive-reduction impulse and its seeking homeostasis. He also, following the new school of humanistic psychologists, sought ways to help people move toward self-realization and self-actualization. With Mahler, he suggested that the self emerges out of the gradual crystallization of a separate psychobiological existence from the union of mother and child. Erikson leaned toward viewing the self as expressing itself through the thinking, cognitive processes rather than through the drives of the unconscious id. Erikson also built on the seminal work of Charlotte Buhler who in the '30s described motivational development in stages of self-determination to goals towards self-fulfillment.

Erikson (1959) proposed that the healthy personality must develop on a foundation of "basic trust." This attitude relates both to the individual's concept of self as well as its orientation to the outside world. Trust develops during the first year of life and is dependent on the satisfaction of needs which, initially, must be met by others. Though the satisfaction of psychophysical needs is a basic goal from the beginning of life, the emotional climate in which they are administered is also of primary importance. Adolescence is a time for intellectual expansion and the development of increased ability to generalize, to deal with abstractions such as the concept of time and to engage in logical thought and communicate with others. The central theme of adolescence is that of *identity*, coming to know who one is, what one believes in and values and what one wants to accomplish and get out of life. The early period of adulthood requires attaining a reasonable sense of self-identity so that true intimacy with another person can be established. Individuals who find true-love relations with a partner may move on to the next stage—middle-adulthood—which Erikson calls "generativity." In the final stage of the life cycle people become absorbed in adjusting to diminution of strengths and resources and to confronting the inevitability of death.

In the tradition of Freud, who used his own dreams to demonstrate his theories, Erikson allows us to observe the emergence of his clinical theoretical conception in terms of his own psychoanalytic training and his childhood origins. He skillfully weaves his description of the concept of psychosocial identity into his account of the initial events that occurred in the development of his own self. In spelling out the self's intense occupation in acquiring identity, he also pointed out the dangers to which the self is exposed, particularly the excesses of what he called "the drift into narcissism."

In his book *Insight and Responsibility* (1956), Erikson presents the ethical implications of psychoanalytic insight and the responsibilities each generation has for all succeeding generations, focusing on three orders in which we human beings live, have opportunity for expression and are obliged to respond responsibly: 1) the *somatic* order by which an organism seeks to maintain its integrity in a continuous, reciprocal adaptation of the *milieu interieur* and other organisms; 2) the *personal* order which is the integration of "inner" and "outer" world in individual experience and behavior; and 3) the *social* order jointly maintained by personal organisms sharing a geographical and historical setting. Effective, fulfilled and responsible persons respond in each of these orders or spheres and in this way the self finds its identity, strength and insight.

Focal View

Answers to questions about the self depend greatly on where the questioners are standing and how they are looking.

The infant responds in fresh and simple ways to what is seen in the mirror. As we mature our responses may be physical as for the physiologist or introspective as for the psychologist or pastoral counselor. Estimates and appreciation of the self require much more than a casual glance at people's outward behavior. Account must be taken of our feelings and reason, our intuition and faith.

The self's responses are aroused by stimuli of our feelings. Things excite our feeling response; people stir us even more and with more intenseness. We are also stimulated and influenced powerfully by our own feelings even though we may differ in how we feel—some find a small room cozy and intimate while others feel closed in and uncomfortable. When we look at ourselves we all see not so much what is there but what we *feel*.

To further know the self we need our reason which orders the empirical perceptions of the self. We can analyze its responses as the "output" of thought and behavior and do the same with its counterpart of "input" or stimulus. With our reason the responding self can be defined by its effect on some part of the environment, as a subject depressing a lever, by a specific physical event such as a knee jerk or doing a handspring or, finally, by the meaning attributed to the person's behavior, thought or feeling. Widely differing acts, ideas and emotions in this way can be classified and studied.

With intuition and faith we sense ourselves more subjectively. These two approaches make it possible to respond to ourselves rationally and empirically, as well as romantically and metaphorically. Plato's and the popular conception of the self is as a substance, comparable to the body. Intuition and faith help, as with Kierkegaard, to see the self as mainly intangible, involving "the dizziness of freedom," and in terms of possibilities and decisions made in fear and trembling.

The self is too complicated and vital an entity to be trussed up in a conceptual straitjacket. The cause-and-effect action of a struck billiard ball's response in bouncing off at an angle is simple and direct compared with the responses of a person struck by some experience. The French say that the best way to look at another person is with the heart. We need the quadra-focal view which comes with seeing the self with feeling and reason, intuition and faith. Few of us are sharp enough of mind and senses to monitor our own lives accurately. Our intuitions and reaches of faith help us see more clearly the self's fullness and purpose.

Summary

The observations and therapies of these representative 20th century psychologists, combined with the findings of other careful social scientists, provide remarkable additions to our knowledge about ourselves. In probing the self's nature and multiple ways of responding, psychologists have sought order among facts without needless proliferation of concepts while recognizing that over-simplification may succeed only in caricaturing human nature and that a certain theoretical grounding is essential for understanding the self.

Theorists moved from Freud's naturalistic and individualistic version to Adler's recognition of volition as well as biologic drives and later to Jung's insistence that a causal analysis of psychic phenomena is not sufficient. Historical and social factors must be taken into account. The systematic approaches advanced by these and other clinicians in the 30s, 40s and 50s produced a greatly expanded estimate of the form and dynamics of the self.

In the decades that followed, building on the constructs of the earlier structuralists, the self has come to be seen in new configurations and functions. Previously, for example, the emphasis was on motivation as a sex drive, a will-to-power and other forces that propel and animate the self. Increasing concern came to be placed upon causes arising from hostility, conflict and stress. In recent times large portions of our mental life have been "accounted for" by reflex arc, by conditioning, by reinforcement or they have been viewed as an associational fusion of sensations, images and affections; a dynamic interplay of id, superego and ego; or in terms of some other appealing but skeleton formula such as parent, ego and child.

General acceptance was given the emphasis made by Allport that the self is the individual's core and persons have an urgent responsibility to appreciate its full-orbed aspects and free it to respond. Concurrence is found with Guntrip's assertion that there is an imperative for a reciprocal relation between the self and the other and that we must keep the self strong so that we are able to accept and fulfill moral responsibilities. We can each respond responsibly as we choose, decide and derive satisfaction and meaning from the individual patterns we develop for our being-in-the-world.

The fruit of the combined findings of psychologists and social scientists is without parallel in any other similar span of time. These specialists, some of the best minds of the 20th century, provide not only a broad basis of carefully observed data about the "human document," but they offer a corpus of theory surveying the formidable accumulation of findings about the structure and functioning of the human self.

Regarding freedom to respond and living responsibly, these investigator/theorists, though differing in their approaches, provide a significant consensus: The self is essentially a responding individual. Our freedom to respond ranges over a whole lifetime and our patterns of responding are myriad. Heredity and environmental influences, the ways of how, when and why we were nurtured by family, school and community condition our capacity and motivations to be free to respond. Each self responds in the diverse repertoires characteristic of the individual in a particular culture. Neuroses and psychoses develop when the self becomes fractured and is no longer in touch with reality. Such conditions impede and distort persons' freedom to respond. In nurturing the young and caring for troubled and confused people, psychotherapists have modified older views as they found that blockages in learning and hostility frequently are reactions to frustration and the sense of failure. One effect, for example, was that therapists became less prone than formerly to regard hostility as a cause for feelings of guilt, isolation and self-condemnation. Becoming more fully human occurs as people continue to take responsibility to nurture unitary selves that become strong as they are flexible and meaningful as they find and express purpose.

What is the self? It is a responding human organism, an agent, a function, a personality, an individual, a companion, a creator and a spirit. These differing aspects of the self make their particular responses in ways that are alive, directional, unifying and creative. In the process the self searches for energies, goals and an order beyond itself.

The responsible person seeks to be at one with the inner self, others and the Creator. The self is a unified, whole being that can look at itself and at the world. In responding to time, for example, the self has periods, sequences and cycles of birth, growth and death. It can tell about its responding, reflect on its nature and think about its past and present and hope about its future. In response to space, the outer world and cosmos and the inner reaches of mind and soul, the self serves as the matrix within which growth, creativity and union develop. Confronted continually with options, the self must respond by choosing and deciding. The responses of the self, then, do not originate out of nothing in some general place, but they are the fruit of persistent cultivation of intention and relationships.

The self is in a continuing process of clarifying its nature and identifying its goals. How can the self face the world's disintegration, disaster and threat of nuclear extinction with a movement toward synthesis, cooperation and fulfillment? Can we come to a full recognition of our interdependence with everyone and everything else on this planet? Can we locate the evolutionary psychology that can facilitate courage and patience, wisdom and compassion—qualities needed in a time of paradigm shift and planetary crisis?

C H A P T E R

Locating One's Self

In the cool of the day the Lord God called to the man saying, *"Where are you?"* And the man said, "I heard the sound of thee in the garden and I was afraid, because I was naked; and I hid myself" (Gn 3:9).

O Self, *Where are you?* This foundational question about the location of the collective self has been asked since the dawn of human consciousness. In the Genesis account one reads that when given freedom, Adam and Eve chose their own way over the Creator's. Imagining that cleverness and ambition are the final word, they did not eat from the Tree of Life, they ate from the tree that is deadly to self-respect and peace of mind—the Tree of Knowledge of Good and Evil. This exposed them to malevolent spirits that stirred hatred and suspicion instead of eternal righteousness. Self-will and rebelliousness inevitably confront that plumb-line for behavior. Before the calm and justice of the Maker, Adam and Eve suddenly became embarrassed and ashamed. "They knew they were naked." With the beginnings of awareness we found we had a Self bigger than us to reckon with and that we had to locate our self in reference to the Other. In orienting our self to the Other we confront our responsibility in the place and time of our lives.

The established philosophic systems and structures of communal relations of pre-modern eras supplied ready answers to what was unique about human beings and provided accepted patterns of individual conduct. After the Renaissance the great metaphysical systems of Aristotle, Aquinas and others that viewed human beings as philosophical and religious animals waned. Western civilization struggled with conflicting assessments of the nature and location of the self. In 18th century England, Protestants closely followed biblical assurances that human beings were "created in the image of God" and had a status "a little lower than the angels" (Gn 1:26; Ps 8:4). These Puritan devotees were openly narcissistic about two beliefs: the inner workings of their souls and methodically increasing private wealth. A resolute, but often unbending, society developed with these compulsive Protestants trying to find the dual "location" of their selves. Yet as history demonstrates, the tensions of that turbulent time gave rise to one of the most advanced and wealthiest societies ever known. To them the ambivalence of self-centeredness was not the fifth horse rider of the Apocalypse, but rather one of the guiding forces of that period in English history.

Since the 19th century, the American's colloquy with the self has become increasingly pressing. Much of this contemporary search for self stems from the independence of the Puritans and early settlers in the New World. The American pioneers who moved West and the czars of industry were known as "rugged individualists" and "adventurous selves." In the New World people became increasingly obsessed with locating their own self—getting a bearing on where they were going—seeking more coherent estimates of what they thought was genuinely human.

In our day the urgency to locate the self has moved from a back burner to a front burner priority. Considering the tumultuous happenings of the late 1960s, Carl Jung told an interviewer, "The world hangs by a thin thread and that thin thread is the psyche or self of human beings." The need to accurately assess where we are has taken on deeper personal meanings and broader social implications. A host of people strive frantically to situate the inner self and the self that bonds communities. When they ask, "Where are we now?" and "Which way is forward?" it is not simply the structure and function of the self they are troubled with, it is the self's location.

Anxiety over locating the self is neither new nor limited to England or America. Throughout time, people recurrently exhibit frantic concern over the identity of the self and their destiny. Candide did not exactly live in happy times, nor did the ancient Greeks whose acrid wisdom Nietzsche quotes in *The Birth of Tragedy:* "Best is not to have been born at all; the next best is to die as quickly as possible." Civilized life has often been experienced as a borderline condition in the process of getting worse and history is ultimately the story of bad times. "The travail of self discovery," writes Paul Zweig in *The Heresy of Self-love,* "is the need to shape a human response to a world which we have neither wholly made nor wholly received; the comfort of locating one's own self on the difficult map of the emotions; these common impulses have shaped our cultural traditions."[1]

In the 1980s after the self-wrenching struggles over civil rights, Vietnam and other justice issues, many Americans tended to retreat to purely personal preoccupations—a trend brought about by something deeper than do-it-yourself motivations. With increasing mobility of populations and the erosion of the nuclear family, many lost the sense of historical continuity, of belonging to a succession of generations originating in the past and stretching into the future. The quest for immediate and personal fulfillment became the prevailing passion. This self-centered drive to live it up *now-*

---

[1] p. 265.

for-yourself without regard for predecessor or posterity was a strong reaction touted by a fierce "me-myself-and-I" cult advanced by steely characters found in Ayn Rand novels.

Ours is a time when tradition is broken and cannot be rebuilt along old lines. The cultural structures that served to define what is uniquely human have been swept away. The suicidal escalation of preparations for a war of annihilation and the decline of moral and religious influence is part of this search for a "satisfying sense of self"—also expressed frequently in a hedonistic chase for happiness and an unbridled pursuit of self interest. When it becomes an exaggerated pursuit for what pleases *me* and does not give appropriate consideration to others, the foundations of groups and communities are threatened. A social norm premised on the idea that all people can have their own choice simply does not work.

In our lifetime, confidence in progress has gradually given way to a widespread fear of and superficial adjustment to change and a suspiciousness concerning faith itself. Identity problems and the symptoms of identity confusion have changed accordingly. We alternate between denying our foibles and failures with becoming preoccupied by them. Our simplistic moralisms are no match for the harsh realities we face. Many voices, often conflicting, try to describe what is genuinely human, but few offer realistic guidelines or have the power to reveal our inner selves convincingly.

Responsible Search for the Self's Ecology

Our personal ecology includes the self's physical, cultural and spiritual embodiment. To be alive is to participate in the interdependence of the environment, our culture and the world of the spirit.

File cabinets of psychologists and counselors are filled with stories of individuals who have struggled in vain to "locate" themselves within their personal ecologies. The replies of concerned or desperate persons when asked "Where are you?" reveal the temper of the day. Frequently varying degrees of dissatisfaction are expressed regarding the roles into which persons are cast. Work provides us with a livelihood, a sense of belonging and often the chance to express creativity, but it also confronts us with problems of competition, monotonous routines and insecure tenure. The latter, referred to by Europeans as "work or relationship disturbances," often prove disruptive to the self. Unfulfilled neurotic drives or a fruitless search for a deep and trusting relationship may lead to despair.

The question of origin of birth often looms large in individuals who are driven to be both original and honest. Adopted children find themselves haunted by questions of the identity of their natural mother or father. The instances of our attempts to "locate" our self are endless.

High schoolers and college students, when sharing "where they are," often disclose explorations they are making into their expanding horizons. Mixed with a geographic restlessness and a need to find ways to express their zest and excitement, they seek more suitable "locations" for their selves, that is more secure identities and patterns of life. Wanting to leave behind childhood roles, they stand at the threshold of an uncertain adulthood, often trying to recover some as-yet-undeveloped childhood strengths. For young people in societies that provide meaningful rites of passage, the personal identity crisis will be silent and contained.

For other young people living in periods of collective strife or epidemic tension, their adolescent identity crisis will often leave them seriously emotionally disturbed. Living in chaotic conditions accentuates the conflict inherent in the adolescent developmental process, inducing individuals to "give in" semideliberately to their most regressed or repressed tendencies. Young people are particularly vulnerable to *fears* aroused by new facts and to disappointments over the unfulfilled promises pervading the time in which they live. Anxieties are provoked by symbolic dangers as a consequence of the decay of existing ideologies. On the one hand they repeatedly test the limits of new relationships and social boundaries, on the other hand they *dread* facing an existential abyss devoid of spiritual meaning. All the while they know they must work out life plans.

Mike, a high school athlete, answers the question, "Where am I?" candidly: "I'm trying to keep up my grades, stay on the team, keep off of drugs and booze and keep from getting a girl pregnant." Sonja, a Russian exchange student, finds herself enthusiastic about the opportunity to study abroad but reports, "Back in Leningrad I waited two years for an apartment, three years for a permit to buy an auto and four years for a visa to study in the U.S. So I'm frustrated with the slowness of *perestroika*." Pedro, a 23-year-old hunted El Salvador rebel, speaks with urgency about where he is: "I'm doing everything I can to find sanctuary."

People in mid-life face other kinds of adjustments. Developed in our formative years, our poor work habits and awkward social skills begin to catch up with us and impair our functioning in adulthood. Affiliations and associations, essential for correction and reinforcement, all too often are blocked by inhibitions, shyness or suspicions carried over from youth. New crises continue to pile up: health problems, financial pressures, disillusionment and religious doubt. Often those in midlife find themselves swamped by numerous responsibilities of life with little time or energy to explore life's pleasures. Both pain and frustration accompany the struggle to live up to the expectations of those around us.

During these years even love, so difficult to approximate, becomes increasingly problematic. Ideal images of fulfillment as sexual beings, spouses and parents are confusing and remain frustratingly unrealized. Disappointed, those in midlife question love and search for a love that binds together the relationship of responsible vocation, creative affection between spouses, family and the wider community.

Is this special devotion and mutuality really working to subdue life's antagonisms? If love is a basis of ethical concern, how can love also be joint selfishness in the service of some territoriality, be it village or country? Love that was once a star may become an ominous shadow.

Nevertheless we continue to yearn to belong to a caring relationship over and above sexuality. Love elevated to a dominant virtue of the universe is particularly sought. Ours is a longing for intimacy that is rarely given or received. This haunting hope is described by Erik Erikson as the *mutuality of mates and partners in search of a shared identity* which lives on and deepens.

As the years pass, concerns spread out, as do our bodies. Goals become more inclusive and less particular, more diffuse and less clear. After age 55 the sense of the *passing of time* becomes exaggerated. Signs of aging, real or imagined, become more prevalent and thoughts of an early death begin to creep up. Long-smoldering and unattended "negative identities" surface. The sum of all those long-put-down and submerged identifications begin to emerge. An accumulation of blighted hopes over not achieving the promise of an assured wholeness may in later life explode in expressions of rage. Being denied a chance of communal integration, we may resent being made to feel like a delinquent or continue to live on old battlefields.

It was thus for Victor, a 56-year-old Vietnam veteran, still tormented with ghastly dreams. "The terrible nightmares of death in the jungles will not go away. In the war and in 25 years of remembering it, I've lost my innocence, my sense of justice and humanity and dignity without gaining anything. The wisdom and healing that age is supposed to give has never come to me. Inside the hollow husk of my being, a persistent anger smolders."

In our Location, How Forsaken Are We?

The disease of locating our self in feelings of being forsaken is contagious. Though we have the psychic strength to avoid neuroses, many suffer from a more vague, less tractable condition characterized by feelings of inner emptiness and low key uneasiness—a sort of lifelong psychic cold. To preserve our self esteem, we seek what appears to be a safer location: we may gather our reserve sense of self esteem and retire to some inaccessible place in our minds and no longer relate with others. In such times of discouragement and anxiety we may hesitate too long to ask for fellowship and rekindle our lost faith. Like Dostoevski's Ridiculous Man, we retreat from our isolation into a euphoric vision of love. But then our fantasy betrays us; the germ of isolation finds us again making our guilt and loneliness even greater than before. At this point, like Dostoevski's character, we become truly "ridiculous." Awake from the dream, we set out on a foolish course which obeys another equally imperious logic. We advocate the loving relationships we dreamed of, but we remain destroyed and abandoned. We find a way to do a new thing in our life: to speak to people instead of to our fantasies. By becoming "ridiculous," we try to become sane.

Perhaps we *are* sane when compared with Romero who introduced himself to me realistically as to his location: "Darn right, I know where I am! In hell!" At 27 years of age, square-jawed and chunky from weight-lifting while wiry from martial-arts training, he entered my jail office with ankle-shackles clacking and handcuffs clicking. "I'm down in this end-of-the-line hole," he said in broken English. "These here chains and cuffs burn more than my ankles and wrists; they tie up my guts and spirit." He paused, "Better keep your finger on that (alarm) button over 'der. 'Dey don't have me chained for nothin.' "

His warning carried authenticity as his three murder charges attest. With the blood of his father's slit throat still on his hands, he "did in" his mother the same way. Shortly afterward, he drove a dagger through a neighbor's heart.

Romero's thick case folder on my desk chronicled the chaotic and sordid life of an individual attempting to "locate" himself. Conceived in lust and disgust he was rejected even before he came into the world. His mother was a prostitute who denied him even the crumbs of affection, cursed him when he was sick and regularly slapped him around. The conniving man who sired him was a pimp and a "slave-runner" supplying young Mexican servant girls for wealthy Anglo families. He despised Romero and consistently abused him. His maternal grandmother occasionally took him in and fed him. Abandoned, with no semblance of nurturing from family or friends, he fended for himself in the back alleys and street corners of the ghetto. With no one responsible for him, he learned no social responsibility.

Schooling was spotty as Romero played hide-and-seek with police and truant officers. At twelve he joined a gang and started using drugs. Quickly he became a pusher and before long participated in knifing rivals. On his 14th birthday the authorities arrested him for assault with a deadly weapon and sent him to juvenile hall for nine months. Since then he has been in and out of prisons.

At a cost of further warping his self, he survived the forces that could have wiped him out by doing violent and crazy things. He fought all authority, especially those who held the power of life and death over him. Fired by deepening distrust, he retaliated with destructive acts that steadily became more vicious and uncontrollable. It was as if society shackled him with hate, anger and the "profound alienation" that Erich Neumann, Erich Fromm and a host of other social scientists have documented. Small wonder Romero's mental status report reads: "Orientation to place and time intact, but orientation to people and self radically disordered; recurrently manifests hallucinations with grandiose content, persecutory delusions, recurrent ideas of reference and other bizarre ideations; he exhibits severe negative emotions, particularly anger that erupts uncontrollably and explodes in violence; no family or significant peer relations."

And what is Romero's location now? He shouts his name trying to become somebody in the real world. When he walks down the gauntlet of the aisle through the tiers of fellow inmates, he holds his head high. He is aware of the special status a triple murderer has. He is shackled and handcuffed and escorted with a guard on each side and one behind him with a cocked gun. "I'm in the bottom of hell! So what!" The isolation of solitary confinement gouges more deeply at his violent rage and rots his heart. He savors dreams in which, with satanic egoism, he relives seeing his parents' blood spurt as he slits their throats.

His is the story of Narcissus in reverse. In refusing to love anyone but himself, Narcissus loved himself to death. Romero cultivates the death his consuming hate promises. He says, "The torture of this hell is killing me, so I have a no-fail plan. At the court sentencing, I'll charge a marshal and in a flash one of the others will finish me off with his .38."

Was Romero doomed forever, unable to form normal relationships because his chromosomes were disordered or was he afflicted by some malevolent psychological virus? Is he the product of estrangement from those who should have loved and cared for him? Is his the lot of children who are never shown values or positive emotionality? In Romero's situation we see a tragic example of how society cripples people instead of nurturing them.

In the 19th century, the French writer Alexis de Tocqueville observed a paradox about the burgeoning American democracy: the country whose goal was to create a noble balance between an individual's freedom and social responsibility also tended to enclose its citizens in an isolation that had devastating psychological consequences. This tragic and corrupting process was described by Karl Marx as the kind of profound social "wound" referred to by Johann Schiller (and Thomas Carlyle after him).

Romero's story gives some inkling of the impoverishing effects of the political and economic institutions and the dehumanizing pressure of misery and insecurity. He exemplifies the psychological wounds that can be inflicted by impersonal authority and the difficulty in modern society of forming intimate and genuine relationships. Romero's way of "locating himself" brings up frightening omens. In closed rooms without alarm buttons, people like him arouse a formless terror. We shrink before such manifestations of evil at work. Our deepest feelings confirm the poet Dryden's lines, "Our malevolent stars have struggled hard; / And held us long asunder."

Clutching all that is "healthy" within us, we withdraw from Romero's abyss. But the wolves of his hellish tumult and violence tear at our comfortable complacencies. While we may not have fallen into such an underworld, we keep it flourishing by our contributions and our neglect. We are not mad, yet we live in the shadows of madness and it reminds us of the precarious location of our selves. Who among us is totally sure of their orientation to people and self? Who among us is confident of contributing sufficient love in relationships?

In the knowledge that such a pressure-cooker of negative feelings exist, we begin to understand the meaning of what the Bible describes as people possessed by "evil spirits." Romero reminds us of characters like the unrepentant thief on the cross beside Jesus. His life exposes a frightening new darkness in the human soul and causes us to question whether good can triumph over evil.

Occasionally demonic spirits do "possess" people. Though we live in a practical and pragmatic age, our hesitancy to consider satanic forces must give way to acknowledging the evil we see, hear and sense. Whether we believe in a personal devil or not, certain irrefutable evidence points to the work of a satanic force. Inordinately strong demonic powers enter and take over persons, wrecking their lives. In ancient Israel such deranged people were considered unsavable and were chained and isolated in grave yards.

Locating Personality: Clarifying and Unifying the Self

Threatening personal and social cataclysms do not only come from deranged people or criminal networks. To achieve a wholesome society it is not enough to scapegoat only the psychotics, organized crime or nefarious individuals.

We must try to avoid detachment and dehumanization and reach beyond the stereotypes. To locate the self we must also deal with the ambiguities within our own personalities. Taking a look at America's other *bêtes noires* we see the reign of "corporate martial law," the ruling principle of greed operating on Wall Street, Black poverty and disintegration in the ghettos, white destitution in Appalachia and a growing dependence on illegal drugs. Everywhere our inner confusions beg for clarification.

The so-called "Gerasene demoniac," who lived among the tombs when brought to Jesus identified his own derangement: "My name is Legion, for we are many."(Mk 5:9) His was a shredded self seeking unity and wholeness. He was saying: There are many persons in me pulling in opposite directions. There are many clamorous voices in the town meeting of my mind, with no gavel to bring them to order. The Gerasene's life was chaotic, torn not so much by physical disease as with emotional disintegration and his life was an anarchy.

A persisting metaphor is the biblical description of the consequences of this terrible fragmentation of the self which provides an arresting picture of humanity like lemmings, or as in the biblical account—demented swine—charging off a steep cliff to destruction. This picture fits with tragic closeness to many human crises and paints a soberingly dark background to our future: in prosperity and in adversity it is the same blind rush of humanity off the steep cliff of greed and ruin. Several of the weaknesses to which the self is vulnerable are at work in this prospect: denial of the doom toward which we are pointed and lack of vision. Such a blind stampede of the unexamined and undirected self threatens all nations and all peoples.

The self manifests perplexing contrasts such as the tendency towards both euphoria and depression, acceptance and rejection. Only as such polarities are worked through can we move to locating our personality with a realistic and integrating self-image.

In seeking clarification and unity within its polarities, the self must resolve the distortions and conflicts in the way it perceives. Our self-image determines, in large part, how we feel, think and react toward ourselves and the world around us. Our self-estimation conditions the way we appraise others and the environment and establish bridges to the world outside. The relation between the self and the world remains both elemental primitive and fundamental in the formation of personality. The formidable problems involved in continually reconciling the self and the world requires an integrated and responsible self.

As the self takes in data from the world, concealment and distortion frequently occur. When our formative experiences are seen inaccurately, our lives become skewed and unbalanced. Experiences that mold us include what our senses take in as well as tensions arising out of the contrast between thinking and feeling, imagination and intuition. Distortion in interpreting these phenomena can hinder the development and functioning of the self.

Was not human life designed to have its parts with all its contrasts and ambiguities somehow fit together coherently? Fragmentation keeps us unsettled and anxious. What we call "life" is more than an isolated, pulsating biological episode. It is a holistic system with complex processes of experience and reaction to stimuli. This interplay will be disconcerting and disruptive to the self if it is fragmented or aimless. The location of self must be within the mutual influences of the processes of thinking and feeling, imagination and intuition. The responsibly located self is one that faces and works within these tensions.

If our contradictions and polarities are unattended we continue, as it were, unfinished. When we use the pronoun, "I," we derive all sorts of personal meanings, but the noun, "the world," often conjures only a vague and distant image. There may be an original harmony between world and self which is reestablished in the act of experiencing, but it is elusive and requires our conscious and continuous effort.

When we flag in this effort, we locate ourselves in a condition where we are not our true and genuine selves. To become more genuine with a better located self, we must come closer to realizing our potential. We need to become more nearly "what we really are." Becoming more fulfilled may necessitate correcting our unrealistic or overly idealized self. This entails guarding against generating expectations which life cannot fulfill. When they remain unfulfilled, the resulting despair can become devastating.

The more realistic locating of self is helped by the functioning of culture. Our language gives a shape to the otherwise amorphous communication between people. In our "civilizing" process we realize our selves only approximately; we never attain the ideal. Those who persevere in working through their "grandiose selves," deficient and insufficient as they are in their uncorrected and narcissistic condition, receive an unusual bonus. They gain refinement and emotional deepening in the reach for more genuine relatedness and acceptance as worthy parts of a community and feel within themselves life forces which empower them to explore and grow. They experience an increase of "object love" as they reach out lovingly to others.

Though it is difficult to maintain a dialectic tension within these human polarities, when they are clarified and integrated the self is strengthened to stand firm and confident. With adults, the self works through obstacles to self-growth, whereas in childhood we lacked sufficient confidence and perspective. We learn to convert our narcissism into healthful self-esteem and transmute the powers of our parents and heroes into a set of internal guiding values and goals.

By engaging in loving and concerned relationships (provided by therapy at its best and religious discipline at its fullest), we give more love toward others as well as more concern for ourselves. With a more positive self-image and more realistic guiding ideals, the self is richly enhanced and becomes capable of more empathy for others. Its capacity for initiative and creativity is increased and its sense of humor, wisdom and balance are enhanced.

The self is challenged to gain control of itself. Action becomes easier to take as we resolve our dilemmas and reach decisions. Locating the self becomes clearer, more definite and directional. Reinforcement and empowerment in regard to locating the self comes by way of faith. Humans are the only beings that can apply spiritual energy to fulfill their ends and to become what they aspire to be.

Consequences of a Narcissistic Location of Self

Viewing our selves is part of "locating" the self. But this necessary self-consideration presents problems. Since the image we see of our self often falls short of what we would like it to be, we prefer to see an imagined better picture. Confusion and insecurity over our identity and inner workings causes us to "see through a glass darkly." Modern technology helps us get a better reflection of self. Instead of being stuck to one place, with the automobile, airplane and the media, we surge to the ends of the earth. But in our fascination with extensions of ourselves, we are susceptible to becoming numbed. Preoccupation with selfish emotional indulgences typically confuses thinking and distorts efforts to situate the self more realistically.

The West has held a millennium-long fascination with the ancient Greek legend of Narcissus, who has become an intimidating paradigm of the moral life. Narcissus, when seen as one who died in the process of loving himself, is deplored for his inhuman solitude, yet admired as a figure of fulfillment and transcendence. When the introspective process suggested in the story is examined, it is disturbing to see how the youth Narcissus mistook his own reflection in the water for another person, an extension of himself. Being transfixed on his reflection in the water and adapting to his extension of himself, as Marshall McLuhan in his book *Understanding Media* points out, Narcissus became a numb, apathetic and a closed self. In binding himself to that reflection he made it into an "idol." The inevitable consequences of that idolatry, according to the Hebrew Psalmist (much like that for the Greek myth-maker), was that, "They that make them [idols] shall be like unto them; Yes, everyone that trusteth in them" (Ps 113). The implication remains strong that the *beholding* of idols conforms people to them.

In our cultural traditions we see recurring variations on this theme. Repeatedly Narcissus symbolizes our longing for inner autonomy—a sort of spiritual Robinson Crusoe. This theme is seen in the fantastic poems of Gnostic sects which competed with early Christianity or a woman gazing into a mirror representing the medieval sin of *luxuria*. In John Milton's reworking of Genesis, Adam became a kind of Narcissus, doomed because he could not live without the "other self" God had made out of Adam's very flesh. In Adam Smith's theory of self-interest, in the radical social criticism of the 19th century, the same cult of self-love surges forth—with a warning note that self-love endangers the fragile fabric of sociability.

Christopher Lasch in his best seller, *The Culture of Narcissism,* documents the ways in which self-centeredness has come to dominate the cultural life of Western societies. The success of his book offers ironic evidence of a public eager for news of itself, even in the form of a devastating critique of its shallow self-preoccupations. It also reflects a common anxiety about our future and our powerlessness to reshape it. Lasch's careful social analysis resembles a morality play. Narcissus stands for a danger that has fascinated as well as repelled us for centuries: the individuals who become so enamored of themselves that society will go untended and God go unloved—or, perhaps more secretly, that each of us will go unloved.

Narcissism is an inevitable aspect of each of our lives. Whether intense self-absorption is pathological continues to be debatable, but in varying degrees it is a universal illness. We all boast about ourselves and mischievously manipulate people who would be advantageous to our hidden agendas. Writers, teachers, psychologists and ministers use themselves to edify others. Popular novelists are skillful in building a narcissistic world of their own. In describing their feelings, thoughts and concerns, they help the rest of us transcend the continual tug of self-regard. The perceptive efforts of these muses represent moral acts, quite different from the actions of the self-exposing hucksters who infest our media world with their exaggerated and unexamined self-centeredness.

The "Narcissistic Personality Disorder" was designated by the American Psychiatric Association in its *Diagnostic and Statistical Manual III* (1980). Characteristics of such people, which are not limited to episodes of illness, but nevertheless cause either significant impairment in social or occupational functioning or subjective distress, include: 1) Grandiose sense of self-importance or uniqueness with exaggeration of achievements and talents and a focus on the special nature of one's problems. 2) Preoccupation with fantasies of unlimited success, power, brilliance, beauty or ideal love. 3) Exhibitionism where the person requires constant attention and admiration. 4) Cool indifference or marked feelings of anger, inferiority, shame, humiliation or emptiness in response to criticism, indifference of others or defeat. 5) Prevalent disturbances in interpersonal relationships, including exaggerated importance of entitlement without accepting reciprocal responsibilities, exploitativeness, over idealizing or devaluating relationships and lack of empathy and ability to recognize how others feel. Two psychologist from the University of California at Berkeley, Robert Raskin and Henry Terry, have developed (1988) a *Narcissistic Personality Inventory* which measures these characteristics and effects they create in the way people interact with each other.

When we locate our personality in compulsive self-worship and self-satiating pursuits, we find ourselves in contradictory circumstances. Though preoccupied with our own desires, we cannot do without others. We look to others to validate our self-esteem. In spite of occasional illusions of omnipotence, we lean heavily on others. The self-absorbed individual cannot live without an admiring audience. As the adage says: "We all play to an audience and cannot live without applause."

Another difficult contradiction which engulfs the narcissist is the perennial struggle between responsibility and irresponsibility. With insufficient self-monitoring, we are insufficiently responsible, aware and concerned. The preoccupation with what pleases ourself paradoxically tends to keep us from the fundamental fact that the self is the basic aspect of experience. Over-concentration on satisfying our desires seduces us into a distorted grandiosity. The narcissist's weak self-awareness and self-control tend to blur the distinction between good and evil, since these opposites are seen only as relative to the self and not as an objective or transcendent truth. Now that such a large portion of the population is without the check of firm religious principles, a massive psychological regression has taken place.

Socially, complete narcissism is disastrous. Its hedonistic characteristics express a retreat from common life to those private pleasures within the individual's reach and those that seem susceptible to self-management. The narcissist, instead of seeing many centers, concentrates on one. When individuals operate on the basis that everyone has their own choice at any time, community cohesion is impossible, for communal life requires that personal desires and aspirations give way to some degree of social needs and hopes. Lasch reminds us that a narcissistic location of the self creates a cynically materialistic culture, which in turn exerts a strongly negative effect on the self. We grow careless about our delicately balanced infrastructures—the basic services and groups needed for the functioning of a community. Taking priority in selfish pleasure, the narcissist destroys the faith so necessary for the growth and vision of the community.

The narcissist's imbalance regarding personal and social relations compounds emotional difficulties and makes them harder to manage. Within the self unacceptable urges and motives contend with more conservative feelings. Outside forces confront the self with tensions. These pressures combine to create conflicts which drive the self in opposing directions. We build, then destroy; we grow, then endanger our health; we intend and need to love, but so often we hate. Such actions and reactions put limits on our individual freedom. The narcissist has difficulty facing and coping with these basic inward and outward facts of life.

Locating the Self within Human Uniqueness

Is there a *human uniqueness* within which the self can be located? Are there distinctive human qualities that enable the self to face and cope with the inner and outer facts of life? Responsibility rests with us to work through the contradictions of the self by balancing our personal and social interests. But the individual's aspirations—worthy or unworthy, altruistic or ego-centered—are frequently compromised and defeated in a pluralistic society that must function ultimately upon consensus. What is the unique quality that enables the self to transcend this and other dilemmas?

The way we approach the meaning of being human, i.e., its "uniqueness," has much to do with whether or not we get at the substance of the self. Answers will not come by enumerating ways to sanitize and absolve our petty acts and wishes. It is not easy to see ourselves objectively. We know more about the moon or the composition of a distant star than we do about our individual and collective inner selves.

With traditional philosophy it was easier to investigate everything except the person doing the investigating. This is the same posture as the familiar cartoon of the man searching desperately for his glasses while all the time they are out of sight on his forehead. Socrates, practical thinker that he was, urged his followers to "know thyself," which could be paraphrased: find out what is uniquely human. Confucius, about the same century, told his disciples: "What the

Superior Person (*chun tze*) seeks is within," or the Superior Person is the uniquely human individual.

Information about what is human comes both from observing individuals in specific situations and from considering philosophic and historical experiences about the self. Modern scholars in the fields of psychology, anthropology and sociology research extensively what is considered exceptional in people. Human beings, the psychologist hold, are known in their thinking, feeling, acting, creating, risk-taking and praying. Sociologists study dimensions of humans considered gifted by observing how people group themselves in families, churches, unions, schools, communities and states. We have been sliced open as individuals and groups by the probing eyes of specialists.

The combined, rapidly escalating findings present an overwhelming accumulation of facts about exceptional human qualities. We have trouble integrating and ordering massive data bases of new information. We also are learning how much more there is to know. Today in confronting more complicated personal and social enigmas than ever, we have had to develop a wide spectrum of new adaptations to comprehend and hopefully solve the problems they present. In going deeper into our selves and penetrating farther into the cosmos, the dilemmas associated with the self seem to increase. In asking why the new knowledge does not give us more security and fulfillment, we turn to philosophers and theologians, only to have them remind us that becoming more uniquely human involves living out our ideals. This brings us another enormous question: What is moral and purposeful behavior?

Paradoxically, helpful as recent empirical approaches to the self may seem, available studies in some ways have contributed to the erosion of the models of the self held a century or even several decades before. Efforts to pinpoint what is distinctly human are made more difficult by the rapid and radical changes that have swept over all nations in the last 150 years. Added to the Copernican, Darwinian and

Freudian revolutions, we have those associated with Marx, Keynes, Einstein, Mao and a host of others whose innovations added enormously to our intellectual growth, the advancement of empirical science and expanded the possibilities of economic and social life.

With the acceptance of each new scientific hypothesis, however, a reduction has occurred in our sense of a secure and stable place in the hierarchy of the universe. Human beings seem demoted, with the essential confidence in the average person's identity shrinking day by day. The more we learned about ourselves, the less we thought of ourselves. Having been dethroned, we have had to make our own place, create our own meaning, establish our own new values—artistically, sexually, socially, politically and philosophically. Experimentation, innovation, novelty and subjectivity became the rallying cries in the search for self-understanding and direction—guides to locating the self.

Many expressions of human beings evidence the uniqueness of the self. Our capacity in performing creative tasks is often singled out. More than skill in purely practical functions, human uniqueness is found in the special ways we understand, think, feel, intuit and experience inspiration and revelation. Also, they show uniqueness in the many varieties and qualities of their responses, not the least of which is their power to draw nature into history and refashion it. Human beings have the capacity to focus their lives on specific goals. They are able to fulfill the purpose of being-in-the-world and manifest intellectual, aesthetic and moral qualities. This is in line with the early Greek philosophers, who held that human uniqueness was evidenced in a person's capacity to think of and show the ideals of truth, goodness and beauty. Also human uniqueness is seen in a person's centering on "the Good" as a goal and cultivating the self's conscience as the watchdog of moral character. At this deeper level, a particular uniqueness is located in the self's insistent search for priorities and appropriate ways to accomplish them. These and other such capacities give human beings uniqueness because of their intrinsic value.

A special feature of human uniqueness occurs in its self-consciousness. The self is aware of its substance and its existence. To have substance and existence is *to be.* To recognize this is to participate in the process of *self-transcendence.* With this capacity for self observation, the self can see its weaknesses and impaired states. At the same time it can recognize and mobilize itself as a flexible and powerful regulator and agent for change. New forms are created out of the self's existing polarities. "To be," and to be aware of it, to sense existence, provides the self with freedom to respond. The self no longer merely imagines or hopes for a freedom to respond, that freedom exists and the self exercises it as value and purpose. A self conservation becomes possible; a unity is achieved between identity and difference, rest and movement, and conservation and change. The self's freedom to respond, however, must fulfill the outside world's demand that its events, powers and changes be appraised accurately. Since human freedom lies within the bounds of existence, people must be faithful to the conditions within their particular place and time. The realization of human uniqueness require that our responses are validated by the checks and observations we make in our mutual exchanges with people.

To be and be free to respond also means to be able to co-create a life-world and a self-in-the-world. This aspect of human uniqueness is the significant process of *becoming.* Human beings have the priceless capacity to become supremely alive in creative moments, achieve new awareness and see possibilities for new relationships. Deeply embedded in the self, an elemental urge presses to realize the promise of such moments and to make its potentiality actual. It is as if the self remains poised, ready to risk investing the energies of its freedom to respond to take the next step toward fuller maturity. The self, as an originating center, sees, thinks, feels and intuits the outside world, then formulates meanings and uses the freedom to respond to invent new possibilities. This response of *becoming*, disciplining our selves to create new forms of living, is radically different from the self-indulgence of narcissism. It is the self recognizing its unique value, its freedom to respond and its particular responsibility to others and to our Creator.

Three differing concepts about "becoming," or the process of self transforming, are suggested by Herbert Fingarette: 1) the notion of *self-discovery*, pioneered by Freud; 2) the notion of *self-creation*, espoused by the existentialists and 3) the notion of *self-realization*, put forth long ago by Aristotle and Confucius. These contrasting maps showing the way towards becoming more fully human provide a general consensus. The first step in the journey is *to decide* on and be open to the venture. Second, *hindering blockages* and conflicts must be faced and resolved as much as possible. Third, recognition of *the differing ways people mature* must take place. Steps include self-action, the self responding under its own power; interaction, where the self is balanced against others; and transaction, where descriptive systems are used to code communication and behavior. Fourth, the *enhancement of the self's value, meaning and loving*—which in friendship is expressed in concern for the self's uniqueness and in therapy by the therapist's modeling of the *concern* to enhance the patient's awareness and courage to change.

Given that human beings have a wide variety of uniqueness and are challenged to mobilize their freedom to "become" and grow into fuller selves, what then are the self's responsibilities?

The Self in Search of its Responsibilities

Eleanor, a 27 year-old engineer in an electronics corporation, told of a growing awareness that gathered many of the loose strands of her life into a new realization of who she is and where she is going. Elatedly she said, "After a two-year struggle, I'm on a new way. It's clear to me that I am ultimately responsible for my life and I must keep working to open my life to a Higher Self. And," she added, "this reality is not ethereal but is very practical and immediate." These were surprising words for a sophisticated, rational and strictly three-dimensional systems designer.

Explaining the quantum leap in self-understanding she had taken beyond rational deduction, she told of her recent odyssey. At a crossroads time in her life, she found the important strands in her life tangled. She began reneging on responsibilities which had become worrisome and meaningless. Distressed and confused, she found it difficult to take an honest look at herself. Friends were of little help because some thought she was "pretty well put together," while others were critical of her taking on more responsibilities than seemed rational. So she sought a counselor who could help her assess her strengths and weaknesses, motivations and resistances.

The insightful and mature person she found encouraged self-responsibility and choice. She was trying to live with the pain of a physical disability and trying to free herself of her dependency on parents who held high expectations for her. Then came the disappointing ending of her relationship with the promising young lawyer she was dating, demands of her program at graduate school, heavier assignments in her recent promotion at work and having to turn around feeling burdened by the adulation of the enthusiastic youngsters on the baseball team she coaches. She described the integrating insights breaking through from her two-year exploration of self with her supportive "guide."

Eleanor's awareness that was bringing her life to a sharpened focus had not come through teachings nor through logic. Her insight, she said, "Was something I 'saw' with an inner knowing. . . . It exacted a price: some tears, new loads to carry, new doors to enter and new responsibilities. These added responsibilities bring more stress, but it's a positive, almost ecstatic stress, because I also see the awesomeness of having the power to choose my life." Her reality testing, in her guided self exploration sessions, helped her take stock of assets and liabilities and clarify priorities.

"In monitoring where I am and where my energy is going, I see fears, doubts and resistances are blocking me. As I invite the will to come in, I'm getting help in developing skills I need for my new responsibilities." In the new position to which Eleanor was recently promoted, her new and more balanced self-confidence enabled her to help humanize the cerebral and often unempathetic supervisor. Together, she and her co-workers were now developing their work unit into a more efficient and egalitarian team. She explains, "I'm paying attention to my innovative and intuitive feminine self. Before when I asked a question, I had to get a rational and immediate answer; now I'm getting better at listening and drawing out the opinion of others. I'm seeing people less as competitors and predators and more as cooperators. I'm concentrating less on obstacles and more on growth. As the game plan for my life becomes clearer, I want to practice 'the Twelfth Step,' that is, give back some of what I've gained."

Each of us in locating our self begins to realize more of our potentials and gains courage to risk opening new doors. In the process we meet new responsibilities and discover we have unexpected strengths and skills to handle them. The manner of our deepening realization of the need to take charge of life may be quite different from Eleanor's. Frequently it is not the neglect of our obligations, but our fear of them which hampers us. It is chastening to realize that we are the only beings who are free to deliberate, decide and take on responsibility. The remarkable reaches of intelligence, intuition, imagination, creativity and the other unique capacities of humans entail also the responsibilities each demands. The irresponsible are vulnerable to sinking into "unbelief" or "un-faith"—the response in which selves turn away from God. If, with pseudo self-realization, we turn inward against ourselves, we lose our essential unity with the ground of their being and their world. In retreating into

244

ourselves and away from freedom and destiny, we deny our emotions, our will and our God. On the other hand, once we get a glimpse of the vastness of our human potential and accept the awesome responsibility which accompanies those possibilities, we are on the way to realizing a fuller and more effective self.

To locate the self is to find the area and scope of one's responsibility, taking seriously the "ecology" of the self—taking stock of and being responsible in the interdependent relationships with the physical environment—being involved with land and sea, trees and forests, flowing rivers and parched deserts and all the other systems of nature while remaining accountable in the mutualities of our social systems. This dovetailing of function (the *how*) and place (the *where*) recognizes that every situation in which the self is located remains permeable to and dependent upon both its social and cosmic relationships.

Our anatomical endowments provide the beginnings of an interpretation of these responsibilities. The central nervous system is divided into two sets of fibers and associated centers. This division separates sensory and motor activities and also accounts for the division of behavior into *acts* precipitated by a stimulus and *interior* impulses motivated by more gradual situational changes. Differing stimuli summon differing responsibilities. Every stimulus creates a small change in the self and calls for new responses under that changed situation. Within that sequence, which B.F. Skinner calls the "reflex process," obligation is derived from behavior inspired by positive reinforcers and turned away from negative reinforcers. When it rewards us with power and prestige, we welcome responsibility; when it burdens us we deny and avoid it. The same stimuli can have different meanings. An electrical shock, for example, when received while repairing an fixture will be experienced differently than that given as a trick in an amusement park or when administered as part of torture. The interplay of reinforcers, impulse stimuli and habit patterns in a single dynamic behavior system calling for our freedom to respond is the arena of responsibility where our acts, simple or complex, personal or social, are weighed in the balance of whether or not they contradict our essential nature and the goals and faith by which we live.

The continuous growth of our personality emerges as a crucial responsibility in locating the self. The "individual self," wrote Roberto Assagioli, "is not fixed and immutable, but is in a continual state of *becoming*." Working to locate our self, engaging in the ongoing process of integrating all our aspects and energies into a harmonious whole like most 'natural' processes can be enhanced by responsible awareness, understanding and specific techniques. Responsibility grows as the exercise of our freedom to respond is extended. Growth in responsibility is enhanced as we harness impulses, strengthen our self and direct and regulate our "becoming" to enrich our relations with family, friends and community. Likewise, with the scope of responsibility expanded, the self moves into a larger perspective.

Responsibility arises out of an intentional self that is focused on moving toward our goals. In the process of finding our responsibilities we work to correct our self's negative tendencies by harmonizing the conflicts within our inner forces. Taking responsibility for the self involves engaging in the process of putting impulses in the service of the *will*. When we express responsibility as will, we begin to discover our real selves. Rollo May describes what happens, " 'I conceive–I can–I will–I am.' The 'I can' and 'I will' are the essential experiences of identity."

The process of self-realization is ongoing, whether we are working at it on our own or with a guiding counselor. When we move beyond mere existence and become involved, through a deliberate choice and act, we are morally responsible. It is a process in which the individual is consciously and constantly engaged. Responsibility begins in awareness of our self and our accurate perception of our surroundings. It continues as a progression in which thoughts, wishes, hopes and prayers become actual.

This progression of responsibility accompanying the expansion of self-awareness was seen in Eleanor. She took a quantum leap in self-understanding when she realized her ultimate responsibility for herself. Recognizing responsibility for the self, however, does not fit usual paradigms, so we repeatedly resist entering situations and relationships that promise transforming experiences. Clinging to old habits and securities, we seek to avoid responsibility and try desperately to "stay in control," keeping the old balances and behavior patterns intact. We can, however, work *with* these resistances, treating them with respect. As we take increasing responsibility for locating ourselves and our life direction, blocks often can be transformed into constructive energies. With discipline we can develop qualities and patterns needed for continued growth and identify with the personal self, letting go of our over identifications with externals and our fractured self.

Within the self the seat of freedom and responsibility—the unconscious—exerts a determining power in our conscious responses. Often one's decision, plan of action, manner of accountability and the other steps of responsible responding are rehearsed in the recesses of the self. When we become aware of the inappropriateness of our words or deeds and feel remorse, we realize subliminal forces at work. Responsible decisions and acts issue less from isolated impulses and more from the combination of the self's inner (unconscious or "subliminal") motives, energies and faith. Responsible responses are called for during special experiences, either negative (suffering, loneliness, despair and meaninglessness) or positive (health, fellowship, creativity and inspiration). Purposeful persons show responsibility in anticipating the effects of actions and correcting present behavior in accordance with such foresight. Healthy persons are aware that when responsibility is disregarded, external surroundings become unreal, relationships become meaningless and internal dysfunction and disintegration threatens the self.

A *plan* for carrying out the choice must be developed to balance the individual's needs, resources and good will. Also the impact of the plan on family, friends and community must be considered. Inner conflicts are confronted and alternatives are sought through imagery, inner dialogue and other such approaches. Journal keeping—recording one's personal journey by regularly writing down thoughts and inner searching—is a fruitful way to cultivate ongoing growth in responsibility. Such catharsis helps to clear out the debris of hurts and angers. In still another approach, the individual can *implement* the choices made and *evaluate* the need for change. New choices should be noted and carried out.

Gathering up and focusing the self's needs and potentials and applying them responsibly to the givens of the world around us requires a overall strategy. That comprehensive assignment entails positioning our self to evoke and develop the *Will* in relation to life issues. The training of the complete will in all its phases and positive aspects becomes one of the essential and lifelong tasks of locating the responsible self. Training the will increases the individual's "capital" or the active quota of the person's total resources.

Roberto Assagioli, in a method he calls psychosynthesis, proposes five stages to cultivate and discipline the will: 1) clarification and unification of purpose, 2) deliberate choosing and deciding, 3) effective and faithful affirmation, 4) planning and organizing of activity and 5) execution of the total act of the will.

The first stage, gaining a "one-pointedness" and rallying the self's powers, is preceded by exploration and integration of the unconscious. The will then presses for a singleness of aim, a sharpening of intention, a gathering of motives and a checking by means of valuation and deliberation. It is a sequence: having decided on purpose, there follows the intention to attain it and the evocation of motivation to empower it. These stages are monitored by valuation, which implies a scale of values which express our philosophy of life and the world. To keep our inner and outer worlds in equilibrium, we need a universal standard of responsibility which acknowledges the responsibility of each individual for the potentialities of all generations and of all generations for each individual. Deliberation, or consideration of the various conditions and circumstance, must take place. Then comes an evaluation or weighing: our acts, simple or complex, personal or social, are weighed in the balance of whether they contradict our essential nature and the goals and faith by which we live.

The four stages that follow take the self's will through a series of practical applications. The *choosing* does not come easily, because decision is an act of freedom which inevitably involves responsibility. The next stage, *affirmation,* involves a living dynamic faith with an assured conviction that empowers the self to take risks in a spirit of courageous adventure. The stage of *planning* calls for the self to organize its activities to move through the steps between the starting point and the ultimate goal or realization of the purpose. A *plan* for carrying out personal choices needs to be developed, balancing the individual's needs and resources. The impact of the plan on family, friends and community needs to be weighed. The next phase, *execution,* pulls together choosing, affirming and planning and works to achieve an equilibrium between them. Two outstanding qualities of the whole will are demanded: first, the dynamic power of a one-pointed, driving energy; second, persistence.

Simultaneously, the self must reach beyond its personal will which is susceptible to exploitation by its own prevalent drives. We move to come under the influence of the *spiritual will* connected with the realization of the spiritual Self. Uniting intention, purpose and loving will, the self takes responsibility for fulfilling its destiny. Our destiny incorporates the communities to which we belong, the remembered and forgotten past, the environment which has shaped us and the world's impact on us. Destiny is not a strange power which determines what will happen to us. It is ourselves as given, formed by nature and history, by our deliberation and decision. Our destiny is the basis of our freedom. Being free to respond assumes acts in which our inner drives and outer influences are brought into the centered unity of our decisions.

The self, having freedom, has a responsibility which is destiny. We all, says Paul Tillich, are responsible for what has happened through the center of our self—the seat and organ of freedom. God, who *is* freedom, incorporates responsibility and destiny. To link destiny with religious beliefs and strivings goes beyond the concept of an inevitable fate to which a person or community is chained. This linkage points to another unique quality of the self—its continual striving to push back the boundaries set by physical, social, cultural and philosophical surroundings.

The self seeks to break out of today's narrow fate into the wider destiny of a more fulfilling tomorrow. One step in doing this is manifest in the self's effort to climb to a higher vantage point—the better to see the self's place in the community and into its own deeper strivings. An inner alignment and attunement to the Higher Self allows self-guidance to come from our highest wisdom and to be in harmony with planetary needs. Grounding this alignment in a sense of personal purpose and in appropriate choices and goals contributes to the tangible expression of Self-realization in daily life. We begin with ourselves, then share with our families, colleagues and friends. Energized and guided by the collective Higher Self, the transformation spreads from our ourselves to these others. As we attempt to give more unified direction to the self's future course, certain basic virtues emerge for the self to incorporate. Orchestrated within freedom and expressed in our choosing and responding, responsibility moves as a melody toward a certain completion.

Searching For The Self's Priorities and Responsibilities

O Self, Where are you? The answers are found within the riches of our many traditions—literary, philosophical, social and religious. They all give high public significance to our most private range of emotions and experiences. Paradoxically, as we learn what these traditions value, it appears that our energies of self-preoccupation are turned against authority and orthodoxy. Also we find that the accumulation of answers to questions about the responding personality greatly expands our range of knowledge about the self.

For Western and Oriental cultures alike, the systematic and philosophic exploration of the nature and location of the self began with the breakdown of a way of life in ancient Greece/Israel and China. In those tumultuous times of crisis for Plato and Aristotle, for the Hebrew prophets and for Confucius and Lao Tze, the key questions posed were: "Where is the self?" and "What should the self *do* and *be?*" The Greeks great discovery of the "awareness of strong personality" appears to have grown out of a combination of sociological circumstances in the *polis,* or city-state. Imbedded in the Greek language we see an individualistic emphasis. The word for "everyone," *hekastos,* is derived from *hekas,* meaning "far-off." Some 700 years later, in Gnostic and other Christian ascetic groups, with the alienation from worldly experience and their extreme reliance on spiritual experience, we find a clear break with the Hellenistic past—thus the roots of the current explosive reaction of an exaggerated emphasis on the self predates Rousseau and the Renaissance. The hero, the saint, the lover, stand out among the images of these cultures, reflecting important strands in each. The deep concern remains—an absolute requirement of self-perfection and a refusal to acknowledge the crippling barriers of "this world." Along with the assertion of the freedom of the self, we find the sharpened awareness of the responsibility of the self.

Particularly in modern Western societies, we are heavily invested in a perennial search for the self's uniqueness and the self's essential priorities and responsibilities. The self-cultivated and aggressively articulate private individual is placed at the center of the public stage where their very presence becomes a political act of resistance, locating the self beyond being swallowed up by society. Within its ecological matrix, the self is vulnerable to misplacing its identity and its authentication. Stranded midway between unpromising forms of the social bond and the icy strictures of an aloneness drained of cultural drama, the self runs the risk of being trivialized and becoming a specialized automaton.

The fullest knowledge and sharpest intuitions about the self's responses may not lead us to a fulfilling life. It is more important that the self, having freedom, can apply this knowledge, feeling and intuition to grasp the experience of the self whose very life comes from the depth of the struggle for self-clarity. The exclusively rational approach does not reach all the remarkable manifestations of the self. We cannot be completely objective or accurate in defining ourselves. We see this in the extent to which people of our generation are absorbed with themselves and permit that absorption to filter the accumulated mass of information about the self. How the narcissist can lack objectivity has been pointed out, for as Christopher Lasch's composite portrait indicates such are "facile at managing the impressions given to others, ravenous for admiration but contemptuous of those manipulated into providing it; unappeasably hungry for emotional experiences with which to fill an inner void; terrified of aging and death."

Once we recognize that the self is greater than any of our bundles of data, we can arrive at several responses to the question: O Self, Where are you? The self derives its sense of wholeness, relatedness and direction from an awareness of the mystery of the meaning of life and destiny. This deeper awareness sharpens the self's moral imperatives and the urgency of its responsibilities. Being free to respond, the self still holds in trust a particular environment, an ecology of its own. The *self* is none other than the story of the individual's life. We have a plot, conflict, a subplot, a beginning, middle and end. Like the traditional novel, the self is a "mirror" and a vehicle rolling down the road of life, reporting reality. The concept of global response and global responsibility gives the self new relevance in the pursuit of ethical and spiritual awareness. The different purposes, decisions, affirmations and life plans of the 27 year-olds described, Romero and Eleanor, sharply etch two contrasting "locations" of the self.

Romero remains the socially disabled and subversive egotist, responding to authority by disqualifying it, drawing from his own hell a still deeper one. As he limits his responsiveness to life by concentrating on hate and anger, he holds precariously to a gossamer thread of self-love. We recognize decisive similarities and differences between the hero and the maniac, the productive citizen and the imprisoned murderer who before his solitude is executed in physical death, sends back a signal across the ocean of his tragic history. Are there inextinguishable flickers of Romero's self that hopefully can pull him back from the brink of his dark abyss?

Eleanor's circumference of life possibilities and qualities, in glorious contrast, appear almost unlimited. Her taking responsibility for self focuses her choice and her will in ways that will accept and develop her unexpressed potential, individually and in her varied relationships. She has disciplined herself to transform patterns of fear and doubt, dependence and insecurity, which held her back from being all she could be for herself and for her world. The constructive steps of "locating" her self, beginning within her heart and mind, spreads inevitably into her family, work and community. These transformations are guided by a Higher Self.

The story of the self is the ever-renewed attempt of cultures to socialize it. We both seek to locate our self and assure it a degree of independence and privacy. It is the story of reversals, of an irrepressible cultural dialectic: exposing the sin of privacy, but out of the struggle creating our most powerful cultural values. We find ourselves today caught in a moral dilemma: uncomfortable with the conformities of patriotism, national honor, and authoritarian religion, yet wary of the old poetry and drama of alienation and its overtones of self-punishment and isolation.

Summary

O Self, Where are you? Where do we stand?

One answer comes from Erik Erikson who says that in our "historical moment," for the first time one human species can be envisaged with one common technology on one globe and some surrounding "outer space." He suggests that the nature of history is about to change. It cannot continue to be the record of high accomplishments in dominant civilizations and of their disappearance and replacement. Joint survival demands that the race visualize new ethical alternatives fit for newly developing, as well as over-developed, systems and identities. A more universal standard of perfection will mediate more realistically between the human's inner and outer worlds than did the compromises resulting from the reign of moral absolutes; it will acknowledge the responsibility of each individual for the potentialities of all generations and of all generations for each individual—in a more informed manner than has been possible in past systems of ethics.

Our selves are strengthened as mutual guarantees are given and received by all whose life-cycles intertwine. Much is learned from the life histories of great leaders who emerged from historical moments and from the life histories of those who decided to follow them. We are challenged by others who are awakening to a need for inner and political liberation and we are concerned throughout with our own life histories, defined by our own past, by the history of our field and by the tasks of the times. Whatever opportunity we may have to transcend the limitations of the self seems to depend on our prior ability, in our one and only life cycle, to be fully engaged in the sequence of generations. Thus the study of those miracles of everyday life, which we have attempted to describe as the emergence of basic values, seems indispensable to an appraisal of the process and strength of the self's participation in the environment and community and must have a place of priority in helping us locate our self more in line with the Higher Self.

Constructive and vital religious experience serves to sharpen the self's awareness of both its freedom and responsibility. Positive spiritual experiences anchor the self and keep the split between body and mind from becoming progressively deeper. The awareness of transpersonal powers strengthens the self's sense of dignity and worth. We need this, for most of us fail some of the time in our life-strategy, experiencing anxiety, depression and guilt. Often we sense danger lying close to the surface of our lives. Sound and committed religious experience affirms timeless values and binds us to a caring community. In order to gain the self, you must lose it.

Christians hold to the conviction that there is a difference between regarding the self as a theater of redemption and regarding the recovery of the self as the substance of redemption. The responding self is responsible to develop and apply its personal endowments, but we must honor the ecology of the self. With our unique gifts we must keep in touch with society, the world and with the awesome ultimate mystery we call God, which is both beyond all things and within each individual. At length we find—in the words of the *Recessional*—that the only thing to save us is a "humble and a contrite heart." The alternative stands that we may then attain to the great hope expressed by St. Paul to "put off the old self with his deeds," and "put on the new self, which is renewed in knowledge after the image of the Creator" (Col 3:10). Then we can affirm positively and celebrate where we are in relation to God.

C H A P T E R

Community and Responsibility

A 90-year-old woman who lives alone told her minister, "Every once in a while I have to get out to the market. On the street and in the store I visit with neighbors. My old body needs food and my inner self needs attention, but I also need to rejoin the human race every so often." We all need regularly to get to the market place, visit with neighbors and rejoin the human race. Wanting to be with others is fundamental to wholeness. There may be a few Robinson Crusoes left, but in our societies they are anomalies. To use a Tough-Love phrase, "Only nuts stay in shells."

Granted, individualism has its place. Americans especially cherish the image of independent citizens who courageously proclaim and work for their convictions. People readily agree that individuals' freedom deserves protection from monolithic proposals that would mass produce identical citizens. Americans talk often of "doing their own thing," "finding themselves," and having a home of their own. Also, they recognize the need to defend a degree of privacy for themselves in which to live meaningfully, as individualists like Virginia Woolf insist.

Nevertheless, in spite of the fact that individualism remains a crucial element in the national mosaic, the reality is that a major part of our activity goes on in relationships, associations and communities ordered by institutional structures and interpreted by cultural patterns of meaning.

Families, neighbors, states and nations surround us with interacting networks that call for our response and in turn give us sustenance and encouragement. Without these associations people become "isolated, single-channeled beings." Most significant events in our lives, small or large, involve the give-and-take encounters with other people. The cry of an infant just born, the wonder of discovery when two young people face one another at the first dawn of love, or the stark reality of death shattering a close companionship—all stir powerful emotions which are validated and kept in balance when others participate with us and share their sensitivities about such experiences.

Individualism, as the social scientists remind us, rests on the insufficient assumption that people are entirely self-contained entities. Extreme individualism undermines social supports and threatens free institutions. It is true, as Paul Tillich observed, "There is no self-transcendence of life except through the polar interdependence of individuals participating in community."

The essential dimensions of our human relatedness are not easily described. We talk of participating and belonging with people. Used in this way, *with* suggests the social essence of being human. The well-worn expression, *togetherness,* stresses other qualities of human interaction and the clumsy Old English word, *mundanity,* gets across the importance of our belonging to a social world.

The Special Connectedness of Community

When the *we* and the *I* interact, *connectedness* is created and when *I* and *you* become involved with each other community is created. The special connectedness of *community* affords fellow humans a genuine relatedness—hopefully one without superficiality or distortion or animosity. Whatever term we use to refer to it, we human beings have an essential communal characteristic to which we must respond. When two or more people participate and keep in touch *with* one other, they affirm their relatedness and open themselves to generate and share unique mutual experiences.

We express our connectedness in paradoxical ways. Our association can be creative and regenerative, also perverse and tending toward exclusiveness or explosiveness. Cooperative projects of citizens produce remarkable achievements in technology, the arts, social sciences and religious explorations. In contrast, subverted community endeavors intensify cutthroat competition which can accelerate into global explosions of world wars. We often feel unable either to understand or deal responsively with our immediate social relations. Uncertain about our connectedness, we find ourselves venting hostility on groups and individuals that are not responsible for our threatened feelings.

In our age of cultural crisis, beset with a pervasive anxiety and sense of alienation, our essential connectedness is fraught with many obstacles. The connectedness of all people, in a world that has become a global village, emerges increasingly as an urgent necessity. Hastened by the communications revolution and our increasing economic interdependence, each member must relate in new ways. In the United States, with the fraying of the political establishment in the 1970s and 1980s, we confront new and more complex questions about our connectedness: Where will a new consensus and the enduring elites emerge to provide cohesive leadership for the future? What social forces will they represent?

The new world we face is a disturbing one. Values and cultures other than our own demand a place in our consciousness. Can we contain that turbulent competition between cultures which ignites development on a global scale, or will the dynamic force of unbridled individualistic competition overwhelm and destroy us? Plurality is the defining feature of the new civilization forming at the end of the 20th century, yet at the threshold of a bright new age we cling to archaic assumptions of chauvinistic nationalism and squander our resources on armaments designed to annihilate other nations. With failed imagination we sabotage and fragment the connectedness we were formed to use creatively and enjoy.

Is this fractured state of our connectedness the new human condition, or is it an interval of redefinition before a higher ethos emerges that both tolerates and integrates plural cultures? Such critical questions, at once philosophical and practical, call for a new wholistic approach. Reconciliation between past social approaches and perceptions and the demands presented by the near future has become urgent. Commitment to develop new connectedness is needed for communities surfeited with information-age technologies which unrelentingly transmit new realities into our cultural space.

Inescapable Social Dimension of Personality

Try as we may to "go it alone," our need to belong and interact with others is never easy to set aside. Even to be alone is to be among those who are of the community of loneliness! We cannot run away far or for long from our ingrained need for community. A semi-retired engineer returning to California, after an attempted escape to a cabin in a remote wild-life reserve in Oregon commented, "There's little chance to be a complete hermit. I moved to get away from crowds and polluted air. All I did was exchange life in a large community for life in a smaller community." He added, "Each of us has to face living in a community, either in cities or in remote areas. Whether 'spaced-in' or 'spaced-out,' much of life's joyous qualities depend on how we respond living with others."

Our need for other people is so great that deprived of them our brain makes images to try to satisfy our yearning. In experiments where talking with and listening to others is cut off, the subjects tend to hallucinate and see or hear imaginary people. If we allow our world to become a vacuum devoid of other people we court emotional illness. Closed persons, who reveal only a small part of themselves, are susceptible to fragmentation and isolation. They are like the lonely husband-father who described his feelings as being "in a plexiglass hemisphere, unable to get myself or my messages through to my wife and children." Emotional health is experienced not only by how we feel about ourselves, but also how effectively and harmoniously we respond to others. Single-channel loners easily become inflexible and tend to feel threatened when faced with demanding social situations.

Sociologist R.M. MacIver of Columbia University suggests there is no community without members having shared interests "wide enough to include their lives." Community is a generic experience, pointing less to the boundaries and sizes of combinations of persons and more to the qualities and goals of their interaction. Within the social forms supplied by tradition and necessity, community provides the large and small arena in which humans live in close proximity, respond to one another and develop some sort of social organization. People involved with others are more able to cope with daily living. Unless those they are dealing with make it more difficult for them to cope, they can seek out others to help them.

Living in the confining straitjacket of social character is not without its benefits. Social structure, like character structure, serves both to limit and channel action of individuals. The social structure protects the individual from excesses and also helps by foreclosing some of the otherwise limitless behavior choices. Choosing social character permits one to live in some sort of working structure. People tend to accept the harness of their culture. It is hard to conceive of another make of harness because they are unaware of constraints.

Their "stories" that emerge in their dreams show how their relatedness offers refuge and helps them go on with ordinary life.

When two or more persons share basic experiences, and give meaningful responses they establish *betweenness*. My awareness of you and your awareness of me draw the two of us together into a *WE*. The *WE* dependency that develops energizes the give-and-take of responding. Also the *WE* experience shared by partners takes place within the larger groups and circles of everyday life. In the sharing of responsibilities found in caring communities, health and wholeness are reinforced.

Personality develops as we learn new ways to function in our common life. In sharing community life we assert our own self and receive back the correction and affirmation we need. The community serves as a backdrop for our freedom to respond. In bouncing ourselves off other people, we find new aspects of ourselves. The reactions that come back to us test and clarify our thoughts and proposals. The essential characteristics of our responding are magnified and enriched in the diverse relationships which community opens to us. We learn new things about ourselves as we respond within communities. The awareness of our commonality serves to sharpen our *uniqueness*. Obstacles seem less horrendous and problems less obdurate when they are shared with others. We assume responsibilities with them, discuss, adjust and help one another tap new personal resources. Responding within our "sociality" puts to use our assets and helps us to compensate for our liabilities.

Relationships gained in community frequently come to us through life's givens. The social dimensions of our living often are influenced by the space and time surrounding us. We discover ourselves and others as we find new meanings and connections with important places and crucial moments.

Our *space* affects the social dimension of our lives because the circles of our relatedness—family, community and nation—condition the space we occupy.

Janet's residence in Southern California includes a number of relationships. As a college graduate, single and aged 28, her primary space is her suburban apartment, which includes two roommates. At work as an executive secretary, her desk is one among seven. This space is occupied by her supervisor, an assistant secretary and four sales persons. Apart from home and work, Janet frequently thinks of and contacts persons important to her in other spaces: San Francisco where her fiancé lives, Indiana where "home" is and Los Angeles where professors and fellow graduate students work in night classes on advance degrees. Each of these spaces are peopled with significant people, who serve as the loci around which her social relations revolve.

Likewise *time* affects the social dimensions of life, for our life is embedded in experiences of the past, present and future. The past reflects our heritage of social relations. Each individual's biography encompasses everything experienced and takes in the personal history which is presupposed in social life. Our past is a backlog of experience from which there is no escaping. Often an area to which we have almost negligible access, our past nevertheless exerts an influence on how we relate. The present offers an immediate expression of our social self as we overlap with the persons before us at any given moment. We can write or telephone other persons we cannot see. Our relations with other people includes the vitality of the *WE* in encounter and the remoteness of those who remain at a distance from us. In turn the future imping-es powerfully on our social self. Consider the intended field of how others influence our projects. We have plans for today, next year and when we retire. The historical future transcends our lives with others and concerns those who will be born after us.

The far future influences our responses less in a strictly causal way, but our interpretive awareness of what will happen long after we die has an important reflexive meaning. The far future, as the past, has a way of coming into the pre-sent through our social relations. We often think of the future and move beyond the present by taking action in the direction of their intentions with and for other persons.

Hope is generated and nourished in community. The quality of hope is not simply an interior strength possessed by a fortunate few nor is it something we possess alone, for basically it is a shared experience. Responsive others are required to discover genuine hope. Hope is born when someone really *hears* us. In the inescapable social dimension of our personalities a great variety of social responses are opened to us. With others we convey and receive thoughts and feelings, touches and hugs and gain the strength of experiencing mutuality. We assume responsibilities with them, discuss, adjust and help one another tap new personal resources.

Dimensions of Response in Community

Human beings manifest marvelous and unique ways of connecting and relating in their associations and communities. People in cities around the world all relate and bind themselves in communities that vary geographically, ethnically and in their traditions. The complexity of our social network compounds the demands upon us to respond responsibly. Far from static, cities with their burgeoning populations and extensive social systems are dynamic and explosive. Communities, like individuals, change, grow and create. This diversity and dynamism of our "sociality" in becoming more complex and insistent compounds the demands upon us to respond responsibly. For people to be responsible is not only to become aware of the nature and meaning of community, but to live in and contribute to it.

The vital networks of interaction in society define common allegiance and require particular patterns of conformity that do not necessarily reduce individuals to isolates. More than ordinary grids or traceries, these human connections are organic. Thus community can be thought of as a womb in which we are conceived and nurtured and from which we emerge into ever-widening relationships that continue to sustain us as we start off in new directions.

These primary sources of association vary in size and scope, beginning with the family and going to ever-larger groups, reaching to nation states and the cosmopolitan whole of our planet. Variance occurs in organization and infrastructures such as work, politics and leisure. Differences also occur in personal maturity and purposefulness in fulfilling useful roles and functioning appropriately in each level of the life-cycle.

The family—the basic unit of human relatedness in our society—provides primal patterns of mutual give-and-take and responsibility. It gives children position and protection, while it affirms and nurtures. It also gives them their earliest values and meanings for emotional growth and interpersonal adventure. Groups, a larger and more diverse unit of relatedness, are a cluster of individuals who get together for particular purposes or interests. The forces and conditions characteristic of groups are many—group acceptance, group response and group consciousness are but a few. Group influences are exerted on goal development through sharing information and identification and making thought specific. Disciplined groups that are accepting, nonjudgmental and purposive provide a fertile base for individuals to gain insight and power to effect personal change.

The political unit, the nation-state, dominates our international community. It is a vast combination of persons who rank loyalty to the collective over individual objectives. John Stuart Mill said that "persons are united into a nation if they are united among themselves by common sympathies, which do not exist between them and any others. They cooperate with each other more willingly than with other people and desire to be under the same government and live within specific geographical boundaries." People unite for mutual safety and welfare and to consolidate the interests and ties that they share.

Underlying the larger political bodies are numerous smaller units or institutions. These supporting entities may be social, political or religious and can be informed by any number of philosophical idealisms. These aggregates of people are controlled by rules, customs, rituals and laws and the pattern of their relationship is defined in such a way as to be relatively independent of the individual. Institutions regulate actions and define acceptable behavior by giving patterns of expected behavior and responsibilities to people. For the health of a community, an essential response of institutions should be not only to answer citizens' questions, but also to generate new ones, and their primary goal is not only to relieve curiosity, but to enlarge it and ignite it. These various institutions give rise to culture.

Culture is the medium in which people relate, for they must devise some generally acceptable set of categories, given concreteness by social institutions, or they cannot deal with life at all. In *Habits of the Heart,* contributing author Robert Bellah explains that "Cultures are dramatic conversations about things that matter to the participants."[1] Less a political unit to which citizens belong, culture involves more the contents of a particular people's ideas and sentiments, customs and morals, habits and patterns of life.

Another elemental response that leads to community has to do with the life roles we grow into. The possibilities and limits of responding to others are conditioned by the roles society requires of us for the stage in life we have reached. These roles of personality are biologically and psychologically anchored, but they are socially transmitted. The shaping of the self is dependent upon the personalities of people around them. Our capacities for responding, as well as our ability to experience and contribute to community, may be impaired by faulty "ego-formation" as we move through these stages. Arrested in our development, we cannot fully respond either

---

[1] p. 27.

to what Harry Guntrip calls "our own lost heart of personality," or to others in our environment.

In infancy our ego-formation is powerfully influenced by the community that surrounds us. Persons are no less real and influential than the physical environment in which we find ourselves. Mothers and fathers, on whom babies depend, determine many of the qualitative features of our response patterns. We experience community by "internalizing" either their love and care or their indifference and rejection. The heritages of genetic development and cultural adaptation are intertwined. In childhood as our community and our responses are enlarged, we gradually become more self-managing. In maturing we gain greater skill and expand our response patterns. At the same time our "super-ego," as Freud held, takes form in a growing center of personality, which guides us in responding to our larger community.

Relating Responsibly in Roles

Fulfilling a role in a social setting gives us status and serves as a channel by which we can meet behavioral expectations. The moderator and secretary of a committee have defined positions. The role of one is to serve as chair and the other is to record the minutes. The role is affected by the group and the group is affected by these two functions and expectations. Both, however, depend on their personality in relation to the group and on the social or cultural expectations.

The stage of midlife according to Gail Sheehy's widely acclaimed book, *Passages,* is the time to move "out of roles and into the self" in order to discover "an enlarged capacity to love ourselves and embrace others."[2] She cites the growing population of senior citizens as an illustration of how the increasing number of pensioned retirees are flowering

---

[2] p. 364.

into new roles, and notes how these retirees often tell of how their work seems to be only a means of achieving a satisfactory private life—a fulfilling "life-style." The more serious among them raise questions about what their freedom and privacy-loving pursuits contribute to their own and their community's fulfillment.

Roles are taken to cope with the predicament experienced when we try to respond appropriately in a social situation. In becoming aware of an event, part of ourselves is engaged as our response is demanded. We need to adopt some position to make it possible for us to relate to others. A workable way of responding is to act on the basis that both the self and the other person *exist* and that each of our responses will probably be determined by our particular stage in life. Belief in others comes from a consciousness that sees others as someone *like us*.

We settle the ego-predicament by either accepting or denying a particular *role*. Problematically, we seek to overcome the tension aroused by trying to rewrite the script, adopting a different role ourselves and changing the role of the other person. Clarifying and accepting a role brings us a sense of control by giving us an "assumption" of where the other person stands and thus having a point to respond to. At that point we can see the individual and ourselves as a unity and begin to map out an appropriate game plan for our responding. The danger here, of "boxing in" individuals, is self evident.

Conformity and Community in Western Traditions

For a sound understanding of our postmodern struggle with community, we must be aware of the contributions of crucial periods of history. To appreciate how people in other times lived in relation to one another and what social structures were developed illuminates both the strengths and strains of community life in our time.

The foundations of Western culture's thought, concerning how people associate, reach back to the reflections of philosophers in the Golden Age of Greece (fifth to fourth century B.C.). In the *Republic,* Plato portrayed people as prisoners in a dark cave forced to look at shadows, projected images on a wall of those outside. They take the shadows as their only experience of those outside. Outside the cave they find the sun illuminating the beings and showing them as they really are. Becoming aware of and participating with these others opens a more diverse community, which in turn cuts the bonds of unrealistic estimates and frees them to grasp truth. Through reason, shared within a community, the deceptions or myths assumed about people can be overcome. Such insights about social relations reached by Plato and other stellar Greek philosophers accompanied the cultural achievements of Sparta and Athens. The resulting creations were expressed in splendid architecture, in dramatic heroes who provided models for free and moral citizens and in communities that were producers of cultures.

Another experience of community that proved formative for Western society's patterns of relating stems from Europe's Middle Ages. Monastic communities set examples of civilized living and served to establish medieval endeavors on other motives than riches or fame. The orders of chivalry held that virtue was a part of the heroic code—a concept derived from Christianity. Residents, strongly interdependent, held moral and aesthetic health in high esteem and sought it diligently. Artisans were organized in guilds, and their position seemed to have been more satisfactory than in earlier centuries.

During the Enlightenment of the 18th century, social theorists tried to make reason and human goodness central for society. The leaders of this movement sought to bring light where there had been darkness, to replace superstition by scientific knowledge of nature. Their method was to begin from phenomena available to all people and move toward rational demonstration possible for all. Bacon, Descartes,

Locke and others pressed for knowledge of the nature of all things. But this objective put them at odds with Plato's powerful picture of the relation between thinker and society. The issue turns on whether the people of the cave are intractable, as Plato thought, or can those on the inside be changed by a new kind of education.

In the 19th century reason gained greater ascendancy. Applied both to nature and the processes of mind, the discipline of reason opened vast new realms of knowledge and technological developments. New views of how people relate in communities were discovered. The new biology brought to the fore the need to see persons and societies in organismic terms. More than mere mechanical systems, human beings were seen to respond and associate as organisms. Eloquent illustrations of the mounting complexity and pressures of people's common lives appear in the key novelists of that century. Melville, Dostoyevsky and others show dramatically how individuals crave social interaction and struggle to find personal identity and the appropriate responses within community.

Melville, in his prodigious portrait of Captain Ahab, developed a character that tackles the Herculean task of responding for the self in society. Humanist to the core, Ahab affirms his relatedness and responsiveness when he says, "Let me look into a human eye . . . . It is better than to gaze into sea or sky, better than to gaze upon God." In the same century, the American poet Walt Whitman provided another kaleidoscopic picture of the facts and fantasies about responses people make as they relate. He resonated with nature and society and in his poetry he was expressing the truth, not only of himself, but of the world. In his writing and his public life his responses were guided by his search for a sense of belonging. He wrote, "I am always conscious of myself as two—my personal and my social selves."

In the 20th century Camus, Sartre, T.S. Eliot and other creative writers were deeply disturbed by the loss of social cohesion and a sense of belonging. These contributed new chapters in the story of people's relating as they wrote of people possessing a subjective life, often at odds with traditional communities. Through this "exile" motif, they showed humans as attaining existence only when they are living out what they purpose to be.

The central problem for the responding self in community is to find meaning and reason in existence. Camus presents strident and bold characters to illustrate the two positions of the nonconformist and the outcast. In *The Stranger* we find a man whose relation to society is absurd. Arrayed against the traditional community and the transcendent, he claims "I rebel, therefore I exist." The dual response of exile and rebel also is found in Sartre's *The Flies,* in which we find an Orestes-like character who takes guilt upon himself, since value is simply the meaning one chooses.

Gabriel Marcel, a contemporary Catholic existentialist, stresses the importance of observing the objective reality in human relating and the search for subjective responses. "When somebody's presence really makes itself felt," he noted, "it can refresh my inner being; it reveals me to myself. It makes me feel more fully myself than I would be if I were not exposed to its impact." This view holds that in the immediacy of face-to-face encounters, *Thou* comes through with undeniable force. The "Thou" of encounter is more intimate than the "you" alone. The "Thou" of friendship and loved ones is a specified recognition of a mutual responsibility of the self through being *with the other person.*

These writers of the first half of the 20th century, despite their subjective grounding and expressive individualism, sought an alternative to the either/or position of alienation. They found an answer in the position defined by Martin Buber of the "narrow-ridge," which entails learning to respond responsibly to each *person* and *life situation.* The contemporary responder in community is charged with finding a relation to reality. The uniqueness of the individual is rooted in spontaneity and freedom. To walk the narrow-ridge is to participate in life as responsible persons.

The various movements of thought and political-social trends converged in the late 19th and 20th centuries to create new ways of connecting individuals to communities. Paradoxically it was only as societies matured that it became possible for individualism to flower. Individualism and autonomy arose within traditional social structures in which the moral and psychological necessity for being together and creating a social order was taken for granted. As individualism became more sophisticated, people found themselves both in tension with and dependent upon community.

The elevation of the rediscovered self brought important social changes, contributing to the rapid development of the physical sciences and gave individuals a broader role in society's decision-making and future-ensuring processes. The contrary effect on individuals is their increasing vulnerability to alienation. They need the community they pulled away from as well as flexibility in approaching problems of how to get along with one another. Thus individualism both threatens and reinforces community. On the one hand, rebellious and nonconforming individuals tend to undermine the bonds that hold communities together, while on the other, the mandates of our postmodern era demand the strengthening of our communal relations and structures.

Philosophers and Social Scientists View Community

Philosophers and social scientists of the 20th century have been much concerned with the question of how communities can best serve and nurture individuals. In addition to their aim to reconcile the tension between philosophy and practice, they have sought to deal with the struggle between individualism and community.

Alfred North Whitehead and John Dewey, applying differing overviews to social behavior, illustrate how 20th-century philosophers give coherence to the relation between thought and action in social organization. For them the unification of thought and action depended on how honestly the uniqueness of both are recognized. They found the two forces to be complementary—not separate. When thought and action are divided, individuals tend to be cut off from community. They further believed it is *time* that binds our experience in crucial ways, for time brings disappearance and death, which threatens the security of the individual and the stability of the group. Time also brings birth, which represents the continuance of life. Similarly, time binds thought and action. Whitehead pointed out that thought can be more easily systematized than action and hence more quickly detached from action, yet it is time that works to keep behavior under the control of our thoughts. Insofar as the community serves as a conservator of thought over a span of time, community serves as a guide to action.

Comprehensive judgments of the ways people relate and organize their society are found in the probing social critiques of innovative analysts of society like Max Weber, Karl Marx and Thorstein Veblen, who pointed to what they considered of utmost importance: the fundamental revision of the social order. Max Weber, a great scholar, saw a severe threat to community in the 20th values. People, he claimed, show no basis for decision, no criterion for responding in groups and communities other than their own personal will and integrity. Karl Marx was fired with a messianic zeal to forge a mighty structure of human responding through community in social action.

An insightful American social scientist, Thorstein Veblen, focused attention on human responses within the continuing class struggle and saw this deep tension to be at the center of contemporary history. Analyzing the responses of industrial technology in tension with institutions of business and juxtaposing bureaucracy with a secular disenchantment of the world, he described the responses of regard for reputation as follows, "the striving to be better than one's neighbor," "the struggle for respectability," and "the drift of the selves in the drift of modern societies." Each of these trends prevents the individual from fulfillment and jeopardizes community.

The insights about people relating in community of these specialists demonstrate a commitment to humanistic ethical concerns. These specialists have a strategy of applying learning and cognitive theories which give us practical "conceptual maps" that help us understand communities. Common problems associated with social responses are clarified. In identifying a "systems approach," today's social psychologists reinforce the study of a pluralistic view to understanding and guiding responses of people in social situations. With their "field theory," which requires getting the "big picture," they supplement the work of other social scientists who are working to get a handle on our increasing interdependence, nationally and internationally.

Social psychologists, involving themselves with individuals and communities, have helped mental health workers identify the influences that contribute to either emotional health or illness. They explore ways to determine what conditions nurture emotional well-being. Instead of assuming that mental disorder is a *private misery,* social psychologists reinforce other specialists who hold that the trouble and cure are related to the person's relationships and that tensions between the requirements of communities versus wishes of the individual can be worked through. They also indicate ways to reduce the isolation of the mentally disturbed and bring them back into the community as worthy human beings.

As comprehensive as current social theorists' descriptions and analyses of community may be, conditions in the postmodern world demand they be stretched to include new dynamic realities. The new multicultural reality that characterizes "community" at the end of this millennium makes an approach from the perspective of Western cultural values, including Greek philosophy, questionable. Each of the fastest growing cultures in this country—the Hispanic and particularly the Asian—has something to bring to the new pluralistic culture being created. The Korean community in Los Angeles owes nothing to Greek culture. Their diligence and discipline, not to mention their familial loyalty and esteem of education, know nothing of Descartes, Weber and even less of Plato.

The issue is not value relativism. We cannot jump to the conclusion that values are broken down. We are in a period of transition in which the fact of values is broader. We are leaving behind the time in which we accepted only one set of values as the truthful way of living and are moving into the period in which we will have to accept values which represent other cultures that are not "worse" than ours, only different. This transition is immensely difficult because the nature of our minds is ethnocentric. The mind of future people in community, however, will be polycentric. With these considerations we need to sketch the chief features of the community in the postmodern world.

Community in the Post-Modern Era

Americans' experience of community has changed radically in the 20th century. We have moved from the local life of the 19th century, in which economic and social relationships were visible and morally interpreted as parts of a commonly accepted sense of the expanding nation. National unity was based largely upon a religious, ethnic and racial homogeneity. In the new century we moved toward becoming an advanced industrial nation with an aging white population and a birth dearth. The 1970s and 1980s brought radical and accelerating demographic changes, largely the result of Hispanic and Asian immigration and the upsurge of minority populations. Simultaneously, we have participated in the melding and increasing complexity of systems of economics, politics and culture. One telling result has been that social status has come to depend more on a national occupational system and less on local social settings. Combined with these changes, a degree of freedom has emerged in private life that would have been inconceivable a generation ago.

Community today extends from an individual's experience all the way to the complicated multinational corporations which wield global influences. In the most immediate experiences, "life-style" serves as one way to describe postmodern societies. In the Western world the relative availability of automobiles, consumer goods and a variety of appliances in homes provide one of the earmarks of contemporary society. With this has come a standardization and regimentation of human as well as material resources. Life-style easily becomes the appurtenances of what *Life* magazine calls "modern living" or what Bellah notes in *Habits of the Heart* as "the celebrating of the interdependence of public and private life . . . rendering the mode of living segmental by elevating the economically well-off into a narcissistic similarity."[3]

The results are that the economics we used only a few decades ago are too conventional and narrow to encompass the realities of today's intertwined financial settings in a world with plural centers of power. Consider the evidence found in leveraged buyouts (L.B.O.) which have their roots in the 1970s, when investment boutiques like Kohlberg, Kravis and Roberts discovered that smallish, old-line industrial outfits could be bought cheaply (mainly on borrowed money), slimmed down and eventually resold at a smart profit. Respectable Wall Street found these maneuvers a little shady at first, but the huge returns earned by K.K.R. and other firms gradually turned skepticism into manic enthusiasm.

The larger economic picture—global and historical—is perceptively spelled out by Jacques Attali, a French economic theorist. His study of the broad rhythms that underlie and transcend the struggles of particular periods, lead him to point out that the world has always moved from one dominant order (community in its widest sense) to another. The

---

[3] p. 72.

largest part of history, however, is occupied by intervals between two orders. The order breaks into crisis when the costs of maintaining increase beyond the capacity to produce and pay the bills. The costs increase because demand for services increases with affluence, while the productivity level of delivering them does not. The period between orders goes through stages of "socialization," "amortization" and reorganization.

In the first stage debt, be it public, private or international, increases to cover the mounting costs of supporting and protecting the dominant order. Eventually the debt is cancelled by inflation, moratorium or bankruptcy. There follows the beginning of the organization of a new order through the introduction of the new cost-reducing technologies. Considered from the angle of economics, Attali maintains, the United States at the present is in the midst of a transition from the old world order, centered in New York, to a new order. We have just finished the socialization stage and are in the middle of an amortization stage where mounting debts cannot be paid. The big question becomes—will the core of a new order emerging in the Pacific Basin be in California or Japan?

Japan is strong and other countries such as Korea and Taiwan are moving from the periphery into a new affluence characteristic of a core region. America is not as powerful and rich as it was from 1945-1975. We are living in an unsentimental age for which we are not particularly well-suited and are entering a highly competitive world in which knowledge and human resources, not military might and natural resources, will be the dominant aspect of power. Applied brain power, as exemplified in the rise of the Japanese, is more important than natural resources.

The contemporary political-economic state of our country, according to Daniel Bell, Harvard sociologist, revolves around two axes: One is an economic axis divided by the left and the right. The other is a cultural axis divided by traditionalist and modernist attitudes." He suggests that translated into political terms, the class can't reform: the interaction of economic and cultural life in America tends to cancel out the ability to form a consensus.

Robert Bellah and his associates describe the post-modern period as being an "entrepreneurial and psychological ethos." Like other estimators of the functioning and dynamics of society of this era, they focus on the dominance of the manager-entrepreneur and the permissiveness espoused by psychotherapist and the professional. Challenges to that ethos come from those left out of that prosperity as well as from those who, while its beneficiaries, criticize it for moral defects. Some challengers appear motivated by a desire to transform the whole society, others echo the old ideal of the independent citizen.

Considered from the angle of international relations, we see the same confluence of political, economic and cultural forces combining to complicate solutions to the escalating problems. A look at the explosive conditions in the Middle East shows us the complexity of the network of difficulties. In the past Washington policymakers have successfully kept separate issues of geographic subdivisions, such as "North Africa" or the "Persian Gulf," and issues like "oil" or the "Palestinian problem." However, these issues are now irrevocably entangled. As in other theaters of international tensions, the dynamism and concurrent problems are vastly broader. These difficult problems include cultures, peoples and beliefs from other continents and civilizations.

Coupled with the international problem, many Americans are unsuccessful in finding life-style enclaves that encourage their authentic selves. A careful examination of the thinking of much of the middle class shows that it is based on inadequate social science, impoverished philosophy and vacuous theology. We discover ourselves not separately from other people and institutions but through them. "We never get to the bottom of our selves on our own," observes Bellah. "We find who we are face to face and side by side with others in work, love and learning."

Within this new society, individuals can only rarely and with difficulty understand themselves and their activities as interrelated in morally meaningful ways with those of different Americans. Instead of directing cultural and individual energies toward relating the self to its larger context, the culture of managers and therapists urges a persistent effort to make "of our particular segment of life a small world of its own."

Summary

"Personality," as H.S. Sullivan says, "is the relatively enduring pattern of recurrent interpersonal situations which characterize a human life." People must be viewed as part of the interplay of two or more personalities rather than as a separate entity. They are unique individuals, particular biologically determined structures and response patterns. But as individuals, each one interacts with specific other individuals and groups. Their personalities are markedly influenced in specific interpersonal experiences. The social connectedness individuals find in communities gives them form, energy and identity and is essential to happiness, self-esteem and moral worth.

Each of us is inextricably involved with other persons in families, communities, nations and cultures. The structures and processes of these units are both life-giving and life-taking. Our community asks from us conformity to the patterns and histories of its organizations. The task of responding adequately to problems of relating are many and steadily become more intense and complicated.

We live in an impacted world of imperfect people. It is inevitable that some of us will, knowingly or unknowingly, intrude on other's space and time, even when they are vigorously defending it. There is no escaping the historical urgencies that push from all sides as we interact in communities. Still with all the demands and confusions of community, we must continue to relate and respond. The bottom line of being human is that individuals cannot long escape one another.

In the experience of community our awareness of space and time is sharpened with new significance. Whether it involves a trifling glance or a momentous encounter, each interaction offers an instantly accessible capsule of social awareness. The meaningful places and moments of inter-action not only include our perspectives, but those with whom we are interacting. In the intensity of immediate experiences we want persons to empathize with us, share our feelings and exchange ideas. We need to find and keep our individual identity, but we also need feedback and reinforce-ment. The moment is lost when anonymity enters as either of the persons hides their real intentions or feelings.

The problems of relating in the family of nations confront-ing the United States today have become complicated. Solutions now require much more than merely ascertaining our own role and that of others. Each element— family, community and nation—has become increasingly intricate with more interlocking responsibilities and demands. Each role that make up the infrastructures has become complex at an accelerating pace. Each strand of society's history seems to be competing for new expression in the forging of the postmodern societies. The elements, functions and historical strands of communities are but a few of the dynamic factors involved in our over-populated society. We have created a society vastly interrelated and integrated economically, technically and functionally.

"To get our act together" in our relationships, our task is at once personal and immediate, as well as national and global. Each individual must be disciplined to be in tune with others. This is the special work of nurturing families, suppor-tive groups and affirming communities of whatever size and sponsorship. The health of a family or group depends upon what assets or liabilities the individual member brings to the social structure. The functioning social entity is inevitably affected by the influence of each personality involved.

As enlightenment about human nature grows, we see more clearly our responsibilities to our community. This places an additional demand that we function knowingly and respond appropriately. In the present sociopsychological context,the concern must be less with fantasies or intellectual ideals and more with the power and creative direction religious convictions contribute to the general social consciousness. We are challenged to make responses that use everyday experiences as prime data for higher meanings. To nurture and communicate these higher meanings is the particular responsibility of the "religious community." At the same time the religious feelings of people in the street need to be enriched, genuinely rooted and positively expressed in our behavior. Both values and cultural legacy are manifested in the choices we make regarding our social life-styles.

We grow as individuals as we become aware of our interdependence and improve our skills of interacting with our social environment. We become whole as we become part of each other. In recognizing and responding to our associates in community we find the scope of our responsibilities to them. As we become more responsive to and involved with others in responsible ways, we are more able to cope with setbacks and take hold of new opportunities. The degree of self-disclosure which we are given to make to others is variable with time, place and person.

Fundamental among our responsibilities is rediscovering our moral and religious traditions and recognizing how they still speak to our present need. We are entering the period in which we must accept values of other cultures which are not "worse" than our values, only different. Plurality is the defining feature of the new world community. In this new world, values and cultures other than our own are demanding a place in our consciousness. Every system and community that does not admit plurality as the new way of life with new responsibilities for each individual and each people will find itself self-destructing.

C H A P T E R

11

Responsible Social Ethics

Questions about the interactions of persons-in-community
challenge both the application and validity of our ethical
assumptions. To question the responses we practice demands
that we become honest about the guidelines we use and that
we clarify our beliefs. We find many excuses to avoid locating
and applying our deepest convictions. Our search for reliable
guidelines uncovers the ambiguities which are characteristic
of our predominantly secular society. With consumerism and
technological innovation ascendent, the pull to use affluence
and success and status as our guidelines is insistent.

Selfish Motives Supersede Higher Principles

In practice, we find it hard to sort our goals and even
more difficult to find principles higher than our own selfish
motives. Consequently we look for easy answers and quick-
fixes. Applying altruistic feelings of compassion and concern
seems impractical in an entrepreneurial society that often dis-
regards mutual obligations and sees people as instruments
instead of citizens of the world sharing a common life. Not
only on Wall Street is "being hot" deemed better than being

good. Acting according to our deepest convictions more often than not is costly. The martyred Archbishop Oscar Romero declared 30 days before he was assassinated, "We in El Salvador well know how any dissent against the present form of capitalism and against the political institutions that support it is repressed with ever increasing violence and ever greater injustice—inspired by the theory of national security."

Modern Western culture points us in different directions— toward the exploitative, competitive and self-aggrandizing. Thus conditioned and committed, we prefer to side-step deepening our convictions and avoid drawing on them to answer ethical questions that arise in the responses we make.

Personal decision-making cannot be avoided long. Serious ethical questions press us. Are we to respond with polite and accommodating behavior? Should we be honest and express exactly the way we feel? What can we do about our contradictory feelings that often are passive and self-centered instead of confident and generous? What principles will guide our responses to we interact with? In the face of controversy and possible violence, will we manage conflict and negotiate for better solutions? What social problems should we tackle to fulfill our responsibilities as citizens? If we claim to be working for improving society, how can we direct our responses to keep them from becoming disconnected and selfish maneuvers?

As we attempt to tackle problems on a larger scale, we confront a world which is daily becoming more interdependent, presenting us with complex and difficult choices. People in developing countries, struggling to modernize while preserving their culture, find improvement painfully slow and uneven. A few profit, but the majority remain frustrated in their marginal roles, facing difficult changes as they await the creation of the new order. Decision-making in their families and neighborhoods present perplexing discrepancies and conflicting demands.

People in Western societies caught in rapid transition also face new ethical questions. In the process of radical change neuroses increase and interpersonal violence spreads. Those who do not accept the social prescriptions are branded "deviants" and incarcerated. The craving for relief by means of messianic leadership deepens. As a consequence much effort is spent to socialize people and train them for roles that are unresponsive to basic human needs.

Is the answer for nations to curtail the freedom of their citizens? Cross-cultural studies show that severe regimentation and strictly required conduct generate frustration in many societies. Austerity is found objectionable in as different situations as Catholic orders, a generation after their foundation, and in Soviet communes, a decade after the revolution. Contemporary Israeli kibbutzim, now 40 years after their establishment, are facing a severe restructuring in order to survive. Utopian aspects of sharing and sacrificing are being replaced by individual decision-making and arrangements that encourage members to go it alone.

Yet unbridled libertinism leads to excesses that spawn crime, child abuse, drugs and pornography. When narcissism goes unchecked, the struggle for human rights and participatory involvement in the community are neglected. When self-interest prevails and relationships become exploitative, democracy is undermined. On the other hand, democracy grows when commitment to responsible politics is encouraged and personal and institutional religion occurs is vital.

To live is to decide in the face of ambiguity and diversity of ethical dilemmas. The discrepancies between our inclinations and what society demands present difficult problems in decision-making. The malleability of human nature that allows these disparities, frustrates individuals with imperfect socialization and troubles communities with inadequate social control. The frustration is both disturbing and poignant because we are living in a seminal period of history in which many traditional elements of national and international affairs are in flux simultaneously. The situation is pliant to an unusual degree, presenting us with historic opportunities.

Nevertheless, in spite of marvelous new opportunities, choosing remains a problem. Ethical decisions have become increasingly complicated and confused by the covert fluidity of values. In a group-therapy session, when a 52-year-old mother of five was asked how she chose her responses, she gave the quick answer, "When I must decide on questions of right and wrong, I know the difference, my conscience tells me."

"Fine," the others praised her, "and we hope your conscience is sensitive and well-honed. But what if the dictates of your moral compass don't agree with ours?"

As important as the conscience is, in itself it is not enough. The predicament conscience is often caught in, both in theory and practice, is between ethical irrelevance and relativism. Regarding this dilemma of ethical decision, Bonhoeffer in *Ethics* suggests, "The conscience which has been set free is not timid like the conscience bound by the law, but it stands wide open for our neighbor and for his concrete distress."

We easily fall into too-narrow notion of the place of moral argument. Politics, in the broad sense, has to do with the foundations, structures and ends of human community. In terms of the quality and direction of our social life, the commanding need is clear. Personally we have to make decisions within the perennial tension between individualism and community concern. To develop strategies to capitalize on their strengths, both persons and nations need clear goals. The development of goals, in turn, depends upon having a guiding ethos where the crucial question is: Can we develop a substantive conception of the common good and recognize that morality and politics must be mutually supportive?

Ethics continues to be "normative," a guiding principle for action, but it is also "descriptive" in the sense of providing an account of the transformation of the concrete stuff of behavior. Clearly defined goals do not emerge automatically, but develop in the reflective process of reason, experience and faith in meeting life situations. In relating, we strive for certain balances of trustworthiness and mutual rights and obligations. The concept of "ethics" must be regarded as more than a moralistic principle. It must be an ethical dimension rooted not in culture or morality, but in the condition of mutual merit and obligation between people. To keep relationships in ethical balance, persons are challenged to show their concern for the interests of everyone involved. It follows that justice is not a juridical concept, but an ethical one. A relationship is "fair" if there is a balance in the giving and receiving of rights and obligations. At the deeper level of religious conviction, the circumstances, motivations and structures of action are guided by the concrete, personal and purposeful activity of God.

Our Personal Stake in Making Culture Responsible

Making responsible decisions within life's dilemmas is difficult as people meet varied situations at different stages of life, balancing the demands of community with personal inclinations. One pull is to work for the common good, and another is to respond to what they feel will enable them individually to live meaningfully. In our responses to family, neighbors and co-workers, we find that working to make community and culture more responsible is a corporate enterprise; it is also the work of individuals.

Kay Coles, 22 and former runner-up for beauty queen in her northern California county, now is a junior social ecology major in a state university enthusiastically preparing for a career that will "help to improve the world a little and assure me of some degree of financial independence." On campus the BMWs her classmates drive plus their faddish garbs, weekends to Palm Springs or Lake Tahoe are constant reminders of the affluent society in which she lives. Her training to become a "social ecologist" keeps her busy with seminars and field trips aimed at dealing with the complex environmental issues that confront our planet. Studying how different people live in the intricate web of physical, social and psychological environments, she learns about how they develop and act, but she also notes evidences of social disruption: the impact of divorce on child development, the causes of hyperactivity, the effects of stress and pollution on physical and psychological well-being, as well as white collar crime.

Kay strongly disagreed with Dan Danknick, an assembly speaker on campus who maintained that since Americans had to fight the British, the Indians and the Spaniards to get the excellent land we have, we were not obligated to help other nations with their hungry. Furious at this chauvinism, she wrote a strong letter to the editor of the campus *News:*

> True we battled for our land, but at what expense? Are we proud that we killed Indians and drove them off the land that we stole from them? Are we happy that our crops were prosperous because we enslaved and dehumanized the Blacks? Industrialized nations prosper by exploiting Third-World countries of their natural resources and labor. It's time we gave something back to them. America could not have become the great "Melting Pot" without the contributions of other nations. America was formed by taking the best of other cultures. When we help other cultures to become strong, we strengthen ourselves. Mr. Danknick says he agrees that we should end world hunger, but he asks "what do we get out of it?" Do we need material reward for doing what we as human beings have a responsibility to do anyway? Obviously, Mr. Danknick has never helped anyone in real need; otherwise he would have received the reward of an overwhelming feeling of love and fulfillment that no amount of money could replace. It is time for America to live up to its responsibility as a leading world power to help end the tragedy of world hunger.-K.C.

In reviewing her "opinion," Kay commented, "In 18 months when I have to earn my own keep, I'm not sure of where I can find a position that will pay me to work on some of these social problems. The job opportunities may be limited if I keep riding my white horse but I hope to find work where I can apply my convictions."

Stewart and Alice Robins, both in their early 30s, live with their two bright and well-mannered daughters in a predominantly Black community near where Stewart was raised. A counselor at a church summer camp 16 years ago, noticing Stewart's quickness of mind and leadership qualities, kindled his resolve to aim for a college education. The odds against him realizing his hopes were great: his father, with only seasonal work as a laborer, barely kept food on the table for his wife and six children. His mother, a part-time maid, needed Stewart's help to care for three younger siblings. His eldest brother was "freaked out" as a lost cocaine addict, and his next older brother was serving a ten-year sentence in the penitentiary for drug trafficking. Pulling away from his high school drop-out, drug-using gang mates was, as he explained, "very sticky." But Stewart, reinforced by his old counselor, persisted with his plan and with the encouragement of a lenient registrar, was able to enter LaVern College. Much hard work followed, but he earned a diploma in business administration.

Both Stewart and Alicia encountered rebuffs seeking positions where their training could be used—they were either "over-qualified" or they "lacked experience." Four years ago Alicia was hired by a social work agency and Stewart, on his fourth attempt, won a permanent position in one of the Los Angeles city departments. With accumulated savings they invested in a two-bedroom house in Long Beach hoping to serve as change-agents in the old community now turbulent with competing Hispanics, Asians and Blacks. Over the following years the waves of vandalism, drug abuse and racial conflict increased. Once when violence exploded the immediate neighborhood was rocked with a series of vicious gang wars, and in, one of these shootings, the Robin's home was caught in the cross fire. Had the shots not been with "cheap bullets," they would have penetrated the plaster of the little girl's bedroom. The event shattered their resolve to live and work for improving the neighborhood. They decided to move to the suburbs and, through P.T.A., church and other community groups, continue as responsible agents for social change.

Another attractive couple, Rich and Sherry Johnson, live with their three teenagers in the suburbs. Respected and successful in their careers, they are seen by friends to be sociable and congenial. Not so. In the inner-community of their family, their decision-making had become antagonistic instead of mutual. No longer do Rich and Sherry share their hopes and dreams or their hurts and dissatisfactions with each other. Their interaction soured to the point that they separated two months ago. In counseling sessions they demonstrate what spoils mutuality: persistently poor communication, failure to manage and resolve conflicts, growing insensitivity to the emotional needs of the partner and abandonment of appreciating and reinforcing the other.

Rich talks along one line; Sherry pursues another. When Rich starts to express his deeper emotions, Sherry attacks with a barrage of old complaints. He turns silent and suppresses his discounted feelings. At loggerheads on issues of how to spend their money, manage the children, or correct their lack of intimacy, they blame one another and avoid working to resolve their differences. When Sherry is in a more amiable and conciliatory mood, Rich tends to clam up. "Most of the time," Rich notes, "we are out of sync with each other; neither of us respecting the turf, much less offering support, of the other."

Rich, 43, is highly regarded in his sales office for the way he smoothes out difficult customer demands and complaints. "On my job," he explains, "I work through complicated disputes, but at home my efforts seem to make matters worse. Defensiveness and sarcasm aggravates the tension and when I approach Sherry with affection, she pushes me away telling me she's stressed out and tired. The opposite of my mother, who respected Dad as head of the house, Sherry challenges my authority. Instead of listening to my proposals about managing the house or our children, she reasserts her plan for what must be done. Demanding her way, she's unwilling to discuss our difficulties."

Sherry, 42 years old and the only child of parents who were divorced during her adolescence, is both a conscientious mother and an efficient executive secretary. At home she runs a tight ship. As a spouse she feels, "Rich still holds on to the dead-as-a-dodo idea of being a domineering husband and father and having a dutiful little cook and housewife. He can't accept my role as a liberated woman. He doesn't listen when I try to tell him my feelings about authority and standards for our family. Worse than 'out of sync,' we're not on the same wavelength."

Rich and Sherry's denial of the other's needs and their strife-ridden communication keeps them from negotiating differences and rediscovering their lost harmony. Busily protecting themselves, they find it difficult to be aware of the feelings of the other. Frustrated by the increasing complexity and pain of the untended issues in their relationship, they make matters worse as they throw demeaning lists of faults at the other. Questions of "right" and "wrong" are abandoned; each spouse simply knows that the other is wrong. Both are individually guided by accurate moral compasses. Both are honorable, trustworthy, brave and respectable. Both had parents who were church members and brought up Rich and Sherry in the Christian faith, but they now find their moral and religious convictions insufficient to help resolve their distressing relationship. They recognize that divorce, instead of solving problems, would devastate their self-esteem, compound their personal problems and create deep emotional difficulties for their three adolescents, but they are riding the unstoppable roller coaster of dissolution.

Another couple, Lester and Jane Abrams, have succeeded over their 20 years of marriage to deepen both the closeness of their relationship and grow in their community service. Over a decade ago they bought a home in a fast-developing Southern California city and began participating fully in community activities. "Concern for the democratic process," Lester explains "is part of my heritage and graduate-school training. My grandparents emigrated to America from Central Europe and started immediately to take part in the growth of the community where they settled. I followed their example when I got to the Berkeley campus in the 60s and rode 'the wave of privileged vision' as one of the eager Students for a Democratic Society."

From their Orange County home Lester and Jane joined with neighbors who believed that responsible citizens implement values they cherish rather than simply accept their community as a mere geographic convenience where people quietly live out isolated lives. Jane took an active part in the work of agencies and schools and decided to finish her college and enter the medical school of the university located nearby. Lester, an attorney who majored in public law at Harvard, found ways to work within the political processes of the local government. A few years later he won a seat on the city council and within a year was named mayor. Jane, in turn, completed her training and opened a practice as a pediatrician in the community.

In his office Lester Abrams found that in spite of problems arising from their city's rapid growth, opportunities arose to infuse values he counted important. New schools were built, both private and public, and new industries and businesses were begun and given incentives to expand. "Delays, mistakes and lost opportunities," he acknowledges, "have hampered our efforts to extend community betterment programs. Our delay in launching a latchkey project led to a crisis in child-care centers. We made a mistake in proposing to utilize an unused animal shelter to provide a hostel for the homeless, yet as citizens become active and responsible in an open democracy, the more easily the city solves its complicated social problems." He tells with satisfaction how committed citizens—not just the city council—cooperated to build a durable community where people of diverse cultures, lifestyles and economic circumstances live.

In spite of these gains, resistance from special interest groups have blocked worthy projects. Powerful land owners fought Lester's efforts to maintain space and greenbelts, claiming that in restricting growth the city council was obstructing progress. Paradoxically these same critics argue that Lester pours out more oratory than action. He responds that his lectures on city government at the university are realism, not rhetoric and reiterates his theme, "If democracy is to thrive in the U.S., it must be facilitated in the civic centers of America." He stresses that city halls throughout the country must share with the federal government the responsibility for vitalizing foreign policy and halting the arms race, which is systematically looting the nation's cities to the tune of one trillion dollars a year! Abrams admits, "I deliberately put issues in emotional terms because it takes heat and expanded vision to arouse people to face local needs and to become involved in halting the nation's march toward nuclear annihilation."

At 55, Dr. Buck Jones, founder and director of the East St. Louis H.O.P.E. (Helping Other People Emerge), is a Black, United Church of Christ minister who works for a community larger than his particular congregation. From his parsonage on a knoll in the center of the city, he points out that wherever America's troubled cities are headed, East St. Louis will get there first. Throughout the '60s and '70s employers and employees moved to surrounding towns leaving behind a population unable to support the city with their taxes and unable to pay for needed services. To trail Dr. Jones only for a few hours is to face the stark realities of militarism, racism and poverty in the largest all-Black city in the country—where boxcars carrying highly explosive Trident missile propellant stop longest en route from Oakland, California to deployment at Kings Bay, Georgia.

For ten months, the City of East St. Louis has been unable to pick up its garbage, so it is piled up in vacant lots, on curbsides, in abandoned buildings and in alleys. Health officials have warned that the invasion of roaches, rats and flies feeding on the garbage could lead to an epidemic of communicable diseases. As America spends billions of dollars to develop nuclear weapons, East St. Louis cannot afford $250,000 to pick up its refuse. The town is confronted with the realities of poverty, poor health care, crime, 42 percent unemployment, 73 percent of the residents on some form of welfare (not because they are lazy, but because jobs are so few). Black teenagers in this and other such ghettos cannot find jobs and turn to the self-destruction of drugs.

In walking to the soup kitchen that Rev. Jones' organization operates, we pass rows of abandoned houses. Buck points out that 60 percent of the area's housing is substandard. The city has over 3,000 such buildings, all targets of arson and hiding places for thieves, muggers and child molesters. "The situation is a disgrace," he asserts. "As a nation we are spending $85 billion for the Trident submarine and missile system when people are unemployed and living adjacent to burned-out and gutted buildings."

We stop at a dilapidated and musty-smelling tenement to call on a 29-year-old single parent, mother of three. She verifies what we had heard: mothers sometimes put bread out at night to keep the rats from biting their sleeping infants and stuff cotton in babies' ears to keep the roaches out. Dr. Buck explains, "As we increase our military spending, children in East St. Louis go to bed hungry, sick people are denied health care and some are forced to choose between heating and eating. In this region over 15 thousand people are homeless because of the acute shortage in housing. Frequently renters pay as much as $325 a month for a house not fit for animals."

At the makeshift soup kitchen, a cook greeted us. Mopping his brow with his large red handkerchief, he showed us the flood-line—a dark, waist-high stain on the walls. Two years before on a pleasant evening, while children played in the streets and the elderly were gossiping out on their porches, the earth began to tremble. Manhole lids shot off. Water backed up in basements, sinks and bathtubs and water began to cover the streets. People had to run, crawl and swim to escape with their lives. A 25-year-old floodgate had broken and the Mississippi River rushed into the homes. More than 12,000 were displaced for five months. Most were low income people who had no insurance and lost all their belongings. East St. Louis could not afford a new floodgate—not even the cost of one missile—that would have saved its citizens from much agony.

In Buck's office we noticed a framed placard saying: "Non-cooperation with evil is as much a duty as cooperation with the good." Buck explained that it was a Gandhi saying picked up by Martin Luther King, Jr., and later included in the Nuremberg Principles. "The message for us is clear: the evil of the Trident, much like South Africa's apartheid, is dependent upon our cooperation. We have to choose: we can cooperate with evil or resist, be silently in complicity or actively loving. What would it mean if we really were acting together through love to stop this train which is running over us all?" He continued, "I'm convinced that love empowers, liberates and changes things. We can fragment our understanding and thus weaken our response, or we can see the bigger picture and work together as a united movement for justice and peace." His final words were: "Remember, our responsibility is to keep the faith!"

People Trying to Practice Their Convictions

In these five differing situations we see people "doing ethics." They demonstrate not so much how to dance the minuet of protocol, but more how to struggle and apply their convictions as they encounter the hard facts of human existence. The task remains the same: to meet immediate responsibilities by relating convictions to the changing facts of life. The questions each raises about family, neighbors and coworkers reflects questions we all face. Communities differ, but in each one, we find struggles with which we can resonate.

Obstinate problems are often difficult to clarify and hard to solve. Kay is trying to integrate the new knowledge professors offer and the convictions with which she was nurtured. Stewart wants to protect his daughters from gang-war bullets and to halt forces that turn a city into a fortress or a wasteland. Rich and Sherry wonder if there is an alternative to a painful divorce. Lester Abrams, as mayor of a burgeoning new city, seeks to discover and apply ways that will provide effective governance, and Dr. Buck Jones ministers to people suffering economic, racial and psychological deprivations. The answers they reach are simple but profound, enlightening but sobering. In the ways they confront their situations we see not so much the proclamation of beliefs, but the search for viable guidelines. We find less "normative" and more "descriptive" ethics. On the surface these people are concerned with harmonizing ethically ambiguous situations with their surest convictions.

What about conscience? Did these persons have an inner ethical compass to serve as a reliable guide to action? The conscience is no clear and certain interpreter of the will of God or of the ethical choices incumbent upon one in obedience to that will. The ethical reality of conscience requires a context or community within which the conscience can give behavioral shape to free obedience.

Thus, the questions surrounding conscience demonstrate that Christian ethics, both in theory and practice, has been haunted by the dilemma between ethical irrelevance and ethical relativism. Frequently we are clearer about the whys and wherefores of the ethical confusions we find ourselves in, than we are about how we can apply a Christian line of action to the situations. The problem is whether ethical behavior can be clearly defined and convincingly related to the decisions of life. The task is to try, by systematic ethical analysis, to set out the terms in which problems of living may be stated and resolved.

In viewing the profiles of these few we see that to live is to make ethical judgments continually. As they select behavior considered "wrong" or "right," we note how difficult it is to decide responsibly amid the dilemmas occasioned by the ambiguity of daily experience. Their struggles in deciding also show how, whether they realize it or not, they engage constantly in practical ethical reflection—evaluating the correctness and appropriateness of their decisions.

The nature of "doing ethics" is not so much a speculative question about which among many rationalizations can be summoned, but an urgent question affecting what reflective persons are doing in the world. The one "who does not know such facts," observes Paul Weiss in *Man's Freedom*,[1] "who does not know that peace is good, that the world is not the best possible and should be improved, that love is better than hate, is insincere or mad." Furthermore, every concrete ethical question involves determining what is to be done with reference to a certain pattern or context of relations. For those who accept the Christian faith, the aim needs to be to rethink what that faith implies with regards to their behavior.

Human Response and Ethical Dilemmas

A variety of dilemmas confront people as they relate to one another in the present cultural crisis. Our post-modern period presents complicated personal and social problems that are exaggerated because it is a time of radical transition. The incredible has become the expected and the outlandish, the norm.

Along with technological achievements and artistic accomplishments, we live in societies where children are abused, persons are raped and mugged, individuals are starved and alienated and the elderly are relegated to smelly convalescent residences. We are beset by the necessity of responding, through tax-supported programs, to other socially catastrophic problems: drugs, the breakdown of the family,

[1] p. 179.

the epidemic of violence, the increase of the severely mentally disturbed huddling or howling on our streets plus the new phenomenon—homelessness—displaying an intensity of visible suffering and disorder unprecedented since the long lines of the Great Depression. A recent report in San Francisco newspapers describes how the social effects of crack, joining with the health-care costs of the AIDS epidemic, could possibly bankrupt the city. Neither of these were even heard of ten years ago and yet today they pose a substantial social and economic threat.

We must reckon not only with the problems of people of other cultures, but with their differing beliefs as well. The reckoning requires much more interaction with other belief systems. What is more, these other religions are also in the midst of their own crises and times of transition. In each of the world's great religions we find a widening chasm between faith and consumer-dominated societies. In reaction we find the upsurge of strident challenges of fundamentalism in Christianity, Judaism and Islam.

The upheaval, caused by affluence, on tradition and community, as well as the Keynesian emphasis on a credit and consumption-led growth, spills over onto the cultural side. If restraints were off on the economic side, why not in one's personal life? Libertinism in codes of private behavior are matched, paradoxically, with political conservatism in the wake of stagflation and the dislocations of the internationalizing information economy. Issues such as sexual preference or abortion intersect with the deeply held religious commitments of others who are in the same economic situation. Politically considered, these preferences are non-negotiable, distorting classic expectations and allegiances of left and right parties. In the U.S. the fallen authority of the Establishment started with the breakup of WASP hegemony, just as patriarchy and male domination gave way to the changing status of women who increasingly entered the work force and organized the feminist movements.

Predicaments come from the way life in society involves contradictory demands: some forces pull while others push; a period of curbing narcissistic impulses is followed by a time of expressing them; while conforming to social norms one day, we challenge them the next. Where there is freedom to explore and create, persons cherish the recognition and concern they experience; where they are molded rigidly to fit narrow roles, relationships frequently bring feelings of rejection, devaluation, anger and hate. In encountering one another, people steadily struggle to achieve a mutual acceptance. An ethical corollary to these ambiguities leads to the human tendency to ignore or mute the voice of conscience with our rationalizations, so that persons "acting appropriately" in a particular social situation may go against their own standards and values.

The intransigent dilemmas found in the family show the pain of Western culture's crisis. Divorce courts are full of couples that could not (or would not) develop a working one-to-one partnership, much less the spirit-oriented healing and reconciling qualities that lead to a fulfilling relationship. The 13-year-old daughter in a conjoint therapy session capsuled one family's faulty relating when she blurted out, "We are all fouled up. All four of us go our own way at the expense of the rest. We are unwilling to let go of our own selfish ways. We've got to stop tearing one another apart and get our family act together. We've got to risk changing and get some give-and-take between us."

Similar difficulties shadow response patterns of institutions. No agency can fulfill all human needs and expectations; as in all social endeavors, some come out ahead, others lose. However, the large organizations, which make up society's infrastructures are susceptible to special bureaucratic breakdowns that present serious ethical issues. The hierarchial nature of institutions creates inequality between individuals and groups and leaves unresolved conflicts to fester and erupt. The need for the centeredness that leaders provide presents the dilemma of how subordinates can be given fair and just treatment.

Another ambiguity arises from the paradoxical nature of the law which is purposed to establish justice, but frequently awards it to the privileged and wealthy. Jurisprudence often tends to get bogged down in intricate torts which, instead of searching for the fundamental rights and wrongs of the case at issue and recommending more realistic response patterns, tends to administer a "justice" dictated by current ideologies and political expediencies.

Ironically, religious bodies are not exempt from the ambiguities which face secular institutions. Churches, synagogues and temples have difficulties relating to established political power arising from their dual character as institutions in the world and as bodies of individuals acknowledging a moral imperative derived from belief in a power higher than itself. Institutional Christianity confronts the problem inherent in all institutions—the danger of misusing the secular power it inevitably accumulates by virtue of its high ideals and positive goals.

Ethical Dilemmas for the United States

What are some of the conditions today that challenge ethical decision? What does a critical testing of reality show? A painful starting point is the warning of the Pulitzer Prize-winning author David Halberstam who believes we must discard the arrogance of success which has blinded this country to the abilities of nationalist guerrillas (Vietnamese) and economic competitors (Japanese) alike. What happened in Vietnam and what is happening in our industrial core today can be traced to the hubris caused by history's favor. We did not see the changing world. We did not give credit to other nations for being talented or for working hard. We squandered resources. Our business practices became astonishingly insular. We are entering a highly competitive world in which knowledge and human resources, not military might and natural resources, will be the dominant aspects of power.

America's competitive edge in world markets is seriously threatened because it is failing to educate its large population of Blacks and Hispanics, with the result that America will soon have an even larger part of its population illiterate and underproductive—a permanent underclass. No nation can carry ten to 20 million people in an underclass and still remain competitive. This question transcends civil rights, Christian compassion and national ideals. The growth of a permanent underclass has reached the dimensions of an American survival issue. How does America compete in the world? How does America penetrate technological barriers? How does America keep civil order or maintain its centrist political values? How do we do any of these things if we fail to bring our growing minority populations into the economic mainstream?

Although Americans need to worry about the trade deficit, this is not the main problem. We need also to concentrate on domestic factors. For decades we have under-invested in our physical, human and knowledge capital. We have happily supported taxation and government spending priorities that have encouraged a live-for-today attitude. As a result, we have the lowest national savings rate among the advanced industrial nations. Americans who worry about the fact that foreigners are buying up the country's prime real estate and productive assets should worry instead that we have put them up for sale in order to live well now without investing enough for the future.

Economic growth of America is further threatened by the changing pattern of the distribution of income. In 1985 the top 20 percent of Americans earned 43 percent of the national income—the largest percentage earned by that group since World War II. The bottom 20 percent earned only 4.7% of the national income—the smallest percentage in 25 years. As we build weapons of destruction, 32 million Americans live below the poverty line, a third of all Black and 28 percent of Hispanic Americans are poor. In his book, *The Ultra Rich*, Vance Packard reports, "The top five moneymakers in the financial community in 1986 made 6,542 times the salary of the average full-time American worker, $13,451 compared to $88 million. The wealth of the 400 wealthiest individuals cited by Forbes now equals the savings that all Americans have in commercial banks."

These facts suggest a new polarization along income lines primarily a result of a transformation in the American economy. We've lost millions of jobs paying $12 and $13 an hour and replaced them with millions paying $5 and $6 an hour. We've shipped millions of jobs offshore and continue to lose our basic industries. The economic growth rates have fallen by half, exacerbating the industrial dislocation. In 1973 eleven percent of America lived under the poverty line and the growth was four percent per year. In the 1980s our growth rate was two percent. As a result, poverty has begun to grow again to 15 percent. San Antonio Mayor Henry Cisneros observes, "Think of the human waste that occurs when large segments of our society no longer participate politically and economically in our democracy."

Another element in the crisis of American culture is found in its diminishing middle class. Often downward mobility takes on a communal character. When steel mills close their gates, oil fields fall silent and farms experience epidemics of foreclosures, downward mobility engulfs entire communities. The blight spreads from the shuttered factory to the town beyond its gates, undermining the firms that supplied it along with the restaurants, supermarkets and clothing store where workers used to spend their money. The public sector struggles to support schools, police and fire departments on a reduced tax base.

The connection between a community and its industries runs deeper than paychecks and tax revenues. The manufacturing plant becomes a moral bedrock, an institution that anchors a town's special character and weaves the fortunes of many generations together. When something so fundamental to a community's sense of self disappears, the consequences are more than economic—they call into question deeper commitments of loyalty, stability and tradition. A plant closure becomes the focal point for evaluating the kind of world the workers inhabit and the shutdown is viewed as a harbinger of symptoms of industrial transformations that victimize the workers and their family.

"Feelings of anger or dismay, a sense of injustice," are the responses to downward mobility, reports anthropologist Katherine Newman in her book, *Fallen From Grace.* "They worked hard for what they had, deferred gratification when necessary and sacrificed when called upon by their country or their families." The disappointment turns into bitterness. One plays by the rules, pays one's dues and still is evicted from the American dream. There simply is no guarantee that one's best efforts will be rewarded in the end and eviction avoided. Newman explains how the downwardly mobile middle class has been betrayed by market forces and by the ambitions of political figures. Hence downward mobility is not merely a matter of accepting a menial job, enduring the loss of stability, or witnessing the evaporation of one's hold on material comfort—it is also a broken covenant.

The true cost of downward mobility cannot be measured only monetarily. Beyond the psychological damage, it ultimately undermines society's values and threatens prosperity. Downward mobility adds up to a monumental waste of intelligence, motivation and aspiration. A nation built on ingenuity, skill and devotion to the work ethic cannot afford to suspend so many able people in perpetual limbo. They should not be left to suffer in silence or in self-loathing; there are too many of them and they represent far too important a repository of experience and capability.

Another closely related condition contributing to the crisis of American culture is the frequency of failed expectations within community life. Often more psychological than economic, these wishes and hopes when dashed produce disappointment. This is not only an American phenomenon.

In Japan, a look under the kimono reveals a world where many managers see their own lives beset by institutional rigidity, murderous competition and—in recent years—rapidly diminishing expectations.

In whatever culture, disappointment and hurt are especially painful in more intimate relationships involving greater emotional investment and vulnerability—as when partners violate their pledges to one another and engage in damaging narcissistic power games. Likewise in social relations we often find our trust in reason, decency and honesty betrayed and see that we cannot assume that every encounter will be guided by *rationality*. Often a reachable goal is a romantic dream. Where there is freedom to explore and create, both individuals and communities can give and receive recognition and appreciation more readily. Where serious ambiguities prevail, as in our society, that needed validation is blurred and the basis for responsible decision-making is confused.

Violation of ethical expectations in politics often appear to be more the rule than the exception because in the art (not the science) of managing the affairs of state, leaders feel justified in carrying out partisan or factional intrigue within a given group. The Government Accountability Project (GAP), a watchdog citizens group, in one week reported on government neglect or violations: in Bay City, Texas, a nuclear project was found to contain 600 safety-related irregularities as a result of a "major quality assurance breakdown;" in Maryland a high ranking official, Louis Clark, was fired from his job because he blew the whistle on a company's unsafe handling of hazardous wastes; and widespread neglect was discovered in the Department of Agriculture's mandated program of inspecting processed meats.

The wake of the Reagan administration is strewn with unresolved political dilemmas. Of Ronald Reagan the *Washington Spectator* observes, "He was never the manager of government or chief policy maker, except in the broadest sense—his anti-communist and 'trickle down' views."[2] The *Christian Science Monitor* states, "Perhaps not since the tragic era of the robber barons a century ago has the unsavory aroma of political corruption been so pervasive throughout Washington." Reagan's closest advisers, Michael Deaver and Lyn Nofziger, along with his military aide, former Admiral John Poindexter with his assistant, Lt. Col. Oliver North, were convicted. Former Air Force General Richard Secord and the attorney general resigned under a cloud. The sleaze did not start with the Reagan Administration, nor will it end with the Reagan Administration.

The breakdown of traditional authority structures produces voter apathy, unprecedented heterogeneity and an excessive tendency to litigate every conflict. With the neglect of citizens' responsibilities we have moved away from the political center toward paralysis and gridlock. American society is becoming so culturally diverse the center can no longer be held together by the older elites with their school ties and cocktail parties. "The notion of social authority," Daniel Bell warns, "is pretty much gone in this country. That's why we have the rule of celebrity, of notoriety and personality."

Richard N. Goodwin, author of *Remembering America,* warns that we cannot attack difficulties of the magnitude and complexity such as our nation confronts through the present political system. "The hierarchy of both parties," he claims, "has been thoroughly corrupted not only by the private economic bureaucracies that rule social life, but also by those who comprise them."

With few exceptions, political leaders have been absorbed—psychically, spiritually and in action—into the controlling centers of wealth to the point where they identify the desires of large enterprise with their own function as public servants and with the fulfillment of their personal ambitions.

---

[2] January 15, 1989.

New and innovative structures of governance and goal-setting need to evolve, but the country's brain and energy power are not directed in this endeavor.

The weakening, by corruption or subversion, of politics is particularly threatening to society. In the broad sense, politics has to do with the foundations, structures and ends of human community. What happens in the world has relevance insofar as it makes human community possible or problematical. The dynamics of change in the world are compounded of natural processes and social forms and make political analysis and responsibility imperative if human life is to be worth living.

The U.S. is aware of the strength needed to mobilize political responsibility; our history has been one of working out pragmatically mixed approaches to complicated political and economic questions. What cultural crisis means in this regard is that it is terribly difficult to capitalize on the elements of health, because the framework within which civilization is understood appears to be so ambiguous or inadequate that making clear decisions in practical affairs is impossible.

Many of the bonds cementing community in other times no longer hold in this post-modern era. With the new freedom, a part of community was lost. In marriage, romantic love has traditionally been the basis for the choice of a life partner and the condition for the continuation of a life-long bonding, but it no longer guarantees a genuine and durable community-relationship. Similarly, the intense commitment of political activists or conservative evangelicals may denigrate the very community they seek. In other generations most groups in America included an element of community as well as an element of life-style enclave, but no longer is this the case. In a time when work is seldom a calling and few of us find a sense of who we are in public participation as citizens, the life-style enclave, fragile and shallow though it is, struggles to fulfill the essential sense of identity with a community that individuals need.

Crucial Ethical Issues within the Global Village Earth

In the family of nations during the 90s it is an uncontested fact that each country is fast becoming increasingly dependent on the others. Equally clear is that our habit of projecting onto the relations of nation-states our inner jungle philosophy is suicidal. If we continue to harness our paranoid feelings to the armaments that the accelerating tempo of technological industrial organization is capable of producing, we will continue to squander irreplaceable natural and human resources. If we continue to make these armaments available at points where they can do the most harm, we are setting the stage for a nuclear holocaust. If we parlay human suspicion, greed and egoism into a jingoism we hasten that outcome. No longer can each state cling to old, deep-seated presumptions of its own superiority and a corresponding resentment against any other's presumption. The critical test of reality can no longer be neglected, by-passed, or allowed for unconscious reasons to be avoided.

For the U.S. this means we must critically test the reality of our policy toward our neighbors to the South—lands soaked in blood and with crushing burdens of stagnation, unemployment and low productivity—and focus on our sense of what is right and wrong behavior of nations. What does it mean to the people of Central and South America that today Americans casually speak of Central America as "our own backyard?" What does it mean that those of European descent—a plurality of the people of the U.S.—that their comfortable life-style is largely built on the backs of our neighbors to the south and the rest of the Two-Thirds World? Are we willing to see how an ideological obsession with Nicaragua has blocked out any vision of the fragility of democracy and the movement toward democracy in Latin America in the face of overwhelming economic problems? Are we ready to face the ways in which the Iran-Contra scandal poses a moral challenge to this nation, endangering the strength and integrity of our democracy? Are we willing to recognize that hidden within these crises are extraordinary opportunities for citizens to meet the challenges, expose the truth and change this country's course?

The U.S. is challenged to bring forth a clear-cut course that is more than a compromise between various positions. We need to talk not only about a final condition called peace, but also about a process in which we ameliorate situations, move them to more stable conditions, and never pretend the process is finished. When we attempt a more critical testing of reality about the crisis of our culture, what do we find? The ethical issues are planetary. It is not only a Soviet problem, a North or South American problem, a European problem, or an Asian problem; it is a structural problem of the world.

In helping to improve the ways people communicate and get along, we must both go "beyond" and get "under" our own particular culture. The trail may take us from New York's rotting inner-city to Los Angeles' bustling Koreatown; from Beijing to Buenos Aires, from dilapidated Cairo to Paris; from the financial bubble of Tokyo to depressed Mexico City. It's not a passing fad that prompts social theorists to urge that we respect the plurality of cultures and take into account the influence of the cultural sentiments that have been so thoroughly absorbed as to remain unexamined "background phenomena." George Bernard Shaw's quip is to the point: "The Golden Rule is really–'Don't do unto others as you would have them do unto you–their tastes may be different.' "

A major symptom of the cultural crisis of our time is the inability of modern nations to conceive practically of peace and economic stability at the same time. It is not that a majority of people do not desire both, but they are unable to see their political and economic problems in such a perspective that both appear to be simultaneously possible. A more subtle dilemma is that freedom and an adequate standard of living appear to be antithetical in our day. It appears that the mastery of our own historical destiny is in jeopardy: modern

humankind is becoming the prisoner of technological enterprise. Transportation, communications, the production and
marketing of all the necessities of life require a high organization of capital and personnel. Therefore the ability of any
individual to affect the process, or even to handle one's own
affairs with any real independence of the process, becomes
relatively impossible.

When the structure of society and the general sense of
self-fulfillment is shaky, people's thoughts, relationships and
actions have no sure foundation of confidence. The expectancy which focuses social life is blurred and anxiety results.
Whether a question of American foreign policy or of the role
of the family in an urban technological society, there is no
clear perspective to enable people to make accurate decisions and to take purposeful action.

What are the much written-about and analyzed old "perspectives" we have used? The two presuppositions are,
1) that by an objective relationship to whatever concerns us,
we are able to control, manipulate or at least adjust to,
circumstances satisfactorily; and 2) that individual self-fulfillment through economic acquisitiveness is the means whereby
a healthy society lives.

But post-modern society is losing confidence without
realizing it. We have hitch-hiked on a long series of technological and scientific victories at the expense of the structure
which made possible the winning of these victories. In the
face of these ethical questions, whose impact ranges from
individual to international, not a few seek to escape from
having to relate to people. Others despair over the ceaseless
harassments of society. Overpopulation is surrounding us with
more people. Queues are longer in New York City, Tokyo,
Moscow and Paris for subways; bumper-to-bumper traffic
aggravates the world. Pollution, congestion and rabbit-warren
housing, though eased in the U.S., is becoming increasingly
oppressive in Shanghai, Calcutta and Mexico City. The cry of
moral nausea, disgust with the established order and despair
for its reformation, fuels profound anxiety and erupts in

protest. Rapid social change weakens the moral consensus of society and magnifies the problem of persons—particularly adolescents—in finding an identity for themselves.

People are deeply worried about the legitimacy accorded evil, instead of mobilizing constructive action for the good. The evidences of the cultural crisis highlights how desperate people are to find some guidance for meeting the ethical issues they confront. People cannot lay hold of the full significance of the dilemmas they encounter and when these are not clarified so as to be dealt with, their persistence increases their confusion. The search for these and other options indicate that people are not prepared to analyze their culture critically.

Ethical Concerns of the Social Sciences

The issues in decision-making are much the concern of the social sciences which must take account of the fact that humankind is free and unpredictable in a way in which atoms and molecules and planets are not free. Ethicists assume that people are responsible for their actions—within limits of their freedom. The degree of freedom is a prime concern of psychology, sociology and theology.

The social science disciplines deal with questions of motivations and the goals people pursue as well as what motivations ought to be and which goals people ought to pursue— continual ethical inquiry. The theories and programs of social science disciplines reinforce and sometimes challenge the values developed by ethicists. Anthropologists have found that in searching for what a primitive tribe held to be responsible communal living, they gained a crucial tool for understanding that tribe. The mosaic of why people did or did not get along became clearer and more distinct through the study of what was considered responsible in human biology, language, technology, social organization, ways of adapting to the physical environment and what aspects of institutionalized behavior are variable cross-culturally.

Responsible communal interaction forms the backbone of studies of human functions in many areas. Medical sciences show how health is a matter of responsible communal interaction: the human body, protected by the epidermis, gains energy and vitality from the responsible functioning of its highly developed homeostatic systems; and public health depends heavily on the society's responsible research in epidemiology, as nations discover in their efforts to combat the AIDS epidemic.

Similarly, studies in education and ethics show that the preservation and transmission of culture and the inculcation of values and the spiritual life require responsible communal effort and support. It has been shown that imparting values and beliefs is less effective in the young who have not experience trust and love and have not associated with nurturing and believing adults. Experiments in psycho-biology and religious education demonstrate this educational-moral emphasis of a responsible community enhance well developed and integrated selves. In such a society they have been encouraged to be and act rationally and to accept moral responsibility.

Ecology, as a biologic and environmental science, has close connections with ethics and philosophy. There is no way to keep them separate, asserts Stephen Toulmin, since every ecological "fact" has ethical significance.[3]

James Bellini in a Sierra Club publication, *High Tech Holocaust,* writes, "Acid rain is destroying our forests, contaminating our water supplies, changing our climate, eroding irreplaceable historic buildings and, we are now discovering, causing the slow wasting of humankind through corrosion of our own body chemistry." Reading his book one is overwhelmed by the lethal ailments generated by our industrial age. The destruction of the planet and its resources, the poisoning of the air and water on which we must all

---

[3] *Return to Cosmology,* p. 265.

subsist present inescapably hazardous consequences to all humanity. We unleash poison into the fragile envelope of nature that sustains us in order to make money—or so that some can make money. The trade-off is simple: We can reduce present profits in return for life.

Ecological concerns present unavoidable ethical issues. Our desire to "conquer" nature makes our culture differ starkly from those of the past that sought harmony with, not dominance over, the precious systems of the earth and for whom its creatures and its habitats were sacred. Even though we have the skills and resources to correct the ecological travesties we have committed against our environment and make the planet earth livable again, the issue is whether we have the will to forsake war and greed and attend to the future.

The Swiss serve as an example of what can be accomplished in improving their ecological practices. They decided to act on the conviction that humans and nature *can* live together and correct the cumulative damage to the earth caused by pollution. What they have done to preserve the ecology of their land serves as a model for other nations. In the last decade the Swiss have achieved this near miracle through political will, legislation, massive application of available technology, state-of-the-art resource and waste-management systems and intricate program coordination at the national, cantonal (county/state), communal (municipal) and individual levels. Theirs is an achievement in social ethics and the key to success has been the high degree of cooperation among all parties concerned. "I think that it is a problem of politics rather than techniques," was how Hardi Gysin of the Federal Office puts it. "The technology has been known for years, but if each little village makes its own decisions, then implementation is impossible. The cooperation and work of the entire population is essential."

What about the relation of psychology to ethics? Ethics has an important reliance on psychology which sheds light on the ethical problem insofar as questions of motivation and

the effects the choice of particular ends or goals are concerned. The decisions of psychologists, as to what aspects of
human behavior they choose to investigate and the direction
in which they seek to influence the personalities of their
clients, involve ethical considerations of the utmost importance. Psychology, in analyzing human behavior, deals with
the process and dynamics of decision making. Psychology
helps clarify people's psychic needs and the complexity of the
motives involved, but it does not provide an answer to the
crucial moral question: What is humankind's true good and
toward what goals ought our actions be directed?

Consider the case of a child molester. Sociological, legal
and in most instances religious norms would meet such
behavior with disapproval, punitive action and certainly
judgment. The psychologist in no way would sanction such
behavior, but sees the ethics as what can be done for the
client and the family in such a situation. Understanding may
come from psychoanalytic and family systems theories. Often
adults who sexually abuse children are repeating their own
childhood trauma in some form. Child sexual abuse can also
be understood as a symptom which functions to elicit a limit-
setting response from a strong, warm parental figure. With
molesters, we are dealing with a pathology of the self—they
have been so damaged by abuse or deprivation in their
childhood that their object world is severely deficient. Child
molesting can be a desperate attempt to establish human
connection and get rid of internal anguish.

Severe fragmentation of the object world results from
unintegrated view of the external world absorbed into
oneself. The molester develops the sense of having a "rotten
core," a feeling of inner badness. Molesters are fragile,
sensitive persons, fragmented with the threat of psychosis and
acting out. For the psychotherapist, the ethical issues require
moving beyond "understanding" the dynamics of this human
being to treatment. Kohut says that treatment must be
characterized by nonsexualized affection and nonhostile
firmness. Alice Miller says that the therapist should always

take the side of the abused child in the psychic structure, so as to validate the hurt and rage produced by the childhood trauma. These clients are narcissistically vulnerable requiring consistent and nonpunitive empathy, firmness in setting limits to impulses.

With ethics as with psychology, sociology looks first to the ways individuals and societies interact and organize themselves. Concerned as it is with human behavior, the discipline must also study peoples' decision-making and even make recommendations about their goals. The discipline cannot avoid the question of how *ought* the patterns of behavior which are adjudged normative in a particular culture themselves be changed? The task of moral evaluation, choosing between cultural norms, is of a different order from the empirical one. Here we are faced with the question of how ought the customary morality be changed? Conventional religion in America has frequently been guilty of sentimentality, expressing emotions unrelated to the empirical facts. Responsible social ethics may be defined as "the study of *what is* in light of *what ought to be*."

Sociologists in studying social processes explore what a society holds to be responsible responding. The socialization of individuals from infancy to adulthood emerges as a crucial concern. Responsible socialization is seen as the intergenerational transmission of culture, the acquisition of impulse control and role-training for social participation. The operation of these three essential factors cannot be taken as self-evident. Full account must be taken of what the community considers to be "responsible," how this is taught and whether in their interacting persons truly learn to live "responsibly."

Responsibility and Community Living

How does a community arrive at concepts about what it holds to be responsible and what difference do such concepts make in community living? The answer is found in what the community considers to be of *value* and what it holds to be its guiding social ethics. A society's higher goals and the manifestation of its positive qualities depends on how completely and honestly its citizens live by their system of value.

In Western societies gold and diamonds, health and happiness, knowledge and skill are all viewed as having *value*, certain things with more than others. Each of these evaluations include a social content and have to do with relatedness. Granted, there is a personal component of values, but a large share of these have to do with person's relatedness to creation and the Creator. Value is more than the justification for what a particular person does, thinks or dreams; it involves asking whether some things are more worthy than those I want and am pursuing. Virtues such as honesty, veracity, friendship and love receive their common *value* from communal directives.

But how can there be responsibility to both self-interest and the demands of society's moral values? Each person has the obligation to be aware of a system of values and to continue in the process of finding and acting on the basis of the community's system of values. Values flow beneath the surface of our consciousness like great Pacific currents. To talk about the responsibilities of individuals and communities invites the study of the prevalence, content and source of our values.

The expression of values is found in every aspect of our lives. Values affect occupational selection and personal goal-setting. These choices are influenced by how much stress is placed upon the development of drives for achievement, motivation and aspiration. Vocational choice and identity have much to do with social status. Behavior, thoughts, feelings and aspirations are directed toward the realization of what individuals value. As people pursue their differing wants they order their choices by values. What they prize, or consider of worth, is what they value. What they value is given special attention and becomes a goal with a higher priority. To hold one's obligation as an important value is to live responsibly.

G.K. Chesterton once quipped that a wise landlady had better know not only her roomers' financial solvency, but how strongly they value their obligation to pay the rent. In a world beset by unfulfilled promises, crises and violence, we need to reexamine our commitment to ethical standards. To understand life and live it responsibly is to look seriously at what we consider to be of value.

The meanings and expressions of *value* are many. Much depends on the context in which the words are used. Value, in the market place, is the monetary worth of an object or service. Businesses seek to assure the public that what they offer is of value. The mention of "value" is intended to catch and hold the buyer. Value is the utility or merit ascribed to something. If we give the valuation "good" to a wine we make an empirical statement—"I've tasted it and like it." The meaning may be "it has value in slaking my thirst," a means-end value, or used by a wine merchant, may convey "this wine sells well" or belongs to a vintage considered superior.

Complicated problems surround determining values for human behavior. Setting values on objects is comparatively easy. Objects can be sorted and graded according to agreed standards. Setting human values is vastly more complex for this involves personal and social aspects. To set values and determine conduct accordingly one must appreciate the differences of others and be considerate of the values held by parents, friends, colleagues and the community. A "good deed" is an action that agrees to some given standard—to an ideal we use as our model or to an imperative stemming from our set of values. Value may be defined as that aspect of motivation which is referable to standards, personal or cultural, that do not arise solely out of immediate tensions or immediate situations. "A value is not just a preference," observed the anthropologist C. Kluckhohn (1952), "but is a preference which is felt and/or considered to be justified morally or by reasoning or by aesthetic judgments, usually by two or all three of these." Judgments about music or art have to do with values that are closer to moral value judgments than to empirical observations. Instead of saying that a goal *has* value, in this usage, a goal *is* value. Similarly, instead of saying the "good" has value, we say the "good" is a value.

The concept of *value orientation* is elaborated by two university professors, Talcot Parsons and Edward Shils, who suggest that patterns of value regarding approved behavior, people's relation to nature, each other and a Supreme Being, have been singled out as the most crucial cultural commitments and systems of action. Cultures, they hold, have value standards—cognitive, appreciative, moral. These standards are "acquired by the actors living in these cultures." Value-orientation, or the organized core of personal value, is a set of linked propositions embracing both value and existential elements. The constant reciprocity of the individual's unified value core and one's perception of others serve to strengthen identity and self esteem. People choose what is least or most wanted according to where they place themselves on the value continuum. This is their particular *scale-of-values* and what they consider good, better, or best is relatively enduring and is maintained even in the absence of external reminders. Values are not the concrete goals of behavior, but are aspects of these goals and appear as the criteria against which goals are chosen.

Life is a process of coming to find what is valuable in the decisions we act upon. Regardless of what ultimate values may exist, there is an interior component of one's *sense of value*. We search for value in ourselves and in what our intimates consider of value in order that we can gain their approval and acceptance. We search for value in the world and ultimately in our faith. Finding value in something is a complex and tentative judgment, one which we cannot avoid. Our lives are spent defining and redefining our values, never quite having fully applied them continually discovering the need to move from narrower to broader values. The process of evaluation is not a matter of matching an object or event to dependable criteria of judgment, but of finding out its value. This is the imperative of continually refining and testing our personal and social value systems.

The values we hold come largely from emotional and ideational influences as we grow. Our individual goals have arisen in the context of small group experiences. Families, peer groups and education all play important roles in forming our values. To a degree values arise out of our needs. When I am hungry and thirsty, food and drink have value. When I am cold, heat and clothes are of value. We experience a progression in the process of evaluating. We move from window shopping to wondering if we should buy and finally decide to make the purchase—living out the exercise of deciding on the basis of our values. Values also develop out of conditions of the community's needs. In early America the values which emerged were functional—hard work, rugged equality, self-government and frugality—all bound by a strong sense of life in common, sustained by familial ties and religious beliefs. A value is an acquired human quality. In times when the communal bonds that generate values among citizens are eroding, values tend to fade and/or become confused. The efficiency of values will be more secure when they have strong cultural support.

As central as they are, values are problematic. Basic questions surround the values people hold or do not hold. Which are to be chosen among the many competing values? Are values fixed points, or is there a continuum of what is good, better, or best? Is value relative or stable and enduring? Is value maintained in the absence of external reminders? Differences in values easily lead to strife which can end in division. Where value is placed exclusively on concern for personal power and aggrandizement, relationships suffer. We ask how differences in values can be handled.

Deciding between values presents a series of difficulties. A generally accepted consensus of central values, neat and clear, is hard to find. We confront a plethora of value systems, but the bases of existing moralities are in a state of flux. Then there is the failure of people living up to the fullest of their knowledge, will and aspirations. Confusion of values occurs as the natural split between theory and practice widens into a chasm. Lip service may be paid to the values of authority, while behavior contradicts them. Religious people may love their neighbors on the Sabbath and spend the week competing, demeaning or even chiseling them. Self-styled patriots who champion the freedom they have fought for may deny freedom of speech to dissenters whose concept of patriotism is contrary to their own.

The training in how to find values and keep a balance about values is rarely consistent. Our youth today receive contradictory messages: parents offer one set of shoulds and should-nots, as do the schools and the media; the church proclaims its own ideas, and peers offer yet another view. Adults are conflicted in matters of values in crucial areas: work, politics, religion and family. Widespread emotional instability often throws out of kilter the process of valuing. Whose values are we to accept and follow, and how are we to keep our powers of discrimination sharp and our commitment to values firm?

An essential reaction in dominant endeavors of contemporary searches for personal and social value systems is a fundamental challenge of traditional approaches which are seen as bankrupt. Kenneth Underwood, a campus minister, puts it this way: "We are in grave need of knowledge. Not so much in terms of how we think people in various positions of responsibility ought to act and what they ought to bring to their actions in the way of religious principles, but of knowledge that tells us the actual basis or grounds of action of persons in the major institutions and professions of the society."

To understand and apply values requires an appreciation of the long history of philosophy and religion with respect to seeking foundations for a viable set of values. Serious thinkers in their reach for a whole view of the world and the Creator, to use Carl Sandburg's phrase, always have been "looking, looking, looking" in disciplined search for what is of value. Philosophy, dedicated to a reasonable search for meanings and significance within the totality of life, arose out of concern with the nature and applications of that which is of value. Through the centuries philosophy and religion have been the makers and custodians of traditional values. An examination of these values and proposals for their application provide a solid basis for meeting moral problems. Distilling the essence of our diverse value-seeking is an enormous but rewarding undertaking.

Philosophers and clerics have consistently held that moral principles are involved in all human relations and function in collectives. Influential thinkers as diverse as Confucius in sixth century B.C. and Ludwig Wittgenstein in the twentieth century A.D. focus their teachings on human relationships within the family, with neighbors, rulers and with the Supreme Power. The goals, guidance and prescriptions provided by ethical norms hold communities together. Over millennia historic religions have developed beliefs and ethical systems that clarify, regulate and undergird the values by which persons live in community. Religion in many ways serves as an indispensable binding force for societies. The very root of the word religion in Latin means "to bind together."

Human relatedness according to the Hebrew-Christian tradition unites the practical (phenomenological) and the spiritual. Our interdependence and the nature of required social behavior are central themes in the Bible. Human relatedness came "in the beginning" as the culmination of Creation. Adam *and* Eve together assured the fuller reaches of humanity. With them the possibility of freedom, the capacity to *choose* and *act* morally, was a significant original endowment. The family was the continuing earthly unit supporting the social body. "We are our brother's [and sister's] keepers," both bonded to and responsible for others. Later, the covenanted group, or chosen people of God, came to be the core structure of community, the social womb where relatedness began. The cutting edge of the great Hebrew prophets was the conviction that all human actions stand under the judgment of God, which established a kind of built-in principle of social criticism.

The centrality of human relatedness continued with the rise of Christianity, stemming from the Hebrew tradition which renewed the emphasis on people's responsibility to one another. In the life, ministry and sacrificial death of Jesus the existential and the eternal were fused (in the Incarnation). In Christ, the God-human, the ultimate bonding of persons was demonstrated. Thereafter within the beloved community, *koinonia,* which is "the body of Christ," the core of "the Kingdom of God on earth" was assured. Support and guidance came from the legacy of the faithful who had died and provided a surrounding "cloud of witnesses."

In becoming aware of self, others and God our spirits are awakened. Essentials of relating are brought out and empowered with such qualities as self-decision and social responsibility, the possibilities of either hurt-guilt-fear-anger or concern-empathy-openness-love and the inescapable commitment to act responsibly within community. Christian response is governed by the conviction that there is a unique dimension in human nature standing above physical nature, social groups and culture. This dimension provides the quality of obedient love and is a three-sided responsibility: love of God, love of neighbor and love of self. This special quality of love dignifies humans and accounts for their superior spiritual nature, while giving them a compelling moral imperative.

Although moral principles are involved in all collective relations, the application of ethical norms is limited by the vagaries of human nature. Individual persons may be moral in that they are able to consider interests other than their own in determining problems of conduct and are capable, on occasion, of preferring the advantages of others to their own. Their rationality prompts them to a sense of justice and discipline and may reduce egoistic inclinations, but these achievements are more difficult, if not impossible, for societies and social groups. Although government serves as the seat of authority, the community is without the unity, centeredness and focused will which is characteristic of the individual. In groups there is less reason to guide and to check impulse, less capacity for self-transcendence and less ability to appreciate the needs of others and express more unrestrained egoism in their personal relationships.

Reinhold Niebuhr in his book, *Moral Man, Immoral Society* (1932), claims, "Human collectives, races, nations and classes are less moral than the individuals which compose them and justice between groups can therefore not be achieved purely by educational means. Injustice must be resisted. The problem is to find forms of resistance which will not destroy the meager resources for rational and moral action which groups do possess." Conflict, he asserts, is inevitable and power must be challenged by power. When collective power, whether in the form of imperialism or class domination, exploits weakness, it can never be dislodged unless power is raised against it. If conscience and reason can be put into the resulting struggle, they will only qualify, never abolish, the injustice. Helping to improve the ways people get along together is but the beginning of responsible community living. Therefore the reinforcement that comes with the exercise of social responsibility is essential for growth toward justice in any community. Crucial is the role of personal religion, which keeps values under the judgment of God, exposing partiality and demonstrating the consequent need for the mercy of God.

For Christians, the mercy side of the Creator is the unconditional love of God. The challenge is for people, though harassed by ambiguous demands within conflicted communities, to exercise not only their rationality but also their convictions about Christian obedient love in devising what should be done in relationship with other persons in the common life. Christians are not always faithful to the moral imperative given them. It is easy to be entangled in culture and fail to carry out the primary responsibility to God's kingdom. The church has not always proclaimed the meaning of God's rule.

The deep-seated and energizing values and moral principles of humanity are immersed in the perplexing dynamism of freedom. Both social scientists and ethicists agree that persons are free to respond. Autonomy is not canceled out by the determinisms that impinge on it, but is made possible by them. Assuming that we are free to respond, we are challenged to develop a science of responding that does justice to our freedom.

The appeal of freedom's dynamism is inestimable. Its measure for contemporary America lies in the freedom to arouse the imagination of the entrepreneur and its citizens' faith in the future. It is this freedom that attracts immigrants. The combination of cultures enriches individuals and communities increasing the sense of opportunity, social mobility, artistic expression and even spiritual search. An expanded freedom also comes from the creative alchemy of a diverse culture, where Hispanic family values and Asian group loyalty meld with the rational individualism of Protestant America.

Western culture understands freedom to be the absence either of political coercion or of economic pressures, but in both cases its reference is to the "rights" of individuals to be self-determining. The contemporary crisis raises the question whether this understanding of freedom is broad and deep enough to describe human existence. In comparison, the New Testament sees freedom as the result of adoption into the family of God. Eduard Heimann observes that "Christian freedom, which ultimately is the freedom to obey God . . . has become the freedom to use one's superior intelligence, cunning, financial strength, social connections to gain advantages over one's neighbors." Thus, this fuller-dimensioned freedom goes beyond the notion of maximizing one's income under varying conditions. Freedom under divine discipline always includes justice and responsible community. Prayer itself is an act of our freedom, even though the prayer is for a greater power to come to the aid of that frail freedom.

Human freedom, Paul Lehmann notes, "has been precariously caught in a squeeze between an *autonomy* which identified . . . freedom to decide with freedom of choice and connected the knowledge of good and evil with the internally directed exercise of the will and a *heteronomy* which identified the knowledge of good and evil with an imposed order of stability and connected . . . freedom to decide with assent and adherence to externally directed rules and regulations." The bond between moral knowledge and moral action gave a crucial meaning and function to conscience. The dilemma between *autonomy* and *heteronomy* has all but rendered the conscience ethically expendable. Because the problem remains, the conscience continues to haunt sensitive people with the possibility of a link between the knowledge of good and evil and the freedom to decide on the basis of that knowledge.

Communal Solidarity and the Just Society

The fact that the warp and woof of our conscious and unconscious existence is largely determined by social conditions, makes communal solidarity the foundation for a just society. Thus peoples are interrelated and individual actions have far-reaching affects upon the lives of others. Our communities form the womb in which we are conceived, nurtured and from which we break into larger relationships. After the family come the influences of schools, workplace, the nation state and the cosmopolitan network of our sustaining earth.

The quality of the individual's identity and autonomy in a particular age depends on the social character for that age. The sequence is described by Erich Fromm as "the role of social character types in the historical process." In Western urban societies with growing economic abundance radically different characteristics appear from those of our ancestors. We have lost the sense of community so typical of rural existence. The impersonality of city life and work has deprived us of the sense of "belonging" treasured by earlier generations. The media and competition with peers educate us on accepted attitudes toward friendship, productivity, leisure and consumption. Politics and work have become consumable. Society catches us up in a network of interaction that requires developing patterns of conformity with the class character in which we are located.

Consequently in Western societies we live in at least three planes. As David Riesman pointed out in his book, *The Lonely Crowd* (1950), "we are adjusting to our history, facing a new centrality for politics and constantly expanding our dream of the good life." On the first plane we are dominated by modes of conformity in several successive periods of our history: the medieval, the near-contemporary industrial and now the post-modern, in which, though we continue to be absorbed in the "age of production," we have entered the "age of consumption." In politics, the American middle class often deals more with myth than wisdom, investing more of its emotional commitment than its reason and sense of justice. We neglect correcting the myth that we have a "ruling class" free of entanglements with special interests. Or we cling to the idea of the community, which assures us of the "good life," in which we can feel free and be free. We are conflicted as we try to coordinate our life on these planes.

In our post-modern society, the development and exercise of the freedom to respond gives evidence of new limits brought on by the increasing complexity of our life-styles. The range of our possible responses is integrated with cultural systems of action, comprising symbols and codes that are organized and incorporated in art, literature, accumulated bodies of academic knowledge and religious doctrines. These systems provide the stimulus and guidelines for our normal patterns of behavior leading to the development of roles and institutions—all of which seem to grow more involved and complicated each year. Under such conditions creativity is expressed not only by innovative ideas and plans, but also by transmitting them to others.

"The way to change the world," affirms Robert M. Pirsig in *Zen and the Art of Motorcycle Maintenance*, "is not through a bunch of social programs for others to carry out, but through our own 'heart and head and hands' and work outward from there." He holds that group values will not be right until individual values are right.

The "helping professions" serve to increase our understanding of the potentialities in our relating with others, but we cannot be blandly optimistic about the capability of these disciplines to change societies. Technology may outdistance sociology and culture and blow us up. Irrationality may get ahead of rationality. Hard-nosed realists say we cannot count on an unseen hand having stacked the cards in our favor.

The person of faith disputes this pessimism, recognizing a judgment against all pretensions to overly simple solutions and yet maintaining a faith that beyond judgment there is always the message of hope for the contrite. The committed Christian is convinced that personality and community are rooted in the fact of a Spirit Presence. Prophetic religion holds that God is in control, affecting one's relationship with others and with communities. The added dimension is that of a person-to-person encounter in prayer which transcends ordinary experiences in intensity and effect, but which neither extinguishes nor disintegrates the core of persons and communities. The Hebrew prophets taught that all political and social constructs are found wanting when measured against the yardstick of divine justice. Human constructs stand in need of continual critique.

Summary

Convictions about ethics develop in the reflective process of reason, experience and faith while meeting life situations. These convictions do not occur in isolation, but come about in the process of a continuing give-and-take between self and community. The current crises surrounding us challenge us to see the "public interest" as an integral part of practical politics. The elevated talk of tolerance does not seem to do the trick. Deeper than the inadequacies of euphemisms and lip service is the problem that rhetorical recipes, in themselves, are not self-interpreting or self-implementing. Laudable as "tolerance," "cooperation," "consideration," and other such conditions sound, in themselves they are no substitute for a guiding ethos that provides vision of the common good and its application.

Ethical convictions about how people can function effectively in relationship do not come as a gift of nature, but rather grow as patterns of response which individuals and communities must achieve. Since personality does not occur in isolation, guided social action is part of the process of self and community fulfillment. This kind of factual search for the genuinely better course of action, coupled with the journey of faith, provides a supremely important discrimination which is the life of committed religious persons. We serve a God who is absolute, but our service is relative. Amid the relativities of our day-to-day responding, it is crucial for us to respond to the absolute and give our response to God.

Surrounded with a disorienting fluidity of values, what are the responses given? In the end it is the power of the guiding ethos shared with the world, and not on its force of arms or the opulence of its economy, that the greatness of America depends. Lacking a sense of mission, our nation will likely flounder and lose hold of its true identity. Only by rediscovering our revolutionary charter and applying it to the realities of the post-European world can the U.S. in its third century enjoy a renaissance equal to the great vision of its founders and develop the potentialities of its people. Moving along that higher ground depends on one's quality of life and purposeful work in communities.

These questions are critical because the survival of community depends upon human interaction that is optimally reciprocal and mutual. As the search for the "good," ethics is of crucial importance in community life. Urgent questions are: What kind of society best embodies and enhances the optimal interpersonal interaction held as the ethical ideal? What kinds of social structures frustrate them? The pursuit of this social arrangement involves a large measure of pragmatic judgment and testing among existing and possible arrangements and systems. Often there is no way of judging before the fact whether a given structure will be good or evil or degree of "goodness."

Christians affirm that the relation of each to all, through God, is real and objective—at once an immediate and an eternal relationship calling for a particular relationship with God and with each other. Meister Ekhart suggests: "Those who are wholly surrounded by God, enveloped by God, clothed with God, glowing in selfless love toward God—such persons no one can touch except they touch God also." Such lives have a common meeting-point; they go back into a single Center where they are at home with God and with one another.

The "blessed community," formed from the unity of individuals of faith, is far deeper than current views based upon modern logic would suppose. The blessed fellowship reaches behind these intellectual frames to the immediacy of experience in God and seeks contact in this fountainhead of real, dynamic connectedness. The quality of a healing community and its unique vivacity can contribute to restoring mental health for individuals and societies. This fellowship is more profound than democracy conceived as an ideal of group living. It is a theocracy wherein God rules and guides and directs the listening children. The center of authority is not in humanity, not in the group, but in the creative God.

The degree of self-disclosure to others is variable with time, place and person. But "we, from our end of the relationship," affirms the Quaker philosopher Thomas Kelly, "can send out the Eternal Love in silent, searching hope and meet each person with a background of eternal expectation and a silent, wordless prayer of love." For until our life "is shot through in every relation and even in death, with Eternity, the Blessed Community is not complete." The completion of the response of self-disclosure and responsible at-one-ment in community awaits the final pooling of joy and love in God which is accomplished in the silences of the Eternal. Short of this, friendships, partnerships, marriages, are incomplete. Personal relations which lie only in time are open-ended and unfinished to the soul and community that walks in holy obedience.

Health and Wholeness as Trusts

Health and wholeness come to us both as gifts and as responsibilities. Without a minimal degree of health, we cannot live, and without a sense of wholeness we do not live optimally. With this combination of vitalities, we are able to meet our needs and wants and fulfill our responsibilities and hopes. These two essentials for life empower the complex web of personality. As highly prized natural potentials, persons of all cultures have sought health and wholeness to fulfill their uniqueness and completeness. It is the experience of the race that the trusts of health and wholeness require responsible care and nurture.

Health and wholeness are difficult to describe and measure. Though not altogether synonymous, they join in making the basis for a full and optimal life. We think of health as specific and immediate, wholeness as more global and a quality to be cultivated. Both are conditions that become especially appreciated in their absence. When head or stomach ache and shoulder and toe hurt, we feel the lack of health. On the other hand when body parts function harmoniously we acknowledge that we are "healthy," a condition we too often take for granted.

Sometimes we slip into hypochondriacal thoughts and begin to imagine symptoms. But most of the time the whole self directs feelings and energies against illness. To recover health when we lose it is to rediscover the natural harmony that is rightfully ours. Subjectively, we express what can be called "health-conscience"—the effort to discount symptoms and evidence a degree of physical and emotional well-being. We devise regimens of exercise, vitamin taking and "slim-trim" dieting to show that we have healthy habits and wholesome attitudes toward the self.

Health and wholeness have to do not only with body parts and systems, but also with mental, emotional and spiritual well-being. A helpful analogy given by Evarts Loomis, a physician who suggest, "Every cell in the human body has its own level of consciousness and is, as it were, a member of the body's orchestra and responsive to the direction it receives from the mind of the person." Emotional and spiritual health, as well as physical health, are positive states and not the mere absence of illness. Mental and emotional health are fluid states of well adjusted persons stirred with a zest for living and self-realization.

These conditions may be obscured by bodily illness or faulty thinking, as well as anemic emotions or unfounded faith. Just as health has the enemy of disease, wholeness has the enemies of separation and alienation, incompleteness and brokenness; and love has the enemies of hatred and conflict, rejection and indifference. Preventive measures against the obstacles to health and the journey toward wholeness emerge as commanding ethical responsibilities for individuals and societies. Health may be compared to the purr of a well tuned motor. Wholeness can be likened to the achievement of a great symphony, performed by talented musicians and directed by an accomplished conductor, who appreciates each member of the orchestra.

The perception and search for *wholeness* begins with our first awareness and continues throughout life. Wholeness

starts with a healthy body and involves persons in a continuing growth process moving towards integration and completion. The effect proceeds not from the parts singly, but from
all of them in combination. Greater than its parts, the whole
draws people toward fuller and more ultimate living. Although we have many distinguishable parts, we are a union
and we seek the unitary nature we sense. It is with our whole
selves that we interact best with the environment—with
nature and with others.

The fact that we were created in the image of God for
health and wholeness provides us with very significant
possibilities. In creating human beings, God endowed us with
the capacity of love. Love in humans is a reflection of the
love of God. In our journey toward health and wholeness,
love serves as both a quality and power. In love the whole
being's movement is toward another in seeking to overcome
sickness, incompleteness and separation.

Health as Problematic

The achievement and maintenance of personal and social
health presents very complicated problems. Our investment
of time and resources in matters of health is tremendous and
looms as a major concern for both individuals and societies.
In the last decade surging "illness-care" costs tops the list of
priorities confronting legislative bodies in the U.S.

The escalating expense of medical costs runs wildly out of
control. Each of us now spends an average of $1,200 per year
for such services. The price of illness-care doubles every five
years with incalculable social effects of sickness. The matter
is more complicated than it might seem. The pain associated
with the faulty functioning of the self is not always experienced by the ailing individual. This is particularly true with
contagious diseases as in the current AIDS epidemic. The
emotional and financial cost of care for the senile and the
terminally ill becomes increasingly burdensome.

The admirable advancements of medical science have reduced the dangers of many life-threatening diseases, but more than half of the patients seeking medical help suffer from psychological conflicts they have been unable to solve alone.

Inadequate management of the emotional traumas associated with physical illness hounds the present system. Too often we overlook the fact that human beings also have minds, feelings and souls which may be out of kilter and physical illness can be accompanied by persisting questions like: Why does this happen to me? Have I brought this illness on myself? or Why must I endure this helplessness and this treatment? All this is coupled with panic over the frightful expense of hospitalization. Many emotionally afflicted people require special, sometimes long term care. These individuals are not only a burden to themselves, but to the many who cross their paths.

Specialists in both the Two-Thirds World and the West find the American health-care system overrated. They point out that the ten most frequent causes of death among the U.S. population in the early 1900s have been greatly reduced by controlling the infectious killers: tuberculosis, typhoid, diphtheria and influenza, but in their place today we find cancer, heart-disease and stroke. Thus we merely substitute one set of killers for another. Douglas M. Castle, a former E.P.A. administrator, noted with the cost of health care in America now at $150 billion a year, with most of this going for after-the-fact attempts at treatment and cure, renders it imperative that we need to reorder our national and individual health priorities. He points out, "How much more health and cost-effective it would be to place more emphasis on prevention—on keeping harmful materials out of the air, water and soil—and out of our people."

The current personal health system, or "non-system," is plagued by serious difficulties. One is the inadequacy of basing a massive and sophisticated profession chiefly on the idea that health is the absence of disease. This negative view avoids the larger problems of public health. Another difficulty arises from the fact that "health institutions" leave a significant segment of America's health problem unattended. Some of the problems stem from directing medical care towards treating diseases instead of stressing a more wholistic approach. Most forms of treatment neglect to take into account that it is not just a stomach which gets sick, but rather a whole person who falls ill. Beyond this there is the unfairness of the present medical delivery services.

In many cases it is either the poor or the rich who have access to medical care excluding the middle income groups. One of the largest difficulties arises from the astronomical costs of sedical care. The excessive financial burdens of the system becomes almost unbearable for the individual and distracting for medical professionals who must increasingly spend time "marketing" their services.

Other serious problems with the current illness-care system arises from its tendencies to become itself a dinosaurian bureaucracy on the one hand and to infantilize the ill on the other. The profession has become intensely entrepreneurial as well as healing. Medical schools, research centers, hospitals and physicians in private practice have become increasingly burdened with paper work, collecting fees, operating offices and making investments. Maintenance of quality professional services becomes more and more difficult.

Likewise Western medicine discourages adults from taking charge of their own lives. Patients are made dependent. A person lying down is dependent on someone standing up. Health care systems often depersonalize the patient and the solution to the problem of finding a balance between pampering and neglecting the patient remains difficult to achieve. Significant care is added when those in attendance go beyond their medical procedures and help patients feel they are part of the forces of health working to return them to wholeness. When health care workers and attendant clergy cannot see beyond the disease, they become as much a victim of the disease as the one who is sick.

Another problem connected with our health-care delivery system arises from the demand for the "magic" of pills. Health professionals are cast in the role of "pill fairies," who must possess omnipotence and infallibility. Problematically, prescription drugs have become one of the leading causes of death. In the U.S. drug-related deaths rank number eleven on the list of killers. Medical professionals are affected in the backlash, experiencing burn-out, developing ill-temper, abusing medication themselves and even finding themselves pushed to suicide.

The development of comprehensive health-care education and many other preventive measures need immediate attention. Modern medicine's breakthroughs in pathology, surgery, innovative treatment procedures and other advances, number among the remarkable achievements of this century. The next large scale innovation to achieve fuller and more optimal lives challenges the medical profession and society to take more responsibility for more effective programs of prevention.

A major five-year study at the Carter Center of Emory University in Atlanta recently identified 14 primary causes of premature death for which preventive action can be taken. The six risk factors most frequently cited were tobacco, alcohol, injuries, unintended pregnancy, lack of preventive services and improper nutrition. Tobacco was identified as the single leading cause of death—1,000 deaths in America each day, all of them preventable. Alcohol, the second most important risk factor, can also be reduced. We can turn ourselves into a healthier nation by making more effective use of the knowledge we already possess.

Similarly, human well-being can be enhanced through the improvement of mental health by means of increasing the opportunities for psychotherapy and developing widespread preventive programs. One such area is an increased need for information on stress reduction. Stress, experts tell us, is one of the most disturbing emotional experiences that upset the delicate balance of health. Taken from the physical sciences, where it refers to the application of a force that weakens and distorts a body, stress has been applied to extreme psychological pressures that are emotionally disruptive.

Relatively new in Western medical research, the concept of stress has proven useful in measuring an organism's imbalance and is found to cause trouble in the interplay between mind, body and spirit, undue and prolonged stress damages individuals as well as relationships. In his pioneering research Hans Selye found that in stress life-assuring functions are pushed to extremes and become impaired. Prolonged stress suppresses our immune system and its natural defenses against diseases. The overloads of stress in Western societies arise from emotional traumas, prolonged frustration and exposure to serious environmental hazards. Physicians also tell us that cancer, cardiovascular and other degenerative diseases characteristic of our time are connected with excessive stress.

Preventive measures are needed to teach people responsible ways to confront the bodily and emotional imbalances caused by stress. Hans Selye and others point out that stress can be controlled and reduced by monitoring reactions to its several stages: 1) the alarm reaction, 2) the stage of resistance and, 3) the stage of exhaustion. In stressful situations we tend to tighten up, lose our usual flexibility and restrict the functioning of body, emotions and thought. Learned stress reduction techniques exert a positive impact on the mind/body system and help control the disease process caused by the accumulation of excessive anxiety, guilt and rage. Preventive help comes as we understand how we allow stress to accumulate, creating conditions that make us vulnerable to illnesses.

Every program designed to better a nation's public health must take seriously world health problems. The World Health Organization addresses the gargantuan problems of illness, physical disability and malnourishment that are such great enemies of human betterment in the Two-Thirds World countries. The need is to develop a public health leadership group which can implement and greatly extend changes.

Health-Care Systems of Other Cultures

Enlightened and helpful lessons can be learned from the experience and practice of other cultures. In earlier societies, the health care emphases appear to have oscillated between stressing how the separate parts and the whole person exist in relationship with nature. At the same time, we find a reliance on people's conception of nature and the cosmos and we see responses to values and spiritual disciplines.

People from cultures that have not had the benefit of modern medical knowledge tend to see the source of illness and the process of healing as associated with forces belonging to the spirit world. In such cultures a variety of healing rituals and shamanistic practices develop. It was believed that illness resulted from some disharmony with the cosmic order of which people are an integral part. Causes of disease are linked with the person's social environment and the active intervention of ghosts and spirits. The shaman serves as the agent who enters into a non-ordinary state of consciousness to make contact with the spirit world on behalf of members of the community. The shaman, instead of looking for bacteria or physiological disorders, will allegedly consult witches and sorcerers to find evidences of jealousy or wrongdoing or failure to keep the moral order by the ill person, or by a member of the patient's family.

Shamanistic approaches aim to reintegrate the ill person's condition to both the social and cosmic order. Healing rituals often try to raise unconscious conflicts and resistances to a conscious level where they can be expressed and resolved. Shamans used techniques such as group sharing, psychodrama, dream analysis, hypnosis, guided imagery and psychedelic herbs for centuries before they were found by modern psychology. One marked difference remains: where psychotherapists help individuals construct personal "myths" with elements drawn from their past, shamans provide them with a social "myth" not limited to personal experiences. In Jungian terms, the shaman works with the collective or social unconscious rather than the individual unconscious.

In ancient Greece healing was considered to be a supernatural phenomenon associated with a range of deities. Hygeia was venerated as the goddess of health and personified the belief that people would enjoy good health if they lived wisely. Hippocratic approaches to illness and health brought a radical new orientation that advanced the conviction that illnesses are not caused by demons or evil forces, but are natural phenomena that can be studied scientifically and influenced by therapeutic procedures. The "new" Greek health practitioners (fourth century B.C.) rejected as quackery the magical and often "verbal" therapies common to earlier cultures and relied on management of the *physis*. The role of the physicians of the new "naturalistic" medicine was to assist nature's healing power, inherent in the organism. The parent of modern Western medicine required a state of balance among environmental influences, personal ways of life and the components of cosmic forces.

In ancient China, significantly, the main themes of Hippocratic medicine were duplicated. Unlike the early Greeks, the Chinese were less interested in causal relations than in studying happenings in a particular time without consideration of historical data: they were concerned with "synchronic" patterning of things and events. Shun Yu, an early Chinese practitioner, explained this dynamic thinking: Things behave in particular ways not necessarily because their positions in the ever-moving cyclical universe are such that they are endowed with intrinsic natures making that behavior inevitable. The cosmic patterns were mapped out by means of a complex system of correspondence with such crucial influences as the seasons, atmosphere, colors, sounds, parts of the body, emotional states, social relations and other such phenomena. As in other early Chinese traditions, the equilibrium sought was a balancing of the *yin and yang*. Natural, social and personal universes are in a state of dynamic balance with all their components oscillating between these two archetypal poles. An equilibrium within the vital forces surrounding individuals and the derivative medical practice were formalized in the early medical classic called the *Nei Ching* developed during the Han period (206 B.C.—210 A.D.).

The body, according to the Chinese, was considered in terms of the functioning of its interrelated parts rather than in its anatomical details. The picture of the lungs, for example, includes the two lungs and the entire respiratory tract—the nose, skin and secretions associated with these organs. The individual organism, like the cosmos, was seen as being in continual, multiple and interdependent fluctuation. The patterns were described in terms of the flow of *ch'i*, a "gas" and not a substance, which keeps a person alive. Imbalances and hence illnesses come when the *ch'i* does not circulate properly along the pathways called *ching mo* or "meridians."

The causes for such imbalances are multiple: poor diet, lack of sleep, lack of exercise, being in a state of disharmony with one's family or society. Illness is seen less as an intruding agent and more as due to a pattern of imbalance. Both health and ill-health are seen as natural and as being part of a continuum—aspects of the same process in which the individual organism changes continually in relation to the environment.

In traditional Chinese medicine the healer, more than a manipulator of symptoms to relieve pain, is a sage who knows how the patterns of the universe work together. Each ill person is treated on an individual basis. Diagnostic methods are necessarily lengthy and require the ill person to participate actively by contributing as much information as possible about personal life-styles. Reliance rests heavily on subjective judgments based on the healer's senses—touch, hearing and vision—through interaction with the ill person.

Whether or not the Asian medical model can be blended with a holistic approach to health in Western cultures remains in question. The Asian reliance on the subjective knowledge of the ill person conceivably can supplement Western medicine's tendency to depersonalize disease. One synthesis is found in modern Japan where subjective experience is valued and linked with rational deductive thinking. Asian *kanpo* healers would not take an ill person's temperatures, but would note their subjective feelings about having a fever; herbal medicines prescribed would be measured only approximately in little boxes without the use of scales. Western healers find it difficult to incorporate into their concept of health the more intuitive traditional Asian view of the body and disease.

Responses that Open a Broader View of Health

The achievement of a more effective system of health care must begin with the integration of the various approaches into a more holistic view of health. Health, rather than an absence of illness, must be seen for what it is—a wonderful balance and vitality. Neither a neutral nor final state, the condition must be experienced as a dynamic participation in life. It is a condition which enables persons wholeheartedly to enter into creative projects and purposeful relationships. The vigor and enjoyment that come with health gives individuals a sense of confidence and lends the feeling of being a part of a larger community and a larger purpose.

The human constitution includes systems that make for health. Developmental psychologists describe our constitutions as channels of energies—flowing in, coursing around and flowing out. Health results with an optimum intake, a satisfactory inner assimilation and energies effectively moving out into the environment. When the flow is regular we feel healthy. When eating, digesting, exercising are impaired by injury we feel ill. The resulting "illness" is not so much "punishment" visiting us as it is a warning that our accustomed way of life is out of balance and needs correcting. Ill persons are helped not only with medication and surgery, but with the knowledge that improvement is a powerful drive of the body and a genuine concern of the healing team. The ill need to be reassured they can move through sickness back to physical wholeness and to a deeper self-realization.

Within each of us a deep reserve of biological, emotional and mental strength presses for health. Those who work with them notice how the sick struggle to regain health. The great abuse our bodies and personalities can take and the rapidity of their recovery provide indications that we are made for health. Similarly, traumatized emotions and confused minds strain to recover stability and clarity. Along with facing the external forces and conditions that may cause illness and death, we need to live in the confidence that what may be called a "kingdom of health" resides within each of us. It is reassuring to recognize that our bodies are naturally sound and that homeostatic immunization systems function continuously to maintain health.

Recommended disciplines that help maintain health are many: the regular intake of nourishing food in adequate, but not excessive quantities, with an accompaniment of positive mental outlook; regular and guided physical exercise; relaxation practices; free expression in music and the arts; consideration of one's spiritual life and meaningful service to others.

Russell Dicks and the Richard Cabot, two specialists in the health sciences, outlined a philosophy of health based on their experience at the Massachusetts General Hospital, Boston. More than a prescription, they set forth a singular image of health, which affirmed that humans are created for health. People become ill when destructive bacteria or disruptive emotions block the healing forces. They proposed putting eight positive emotions against eight disruptive emotions. Their list, from their years of experiences with ill people struggling toward health, included movement:

1. from anxiety to faith	5. from loneliness to love
2. from hostility to joy	6. from pain to courage
3. from guilt to self-awareness	7. from boredom to creative work
4. from despair to hope	8. from rejection to acceptance

They observed that when the mind and emotions were pulled back from the brink of destructive actions to a positive outlook, the body's battle for health was strengthened.

Wholeness is the goal toward which health reaches. Striving for wholeness is more important than the removal of illness. Illness is the lack of wholeness. The self, or the central part of the person, loses a sense of unity. The personality's willing, suffering and choosing falls into conflict. When in bed, enervated and racked with fever, this central part of a person experiences sickness in mind, heart and soul as well as in body.

The complex inter-relationship and amazing unity of the self, that total personality, makes health a matter of its wholeness. Physical and emotional disorders alike affect the health of the whole personality. Depression, anxiety and guilt can cripple and overcome the healthy body and render us unable to function. Research on the body's intricate immune system indicates that defenses against disease are seriously weakened by mental confusion and emotional instability. If any part of our nature is threatened, denied or undernourished, we suffer throughout. The word "health" is derived from the old Saxon word "hal," from which we get the words "hale" and "whole."

This more inclusive conception of health reaches beyond achieving "peace of mind" and adjustment to social demands. Peace of mind as a standard for wholeness may amount to an anesthetization of the individual's higher sensibilities to self or surroundings. The great among the race have never had much peace of mind for they were painfully aware of their own inner conflicts and suffering of others around them. Adaptation as a standard of health is also misleading. Those who adapt to a sick situation or community become part of that sickness. Health may then consist in a movement from within that results in what appears to be maladaptation to one's surroundings and way of life.

Within each organism, and especially the human being, we find an awareness that senses its larger nature and life goal—an inner center that knows what constitutes wholeness and feels pointed towards it. The Chinese remind us that we cannot know we are ill if we do not have some awareness of the better state of wholeness. When our ego-consciousness becomes related to our inner core, we move toward physical and emotional health and the wholeness of our personality.

The movement toward wholeness may bring conflict and stress instead of peace of mind or social adjustment. The journey guarantees not happiness but growth. Instead of wealth or achievement, wholeness promises the development and integration of the emotions, mind and spirit.

Wholeness is more a process than a condition. Our life must have a "story" or consistent theme if we are to become whole. People move toward wholeness as they offer the composite of their efforts, much like composers present an accumulation of their opuses. Wholeness, as a process, calls upon each of us to face the string of life's difficulties in ways that grasp the meaning in the pattern of events that form our lives. Human wholeness begins with the cooperative functioning of a person's organs effectively uniting both physical and mental processes.

At times we see chiefly our "parts" rather than our "whole." Looking into a microscope we see cells, supporting fluids and structures, many separate and intricate units, complete in themselves exercising their own functions and properties. In the morning, looking in the mirror, we see a totality, all the parts put together, covered with skin and encased in a single unit. We can touch our chest and know our thumping heart is part of the cardiovascular system, but looking at ourself we see ourself in our entirety, as a Gestalt. We are more likely to be concerned with the parts of the body causing us pain at a particular time. If the illness is emotional and we are concerned about our depressed and anxious feelings, we try to isolate some part of ourselves that may be out of kilter. We become increasingly concerned with the welfare of our "wholeness."

In the conception of "synergism", the biologist offers a unique view of wholeness. The reference is to a process whereby the parts of an organism interact to achieve an effect of which each alone is incapable. They function as agents of the whole and together bring about another and new whole. Arthur Coulter, a North Carolina physician, talks about "the synergetic mode" of a person's life-giving holistic drive—a condition of individuals programmed to attain greater wholeness. When this mode is "turned on" in the human mind, a new and higher level of functioning comes into being. Likewise, theologians advance a doctrine of synergism where people are "regenerated," combining surrender of the human will and the workings of divine grace.

Synergetic forces, by integrating behavior, reinforce the human movement toward health and wholeness. In converging upon a single and coordinated response mechanism, a health consciousness is activated. Out of it emerges a higher level organization. The parts of a jigsaw puzzle, randomly arranged, are simply a collection of objects. When fit together in the new whole we say the puzzle is solved. In the same way a musical chord gives a richer tone than a single note. A chord is more than just several notes sounded together; it is an emergent whole, having a quality that is absent if the notes are sounded separately. People striving for wholeness experience this as a sense of total well-being.

The social application of synergy is significant. In 1941 anthropologist Ruth Benedict spoke of "societies with high social synergy where their institutions insure mutual advantage from their undertakings and societies with low social synergy where the advantage of one individual becomes a victory over another and the majority who are not victorious must shift as they can." Two social psychologists, James and Marguerite Craig, capitalized on the power of the striving for wholeness and introduced an antidote to the sense of powerlessness so many feel today. These researchers assert that power in itself is neither good nor bad; it depends on how it is used. It is possible, they contend, for people who lack coercive power or those who dislike using it to develop and apply synergic power—the capacity of people to increase the satisfactions of participants by intentionally generating more energy and creativity. The application of this power rallies and coordinates human forces to co-create a rewarding present and future.

The holistic view of health includes a social and ecological dimensions—the individual's relation to community and environment. Kurt Lewin, a Harvard social psychologist, in studying the influence of these external dimensions, demonstrated how both the social and physical environments are transformed into goals, barriers or boundaries in an individual's life.

Wholeness is also manifested as individuals relate in groups, participating in the larger whole of one's environment and community. Our relatedness, or our social existence, becomes the crucible in which the forging of the whole person takes place. As we play out our particular symphony, within our natural environment and society, we find harmonies of all those from our ancient past who became whole by becoming what they were meant to be. It is there that we find the theme to follow with signs and guides. Our particular personality and our set of life circumstances have never been tried before. Life experiments with us in its ceaseless attempt to bring about new forms. Thus social and personal growth continues, moving individuals and groups toward wholeness.

Wholeness, then, combines the individual's search for greater meaning, purpose and wider involvement in society.

People approach wholeness by harnessing the inner forces of the unconscious and by coping more appropriately with life's outer circumstances. The journey toward wholeness does not continue, or even start, if we stand on the sidelines. Inner and outer darkness and evil must be faced and overcome.

The Form and Self-Transcendence of Wholeness

Personal growth toward wholeness continues as individuals become meaningfully involved in communities and in the environment. To a large extent, the path to, and responsibility for, wholeness remains an "inside job." Parents, teachers and counselors can explain the process and encourage us, but others cannot make us whole. In helping us, they are limited to working "from the outside." Others can facilitate healing and point in the direction of wholeness, but they cannot answer the question, "Why must *I* suffer sickness and injury." Wholeness becomes an orchestrated performance after it has been accomplished as an individual's work.

The enhancement of personal wholeness is the special concern of psychologists and religionists. Psychotherapists aim to help persons clarify the meaning and purpose of wholeness and reduce the obstacles blocking the path to that ultimate goal. Clergy proclaims the unity and loyalty to God, who created human beings for wholeness.

Carl Jung conceptualizes the individual in terms of the reach for wholeness. The self is an archetype and represents one striving for unity, which he calls "individuation." In the process, many aspects of personality are integrated and the identity achieved provides an equilibrium. Though no one ever achieves a complete unification, the self must have a minimum "wholeness" to function. The process of moving toward wholeness presupposes individuation when the self's many expressions and capabilities become focused. It is an occurrence that usually does not take place before middle age. In varying degrees it unifies all the conflicts of the personality.

Jung held that wholeness entailed the practical achievement of becoming more able to cope with life situations while integrating harmoniously into larger systems. He found that "whole" persons develop and find their identity in both "inside" and "outside" orientations; he called these introvert and extrovert tendencies. Similarly, other balances need to be worked out within life's many polarities. Wholeness is approximated in the effective coordination of the essential four capacities of thinking, feeling, sensing and intuiting. An equilibrium needs to be developed in the feminine and masculine qualities and potentials, effectively combining the woman's capacity for relationship and creativity through receptivity with the man's reason and active creativity. A balance must be struck between independence and dependence, between working within a structure and working on one's own.

Wholeness is conditioned in and through time. Jung observed that organisms interact and communicate with one another by responding to and matching one another's rhythms; in this way they integrate themselves into the larger rhythms of their environment. He noted that people move toward wholeness as they participate in the process of synchronizing their life-rhythms with those of others. The Chinese, for millennia, have described the intuitive experience of the simultaneous occurrence of a psychic state with a physical process and call it "synchronicity." The sixth century B.C. classic, *I Ching*, described ingenious ways to get at this elusive "equivalence of meaning." Our thought, feeling and behavior needs to be coordinated with the rhythms of the space and time events surrounding us.

The unifying process of fulfilling our potentials requires continual evaluation and adaptation to life's changing demands. Everything in nature seeks to realize its proper goal and wholeness. Acorns become oak trees and never pine trees, because they can become only what they are meant to be. Humans either become what they are meant to be or are incomplete, distorted caricatures of what was to be their reality. Jung identified this unique movement toward wholeness as the human journey into individuation.

This vital process that presses us toward wholeness guarantees no security or completion in this life time. In the refining process of individuation, persons come to see the thread connecting the events, dreams and relationships that make up the fabric of their existence. In our conscious and temporal life what it means to be the "whole person" may remain out of reach as an ideal, but our unconscious knows what it means to be whole. This knowledge from our Center stimulates the process of individuation. The thrust toward wholeness, as Jung explains, "often tries to produce an impossible situation in order to force individuals to bring forth their very best." Psychologist Abraham Maslow picked up this germinal view of the dynamic inner motivation toward wholeness and did much to bring the concept to the attention of the literate public. His proposals of "self-actualization" and "peak experiences" include this striving for wholeness.

Influential voices in the social sciences see people's propensity to stretch beyond themselves as they reach for wholeness. Maslow identifies this powerful tendency as the human drive for self-actualization; the drive for *self-transcendence;* which is an inner drive to enlarge, extend and enrich the self. This dominant impulse is expressed in our seeking deeper self-understanding and trying to develop new resources and capacities. Such a process of self-transcendence appears in the highest artistic and moral achievements of many great cultures. Classic Greek or Chinese mythologies are filled with characters who exemplified a self-transcendence of their societies, showing powers of being that extended beyond the ordinary. They were willing to risk taking responsibility upon themselves even if it led to tragedy.

Pascal declared our capacity to know our end is one evidence of self-transcendence. Transcendence is evidenced in the purposeful courage of a Columbus sailing into the

Western sea while others stand back in fear. In our hopes and limitations, we know something unknown by the rest of nature. In one sense, we all live beyond ourselves in the use of credit cards, buying today and promising to pay tomorrow, living beyond our means and holding to the faith that the sun will rise tomorrow. We live out of expectations which contain elements of the transcendent. We go beyond our usual role of being agents and doers and live as if certain that our expectations are founded on facts. Only as the future is touched with hope and filled with promise can we continue to live.

Life transcending itself defies the usual approaches of empirical analysis. The movement toward self-transcendence takes us beyond reason and institution. Human beings are more than intellect, and more than the sum of willing and feeling. Beyond all these capacities, we are free to become objects to ourselves; we see ourselves "as in a glass darkly." We see the reflection of self-transcendence appearing in the mirror of how others see us and also as we ourselves gain a consciousness of having greatness and dignity.

Another mark of human self-transcendence, suggested by psychologist Gordon Allport, is our conscience which provides life with the style and goals. Guidance provided by conscience enables persons to move beyond the transitory and immediate to substantive and durable values. Another description of this "inner voice" is given by Reinhold Niebuhr in *The Self and the Dramas of History*. He believes the self is revealed as a transcendent "locus which persists" in the dialogues it has with itself in history. The mystery of our being is embraced in this capacity to stand outside ourselves and engage ourselves through memory and imagination.

The prospect we have of coming closer to achieving a more fulfilled and whole life flows from the inheritance of freedoms that our ancestors strove after for centuries. We are mindful that the freedom we enjoy must be protected and extended to a larger portion of our population. "More than ever before," observes Bruno Bettelheim, a survivor of the concentration camps at Dachau and Buchenwald, "most of us yearn for a self-realization that eludes us, while we abide restless in the midst of plenty. As we achieve freedom, we are frightened by social forces that seem to suffocate us, seem to move in on us from all parts of an ever contracting world." Some respond negatively. It is all too difficult to correct and they wish not to be responsible for either their personal condition or that of society. Fortunately there are others who feel the pull of a more whole life and work to approximate it. They recognize that every time you make a decision, you are taking a risk, because very seldom do you have all the necessary information. By risking the new alternatives they can be considered self-transcending.

We experience self-transcendence in our freedom—our ability to respond on levels beyond ourselves. This freedom is connected to the polarity of destiny which stands over against necessity. Necessity is understood in terms of mechanistic determinacy; destiny points to the situation in which we find ourselves facing the world which previously we did not know. Through freedom we can identify, choose and pursue purpose. We transcend the given situation to which we belonged and venture toward new possibilities. We are free for freedom and from ourselves. We are free to endure pain and deprivation, particularly if that is the price of choosing the new way and of affirming our integrity. Such self-transcendency comes out of the past and points us into the future to produce something qualitatively new.

Self-transcendence is given a crucial place in the thinking of Paul Tillich. He outlined the steps in actualizing potential being which lead self-transcendence. First, the basic function of life is self-integration. From this established center, the self moves out, changes the environment and is changed by it. Second, the function of life as self-actualization is the circular movement of life from a center and back to the same center. It also involves producing new centers, or self-creation. Moving to actualize potential, life goes forward "horizontally" toward new centers under the principle of growth. It is self-transcendent insofar as from life itself a new dimension of existence emerges. A third way in which actualization moves is "vertical," a move beyond ourselves toward the Center of the cosmos.

A more complete self-transcendence occurs when life drives beyond its finiteness. Under the dimension of self-awareness, self-transcendence has the character of intentionality: to be aware of one's self is a way of being beyond one's self. Self-transcendence, holding sacred the greatness and dignity of the living being, is ambiguously united with its smallness, its violability and its profanization. The aim of maturity under the impact of the Spirit provides the content of awareness, gives us freedom to respond and draws us to relatedness. But in each case the aim cannot be reached without an act of self-transcendence.

Health and Wholeness: Our Personal Responsibility

"There's no escaping personal responsibility for our health," asserted the nurse-in-chief of the World Health Organization in Geneva, Switzerland. Dr. Mangay-Magalcus continued, "We humans are funny. We resist self-responsibility when we assume we are helpless, either before the nurse and doctor, or in the face of a 'foreign invader'—the germ. We persist in looking 'out there' for answers, formulas and fortunes only to find that we have them within ourselves all along." Similarly, from the famed Menninger Clinic in Topeka, Kansas, Elmer E. Green, Ph.D, affirms,"Patients must begin to change from passive recipients of medical care to active, self-responsible participants; otherwise our goal of developing an adequate national health system cannot be realized."

Taking responsibility for wellness is an individual and a community imperative. The cost of "illness-care" in the U.S., consuming more than one tenth of the gross national income in 1988, is prohibitive! Responsible reorganization of the practice of illness care must become a commanding concern for each citizen. Professionals and the public must become deeply involved with preventive programs, with the healthy as well as the sick, in social structures, mores, attitudes and values. Medical research projects and public health services need to be greatly expanded. These enterprises help researchers deal with the external conditions that overwhelm the body's protective systems and lead to illness and death.

The health systems provided by society must be designed to reinforce the individual's responsibility for wholeness. Individuals can be held responsible only to the extent that they have the freedom of access to preventive care and medication. Many health problems arise from economic and political factors that can be modified only by collective action. Individual responsibility has to be accompanied by social responsibility and individual health care by social policies. "Social health care" seems an appropriate term for collective activities dedicated to the maintenance and improvement of health. The paradigm shift in health care will involve the formulation of new conceptual models, institutions, leadership and innovative procedures.

Unfortunately many are irresponsible about their own and their community's health: Opportunities for fuller wholeness are daily discarded by millions in favor of substance abuse, suicide attempts or destructive behavior. On the other hand we see unswerving efforts to obtain an education, acquire knowledge, improve the character of individuals and the world. To live responsibly is to continue to direct all phases of life into the balance that is wholeness.

No one is entirely free from degrees of physical and mental illness and everyone is challenged to deal promptly and skillfully with these bouts of bodily and emotional disturbances. These and other expressions of lack of wholeness are more than an aggregate of errors in the body's physics and chemistry. In order to move steadily toward wholeness, we have what may be called a "salvage responsibility" to maintain the vital balance of body-mind-emotions-spirit. This balance empowers the body, enlivens the spirit and protects us from disease.

Living toward health and wholeness offers a creative adventure. Steadily as venturing into wholeness challenges us to strive in innovative ways to become more whole. Creative persons move toward wholeness within their present nature and keep changing as the environment and society changes. There is nothing quite like the inner miracle of freedom and wholeness that takes place as old distorted concepts and attitudes are replaced by healthy and creative attitudes. No one else can really bring these changes about for the individual. As the dynamic and creative attitude toward ourselves and others unfolds, a feeling of wholeness will be its fruit. Less need will be found for outer rules and regulations for our relationships. Encounters with others will be transformed because we will be sensitive and appreciative of the wholeness of others. As we accept our own wholeness, we experience and share more wholeness with others.

The adventure of moving toward wholeness calls for creative ways of fulfilling our responsibility for our own health and our collective responsibility is to help those who are less than whole: the broken and those impaired of body and mind. Our participation in the venture toward wholeness summons creative innovation in dealing with interpersonal relationships. The consummate quality and power that enhances and enriches these relationships moving toward wholeness is a deepened and creative experience of *love*.

Responsible Love: Integrating and Enlivening Power

"Empowered by the forces of love, the fragments of the world seek each other so that the world may come into wholeness," writes Teilhard de Chardin in *The Phenomenon of Man*. Love of this deeper quality enhances one's movement toward wholeness and unites people. In the blending of affection and mutuality in healthy relationships we see the magic feat of two or more becoming one through love. In such richer relationships, unity is generated. Love joins people by what is deepest in themselves and moves them toward wholeness.

"When you love someone," wrote Henry Jones in 1963, "the grass is greener, the sense of smell changes, the music is more memorable. A whole interior world of truth and color and delight is lit up. We feel kindlier and more identified with other human beings." To be empowered by love is to be touched with the summit of the human life-force. We experience familiar things in fresh ways and find value and beauty above and beyond the common standards.

This type of love goes beyond ordinary "caring" which includes attentiveness and solicitousness may make the other person dependent. Love adds to caring conscious energy, truth and hope. Love has a broadening influence on personality development. Edith Weigert, director of the Washington Psychoanalytic Institute, with deep compassion and understanding, describes this in *The Courage To Love.* "Love deepens the busy pursuits of daily living by weight of its fulfilled restfulness; it stimulates the productivity of competition and adds to the ambitions of worldly success the steady, unanxious outlook into infinity." She adds, "Care uses persons and materials for the purpose of surmounting anxiety; love transforms drudgery into useful and meaningful work and directs the flow of life toward destiny." Love melts the impersonal and gives significance to the transient. Within the one-dimensional existence of anonymity, love generates positive forces. Passion is blind; love is intensely seeing and looks into the underlying potentialities, enabling their development. With its unique alchemy, love transmutes the crasser metals of personality into the gold of personal autonomy and social relatedness.

The dimensions of this deeper sort of love are not touched by casual discourse or even grasped by the empirical means of science. The experience of love is more than a topic for a racy newspaper column or the sublimated product of sexual biology. In everyday living love is easily disguised, subverted and distorted.

There are many confusions about the concepts of love. If one says "All's fair in love and war," one does not mean love, but sexual attraction. Often talk about love really refers to romance or sentimentality or a type of hypocritical kindness or shallow altruism. The speech of genuine love is silence. It is trusting surrender which burns the bridges behind it. Love does not need verbal communication, it speaks in look, gesture, embrace, often in overwhelming intensity.

Pitirim Sorokin speaks of love's power as "the great cohesive force of the universe." Love as the affinity of one living thing for another is a biological reality which occurs throughout life. In mammals it is recognized in its different expressions: sexual passion, parental instinct, social solidarity. The "togetherness" is more than self-seeking drawing on the other person, a superficial meeting in which a person easily slips into self-deception and an absorption in role playing. The strong cohesiveness of a genuinely loving relationship results in authentic self-esteem and the movement toward wholeness. This "responsible resonance," as Franz Werfel described it, "is the active capacity for passionately developing the picture of another human being in our inner darkroom." An expression of love need not be confined to giving our affection to one or a few. We may think we have exhausted the natural forms of love with the love of spouse, children, close friends and our community, but a microcosmic experience of love amazingly gives us a touch of universal love that precipitates its expressions until the cascading phenomenon envelops all peoples.

Moral philosophers recognize that feeling must supplement reason so the objectively good can exert a force on our will. Morality, which is meant to have command over the emotions, requires an emotion of its own to do so. Love is consistently held to be "the highest good." Psychologists also accord to love the highest of human motivations. "Loving," says Erich Fromm, in *The Art of Loving*, "is the only satisfactory answer to the problem of human existence." This profound significance of love is explained in another way by Allport who said, "The absolute ideal of love catches up and focuses all the human intentions that experience convinces us are worthy of preservation."

Love in its human expressions is constantly in danger of being pushed aside under the impact of anxiety. As a power, love participates in space, time and destiny. Love experiences space as bountiful, infinite, without being anxiously lost in it. Persons validate themselves in seeking a place in the sun, in working for entitlement. The work of love is to narrow the gap separating people. This is seen in the natural gesture of love, the embrace, *la caresse*, as Sartre describes it. Rilke says, "Home and heaven disappear, only where you are, there is my place." Shakespeare's Juliet expressed the limitless generosity of love, "My bounty is as boundless as the sea, my love as deep. The more I give to thee, the more I have, for both are infinite."

For love time is experienced simultaneously as eternity and as the moment of ultimate richness and fullness. Bergson wrote of it as *le temps veçu.* Love, in the moment of fulfillment, experiences infinity as home and eternity. Elizabeth Barrett Browning spoke of love that endures and life that disappears. In Plato's *Symposium,* Aristophanes says: "Love must see eternity behind and before it." Lovers feel they have known each other forever. The everlastingness of love is concentrated in the present moment as an opening up of existence for the bounty of unbounded potentialities. Love is not an approach to ease the hardships of existence. Love transcends restricting anxieties.

Love as both the binding quality and the ultimate purpose empowers people to become whole. Through love people touch life's most complete fulfillment. Along with the urge to creativity and unity love enables one to move toward the fulfillment of wholeness. Through love we determine our ultimate purpose, and we develop a system of values that reflects our genuine nature. Our internal locus of evaluation allows us to transcend our particular rut and even our particular culture. The decisions we make on the basis of love arise out of the potentialities given by destiny. Persons touched by the unconditional agape love, suggested by the New Testament, gain access to the wholeness Tillich calls the New Being. Anticipation of that fuller life is given in the uniting character of creative experiences. This fullest love, as spiritual power, precedes personal actualization.

Pierre Teilhard de Chardin equates love of this sort with cosmic energy. In the touch of a hand or the look of an eye, a charge of energy passes from one to another and a sense of wholeness is begun. The energy of such unconditional love sets in motion a unique current of thought and program of action. This out-flowing love, Teilhard explains, "Is sufficiently progressive to lay hold of the world, at the level of effectual practice, in an embrace, at once already complete, yet capable of indefinite perfection, where faith and hope reach their fulfillment in love."

Arising from the depth of the individual, love is actual in all functions of the mind and heart and has roots in the core of life itself. Effective in the crucial processes of life, it drives beyond obstacles to effect its aim. Love seeks to overcome the misunderstanding and antagonisms that divide people. Beyond the categories of cause and effect, it is mysterious how two can become transparent to each other in a *we-ness*.

The role of love in the healing process is not only told in the Hebrew-Christian Bible, but also by Indian medicine healers, Buddhist priests and confirmed by our contemporaries who have experienced its power. In the encounters of daily life, with its intrinsic moral imperative, love enriches the individual's relating to others because it participates in an unconditional force that is at once transcendent and unifying.

Love in human beings mirrors the love of the God who created the world to move toward wholeness. Love points persons to the Creator. This relationship to the eternal is characterized by an awareness of the element of "ought to be," and with an awareness of guilt and despair and of responsibility and hope. To appreciate this cosmic relationship characteristic of love takes us to the fount and puts us in touch with the spiritual dimension of love.

Evil: Enemy of Wholeness and Love

The enemies of love-hatred and conflict, rejection and inattention come from more than ordinary "problems," they burst out from the radical reality of evil. Otherwise wholeness and love would not have to struggle against it. Evil aggravates rather than diminishes the concern about its origin and locus and ultimately defies both clarification (by reason) and suppression. No explanation of it is possible, as Kant concluded, and yet its reality cannot be put down. Evil is not a witch's caldron boiling away on some craggy fastness of the barren human story but an immediate and pervading aggregate of negative powers.

The Bible presents evil in the world as a manifestation of God's personal antagonist—never an event, never a mere act, but always a power which seduces and overwhelms people. The malicious use of force in the political world is not due solely to the availability of force but to the lust for power, greed, quarrelsomeness and vengeance. It may be wanton destructiveness but that force is always transcended by a sinister power in the background.

The locus of evil is the conjunction of the will in the exercising freedom within the insistencies of things and persons. One person's freedom is threatened by another's freedom. Each one tries to curtail or destroy the freedom of others. "Love-free-from-purpose" cannot be forced. The possibility of evil arises as individuals claim to have a nature of their own and insist on having their own way, setting themselves in conflict with others. The reason for attempting to explain this conjunction is that evil is what ought not to be. Its occurrence anywhere is sufficient to make pertinent the question of what ought to be and what we can do about it. Kant held that evil is tragic; it is the human struggle between good willed and evil done that makes it so.

Evil is always a creaturely reality. As creatures we are not only its victims but its bearers. It is therefore never wholly an event which overtakes God's creatures. Evil can only exist as a creaturely reality because beyond creation there is nothing but the Creator. It may be neat and tidy to suggest that "after all without evil one could not appreciate the good," or without brokenness we could not appreciate wholeness but that is too easy an accommodation to the ugly facts of life.

There are "valuationally necessary evils," so that we can say health points up the value of life, disease the value of health. Philosophers go a step further and posit an ontologically necessary evil—the evil necessary to make a universe be. The human and cosmic aspects of evil are subsumed under a universe of possibilities and actualities the ultimate referent of which is the absolute good (wholeness and love). To this good, evil cannot be evil unless it can be referred.

We must be careful not to identify ontologically necessary evil with natural evil or human evils. Avoiding the consistency of striving for wholeness and love almost always ends in a spiritual death. Much that proves to be abysmally evil in its ultimate effects does not come from wickedness but from stupidity and unconsciousness. Conflicts rage in the unconscious. The problem of evil is the problem of the conflict of the "creative will" with the "insistencies of things." People are the focus of creative will and the cosmos is the focus of the insistencies of things. The appeal to the universe can hardly persuade one that the life of virtue is an attractive alternative to the continuing triumph of insistency over creativity. Possessing virtue, people still fail to do much that they ought. A speculatively consistent case for the good life in a universe of necessary evil may be the best that reason can do. But this kind of "consistency" is not humanly compelling.

If such a power as genuine love wells up from our depths urging us to wholeness, why are we surrounded by hatred and conflict, suspicions and prejudices between people and wars between nations? How are we to explain the excruciating delay between potentiality and actuality? Why the anxiety of guilt feelings stemming from the discrepancies between unused human potentialities, often directed towards unreachable ideals, and the imperfections of realization?

It is difficult to develop our capabilities for love at the level that really counts—love that is compounded of maturity, courage and hope. Learning to love, like other arts, demands persistence and concentration. It demands genuine insight and understanding. In trying conscientiously to do the good, to strive toward wholeness, we face choices between two or more grave evils. Consequently we must accept our decision as the least destructive course open as our share of the darkness of the world and our own psyche.

"Truth" becomes dangerous since it can be perverted to whitewash the most horrifying acts and attitudes. The ideals of justice, unchecked and unseasoned by mercy, become formidable and relentless. The goal of trust can erode into an illusion and the sharing of love come to be seen as a threat to self-preservation. Even the most intimate opportunity for human trust can deteriorate into accusatory, hostile competition.

People turn away from the striving for wholeness and sharing of love when they shut their eyes to their anxieties and guilt feelings. They lose themselves in being busy or distracted. They forget about their imperfections, their contingencies, their mortality, the tragic aspect of human existence. Thus they lose the authenticity that love and wholeness offers. Their consciences are no longer integrated into their egos and they become heteronomous mechanisms. This turns healthy self-love into a malignant narcissism. No longer true to themselves, they cannot be truthful with others. The spontaneity of the I-Thou encounter is endangered. Under the pressure of unbearable anxieties the I-Thou relation freezes into an I-it relation in which the other one becomes a thing that can be forced. Force mobilizes increased anxieties and defenses against anxiety.

The relation of trust and good faith, so essential to wholeness and love, degenerates into what Sartre calls "bad faith," the owner-slave relation of hostile, envious competition or relentless vindictiveness. The damage to self-esteem this engenders was what Sullivan saw to be "the greatest harm that people do to one another." Such wounds elicit the warning signals and mobilize automatic defenses against the painful experience of anxiety. These defenses become habits of character formation, incapacitating not only emotions, but also perception, cognition and will. In schizophrenic psychosis, instead of the reach for wholeness and the sharing of love, we find a fragmentation of the ego and alienation from interpersonal relations.

The radicality of evil resists the rationality of evil and undermines the striving for wholeness and will to share love. Only when persons can be true to themselves can they overcome the defenses of others and meet them in an I-Thou encounter that respects the authenticity and truthfulness of both partners. The radicality of evil sharpens the urgency of another perspective from which a context may be derived within which to deal both with evil and with good and thereby open the channels that free up the reach for wholeness and the expression of love.

An Inclusive Perspective of Health and Wholeness

Regardless of how responsible I may be in my various roles in society, I am not a whole and responsible person until I have faced the question of trust or mistrust of an ultimate totality. Beyond the potentialities unique to my particular personality, reference must be made to the surrounding biocultural realities and the supporting philosophical assumptions and religious convictions I hold.

Wholeness requires I become aware of and nurture my unique center—which is the repository of my history and my uniqueness—and that I become aware of and nurture my relationship to the ultimate totality.

Our urge to explore the mysteries of life is a healthy growth that requires the steady lifting of our awareness above the limits of our physical sensations, our emotional impulses and our usual patterns of behavior. Growth is marked by an enlarging world in which our sensitivities become keener and more discriminating, minds reach out for more knowledge and truths, relationships are challenged to become genuine and compassionate and spirits hunger to respond to what is more ultimate.

A puppet cannot be a moral creature and our modern knowledge of the forces of the unconscious makes us aware that a far greater degree of self-realization is required of us for moral autonomy than our grandparents, or even than our parents had at their disposal. As long as the Christian symbols were projected onto a living experience, they gave a connection with the unconscious that has been largely lost today. For questioning moderns, the psychological approach to symbols is the only guide when consciousness cannot find the way by itself because these symbols still express the ancient mysteries that had seemed to be lost along with their concrete interpretation.

Hans Jonas in *The Imperative of Responsibility* (1984) describes the "excessive magnitude of responsibility to extend the human vision within the 'utopian dynamics' of technical progress." He asserts that by its snowballing effects, technological power propels us into goals of a type that was formerly the preserve of Utopias. What used and ought to be tentative plays of speculative reason became competing blueprints for projects. In choosing between them we have to choose between extremes of remote effects.

The inescapable choices we now confront concern the total condition of nature on our earth and the kind of creatures that shall, or shall not, populate it. The salutary gap between everyday and ultimate issues, between occasions of common prudence and occasions for illuminated wisdom, is steadily closing. The new nature of our acting calls for a new ethics of long-range responsibility. This new responsibility demands a new kind of humility—a humility not like former humility based on the smallness of our power, but to the excessive magnitude of it, which is the excess of our power to act over our power to foresee and our power to evaluate and to judge.

Confronting the eschatological potentials of our technological processes, ignorance of the ultimate implications becomes itself a reason for responsible restraint. The old question of the power of the wise or the force of ideas not allied to self-interest in the body politic is raised to an ultimate pitch. For the needed enforcement to become practical, the new ethics must find its theory, on which does and don'ts can be based. Before the question of what force, comes the question of what insight or value-knowledge will represent the future in the present.

We chafe under the burden of an impenetrable fate, an intrinsic consequence of the disregard by creatures of boundaries divinely arranged for their good out of the abundant goodness of the Creator. For people, the primary creatures, such an order is one of humanization, since the integrity of their creaturehood is being in fact and in fulfillment what they have been created to be. Rebellion against these limits involves people both in the external and in the internal disintegration of their creaturehood.

Humanization is a matter of obedient freedom, of choice in the knowledge of good and evil. Life must be lived with everything you have and it must be integrated in the process, or you cannot be a morally mature person. No one claims all-out living is safe. If one is to prevent getting hopelessly lost, it is necessary to be far more responsible when one's way leads through the shadow of evil than when it goes through the light. The choice between a known good and a known evil is comparatively easy. The difficulty is to be conscious enough to know which is which in a particular case in this particular time. Since the goal is wholeness, no part, however luminous, has value except as it derives from and serves the totality. The search is for the roots of a fresh possibility. We are challenged, like pilgrims of other ages in times of crisis, to break across the frontier of the tragic conscience into a fresh sensitivity to the nexus of human responsibility in the intimate confrontation between the creature and the Creator.

The well-established stories of heroism, Creation, great deliverances and mighty victories capture the compelling human stretching for a larger perspective. These accounts serve as the tested thread needed to run through life and provide coherence and significance to the fragmented beads of our existence. Ours is a life of scattered baubles looking for a string that will lend meaning to our actions. Without a knowledge of these inclusive perspectives and assurances which ultimates provide, people lose their connections with their deeper selves, their origin and their culture. These accounts offer insights we need to define our fuller identity, our extended relationships and catch a vision of our destiny. Foundational stories and symbols are the necessary key to the suprapersonal mysteries which underlie the life of the ego and are the basis of any true morality.

Four ways in which people are strengthened are outlined by Joseph Campbell in *The Masks of God.* The first relates the waking consciousness to the *mysterium tremendum et fascinans* to the mystery of being. The reconciling force of awe and wonder are required if meaning and truth are to meet and inhabit us. The second gives the self an interpretive framework for the universe, a coherent cosmology that implies safety as well as belonging. The third way reinforces by providing a system of sentiments relating the person to the whole family and the community beyond. In the collectivity of either an unorganized crowd or an organized state, the collective unconscious prevails and the opposites of good and evil lie very close together in the original undifferentiated oneness. Greater responsibility thus rests upon individuals to attain and know their separate uniqueness to assure strength of moral choice and not be swayed by unconscious motives. The fourth recommended way initiates persons into the inner realities of the soul. No detached or ethereal experience, this is the fostering of inner growth and the creation of an environment in which the person can be in the fullest and most whole sense.

Such myths, old and new, activate and guide the individual toward wholeness by giving a fresh awareness of self and of the self as an entity in community. Further substance comes from responsible search for meaning and purpose. The humanitarian, the altruist, the individual devoted to the welfare of humankind become distinct models. Recurrent emphases of these model whole people include qualities of efficiency, creativity, inner harmony, relatedness and transcendence. Aspirations are firmed into intentions and translated into actions. Priorities become clearer and merge into working values. As they become comprehensive these values become powerful behavioral forces. The search continues toward the qualities of goodness, such as justice, righteousness and charity or love. These threads of the unconditional loving persons hold the individual, the community and the world together.

Within this ethical framework the responding individual as the center of responsibility participates in the quality of spirit—which is experienced as a touch of an ineffable force infused by divine power and purpose. "Religion," wrote Alfred N. Whitehead, "is the vision of something which stands beyond, behind and within, the passing flux of immediate things." Insofar as we live by religious conviction, our self-transcendence is empowered by faith in something beyond ourselves, as something real, yet waiting to be realized. From this point of view, the outward reach toward the ultimate and the striving to become more whole have an indispensable and a therapeutic function. Self-transcendence is needed to spur us toward acts and attitudes that link us to the larger wholes of community, church, nation and culture. It is receptivity and responsiveness to the divine influence animating the person.

Current responses to this inner stirring frequently found in Western societies spring from different confidences about the nature of human destiny. Convictions about what is ultimately meaningful varies, with some focusing on deified imperial systems, others on states of "unconditional being," and others on the Will of the Hebrew-Christian God. Questions also arise about how we "know" and how we become aware: by reason, by intuition or by revelation.

These responses fall into three general categories. The first includes religious responses where the self seeks to break out of a universal rational system in order to assert life's ultimate significance. The person may seek to do this individually, as in modern romantic existential thought. In its classical expression it was pursued corporately on a grand scale in the polytheism and imperial religions of Egypt, Babylon, China and later of Rome. The second category, defined by Aldous Huxley as "The Perennial Philosophy," is essentially the approach of mysticism, a heroic attempt to transcend all finite values and systems of meaning, including the self as a particular existence. This way seeks to arrive at universality and "unconditioned being" and struggles with the fact that the universality it espouses does not guarantee its validity. The third category is the religious answer given in the faiths of Judaism and Christianity.

Person's ultimate fulfillment unfolds in the self-awareness that accompanies a dialogue with God. Rationalists and mystics dispute the assumption of a personality in God, but agree on the self and God—communication made possible by the element of the divine in humans. That humans are made "in the image of God" includes likeness in spiritual powers—the power of thought, communication and self-transcendence. Religious traditions furnish examples of self-transcendent persons who have close relationship with the divine, respond to the lofty visions they experience and make righteous and just their behavior. These models—prophets, mystics, saints—are moving influences on others.

Persons move toward wholeness as they respond to the imperative of the divine-human encounter. They are empowered for their life in history, inspired in their achievements and judged for their faulty commissions or omissions. Ordinary persons are made over and given new significance. After God laid hold of him, Moses the tongue-tied murderer became the leader of his people's Exodus. The bereaved and suffering Hosea, touched by God, became the impassioned prophet of God's love. The divine influence wrought profound changes and empowerment in the lives of Saul of Tarsus, Augustine, Francis of Assisi, Luther, Wesley and Martin Luther King. In those who of themselves have little might, the Creator increases strength as they move toward wholeness.

Summary

Health and wholeness come to us as natural endowments of our bodies and personalities. Physically both conditions can be said to be complete from birth. Emotionally, intellectually and spiritually we are in process of becoming more healthy and whole. Both the actuality and the potentiality come to us as trusts for which we have responsibility to nurture and fulfill. The threats to health and wholeness are many and varied, coming from causes that are at once natural, personal and social. This renders both of these vital experiences problematic.

Working for more comprehensive preventive measures against disease and fractures, as well as for health and wholeness, emerge as crucial ethical responsibilities for individuals and societies. To decide for health and wholeness is part of a larger war against evil. As the ancient Chinese have said, we learn about health and wholeness from our illness. The Greeks viewed evil as "missing the mark," suggesting that turning away from the target of health and wholeness is missing the mark." In acquainting ourselves with other cultures, we gain a broader view of health and wholeness. It is important that we continually seek clarification of what we mean by health and wholeness. As we have said, these two processes need to be seen more as a dynamic participation in a varied and rounded life, involving a continued search for fulfillment and purpose.

Responsibility for maintaining health and achieving optimal wholeness is both personal and public. These qualities are not solely from the largess of others, but require continued vigilance and attention. Particular responsibility must be focused on the cultivation of the unique quality of love—the consummate quality that enriches health and wholeness. Just as health has the enemy of disease, wholeness and love have their enemies in evil—a radical reality that must be reckoned with, guarded against and overcome wherever possible.

Relationships must be established with regards to the surrounding biocultural realities and the supporting philosophical assumptions and religious convictions they hold. As people inch toward wholeness they are significantly guided as they respond to the imperative of the divine-human encounter.

The theme of the symphony of life's wholeness, as exemplified in the life of Jesus, was faith in the Father and the power of Love. In his ministry of healing, Jesus was concerned with wholeness. Addressing the chronically paralyzed man at the pool called Bethesda, Jesus gave no diagnosis of a diseased state or description of the breakdown of his homeostasis. Rather, getting at the habit of clinging to illness, Jesus simply asked, "Wilt thou be made whole?" Lasting personal and social health depends heavily on the will to be made whole. Without the consciousness that includes faith and love, it is questionable if there can be a deeper healing and a fruitful striving toward wholeness.

The biblical answer to the self's search for wholeness with a meaning beyond itself poses difficulties for the modern mind. Contemporary ventures into idolatry are proof of the difficulty of containing the collective self within any more general scheme of validity than its own interests. To place some cherished value of the self at the center of meaning is to give oneself to a closed system and shut off the possibility of moving toward wholeness.

We are confronted with evidence that the thesis of biblical faith—that the self is in dialogue with a God who must be defined as a "person"—embodying both the structure of being and a transcendent freedom—is more valid than alternative theses that find greater favor among the sophisticated. The biblical thesis requires a more explicit act of faith because it dares to give a specific meaning to the divine, which is relevant to the partial and fragmentary meanings of history.

Individuals are summoned to function as healthy persons and strive to move toward fuller wholeness. This involves taking into account the attitude of the unconscious as well as that of the ego. As a result, the individual judgment is freedom from the exclusive determinants of the outside situation. The conflict within the wholeness of the individual psyche may be the outcome of the painful tension between the opposites of good and evil. The striving toward wholeness may call for a reconciliation that requires nothing short of a symbolic rebirth.

The role of love in the healing process of reconciliation is told in the Hebrew-Christian Bible and confirmed in our contemporaries who have experienced its power. In the person-to-person encounters of daily life, with the moral imperative intrinsic to it, love enriches our relating to others because it participates in the transcendent unity of an unconditional force. Love in humans is a reflection of the love of the Creator God who created the world for the sake of the fulfillment of our potentialities. Love points persons to the Creator and to an awareness of the "ought to be."

Freedom to respond to health and wholeness is power and spirit; it carries the power and possibility of our inescapable finiteness as humans. This marks the boundary of our selves and leaves persons searching for a connection with a transcendent source of promise and fulfillment. We find it in the adventurous journey of moving toward the God who is Wholeness.

Epilogue

How can the modest consideration about humans being free to respond and having an urgent personal and social responsibility help us cope with the weighty issues surrounding us at the end of this century? In the years after World War I, Irish poet Yeats gave the haunting description, "Things fall apart; the center cannot hold; mere anarchy is loosed upon the world." Midway through the century as the world went up in the flames of World War II, a desperate Thomas Mann wrote, "With what suspense one regards the years ahead! The deliberation of one's responsibility more and more assumes the character of a pastime." Late in the century, Nadine Gordimer from South Africa said, "I live in a society whirling, stamping, swaying with the force of revolutionary change. The vision is heady, the image of the demonic dance is accurate, not romantic; an image of actions springing from emotion, knocking deliberation aside. The time is the last years of the colonial era in Africa."

The time, indeed, is the closing years of an old era. In our private, community and national life, we confront conditions that are whirling, stamping, swaying with escalating change. Western democracies languish. Latin America threatens to "go bust." Affluent and Two-Thirds World nations alike squander their resources upon terrible instruments of destruction. Military and political convulsions erupt and widespread trouble and need deepen. The complicated and explosive aspects of the multiple crises we confront are confounding. Meaning is fractured and certainty becomes relative. Style, or manner of life, becomes confused, making ambivalent demands on persons: alternately exacting strict conformity and socialization then advancing an all-out marketing drive that presses for self-centered indulgence. Foundational values and convictions are shattered. Communities are disrupted and riven. In a time when we abuse and neglect our freedoms, responses are reactive and defensive and the nature and ways of expressing responsibility are complicated and confusing.

In such a century of crisis, responsible responding emerges as crucially important for individuals and societies. The mad dance in which we are engaged is truly demonic. When conviction lags and actions spring from emotion instead of deliberation, things tend to fall apart.

Victor Frankel, recalling his near death in a German concentration camp, identifies responsibility with being "consciously human." Being responsible is being aware of and responsive to the physical world, personality and community. This capability and the decisive exercise of it is an essential part of being human. Responding responsibly applies to how and when persons encounter and cope with concrete circumstances.

Responding responsibly is neither random nor indirect. It is meeting head-on specific moral issues in our ecological home, our individual personalities and our interpersonal relations. The *Dictionary of Social Sciences* indicates that the essential meaning of moral responsibility is answerability—an accountability for failure, the situation of being blameworthy. But responsibility needs to be thought of in more than a strictly forensic way. Although it is answerability to laws or rules, responsibility has to do very much with responses to peoples' calls and needs.

In classical philosophical ethics and moral theology, responsibility usually meant imputability and culpability. Traditionally, responsibility is linked to the process of assessing guilt and to an invincibility in the forum of conscience where response to law, rather than to need, is required of the agent. The emphasis on responsibility opposes legalism, not the law.

Responsibility is more than response to sanctions or action taken out of fear of disapproval. Doctrinaire principles imposed as straitjackets on people is bad faith because it stifles creative moral conduct and social policy. The moral rules and reward-punishments are not all set and people do not need to come to heel and play the game as of old.

Graduate schools of education and business management point out the sad fate of institutions and businesses that fall prey to imitative practices, authoritarianism and rules-bound thinking. Instead, they urge the more responsible approaches of providing freedom, stimulating innovation, encouraging constructiveness. The responsible way invites questioning old procedures and thinking and welcomes new solutions. Responsibility confronts snap judgments and unsubstantiated generalizations with a rational "no".

The more fulfilling and responsible way confronts problems in key areas of our experience: in our environment, with our selves, in our society and in relation to our faith. Realistic questions arise regarding responsible living from the facts of change, the limits of freedom, the uncertainties of the future and the inescapable factor of the high risk of living. There is also the continual tug-of-war between self-interest and concern for the community and between people's shifting behavior patterns and the unchanging principle of loving concern for persons and the social balance.

People live responsibly when instead of losing contact with realities, they become aware of and involved in the world and in a tested faith. Classical moralists condemned *acedia*—mental and spiritual torpor. At the turn of the 19th century sociologists such as Max Weber had much to say about the social evil of "anomie." Early in this century the Spanish philosopher José Ortega y Gasset held that "life is, in itself and forever, a shipwreck. To be shipwrecked is not to drown. The poor human being, feeling himself sinking into the abyss, moves his arms to keep afloat. This movement of the arms, his response against his own destruction, is culture—a swimming stroke." Now at the end of the century, Harvey Cox, in his *God's Revolution and Man's Responsibility,* claims that "sin can best be understood as *apathy.*"

The survival response is the human's responsibility. When culture becomes lush, when it grows excessively abstract and is confused with life itself, these philosophers argue that people begin to feel safe and lose the sense of shipwreck and then lose contact with realities of their environment, themselves and their faith.

Responsibility in and to the World

Living responsibly involves adaptations to life's givens in ways that are both free and critical; innovative but at the same time realistic. To be responsible to the physical "givens" requires confronting the facts of the environment and complying with the demands of space and time while coping with the shifting patterns of history. Substantial questions about responsible living surround the facts of change and the challenge of life's high risks.

Responsibility and change: We live as participants in a stream of continuously altering structures and events. Change, as the observed difference in a given perception with the passage of time, has been a factor in the response of human beings from their beginnings. As Charles de Gaulle said, "The world is undergoing a transformation to which no change that has yet occurred can be compared, either in scope or rapidity."

All change taxes awareness and understanding. With greater awareness and understanding of change we have a better chance of coping with the transformations and may even be able to enjoy and be exhilarated by the new conditions in the making.

Change is neither uniformly bad nor good. Insofar as it brings new options, it offers the opportunity for growth. Coping with change in responsible ways entails preparation for happenings and new conditions. Effective psychotherapy, for instance, goes beyond dwelling on the past. It deals with recognition of vulnerabilities in the present psychic structure and leads to change and growth through particular kinds of learning, incorporating new pathways and abilities into daily life. The therapist takes an active role, encouraging persons to move out of positions of narcissistic inaccessibility, dependency and passivity, using an understanding of past failures and missed opportunities to break out of repetitive patterns of behavior and acquire ego assets leading to enhanced relationships, creativity and personal fulfillment.

Change is an integral part of the Christian's inner "transformation." "If any one is in Christ," St. Paul puts it, "he is a new creation; the old has passed away, behold, the new has come" (2 Co 5:17). The capacity to see both others and Christ in their true light comes from this inner transformation wrought by being in Christ. The change is radical; it goes to the roots of the person's being. The essential difference is an inner change in which thoughts and ambitions are no longer focused inward, but on Christ and on the interests of others.

The new person lives with a changed outlook and transformed values. Instead of being mere doom or suffering, hardship, disappointment and misfortune become the means of God's challenge or discipline, like the tools of the potter which give the cup its shape both for use and beauty. Such change not only makes the world new, but adds to the world its most vital element. The knowledge of Christ and the experience of his love, like the acquisition of a new and transforming friendship, enrich and interpret all other experience.

Responsibility and Life Forces: The functioning and power of life forces are essential facts in the process of change. Motivation for living responsibly can come from the dynamic qualities of natural powers and human powers. These potent and operative forces of the real world that encompass us provide us with what we need to survive. We respond with questions about the near and the far, the small and the great and the earth and the heavens. We admit that our responses to our physical environment are not an acquiescence, but in most cases emerge as a matter of our attempt at controlling them.

The given forms of space and time and freedom and contingency that interlace our experience lay upon us special responsibilities. They enable the mind and senses to lay hold of reality. These forms or categories tie together social and physical happenings and our awareness of them. They make it possible for us to hold in balance the opposing forces we confront. Not always apparent, but nonetheless real, these "realities" or "givens" of being, appear implicitly and explicitly in every thought and feeling concerning our physical and communal life.

When we consider human personality we find theorists stress differing aspects of responsibility for our life forces. These powers are variously described: as having organic and structural quality (Freud); as providing a libidinal energy (Jung); as pushing to counter death-causing anxiety (Horney); as pressure for the development of individuality by giving power to an act of the will (Rank); or as its being a healthy inner drive to overcome one's obsession with self-concern and self-reference (Kernberg).

We see growth bringing change in persons. Life forces can free untapped resources and abilities within each person. It can lead to fuller, more thoughtful, more rewarding ways of living. The many and continual changes families experience in the course of moving through the passages of life are essential to the growth of personality. The response is not acceptance of the life forces for accommodation's sake, but for a responsible, exciting and fulfilling maturing.

Persons engaged in the growth process that are impelled by life forces avoid sinking into purely occupational tasks. As they continue further development of self, they widen their mental horizons and enrich their emotional expressions, becoming more responsible. The goal is to maintain youth's eagerness to discover, to continue being interested and interesting and to continue exercising muscles, mind and sensitivities. The objective is to take time to cultivate those qualities which lengthen and enrich life and bring under control those forces which shorten life. In the process we find power welling up from deeper levels of our humanity and the promptings of the mysterious supernatural world become more real than any regressive fixation on childish fantasies.

Christ spoke of divine life forces as a friend, counselor and comforter and identified it as the Holy Spirit. St. Paul advised us that we "contend not against flesh and blood, but against the principalities, against the powers of darkness, against the spiritual hosts of wickedness in the heavenly places" (Ep 6: 12). But he assures us, "By the power of the Holy Spirit you will abound in hope" (Rm 15:13).

Responsibility and Freedom: The degree to which persons are free to choose remains critical for any consideration of human responsibility. It presents a crucial but a problematic condition: we are both free and not free.

Explosions of new ways and paths of communication have expanded our horizons of knowledge and our potential freedom. But these same developments often jeopardize our freedom. The limits of our personalities and our societies restrict the number of choices we can make within the enormously extended options. Within, we are circumscribed by the limits of our time and energy and by feelings of fear, guilt and low self-esteem. From the outside, our freedom is threatened by political oppression, the likelihood of a nuclear holocaust and other potential catastrophes.

Responsibility and freedom are reciprocal; both need the other. Freedom is not an isolated postulate standing outside the world. It is a condition in which the world and persons are involved. The degree to which human beings enjoy "free will" offers a case in point. When we say someone "wills something" we are implying not so much that free will is externally caused or internally fantasized, but that it is a responsible achievement of discipline and action. Every time we *will* something, our limits must be tested.

If we venture beyond the limits of our own freedom, we become permeable and vulnerable with no shielding skin to protect ourselves. On the other hand, if we fail to venture out with the exercise of our free wills, if we timidly withdraw into our shell, we risk cutting ourselves off from the freedom enjoyed in relations with others.

Our particular identity provides the limits of our freedom: we can take only a limited amount of responsibility. At the same time, the center of our personal freedom (one's free will), though often threatened, continues to carry much responsibility. Maximum freedom is not having a total freedom-from-restraint, but becoming aware and effective within the limitations of one's freedom. In relation to space and time our freedom is limited. Being space-bound, the area of our operation is circumscribed. Being time-bound, the past offers no new choices, but the present offers new alternatives and opens new horizons of freedom for the future.

Responsibility and the Future: The future can be viewed as a never-never-land into which persons can escape from responding responsibly. But that is to deny all that we learn in responding responsibly to the here-and-now. The study of "futurology" seeks to tell us when something may happen, how much impact this event will have *if* it happens and what the possible parameters are for human responses. Studying the *ifs* in this way prepares us to respond responsibly to what the future may offer and opens the door to ways in which human freedom can operate.

The search for a usable future requires the survey of one's discerned past. From history's rhythms and cycles, we can depict and lay foundations for the future. New and more systematic efforts to do this are a far cry from crystal-ball gazing. Taking a responsible view of the future calls for extrapolating the lessons of the past and present.

Moral decisions contribute to such a responsible view of the future. By our failures, we teach the persons who follow us what is to be pursued and what should be avoided. Moving together continuously in time, we all have responsibility for shaping the future. We are prodded by our common experience of the inexorable fact of death. A clearer awareness and a more responsible coping with death leads to the appreciation of the deeper meanings of present existence and yields pointers to the possibilities of the future.

Sentimental nostalgia or nihilistic feelings of marching off the map into nothingness are irresponsible approaches to the future.

To see in death a nothingness, or a "non-being," puts people at great risk. Whether it is met in fear or hope, death remains a complex symbol whose essential features are determined by a person's perspectives on life.

The potential for responsible responding in the midst of change and in the prospect of an uncertain future offers *hope*. For the Christian, hope for the world is found in the life, death and resurrection of Jesus Christ. This hope rests on the conviction that the Heavenly Father, holding in his hands the life forces that will operate in the future, has worked out a master plan toward which all of creation and the processes of history are moving.

Responsibility and Risk-taking: The fact of risk, another unavoidable condition of life, calls for particular kinds of responsible responding. Multiple risks are encountered in answering responsibly the tensions between potentiality and actuality, permanence and change. Taking risks in these contradictions of life entail the possibility of suffering harm and loss. Do we dare let others trust us when there is so much risk? Would it not be wiser to remain apart and not cause commotion? Such questions make sensitive people hesitate and draw back from the risks of deciding and participating. This is the fear of risking responsibility.

Risk-taking is not merely a matter of "fun and games," nor the radicalness of liberals or the high-risk of entrepreneurs. Life at every point carries the chance of failure and imperfection. The risk of what to risk, when to risk and how to risk become increasingly significant as the options in our world multiply. The illustrations of how risks stem from the paradoxes of life are myriad.

The complications and issues involved in risk-taking are dramatically illustrated in current controversies about the sophisticated research in gene splicing. Public discussions of these remarkable breakthroughs have been limited to questions about "risk benefit" assessment. In the midst of conflicting expert testimony on the probability estimates, the "risk-benefit" estimates appears to be an unreliable framework for decision-making because it rests on the assumption that risks are calculable within definable margins of error. The need has been to shift the decision-making process from risk-benefit to an uncertainty framework.

In this and many other fields, it is imperative that a risk-taking discipline be developed. The rule-of-thumb is that high risk brings high yield—or the possibility of failure. The spirit of adventure and the safeguard against stagnation go with responsible risk-taking. Disciplined and purposeful risk-taking powers provide necessary corrective forces in societies. Such confidence in venturing enables individuals to find courage to change one's style of living. High risk is involved in the application of the Christian scenario of hope—it could lead to crucifixion.

Responsibility for Personal and Social Renewal

It has been the theme of this work that the unitary self and communities of selves are challenged to stem the tide of personal destructiveness and the cruelties of history by becoming more responsibly responding persons. This immediately arouses countering questions. What is new about such a grandiose proposal? How can responsibility be pinned on today's individual when so many personal and community dysfunctions are due to natural and historical causes?

Nevertheless, this proposal seeks to reiterate the ways in which individuals and communities are summoned to become more honest and just, more authentic personally and concerned socially and more loyal to and expressive of their deepest faith. Psychotherapy has taught us that the individual who decides out of an integrated and fulfilled sense of identity and authenticity is most able to respond responsibly.

Conditions and functions of responsible behavior have been found to include awareness, capacity for sensitive and accurate perception and objective evaluation. In facing life, persons need to clarify and update their values and continuously renew their faith. Such responsible action lays hold of a sense of destiny—which is not a strange power which determines what shall happen to me; it is myself as given, formed by nature, history and myself. My destiny is the basis of my freedom and my freedom takes part in shaping my destiny.

Reinforcement for seeing responsibility as response has come from many theologians. The "heart of responsibility, or real life meeting," as J.H. Oldham conceived of it, "is relationship to self, others and God." Martin Buber wrote, "The responsible person, the loving person, responds in encounter and dialogue with others and with God."

Responsibility and the Unitary Self: The seat and agent of responsible responding is the individual's unitary self that copes with change and is empowered by life forces. The self alone responds within the limits of freedom and ventures into the risk of responsible living. The individual is a nuclear unit, alive and unique, with the capacity to be free to respond within the full scope of life's varied circumstances: in the context of space and time, in history and community and in exercising feeling, thinking, acting and faith.

As we move through successive stages of life we have the responsibility to keep searching for an accurate and holistic picture of human uniqueness. The two-year-old pointing to her image in the mirror and saying "That's me," is beginning to be responsible for herself. The 15th century philosopher Giovanni Pico della Mirandola gave profound expression to the awareness of the unitary self and the remarkable fact that human beings are free to respond. According to Pico, human beings are unique among God's creatures in that they are not confined to one level. Contained within them is the capacity to rise to angelic heights or to descend to a brutish level. We all, he claimed, have the responsibility to choose our own level.

To the question of how much freedom and responsibility exists within the complicated process of early human development, we have no precise answers. We are barely on the edge of knowledge about the ways personalities come into being. Recent research in child psychology supports the assumption of an initial selective reactivity and self-directive response patterns in the newborn.

At about four to five years of age, there can be seen the first *self-determinations* to goals and ideals in which healthy children seem to evolve out of their own potentials. They begin to realize that what is going to happen in their lives is to an extent the result of their own actions. Later responsibility comes to imply the possibility of foreseeing the effects of one's actions.

As ideas and prejudices infiltrate, responses become increasingly complicated. Persons insecure about their identity may find difficulty in making responsible choices or integrating society's demands into their personality. Those reluctant to mature may blame their heredity or environment and take this as an excuse for avoiding responsibility and accountability.

Response stands as the first element listed by H. Richard Niebuhr in his book *The Responsible Self* (1963). Decision-making, anticipating the reactions of others and, the givenness of a person's continuing membership in an interactive community follow one's initial response. Sartre, in his essay *Existentialism and Humanism*, says that humankind is always the same, facing a situation which changes and requires choice. The psychiatrist Eric Berne said that what we "have to do about problems is make decisions. This is difficult, since people want certainty. All you can do is compute likelihoods. People don't like that." Particularly people who have not faced the degree to which they are free to respond do not like it, because they have not been responsible enough to make a decision to act on the freedom they have.

The extent to which I can change my personality is debatable, but I do have the choice of how I view and express the substance of *Me*. The beginning of my responsibility is to engage in the unceasing quest to be aware, understand and direct this self of mine. The way in which I am aware of and act on, my responsibility defines my uniqueness as a human being. The qualities and processes I express take many forms and are made up of many dimensions.

My identified self or ego is the instrument with which I respond to myself, my neighbor, my world and my God. "Personal integrity," O. Hobart Mowrer maintains, "is more available to most of us than we sometimes wish to think. Many of us are too disposed to hold the external situation more responsible than we should for the moral ambiguity in our lives. We need to stop blaming others and take full-time responsibility for ourselves." Joseph Fletcher, as a "situationist" advocate, adds that responsible behavior is autonomous responding in accordance with the *reality principle*.

Responsible responses face reality and flow from the unitary self. Such responding then has the quality and validity of the individual. Using the symbolism of depth psychology, Fletcher shows that libertinism is control by the id, legalism is control by the superego and situationism or confronting reality head-on, is ego control.

Of such a statement we respond, "Laudable, but not probable." True, the wholeness of the self is neither a disease nor a superhuman attribute, but fundamentally an insoluble mystery. We can only conjecture that the person is grounded in being, in its essence and in its transactional reality.

Clinicians and pastoral counselors in intensive work with people encounter much about the self that is collective clutter, or peripheral trivia, that still does not reveal the substance of the individual. Analytic and intensive depth psychological approaches can bring to light irresponsible patterns and help to reconstitute the unitary self in more responsible ways. A strictly deterministic model of emotional disturbances, however, does not suffice. To be told, "Your emotional disturbance is just like any other sickness and you are not responsible for it and cannot do anything about it; so don't worry and just relax" does not satisfy the troubled self. Fuller journeys-into-self move beyond the externals of life's accidents to what is basic and truly representative (symbolic) of the self. Responsibility is involved in the seed, root, branch and fruit of the unitary self. In these deeper and more substantial levels we locate both the resistances to and the motivation for taking responsibility; we find out how responsibility is alternately blocked and empowered. Our responsibility includes becoming more aware of the extent of our freedom to respond and directing and maximize it in our lives. In the process of becoming more responsible, resistances are faced and neutralized and positive motives and behavior are reinforced. Consequently awareness deepens, self-esteem is elevated and goals are clarified.

Responsibility and Decision: To think, feel and act demand choice and decision. But to decide for something as true or as good means excluding other possibilities. Each decision marks a resisting the temptation to not act. The demand to decide implied in our freedom is embarrassing because we realize that we lack the complete mental and active unity with our destiny which should be the foundation of our decisions.

Deciding is a delicate and often an uncomfortable process that frequently leads to inconclusive actions. To decide and sacrifice alternatives involves risk. No decision can be eliminated; no action can be undone. Instead of right decisions we engage in trials and defeats and successes.

Nevertheless, decision-making is a necessary assertive and creative human process. As Tillich reassures us, there are decisions which are rooted in love, which by setting aside an absolute principle in favor of connecting with a human being avoids falling into relativity. Love overcomes the disappointment of excluded possibilities by enabling the person to reach the heart of another.

Our decisions, arising out of the broad basis of our unitary selves, form our destiny. Making a decision is more than a matter of looking into a how-to-live manual for instructions about what to decide. It is more than proper or even appropriate functioning. Adolf Eichmann asserted in all seriousness that doing his butcher work was nothing but fulfilling his responsibility.

Responsible decision-making is more calling into operation the totality of everything that constitutes the person's being. Decision involves body structure, psychic strivings, spiritual character. Former decisions, communities belonged to, past experience (remembered and unremembered) and the influencing environment all affect decisions.

To decide responsibly is a two-way street. A choice must be made between the *person's nature* and the *larger nature*. Moral decision-making puts persons at the edge of the deepening chasm between self-interest and the demands of the community. In postmodern societies, although choices for individuals have been vastly multiplied, people find the effectiveness of decisions has comparatively little influence on the present complex network of national and international affairs. This diminution of the effectiveness of private voices, together with the increased pressure to conform, render decision-making on the part of individuals less meaningful.

We are placed in the position of needing to register as much subjectivity as possible against global conflicts over which we have no control. "We can now recognize that the fate of the soul is the fate of the social order," says Theodore Roszak in his book *Where The Wasteland Ends.* He holds that, "If the spirit within us withers, we too will lose all the world we build about us." When people intuit and accept this fuller dimension of responsibility, they become convinced that they must participate in the decision-making process. Persons aware of their *response-ability,* who accept the burden of decision-making, become the source of moral law.

Frequently, we operate in a moral wilderness which is the spectral realm created by the going out and the coming in of elemental forces of our personality. The responsibility of decision-making is more than plugging into the hierarchy or lines-of-command of which a person may be a part. It is more than taking orders from above and "passing the buck" on to others.

Making responsible moral decisions calls for considering a wide range of facts, ideals and intention, as well as self-deceptions. A priority ethical question is *when* is a particular action right and *when* is it wrong. The Christian's criterion from the Old Testament is justice and righteousness and from the New Testament is concern and unconditional love.

Decision-making in the personal and organizational revolution that characterizes our day is difficult. Though difficult, it is urgent; deciding to exercise one's freedom to respond cannot be avoided. The four, morally based, considerations of Professor Pierce—tenacity, authority, the *a priori* and the spirit of inquiry—provide a sound starting point. In each of these dimensions the self, within community, must cope with change, life forces, the future, freedom, risk and death.

Helpful as are the healing services in enabling individuals to see and correct personal and community failures, therapy does not assure more effective decision-making. Bettering communications, working through neurotic tendencies and unlearning dystonic behavior patterns strengthen persons significantly. But first the individual must decide to respond more responsibly.

Responsibility and our Social Context: Responsiveness to other human beings is an integral part of responsibility. Interpersonal relations form and sustain the self; the context of the self is person-to-person. The relationship is more than that of atomic individuals making legal commitments to each other, but rather the face-to-face community in which unlimited commitments are the rule. The responsible self, as H. Richard Niebuhr points out "is driven by the movement of the social process to respond and be accountable in nothing less than a universal community."

Insofar as my identity largely comes from the reflection I get from others, I need others. To communicate the essence of my emotional and spiritual need enhances self-fulfillment, releases tensions and builds bridges to other needy human beings. Interaction with others teaches persons to face and manage hard facts of reality. Lessons about constraint and necessity come less from the biological and psychological nature of the individual and more from the fact that persons are social beings operating within a social system that puts definite restraints on irresponsible behavior.

Responsibility is a mode of helping people express and meet this need and to survive in a difficult and confusing world.

In helping one another confront reality honestly and directly there is a gain in mutual trust and the cementing of communal ties. Responsibility is dependent on persons and neighbors who are concretely neighborly. Each expresses concern for the other in their own concrete possibility. They are involved specifically with the other person. The opposite of love, then, is not hate but indifference. It is not possible to be responsible, or responsive, to an abstract principle. We can only respond to the calls and claims of others who, like ourselves, are persons rather than things. True responsibility is response to a call from others.

The individual continues in a tug-of-war between self-concern and concern for others. A degree of self-concern is essential for survival. I must hold my own identity over against the corrosive effects of society. Being self-centered in society is an inevitable aspect of each person's life.

Extreme self-centeredness as in narcissism deprives individuals of the rich benefits of social exchange and support. It also impoverishes society by the absence of the individual's contribution. Likewise, the consequences of societies becoming increasingly self-serving can be disastrous. A society whose morality stresses individual pleasure above responsibility will collapse, for then people attack one another and everyone blames the other for systemic changes which are not in the hands of anyone.

The temper of our age tends to make us reluctant to commit ourselves to past philosophical and theological guidelines for moral decision-making regarding social problems. But in our decision-making about social affairs serious and crucial questions of purpose and value keep hitting us. Other queries are just as specific. Wherein is our responsibility in a society beset by unemployment, inflation and confused foreign policies? Wherein is our responsibility in a society that is corrupt, class-ridden, hypocritical about equality between races, sexes and generations.

This perennial struggle between self-concern and concern for others is the arena of ethics, the field of debate over right and wrong and setting forth recommendations to guide responsible decision-making. In the face of many inhibiting trends in society which curtail the exercise of responsibility, the need to respond responsibly to situations in which we are free to respond becomes imperative. Americans have roots in their heritage of the determined individualism where each person is responsible for themselves. The taking of responsibility is one of the fundamental constructive approaches to life that we are rediscovering from our heritage. In its communal form it is the response of persons agreeing to carry their share of the common load.

To stay alive in a fiercely competitive and often uncaring world, we structure ourselves and respond in order to protect and then to assert our self-identity. In addressing others we look outward to reflect inward. In the contracted world of human exchange we seek confirmation of our self-esteem. Responding responsibly requires more than the protection of either our self-esteem or the corruption within our high vaunted social system. The "whirling, stamping, swaying" conditions which face us are the evil fruits of both the destructive inner forces and the cruelties of history.

When these tumultuous negative forces run out of control, both unitary selves and communities are threatened. Irresponsibility of individuals and communities generates confusion and lack of control; the traffic in irresponsible catchwords that cloud fact and truth, deteriorate from the shady to the violent. In economies allowed to be deregulated, inequitable and inflationary, the rich grow richer and the poor poorer; this leads to loss of jobs for workers, bankruptcy for industries and failures for banks. In the family of nations, preparations for war reach astronomical proportions and dissidents are liquidated.

Personal, social and international threats of this magnitude, make it grossly irresponsible for persons to remain detached, benighted and complacent. Good intentioned and idealistic persons must do more than mouth high-sounding platitudes and fantasize about peace. Parents, employers and elected officials must do more than appear humble and ingratiating while reinforcing outworn systems that support them. Responsibility can not be avoided by rationalizing one's non-involvement or by insulating ourselves from the struggle against the destructive inner conflicts of individuals or the cruelties of history. People are not held accountable for their damaging parents, poor teachers, physical disabilities or painful childhood memories that keep them enslaved, but they are accountable for taking steps within the limits of their *response-ability* to work to transcend the deficiencies of their history.

Does Responsible Responding Assure Renewal and Hope?

Growth in responsible responding—whatever the therapy or spiritual discipline followed—requires confronting reality and the self head-on. Persons disciplining themselves for accountable action train themselves to give honest and direct responses to people and events. Effort is made to be honest not only to the realities coming from the outside but also with themselves.

With heightened responsible responding, what are the odds that in this apocalyptic moment in history we can look forward with optimism? When we experience the difficulties and the slowness of renewal, fundamental personal and social change, we are not only frustrated but profoundly discouraged. Even though the promises of the future are magnificent, pessimism about what is in store is not unreasonable. Not much in contemporary history justifies a great optimism. There is little indication that evil "principalities and powers" will quickly or easily give way to goodness. What prevents a nuclear holocaust? Nothing stopped the explosion in the cosmos near the constellation Sagittarius thousands of light years away. "God writes straight with crooked lines," observed the theologian Anton Pregis. And, whatever the markings are, we had better be attentive to the messages about responsible responding that the creator and governor of this cosmos is sending human beings.

Religious Experience and Responsible Responding

For many people the dictates of their *religion* provide the moral principles guiding their decision-making and the positive hope by which they live. The religion they espouse and the behavior they aim to follow and trust is rooted in the divine itself. With some, their piety directs them to hold that no atheist can be a person of moral principle. Dostoyevsky has Ivan Karamazov argue that except for God and divine law, anything is permissible. The effort to ground moral convictions in the tenets of religion involves both community and individual emphasis.

Buber insisted that to be responsible means to respond, to hear the call or claim of others. Responsibility is not a quality that can be laid down according to set principles, but must be recognized in the depths of the soul according to the demands of each concrete situation. In other words, morality, like the Sabbath, is made for persons, not persons for morality.

Bonhoeffer sees the foundation of the "structure of responsibility to be "essentially a relation of man to man." He saw that life is found by those who set life in the freedom of one's own life. Without this bond and freedom there is no responsibility. He defines the structure of responsible life in terms of "dutyship, correspondence with reality, acceptance of guilt and freedom." More specifically he says, "The question of good is decided in the midst of each definite situation of our lives, in the midst of our living relationship with persons, things, institutions and powers, in the midst of our historical existence."

When the response is given with a responsible weighing out of all the personal and objective circumstances and with the awareness that God has become human, then the deed is delivered up solely to God at that action-moment. Those who act on the basis of their conviction see themselves justified in the idea. Responsible people commit their actions into the hands of God and live by God's grace.

The German-Swiss theologian Gerhard Ebeling of Zürich explains how the responsible self responds to God's offer of love. The response is one of faith or trust so that self-love is no longer necessary. Thus, freedom for others is born in us and it is the capacity to respond to the moral claims of our inner selves and to those of our neighbors. It is freedom to be "responsible" both to God and to persons. This process of responsibility was described by Luther when he said "faith is the doer, love is the deed." Christians, in any case, are commanded to love people, not principles.

Social love, or justice with mercy, is what the New Testament is talking about most of the time. Friendship and romance are valid, real and creative, but they have to be kept in their place. Ralph Harper, in his book, *Human Love,* distinguishes correctly between "human" and "mystical" love. The former is existential and experiential, the latter is a faith commitment. A third dimension of love—the social quality—is the New Testament's principle of unconditional, unrequiting, genuine love.

It is not just by reasoning, by wishing or even by praying that change, growth and love appear; it is by participation, involvement and commitment that we see it manifested. Learning takes place not only cognitively, volitionally or ritually, nor as an automatic result of stimulus causing a particular response, but rather learning, growth and conversion occur when one's freedom to respond is willfully engaged—when persons are responsibly involved in the world and with God. This expression of reality is only rhetorical unless it refers to a person who *is* involved. Theologically considered, this is the supreme significance of the Incarnation: God became personally involved with the world and humanity in space and time.

Persons are free to respond with acceptance or rejection to the affirmations of the religious faith to which they are committed. For Christians the divine is not an arbitrary, harsh despot but a loving, dynamic One who does new things, whose relation to creation is like a parent to children.

It is held that the ultimate way of responding to this inscrutable power in all things is by following the teaching, life and death of Jesus Christ. His claim is unmatched: "When you have seen me, you have seen the Father." He demands a decisive answer, "Whom say you that I am?" By the model of his trust and obedience individuals are directed toward God; in him also God is directed toward us.

There are as many ways of associating Christ with the responsible life as there have been ways of associating him with the ideal or the dutiful life. Those who exercise their freedom to respond and keep in touch with the Son receive strength, nurture and direction from him. People are empowered by the fact that he was also a person like themselves, yet he was able to interpret all actions upon him as signs of the divine action of creation, government and salvation and so respond to them accordingly. He carries out that act to fit into the divine action and looks forward to the infinite response to his response.

The present is enlivened and guided by a Comforter, Counselor and Friend called the Holy Spirit. This power is "closer than breathing" and enters graciously into the lives of responsive people. The responsibly responding person finds deepened sensitivity and healing born of suffering and grieving while wholeness and health are enriched by experiences of joy and creativity. These "fruits of grace" are among life's deepest kinds of loving.

A community who experience these things knows through reason and through these "triune" powers what it should make out of life, what law ought to be obeyed and how goals should be chosen. It also knows that we lack the power to try to live such a responsible life. But it is the community that encourages individuals to try what lies beyond strength and to persist hopefully in a journey that often seems futile, reaching toward the unattainable goal that Christ attained, living a life of obedience that continues to miss the mark. Forgiven, the Christ-follower tries again to obey.

The substance of the faith is that while once we were aliens and alienated in a strange and empty world, while we were once saboteurs of responsibility, now we begin to realize the temporal nature of this world and take responsibility grounded in Christ. We were in love with ourselves and all our little cities, yet estranged from our authentic origins and self; now we are growing in love with the Creator and the creation and becoming responsible in the city of God. We recognize and experience that we are free to respond, for we have an identity and relationship within the universal community of which God is the source and governor.

Optimal and responsible living is made possible when individuals and communities commit themselves to the qualities and values found in this paradigm of responsible personhood. Freedom to respond is exercised within the universal human community. Often praised, this higher and more responsible way is routinely neglected or threatened from inner and outer destructiveness and irresponsibility. In its growing, seeking flexibility and becoming, this higher way is guided by an increasing sense of responsibility. Even though humans often exhibit devilish traits, they are, as the psalmist said, "created but a little lower than the angels."

Jesus' teachings about responsible responding are consistently within the context of the reality principle—always confronting reality head-on. His words about responsible behavior are modes of responses to God and our fellows—not prescribed regulations. He said, "Love your enemies, . . . Do good to them that hate you" (Mt 5:44). "Love your neighbor as yourself" (Mt 19:19).

These are hard commandments to follow. They do not prescribe exact behavior. They call on the unitary self to respond responsibly and to relate themselves to the "other" in outgoing and loving responses. They call for acts that cannot be defined in advance of what love requires in forthcoming human encounters.

In his *Ethics,* Bonhoeffer claims that the individual's responsibility "consists in the adaptation of the concrete form of the divine mandates to their origin, their continuance and their goal in Jesus Christ." He adds, "The conscience which has been set free is not timid like the conscience which is bound by law, but it stands wide open for our neighbor and for his concrete distress." The person who responds responsibly, being conformed to Christ, is "the one for others" and therefore gives for others.

"The loving man," Martin Buber wrote (1917), "is one who is responsible, i.e., capable of responding in encounter and dialogue." Emil Brunner gave a Christian interpretation of these concepts of Buber when he spoke of the ethics of relationship or response and declared that the meaning of human existence as responsible and reciprocal existence is precisely love. Moral guilt lies, not in the failure to obey an abstract principle, but in the failure or refusal to respond to the needs of others. Encompassed in a responsible human being, three kinds of loving responses are found: the human or friendship, the mystical or faith committed person and the dimension of social or community love. Within these dimensions responsible responding includes faith, hope and love. But the greatest of these is love.

"Created but a little lower than the angels," with the gift of being free to respond, we are accountable for expressing the full array of our unique human capacities. We have the choice to decide to work diligently and vigilantly to become more responsible persons. This is our privilege and obligation in being free to respond.

Bibliography

ETHICS

Bennett, John, *Social Salvation,* Harper, New York, 1955

Berdyaev, Nicolas, *Destiny of Man,* Scribners, New York, 1937

Brunner, Emil, *Divine Imperative,* Westminister, Philadelphia, 1947; *Man in Revolt,* Westminster, Philadelphia, 1947

Bonhoeffer, Dietrich, *Ethics,* Macmillan, New York, 1955

Childress, James F., *Dictionary of Christian Ethics,* Westminster, Philadelphia, 1986

D'Arcy, M.C., *The Mind and Heart of Love,* Henry Holt, New York, 1947

Elert, Werner, *The Christian Ethos,* Muhlenberg Press, Philadelphia, 1954

Frankena, William, *Ethics,* Prentice Hall, New York, 1973

Fromm, Erich, *Man for Himself,* Rinehart, New York, 1947; *The Art of Loving,* Rinehart, New York, 1949

Gert, Bernard, *Morality,* Oxford, New York, 1988

Hallett, Garth L., *Christian Moral Reasoning,* Notre Dame Press, 1983

Hebblewaith, Bryan, *Ocean of Truth: Defense of Objective Theism,* Cambridge; *Christian Ethics and Modern Age,* Westminster, 1982

Hutchison, John (Ed.), *Christian Faith and Social Action,* Scribners, 1953

Jonas, Hans, *The Imperative of Responsibility,* Univ. of Chicago, 1984

Lehmann, Paul, *Ethics in a Christian Context,* Harper, New York, 1963

Levine, Maurice, *Psychiatry and Ethics,* Braziller, N.Y., 1972

Moltmann, Jurgen, *The Crucified God,* Harper, New York, 1975

Pannenberg, Wolfhart, *Anthropology in Theological Perspective,* Westminister

Ramsey, Paul, *Basic Christian Ethics,* Scribners, New York, 1950; *Faith and Ethics,* Harper, 1957

Rendtorff, Trutz, *Ethics, Basic Elements,* Fortress, Philadelphia, 1986

Ross, Stephen David, *Moral Decision,* Freeman, Cooper, San Francisco, 1972

Stackhouse, Max, *Ethics and The Urban Ethos,* Beacon Press, Boston, 1987

Sudgate, Alan M., *William Temple and Christian Ethics Today,* Fortress, 1939

Thomas, C.C., *Vision and Revision,* Harper, San Francisco, 1985

Thomas, George, *Christian Ethics and Moral Philosophy,* Scribners, New York, 1955

Troelsch, Ernest, *Social Teachings of the Christian Church,* Macmillan, 1931

PSYCHOLOGY

Adler, Alfred, *Practice and Theory of Individual Psychology,* Harcourt Brace, 1927

Angyal, Andrus, *Foundations for a Science of Personality,* Commonwealth, 1941

Alexander, Franz, *The Vital Balance,* Viking, 1963

Allport, Gordon, *Personality: A Psychological Interpretation,* Holt, 1937; *Becoming,* Yale University Press, New Haven, 1955

Assagioli, Roberto, *Psychosynthesis,* Hobbs-Dorman, New York, 1965

Bettleheim, Bruno, *Love is Not Enough,* Free Press, New York, 1950

Bugenthal, James F.T., *Search For Authenticity,* Holt-Rinhart, NY, 1965

De Nouy, LeComte, *Human Destiny,* Longmans-Green, New York, 1947

Dollard, John and Neal Miller, *Personality and Psychotherapy,* McGraw-Hill

Erikson, Erik, *Insight and Responsibility,* Norton, New York, 1961; *Childhood and Society,* Norton, New York, 1963

Freud, Sigmund, *The Problem of Anxiety,* Norton, New York, 1936

Frankl, Vicktor, *Psychotherapy and Religion,* Simon Schuster, New York, 1947; *The Unconscious God,* Simon Schuster, New York, 1975

Fromm, Erich, *Escape from Freedom,* Holt, New York, 1947; *Sane Society,* Holt, New York, 1955

Goldberg, Arnold, *Progress in Self Psychology,* Guilford Press, 1985

Guntrip, Harry, *Personality Structure and Human Interaction,* University Press, 1964

Hall and Lindzey, *Theories of Personality,* Wiley, New York, 1981

Hamilton, N. Gregory, *Self and Others,* Aronson, New York, 1988

Horney, Karen, *The Neurotic Personality of Our Time,* Norton, New York, 1937; *Our Inner Conflicts,* Norton, New York, 1945

Jung, Carl, *Structure and Dynamics of the Psyche,* Routledge-Kegan, 1960; *Psychological Types,* Harcourt Brace, New York, 1926; *Pscyhology of the Unconscious,* Dodd-Mead, New York, 1927; *Modern Man in Search of a Soul,* Harcourt-Brace, New York, 1933; *Psychology and Religion,* Yale University Press, New Haven,1938; *Psychology of the Spirit,* New York Analytical Club, 1948

Kernberg, Otto, *New Perspectives on Psychotherapy of the Borderline,* Brunner/Mazel, 1978

Kline, Melanie, *Narative of a Child Analysis,* Basic Books, New York, 1961; *Love, Guilt and Reparation,* Delta Books, New York, 1975

Kohut, Heinz, *The Analysis of Self,* International University Press, New York, 1977; *The Restoration of the Self,* University Press, New York, 1988

Mahler, Margaret S., *Separation: Individuation,* Aronson, New York, 1974; *On Human Symbiosis,* International University Press, 1968

Margulis, Alfred, *The Empathetic Imagination,* Norton, New York, 1989

Maslow, A.H. Abraham, *Motivation and Personality,* Harpers, New York, 1954; *Toward a Psychology of Being,* Van Nostrand, 1962

May, Rollo, *Man's Search For Himself,* Norton, New York, 1975; *Love and Will,* Norton, New York, 1969

Orstein, Robert E., *The Psychology of Consciousness,* Viking, New York, 1972

Perls, Fritz, *Gestalt Therapy,* Random House, New York, 1988

Rogers, Carl, *Client-Centered Therapy,* Houghton-Mifflin, Boston, 1951; *Persons,* Houghton-Mifflin, Boston, 1957

Schafer, R., *New Language for Psychoanalysis,* Yale, New Haven, 1976

Singer, June, *Boundaries of the Soul,* Anchor Books, New York, 1973

Sullivan, Harry S., *Schizophrenia as a Human Process,* Norton, NY, 1962

Weis, Paul, *Man's Freedom,* Yale University Press, New Haven, 1950; *Personal Psychopathology,* Norton, New York, 1972

Winnicott, Donald W., *Transitional Objects and Transitional Phenomena,* 1953; *Family and Individual Development,* Routledge, London, 1968

Zweig, Paul, *The Heresy of Self-Love,* Princeton University Press, 1980

SOCIO-CULTURAL and HISTORY

Achebe, Chinua, *The Trouble With Nigeria,* Heinemann, London, 1984; *Things Fall Apart,* Fawcett, London, 1985

Bellah, Robert et al, *Habits of the Heart,* Harper, 1985

Berdyaev, Nicolas, *Solitude and Society,* Scribners, New York, 1939

Coan, Richard, *Hero, Artist, Sage or Saint,* Columbia University, 1977

Coulter, N. Arthur, Jr., *Synergetics,* Prentice Hall, New York, 1976

Cousins, Norman, *Human Options,* Berkeley Publishing, 1983; *Pathology of Power,* Norton, New York, 1988

Dixon, W. Macneile, *The Human Situation,* Heinemann, London, 1965

Dostoevski, F.M., *Brothers Karamazov,* Heinemann, London, 1941

Drucker, Peter, *Management's Tasks, Practices, Responsibilities,* Harper

Ellul, Jacques, *The Technological Society,* Knopf, New York, 1964

Erikson, Erik H., *Life History and the Historical Moment,* Norton, 1975

Friedman, Milton and Rose, *Freedom to Choose,* Avon Books, NY, 1981

Keniston, Kenneth, *The Uncommitted and Young Radicals,* Harcourt Brace, '68

Kroner, Richard, *Culture and Faith,* Chicago Univ. Press, 1951

Kronner, Melvin, *Tangled Wing,* Harper, 1983

Lasch, Christopher, *The Culture of Narcissism,* Norton, New York, 1978; *Men of Destiny,* Norton, New York, 1970

Lifton, Robert, *Home from the War,* Simon Schuster, New York, 1973; *Boundaries: Psychological Man in Revolution,* 1972; *History and Human Survival,* Random House, New York, 1970

Lippman, Walter, *The Preface to Morals,* Scribners, New York, 1932

Marcuse, Herbert, *One-Dimensional Man,* Beacon, Boston, 1964

Niebuhr, H. Richard, *Christ and Culture,* Harpers, New York, 1951

Packard, Vance, *The Ultra Rich,* Little-Brown, Boston, 1989

Roszak, Theodore, *Where the Wasteland Ends,* Anchor Books, New York, 1971; *Making of Counter-Culture,* Anchor Books, New York, 1969

Riesman, David, *The Lonely Crowd,* Yale University, New Haven, 1973

Shaull, Richard, *Heralds of a New Reformation,* Orbis Books, 1984; *Naming the Idols,* Myer-Stone, 1988

Sheehy, Gail, *Passages,* Bantam, New York, 1977

Smith, Page, *Redeeming the Time,* McGraw Hill, New York, 1987

Smith, Brewster, *Social Psychology and Human Values,* Chicago, Aldine, 1969

Tillich, Paul *Love, Power and Justice,* Oxford, New York, 1954; *Interpretation of History,* Scribners, 1936

Tofler, Alvin, *Future Shock,* Random, New York, 1970; *The Third Wave,* Bantam, New York, 1984

Toulmin, Stephen, *Return to Cosmology,* Harper, New York, 1981

Whyte, Lancelot, *The Next Development of Man,* Henry Holt, NY 1948

Wilson, Edward O., *On Human Nature,* Harvard Universary, 1978

SPIRITUAL SEARCH

Brown, Robert McAfee, *Spirituality and Liberation,* Westminster, 1988

Buechner, Frederick, *The Hungering Dark, Harpers,* San Francisco, 1987

Buttrick, George, *Prayer,* Cokesbury, New York, 1942

Frankl, Victor, *Man's Search for Meaning,* Pocket Books, New York, 1963

Kelly, Thomas, *Testament of Devotion,* Harper, New York, 1941

Jones, Rufus, *Pathways to the Reality of God,* Macmillan, New York, 1931; *The New Quest,* Macmillan, New York, 1928

Kierkegaard, Soren, *Purity of Heart,* Harper, New York, 1938

Neill, Stephen, *A Genuinly Human Existence,* Doubleday, New York, 1959

Peck, M. Scott, *The Road Less Traveled,* Simon Schuster, New York, 1978; *People of the Lie,* Simon Schuster, New York, 1982

Ricoeur, Paul, *Fallible Men: Philosophy of Will,* Fordham, New York, 1986; *Time and Narrative,* University of Chicago, 1988; *Main Trends in Philosophy,* Holmes & Meier, 1979

Steere, Douglas, *On Beginning Within,* Harper, New York, 1943

Tillich, Paul, *Courage to Be,* Yale University, New Haven, 1952; *The New Being,* Scribners, New York, 1955

Tournier, Paul, *The Healing of Persons,* Harper, 1965; *The Whole Person in a Broken World,* Harpers, 1963

Trueblood, D. Elton, *The Life We Prize,* Harper, New York, 1961

Ulanov, Ann and Barry, *Religion and the Unconscious,* Westminster, 1975

PHILOSOPHY, THEOLOGY and RELIGION

Barth, Karl, *Knowledge of God and Servant of God,* Harper, New York, 1957; *Word of God and Word of Man,* Harpers, New York, 1957

Berdyaev, Nicolas, *Freedom and the Spirit,* Scribners, New York, 1935

Bonhoeffer, Dietrich, *Prisoner for God,* Macmillan, New York, 1953; *Cost of Discipleship,* Macmillan, New York, 1949

Brown, Robert McAfee, *Theology in a New Key,* Westminster, Philadelphia, 1978

Brunner, Emil, *Christian Doctrine of God,* Lutterworth, London, 1949; *Divine Human Encounter,* Westminster, Philadelphia, 1943; *The Theology of Crisis,* Scribner, New York, 1939

Bultmann, R., *Faith and Understanding,* S.C.M. Press, London, 1969

Calvin, John, *The Institutes of Christian Religion,* Westminster, 1960

Cox, Harvey, *God's Revolution and Man's Responsibility,* Harpers, 1979; *Many Mansions,* Beacon, Boston, 1987

Danto, Arthur, *Connections To The World,* Harper, San Francisco, 1989

Ebeling, Gerhard, *Gewisshat und Zweifel,* Tubingen, 1969; *Glaubens im Zeithalter,* Tubingen, 1970

Eliade, Mircea, *Images and Symbols,* Havervill, London, 1961

Gilkey, Langdon, *Makers of Heaven and Earth,* Univ. of Chicago, 1959

Hall, Charles A.M., *The Common Quest,* Westminster, Philadelphia, 1975

Hutchison, John A., *Faith, Reason and Existence,* Oxford, NY, 1956

Kung, Hans, *Does God Exist,* Vintage Books, New York, 1981

Luther, Martin, *Lectures on Romans,* Westminster, Philadelphia, 1961

Niebuhr, Rheinhold, *Faith and History,* Scribners, New York, 1942; *Beyond Tragedy,* Scribners, New York, 1945; *The Nature and Destiny of Man,* Scribners, New York, 1943; *Self and the Drama of History,* Scribners, New York, 1947

Niebuhr, H. Richard, *The Responsible Self,* Harpers, 1978

Temple, William, *Nature, Man and God,* Macmillan, New York, 1940

Toulmin, Stephen, *The Discovery of Time,* University of Chicago, 1965

Whitehead, Alfred. N., *Process and Reality,* Macmillan, New York, 1930

Index